P9-CQY-022

Twenty-First Edition 2011

The State
of
Church Giving
through 2009

Jesus Christ,
the Church in the U.S., &
the 16 No-Progress-in-Child Deaths Nations,
10 Being 84% Christian

John L. Ronsvalle

Sylvia Ronsvalle

empty tomb, inc.
Champaign, Illinois

The State of Church Giving through 2009:
Jesus Christ, the Church in the U.S., & the
16 No-Progress-in-Child Deaths Nations,
10 Being 84% Christian
by John and Sylvia Ronsvalle
Published by empty tomb, inc.
First printing, September 2011

empty tomb, inc.
301 N. Fourth Street
P.O. Box 2404
Champaign, IL 61825-2404
Phone: (217) 356-9519
Fax: (217) 356-2344
www.emptytomb.org
See www.emptytomb.org/pubs.html for updates and corrigenda.

ISBN 978-0-9843665-1-4
ISSN 1097-3192

The Library of Congress has catalogued this publication
as follows:
The state of church giving through … — 19uu- Champaign, Ill. :
Empty Tomb, Inc.,
v. : ill. ; 28 cm. Annual.
1. Christian giving Periodicals.
2. Christian giving Statistics Periodicals.
3. Church finance — United States Periodicals.
4. Church finance — United States Statistics Periodicals.
   BV772 .S32 98-640917

CONTENTS

TABLES, FIGURES AND ABBREVIATIONS ———————

List of Tables:

List of Figures:

List of Abbreviations:

BEA .... U.S. Bureau of Economic Analysis

BLS .... U.S. Government Dept of Labor Bureau of Labor Statistics

CE .... Consumer Expenditure Survey

CU .... Consumer Unit

DPI .... Disposable Personal Income

EFCA .... Evangelical Council for Financial Accountability

FADICA .... Foundations and Donors Interested in Catholic Activities

GDP .... Gross Domestic Product

GNP .... Gross National Product

IMB .... International Mission Board (of the SBC)

NAE .... National Association of Evangelicals

NBER .... National Bureau of Economic Research

NCC .... National Council of the Churches of Christ in the U.S.A.

NIV .... New International Version of the Holy Bible

OCD .... *The Official Catholic Directory*

RCMUS .... Religious Congregations and Membership in the United States

SBC .... Southern Baptist Convention

SCG .... State of Church Giving

UMC .... United Methodist Church

UNICEF .... United Nations Children's Fund

YACC .... *Yearbook of American and Canadian Churches*

PREFACE _____

Chapter 1 in this 21st edition of the *State of Church Giving* series discusses the vital tradition of voluntary data reporting by church leaders in the U.S. Pastors take time from busy schedules to fill out annual reports. Denominational officials both remind pastors to fill out annual reports, and also aggregate and publish the numbers. While the mission of the church is commonly associated with the work of missionaries and evangelists, the efforts to provide information on membership and giving is also a ministry that benefits the mission of the church in the U.S. Church leaders, researchers, and others who make use of the data must be grateful for the faithfulness of those who provide it.

The publication of the aggregated data from many denominations in the *Yearbook of American and Canadian Churches* is a most important service, continuing a tradition that extends back to 1916. The efforts of Eileen W. Lindner, as editor, have been critical to sustaining this historical data stream. The church in the U.S. continues to owe her a debt of gratitude. She is ably assisted by Elizabeth During and Marcel Welty, who interact with many denominations as the data is obtained and prepared for publication. The *Yearbook* staff continue to offer a professional and collegial working relationship that is greatly valued.

Appreciation must also be extended to the National Council of the Churches of Christ in the U.S.A., and its General Secretary, Michael Kinnamon, for the statesman role displayed in providing this valuable publication series.

Once again this year, other empty tomb staff carried out their many responsibilities even while the writing and preparation of this publication occurred. The understanding and support of this team of individuals who have chosen to live out their Christian discipleship through this organization has not only sustained the local works, but also provided the base from which to challenge the church throughout the U.S. to consider the importance of giving to the mission of God. The support from these coworkers, coordinated by Shannon Cook, as well as from volunteers and financial supporters of empty tomb, inc. is crucial to this effort, and is acknowledged with gratitude.

Joy Bonczek devoted many days to this task, bringing skill and insight to the variety of challenges required to move the publication from draft to completion. We may have been able to publish this edition without her, although it's not clear exactly how. David Anderson, Fred Neumann, and John Jones shared hours of their time in reviewing the final drafts. All these efforts are very much appreciated.

Our prayer once again this year is that the research and information in this volume will inspire and challenge Christians throughout the U.S. to respond to the needs of the "least," with the result that God may receive glory through Jesus Christ and the church (Ephesians 3:20-21).

John L. Ronsvalle, Ph.D.
Sylvia Ronsvalle

Champaign, Illinois
August 2011

SUMMARY _____

The State of Church Giving through 2009 is the most recent report in an annual series that began with *The State of Church Giving through 1989*. These analyses consider denominational giving data for a set of denominations first analyzed in a study published in 1988. The present report reviews data for a composite set of denominations from 1968 through 2009 that includes 27.9 million full or confirmed members, and just over 100,000 of the estimated 350,000 religious congregations in the U.S.

The findings of the present church member giving analysis include the following.

- In chapter 1, per member giving for the composite set of denominations was analyzed for 1968 through 2009. As a portion of income, and in dollars both current and inflation-adjusted, per member giving to Total Contributions, Congregational Finances, and Benevolences decreased from 2008 to 2009. Giving to Benevolences as a portion of income in 2009 reached the lowest level during the 1968-2009 period.

- In chapter 2, data for an additional 17 denominations was available for 2008-2009, allowing an expanded analysis for two years of 42 Protestant communions, with 38 million members. In the expanded group, per member giving as a portion of income, and in dollars both current and inflation-adjusted, also declined from 2008 to 2009.

- In chapter 3, an analysis of data for a subset of mainline Protestant denominations and a subset of evangelical Protestant denominations found giving higher, but a steeper decline in giving as a portion of income, in the evangelical Protestant denominations over the 1968-2009 period.

- In chapter 4, a review of giving and membership patterns in 11 Protestant denominations from 1921 to 2009 found that per member giving as a portion of income began to decline in 1961, and membership began to decline as a percent of U.S. population in 1962. Giving as a percentage of income was lower in 2009 than in either 1921 or 1933.

- In chapter 5, data was analyzed using both linear and exponential regression. Both giving and membership data were reviewed for how past patterns may influence the future for various sets of denominational groups. Per member giving in inflation-adjusted dollars during recession years was analyzed for 11 denominations from 1921 through 1967, and for the composite set of denominations from 1968 through 2009. Expenditures on new religious construction in the U.S. were compared for the period 1964 through 2009.

- In chapter 6, a survey of denominations' overseas missions income in 2003 through 2009 found that, for the group as a whole, denominations' overseas ministries income was 2¢ for every dollar donated to congregations in 2009. The cost per church member for addressing global needs, such as world evangelization and helping to stop, in Jesus' name, global child deaths, were calculated for various church populations. If church members were to reach a congregation-wide average of 10% giving, a low estimate suggests that an additional $174 billion would be available to assist both local and global neighbors in need. If native-born church members in the U.S. were to support international ministry at the level that foreign-born residents of the U.S. send remittances to their home countries, there would have been an additional $362 billion available for international ministry through churches in 2009.

- In chapter 7, charitable giving data for the U.S. Bureau of Labor Statistics Consumer Expenditure Survey, 2009, was analyzed by age, income level, and region of residence. In each category, giving to "church, religious organizations" received the highest level of charitable contributions. Giving to that category represented 74% of total contributions in 2009. Three estimates for Total Giving by Living Individuals in 2007 were compared, the latest year for which the three sources had available data. The data in the analysis was obtained from the U.S. Bureau of Labor Statistics Consumer Expenditure Survey, the Internal Revenue Service Form 990 series, and the *Giving USA* publication, based in part on IRS charitable deduction information for itemizers. The numbers differed by as much as $54 billion.

- Chapter 8 considers church member giving patterns, Jesus' parable of the sheep and the goats in Matthew 25:31-46, and the 16 countries making no progress toward decreasing child deaths, with 10 of the 16 countries having majority Christian populations. The chapter: (1) considers the status and possible prevention of under-5 child deaths, including in the 16 no-progress countries; (2) explores dynamics that may affect church giving, particularly in terms of addressing the needs of the "least"; and (3) reviews signs of hope present in the church in the U.S.

INTRODUCTION _____

A historical series of financial and membership data in the United States extends back to 1916. Church statesmen took a broad overview of organized religion as a major social institution. They collected and preserved the data through publications and archives.

This information tradition continues through the present. Individual congregations initially provide the data to the regional or national denominational office with which the congregation is affiliated. The denominational offices then compile the data. The *Yearbook of American and Canadian Churches* (*YACC*), of the National Council of the Churches of Christ in the U.S.A., requests the data from the national denominational offices, publishing it in annual *YACC* editions.

The data published by the *YACC*, in some cases combined with data obtained directly in conjunction with the present study from a denominational source (as noted in the series of tables in Appendix B), serves as the basis for the present report. The numbers on the following pages are not survey reports. Rather, they represent the actual dollar records included in reports submitted by pastors and lay congregational leaders to their own denominational offices.

By following the same data set of denominations over a period of years, trends can be seen among a broad group of church members. In addition, since the data set includes communions from across the theological spectrum, subsets of denominations within the larger grouping provide a basis for comparing patterns between communions with different perspectives.

In an ongoing fashion, efforts are made to use the latest information available. As a result, *The State of Church Giving through 2009* provides information available to date.

Definition of Terms. The analyses in this report use certain terms that are defined as follows.

Full or Confirmed Members are used in the present analysis because it is a relatively consistent category among the reporting denominations. Certain denominations also report a larger figure for Inclusive Membership, which may include, for example, children who have been baptized but are not yet eligible for confirmation in that denomination. In this report, when the term "per member" is used, it refers to Full or Confirmed Members, unless otherwise noted.

The terms "denomination" and "communion" are used interchangeably. Both refer to a group of church people who share a common identity defined by traditions and stated beliefs.

The phrase "historically Christian church" refers to that combination of believers with a historically acknowledged confession of the faith. The broad spectrum of communions represented in the National Church Leaders Response Form list indicates the breadth of this definition.[i]

Total Contributions Per Member refers to the average contribution in either dollars or as a percent of income which is donated to the denominations' affiliated congregations by Full or Confirmed Members in a given year.

Total Contributions combines the two subcategories of Congregational Finances and Benevolences. The definitions used in this report for these two subcategories are consistent with the standardized *YACC* data request questionnaire.

The first subcategory of Congregational Finances includes contributions directed to the internal operations of the individual congregation, including such items as the utility bills and salaries for the pastor and office staff, as well as Sunday school materials and capital programs.

The second subcategory is Benevolences. This category includes contributions for the congregation's external expenditures, beyond its own operations, for what might be termed the larger mission of the church. Benevolences includes international missions as well as national and local charities, through denominational channels as well as programs of nondenominational organizations to which the congregation contributes directly. Benevolences also includes support of denominational administration at all levels, as well as donations to denominational seminaries and schools.

As those familiar with congregational dynamics know, an individual generally donates an amount to the congregation which underwrites both Congregational Finances and Benevolences. During the budget preparation process, congregational leadership considers allocations to these categories. The budget may or may not be reviewed by all the congregation's members, depending on the communion's polity. However, the sum of the congregation's activities serves as a basis for members' decisions about whether to increase or decrease giving from one year to the next. Also, many congregations provide opportunities to designate directly to either Congregational Finances or Benevolences, through fundraising drives, capital campaigns, and special offerings. Therefore, the allocations between Congregational Finances and Benevolences can be seen to fairly represent the priorities of church members.

When the terms "income," "per capita income," and "giving as a percent of income" are used, they refer to the U.S. Per Capita Disposable (after-tax) Personal Income (DPI) series from the U.S. Department of Commerce Bureau of Economic Analysis (BEA), unless otherwise noted.

The Implicit Price Deflator for Gross National Product (GNP) was used to convert current dollars to 2005 dollars, thus factoring out inflation, unless otherwise specified.

Appendix C includes both U.S. Per Capita DPI figures and the Implicit Price Deflator for GNP figures used in this study.

Analysis Factors. *Chained Dollars.* The analyses in *The State of Church Giving through 2009* are keyed to the U.S. BEA series of "chained (2005) dollars."

Income Series. The U.S. Department of Commerce BEA has published the 13th comprehensive ('benchmark") revision of the national income and product accounts, with the reference year being 2005. The U.S. Per Capita DPI series used in the present edition of *The State of Church Giving through 2009* is drawn from this national accounts data.

Rate of Change Calculations, 1985-2009. The following methodology is used to calculate the rate of change between 1985 and the most recent calendar year for which data is available, in the present case, 2009.

The rate of change between 1968 and 1985 was calculated by subtracting the 1968 giving as a percent of income figure from the 1985 figure and then dividing the result by the 1968 figure.

The rate of change between 1985 and 2009 was calculated as follows. The 1968 giving as a percent of income figure was subtracted from the 2009 figure and divided by the 1968 figure, producing a 1968-2009 rate of change. Then, the 1968-1985 rate of change was subtracted from the 1968-2009 figure. The result is the 1985-2009 rate of change, which may then be compared to the 1968-1985 figure.

Rounding Calculations. In most cases, Total Contributions, Total Congregational Finances, and Total Benevolences for the denominations being considered were divided by Full or Confirmed Membership in order to obtain per capita, or per member, data for that set of denominations. This procedure occasionally led to a small rounding discrepancy in one of the three related figures. That is, by a small margin, rounded per capita Total Contributions did not equal per capita Congregational Finances plus per capita Benevolences. Similarly, rounding data to the nearest dollar for use in tables and graphics led on occasion to a small rounding error in the data presented in tabular or graphic form.

Giving as a Percent of Income. The most useful way to look at church member giving is in terms of giving as a percent of income. Considering what percent or portion of income is donated to the religious congregation provides a different perspective. Rather than indicating how much money the congregation has to spend, as when one considers dollars donated, giving as a percent of income indicates how the congregation rates in light of church members' total available incomes. Has the church sustained the same level of support from its members in comparison to previous years, as measured by what portion of income is being donated by members from the total resources available to them?

Percent of income is a valuable measure because incomes change. Just as inflation changes the value of the dollar so $5 in 1968 is not the same as $5 in 2009, incomes, influenced by inflation and real growth, also change. For example, per capita income in 1968 was $3,112 in current dollars; if a church member gave $311 that year, that member would have been tithing, or giving the standard of ten percent. In contrast, 2009 per capita income had increased to $35,888 in current dollars; and if that church member had still given $311, the member would have been giving less than 1% of income. The church would have commanded a smaller portion of the member's overall resources.

Thus, while dollars donated provide a limited picture of how much the church has to spend, giving as a percent of income provides both a measure of the church member's level of commitment to the church in comparison to other spending priorities, as well as a measure of whether the church's income is keeping up with inflation and growth in the economy. One might say that giving as a percent of income is an indication of the church's "market share" of church members' lives.

In most cases, to obtain giving as a percent of income, total income to a set of denominations was divided by the number of Full or Confirmed Members in the set. This yielded the per member giving amount in dollars. This per member giving amount was divided by per capita disposable personal income.

Giving in Dollars. Per member giving to churches can be measured in dollars. The dollar measure indicates, among other information, how much money religious institutions have to spend.

Current dollars indicate the value of the dollar in the year it was donated. However, since inflation changes the amount of goods or services that can be purchased with that dollar, data provided in current dollars has limited information value over a time span. If someone donated $5 in 1968 and $5 in 2009, on one level that person is donating the same amount of money. On another level, however, the buying power of that $5 has changed a great deal. Since less can be bought with the $5 donated in 2009 because of inflation in the economy, on a practical level the value of the donation has shrunk.

To account for the changes caused by inflation in the value of the dollar, a deflator can be applied. The result is inflation-adjusted 2005 dollars. Dollars adjusted to their chain-type, annual-weighted measure through the use of a deflator can be compared in terms of real growth over a time span since inflation has been factored out.

The deflator most commonly applied in this analysis designated the base period as 2005, with levels in 2005 set equal to 100. Thus, when adjusted by the deflator, the 1968 gift of $5 was worth $22.73 in inflation-adjusted 2005 dollars, and the 2009 gift of $5 was worth $4.56 in inflation-adjusted 2005 dollars.

Data Appendix and Revisions. Appendix B includes the aggregate denominational data used in the analyses in this study. In general, the data for the denominations included in these analyses appears as it was reported in editions of the *YACC*. In some cases, data for one or more years for a specific denomination was obtained directly from the denominational office. Also, the denominational giving data set has been refined and revised as additional information has become available. Where relevant, this information is noted in the appendix.

---

[i] John Ronsvalle and Sylvia Ronsvalle; "National Church Leaders Response Form"; *The State of Church Giving through 1998* (2000 edition); <http://www.emptytomb.org/survey1.html>.

chapter 1

Church Member Giving, 1968-2009

"The King will reply, 'I tell you the truth, whatever you did for one of the least of these brothers of mine, you did for me.' ...

"He will reply, 'I tell you the truth, whatever you did not do for one of the least of these, you did not do for me.' "

—Matthew 25:40, 45 (NIV)

Church Giving Numbers as a Measure of Faithfulness

The third parable in the 25th chapter of Matthew raises a number of interesting and perhaps troubling issues for those who claim to be followers of Jesus Christ.

These topics are considered in more depth in chapter 8 of this volume.

In this first chapter, there is a working assumption about the connection between commands of Jesus, such as that voiced in Matthew 25, and church member giving statistics. That is, church member giving numbers provide an objective measurement of the degree to which church members in the U.S. respond in obedience to the commands of Jesus Christ, the Founder of their faith. In this way, giving numbers display the value church members place on their faith compared to other spending options. The chapters that follow build on this working assumption.

By considering church member giving as a percent of income, a comparison across time is possible. By this standard, one may compare how church members weigh the priorities identified in Jesus' commands with other needs and wants facing the church member. In a related fashion, one may also consider congregational priorities, revealed through spending patterns, by comparing the percent of expenses focused on the internal services to current members, and the percent focused on external activities that take into account the broader principles declared by Jesus in Scripture.

Voluntary Transparency. The church member giving analyses are possible because of a long history of voluntary transparency within the church in the U.S.[1]

The *1916 Federal Council Year Book* began a series of surveys of Christian denominations regarding their "foreign missions" activity. In the *1919 Yearbook of the Churches*, general giving information was added to the foreign missions statistics.[2] The *Yearbook of American and Canadian Churches (YACC)* has continued to publish general church member giving numbers voluntarily provided by denominations through the 2011 edition. For example, information for a set of denominations that include over 100,000 of the estimated 350,000 congregations in the U.S. is available for the 1968-2009 period, largely through data published in the *YACC* series, although supplemented in some cases through direct contact with the denominations. This consistent set of data is useful for identifying, and to some degree understanding, trends in church member giving patterns during this recent four-decade period. Other data for a smaller group of denominations extends back as far as 1921 (see chapter 4). The publication by the *YACC* of voluntarily provided denominational data serves as an invaluable historical data stream, captured faithfully on an annual basis by generations of servant editors and denominational officials concerned about the general good of the church and the larger society in which it exists.

Two Troubling Trends. However, more recently, two troubling developments have surfaced in the voluntary transparency of church communions in the U.S. These trends have occurred at a time when the nature of being a nonprofit is under close review in the U.S.

As observed in a May 2011 *Chronicle of Philanthropy* column: "Charities are under a magnifying glass like never before. Advances in technology have created an era of transparency. No longer can charities rely on just the good will of their name and historical record. Now they must continually justify their relevance and nurture and protect their credibility. Public trust is of paramount importance, and to lose it may mean losing everything."[3]

Five Denominations No Longer Voluntarily Report. A first concern is that five denominations no longer voluntarily report their church member giving numbers.

The *State of Church Giving* series analysis is largely based on a composite set of denominations that published data in 1968 and 1985. By 2009, five of these original 31 communions were no longer making their church member giving numbers public.

The historical data stream is a fragile resource. If the data is not collected on a contemporary basis, it is difficult if not impossible to recover the information in subsequent years. It is therefore a regrettable development that these threads in the giving data tapestry of the church in the U.S. are no longer visible.

1. The Friends United Meeting stopped reporting giving data in 1991.

2. The Church of God (Anderson, IN) stopped reporting giving data in 1998.

3. The newly formed Mennonite Church USA reported general giving data only in 1999, the year it resulted from the merger of the Mennonite Church and

...two troubling developments have surfaced in the voluntary transparency of church communions in the U.S.

the Mennonite Church, General Conference; these two individual antecedent denominations had provided church member giving data back to at least 1968.

4. The North American Baptist Conference stopped providing membership and giving data in 2005.

5. The Evangelical Covenant Church did not report membership or giving data for 2008 or 2009.

In each case, the historical data series extends back to at least 1968, in some cases even further.

Some of these denominations have explained that the central office in that communion has had to cut back on budgets, and therefore does not have the staff to obtain the numbers from the congregations and aggregate them. This trend is a logical consequence of the long-term decline in spending on Benevolences, including denominational support, by congregations (see the discussion on Table 1). Other denominations suggest that the relationship between the national denominational office and the related congregations has weakened to the degree that congregations no longer feel accountable to the national office regarding the reporting of numbers.

Whatever the reason, this trend toward a lack of public accountability by denominations, and thus, through voluntary aggregate reporting, to the society in general, is occurring at the same time that the second troubling trend is emerging.

Proposed Government Intervention. The second troubling development is a possible move toward increased regulation of denominations and congregations by external entities.

The second troubling development is a possible move toward increased regulation of denominations and congregations by external entities.

Traditionally, the church has enjoyed exemptions from governmental control. The church has been regarded as representing many of the higher ideals that have influenced the general social fabric of the nation. The church as a safeguard of these higher ideals, "providing beneficial services for society"[4] related to those ideals—both to members and to the public—has earned various privileges in society, including exemption from taxes and other real-world privileges.

The church has returned this trust from society through voluntary transparency. Reporting of numbers not only demonstrates trustworthiness on the part of church institutions. The voluntary reporting has also served to call the society in general to values beyond one's individual needs, values that emphasize the common, or greater, good. Altruistic spending patterns model a set of values that demonstrate and embody higher ideals. As not only church members, but observers outside the church, consider spending patterns that emphasize "the least" in the U.S. and the global community, the church as an institution serves as a tether to the perspectives that keep the society in general focused on values that insure a broader social context that includes the needs of everyone, especially those with no other voice than the voluntary concern of the church.

Therefore, those who care about the church in the U.S. should regard with concern a move away from voluntary transparency on the part of Christian traditions within the U.S. An unwillingness to be accountable to a society from which the church, as an institution, expects special privileges could lead to the withdrawal of those privileges. Such a change would weaken not only the church, but also the society, which the church is supposed to be influencing.

Yet, there appears to be a trend taking shape that regards the church not as a special entity but as another nonprofit institution that requires regulation. Consider the following recent developments.

Tax-exemption privileges for churches and nonprofits. Some of the developments could affect the tax-exempt nature of the church, as well as nonprofits in general.

1. In a move affecting all nonprofits, including churches, the December 2010 report of the deficit commission advising President Barak Obama proposed the end of the charitable tax deduction available to itemizers, substituting a "12% non-refundable tax credit available to all taxpayers; available above 2% of Adjusted Gross Income (AGI) floor."[5] In July 2011, a proposal to "curb" charitable deductions was made by a bipartisan group of U.S. senators, seeking to address the national deficit and the U.S. debt ceiling.[6]

2. Looking for additional revenue, the City of Boston has previously been asking large nonprofits to make "payments in lieu of taxes (PILOTs)" for a portion of what would otherwise be property taxes. The city now is exploring the arrangement for all tax-exempt organizations. The news report about this development did not mention whether or not churches would be excluded from that expansion.[7]

3. Municipalities are levying "fees" on churches, as opposed to taxes. The fee in Mission, Kansas, specifically is based on a multiplier that combines an estimated average number of roundtrips to a church and "each seat in a sanctuary."[8]

General operations such as pensions under review. Some denominations have pension funds that are "...sufficiently funded to meet future obligations... [and] rank among the nation's largest..." One report indicated that The Episcopal Church, the Presbyterian Church (USA), and The United Methodist Church are in this category. A spokesman for Guidestone Financial Services of the Southern Baptist Convention was also quoted as affirming that organization's stability. However, other denominations report underfunding of their commitments. One mainline Protestant denomination's defined benefit program "has been closed to new participants since January 1, 2010." Denominations have been exempt from enrolling in the Pension Benefit Guaranty Corporation for Federal insurance, and therefore have been exempt from the related regulations. Some observers, such as the director of the Pension Rights center, "a Washington-based watchdog group," have suggested recently that participants in "so-called church plans are far more at risk."[9]

Reporting requirements. The Evangelical Council for Financial Accountability (ECFA) was asked for assistance by Senator Charles Grassley, ranking member of the Senate Finance Committee that has "tax-exempt oversight responsibilities." ECFA formed the Commission on Accountability and Policy for Religious Organizations. "The commission will be tasked with gathering input from the sector and providing feedback to the senator's office, with the goal of improving accountability and policy in the religious sector." Issues that may be considered include whether churches should file the detailed Form 990 or a similar form, whether the clergy housing allowance exclusion should be continued, and whether "legislation is needed to clarify 'love offerings' to ministers."[10]

One news article about this development reported: "ECFA contends that new laws will create administrative burdens and punish all churches and religious groups, even though it believes improper practices 'are not pervasive in the sector,' [ECFA president Dan] Busby says." Senator Grassley has stated that "he prefers self-correction within the industry rather than new laws."[11]

Many denominations continue voluntary reporting of church giving data. The trends noted above could have serious implications for the status of the church in U.S. society, and the church's ability to pursue its own agenda. Fortunately, a large number of denominations continue the rich tradition of making voluntarily reported data available for review by scholars, academics, and members of the general public who recognize the importance of the role of the church in U.S. society. The willingness of these denominational officials to share this information serves as a counterweight to any who would reduce the church to the status of just another institution to be regulated. The faithfulness of these denominational officials distinguishes the church through their voluntary transparency and modeling of self-disclosure, underscoring the basis for recognizing the church as an acknowledged practitioner of core values, and as embodying many of the higher ideals, of society. The information these denominational officials have shared extends the historical data stream through 2009.

Fortunately, a large number of denominations continue the rich tradition of making voluntarily reported data available...

Overview of Church Member Giving, 1968 through 2009

Giving Categories. When a dollar is given to the church, it is allocated into one of two major subcategories, as defined by the annual reporting form of the *YACC*.

The first subcategory is Congregational Finances. This subcategory refers to those expenditures that support the operations of the local congregation, such as building and utilities, pastor and staff salaries, insurance, music and Sunday school materials.

The second is Benevolences, which generally refers to expenditures for what might be termed the broader mission of the church, beyond the local congregation. Benevolences includes everything from support of regional and national denominational offices to the local soup kitchen, from seminaries to international ministries.

Total Contributions is the sum of Congregational Finances and Benevolences.

Giving as a Percent of Income, 1968-2009. The measurement tool can be the number of dollars given, or the portion of income given. To understand how much church members have available to address, in Jesus' name, the needs in front of them, the percent of income given provides a better overview.

Even factoring out inflation, few people had the same amount of income in 2009 as in 1968. This real growth in income is taken into account in giving as a percent of income, since the number of dollars given is placed in the context of the total amount of resources available to the donor. If income goes up faster than the amount of dollars given, in a very real sense giving has decreased in the donor's priorities, because the dollars given represent a smaller percent of the donor's total spending.

If the rate of increase in income slows, and yet church giving remains steady or even increases, then the percent of income given will increase, thus suggesting a sustained commitment to the church even in difficult economic times.

Considering giving as a percent of income provides insight not only into the amount given by church members, but also into the priority that the members are placing on those donations, compared to other categories that attract the church members' spending.

Figure 1 presents per member giving as a portion of income to the church among the members of the basic set of denominations in this analysis, referred to as the composite data set. As can be observed from this chart, giving as a portion of income declined in all three categories of Total Contributions, Congregational Finances, and Benevolences between 1968 and 2009. The overall decline in giving as a portion of income from 1968 to 2009 suggests that the church is commanding less of church members' attention compared to other spending priorities.

The portion of income contributed to the church, as represented in Total Contributions, decreased from 3.11% in 1968 to 2.38% in 2009, a decline of 23% from the 1968 base.

Figure 1: Per Member Giving to Total Contributions, Congregational Finances and Benevolences, Percent of Income, 1968-2009

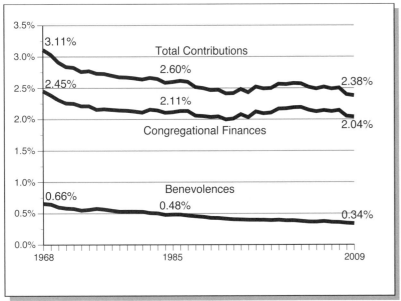

Source: empty tomb analysis; *YACC* adjusted series; U.S. BEA   empty tomb, inc. 2011

Overall, giving to Congregational Finances as a percent of income decreased from 2.45% in 1968 of income to 2.04%, a decline of 17%. In 1993, giving to Congregational Finances began an intermittent recovery from a low point in 1992. However, declines in 2008 and 2009 returned giving levels to those of 1989-1991.

The portion of income directed to Benevolences demonstrated a fairly steady decline throughout the period. Beginning in 1968, the portion of income directed to Benevolences was 0.66%. By 2009, the level had declined to 0.34%, the lowest in the 1968-2009 period. This change represented a decrease of 48% in the portion of income directed to the category of Benevolences.

Giving as a percent of income decreased from 2007 to 2008, and again from 2008 to 2009. These decreases were observed in giving to Total Contributions and the two subcategories of Congregational Finances and Benevolences. The peak of the most recent recession was in December 2007, and the trough was in mid-2009. A discussion of giving patterns in recession years is presented in chapter 5 of this volume.

Implications of Giving in 2008 Compared to 2009. Sometimes the change in the portion of income given can be very small from one year to the next. Yet, because there are so many members involved, even small changes are magnified. To explore the implications of these changes, consider the impact of the difference in the portion of income given to Benevolences between 2008 and 2009. For this analysis, information for the 25 denominations that reported data for both 2008 and 2009 is compared.

In 2008, per member giving to Benevolences as a portion of income measured 0.35%. In 2009, the amount decreased to the lowest point in the 1968 to 2009 period, 0.34%.

The implications of this change can be understood when translated to dollars. The unrounded difference between 2008 and 2009 Benevolences as a portion of income was -0.0061915% of per capita income. When multiplied by the 2009 current dollar U.S. per capita income figure of $35,888, that change translated into a decrease in 2009 of $2.22 given by each of the 27,917,578 members in these denominations. The combination of these individual dollar decreases meant that the composite communions had $62.0 million less to spend in 2009 on the larger mission of the church, compared to the 2008 level.

...that amount could have prevented the deaths of an estimated 65,576 children in 2009—more than the population of either Greenwich, Connecticut, or Palo Alto, California.

Based on available data, it was estimated that $945.96 could save the life of one child under five who is dying from preventable causes somewhere around the globe.[12] The calculated amount of $62.0 million, the aggregate value of the portion of income not given to Benevolences in 2009 as a result of the decrease from 2008 to 2009, can be divided by the cost-per-child-life figure of $945.96. Had that $62.0 million been donated in 2009, and had that amount been applied to address child deaths through the denominations' already established programs, that amount could have prevented the deaths of an estimated 65,576 children in 2009—more than the population of either Greenwich, Connecticut, or Palo Alto, California.

Potential Giving. Another approach is to consider what would have been the situation in 2009 if giving had at least maintained the 1968 percentages of income donated.

The implications of the difference become clearer when aggregate totals are calculated. The levels of giving as a percent of income in 1968 were multiplied by 2009 income. The resulting per member dollar figure was then multiplied by the number of members reported by these denominations in 2009. If the same portion of income had been donated in 2009 as in 1968, aggregate Total Contributions would have been $30.8 billion rather than the actual amount given of $23.8 billion, a difference of $7 billion, or an increase of 29%.

Aggregate Congregational Finances would have been $24.3 billion rather than $20.4 billion, a difference of $3.9 billion, or an increase of 19%.

There would have been a 90% increase in the total amount received for Benevolences. Instead of receiving $3.4 billion in 2009, as these church structures did, they would have received $6.5 billion, a difference of $3.1 billion available for the larger mission of the church.

The difference between the 1968 and 2009 portions of income given impacts the ministry of the church in very real ways.

Chapters 6 and 8 of this volume consider some of the implications and consequences of the difference between actual and potential giving levels among church members.

Giving in Dollars, 1968 through 2009. Per member giving measured in current dollars (the value the dollar had in the year it was given) increased overall from 1968 through 2009.[13] This increase was evident in giving to Total Contributions, and to the two subcategories of Congregational Finances and Benevolences.

Of course, dollars did not have the same purchasing power in both 1968 and 2009. To be able to compare dollars across different years, a deflator is used to factor out the effects of inflation. When inflation is factored out, the value that the dollars had in the same year the dollars were given ("current" dollar value) is converted to the value those adjusted dollars would have in a standard year ("inflation-adjusted" dollar value). The year 2005 serves as the standard year for the deflator series used in these analyses. Applying this deflator series, a gift of $5.00 in 1968 has the value, or purchasing power, of $22.73 in the year 2005, and a gift of $5.00 in the year 2009 has the value of $4.56 in the year 2005. By factoring out inflation, gifts in dollars can be compared across years in a more meaningful way.

Figure 2 presents the changes in inflation-adjusted dollar contributions to Total Contributions, and the two subcategories of Congregational Finances and Benevolences. As can be observed in Figure 2, giving to each of the categories of Total Contributions, Congregational Finances, and Benevolences declined in some years.

Figure 2: Changes in Per Member Giving to Total Contributions, Congregational Finances and Benevolences, Inflation-Adjusted 2005 Dollars, 1968-2009

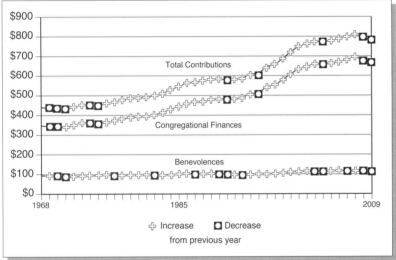

Source: empty tomb analysis; *YACC*, adjusted series; U.S. BEA   empty tomb, inc. 2011

Figure 3: Per Member Giving to Congregational Finances and Benevolences, and U.S. Per Capita DPI, Inflation-Adjusted 2005 Dollars, 1968-2009

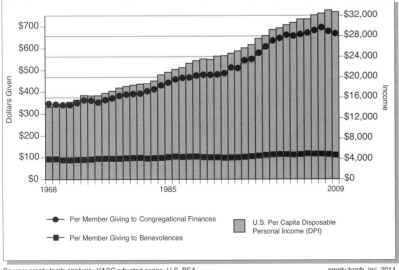

Source: empty tomb analysis; *YACC* adjusted series; U.S. BEA   empty tomb, inc. 2011

Of the total inflation-adjusted dollar increase in per member giving between 1968 and 2009, 95% was directed to Congregational Finances. Stated another way, of each additional inflation-adjusted dollar donated in 2009 compared to 1968, 95¢ was directed to Congregational Finances. This emphasis on the internal operations of the congregation helps explain the finding that Benevolences represented 21% of all church activity in 1968, and 14% in 2009.

From 1968 to 2009, per member giving to Total Contributions increased 77% in inflation-adjusted dollars. However, during this same period, U.S. Per Capita Disposable (after-tax) Personal Income (DPI) increased 131%. The fact that incomes increased faster than giving explains why per member giving increased overall from 1968 through 2009 in dollars, but shrank as a portion of income.

Figure 3 provides a comparison of per member giving to the categories of Congregational Finances and Benevolences with changes in U.S. per capita DPI, both in inflation-adjusted 2005 dollars.

Details of Church Member Giving, 1968 through 2009

The Composite Denominations. The first study that provided a basis for the present series was published in 1988. The *YACC* series publishes church member giving data. Data for the years 1968 and 1985 could be confirmed for 31 denominations.[14] The data year 1968 was selected because, beginning that year, a consistent distinction was made between Full or Confirmed Membership and Inclusive Membership in the *YACC* series. The denominations that published data for both 1968 and 1985 included 29,476,782 Full or Confirmed Members in 1985. The current composite denomination set comprises approximately 100,000 of the estimated 350,000 religious congregations in the U.S.

The present church member giving report series extended the analysis for the original set of denominations beyond 1985. The current report analyzes the data set through 2009, the most recent year for which data was available at the time the report was written.[15] Also, data for the intervening years of 1969 through 1984, and 1986 through 2008, was included in the composite data set, as available.[16]

Financial Categories. Calculating contributions on a per member basis accounts for any changes in membership, either through growth or decline, which might have taken place during the period under review. The dollars given can be considered from two points of view. The *number of dollars given* by members indicates how much money the church has to spend. On the other hand, *giving as a percent of income* places donations in the larger context of the income available to church members, and demonstrates how the church fared compared to other church member spending priorities.

The key general category is giving as a percent of income. This category considers not only the dollars given, but also what portion those dollars represent of the resources available to the church member who gave them. One might say that considering giving as a percent of income reflects how the donation rated in the donor church member's overall lifestyle choices, a sort of thermometer to gauge the warmth of the member's commitment. Therefore, since the point of interest is

Table 1: Per Member Giving as a Percent of Income, 1968-2009

Year	Total Contrib.	↑↓	Cong. Finances	↑↓	Benevol.	↑↓
1968	3.11%	—	2.45%	—	0.66%	—
1969	3.03%	↓	2.39%	↓	0.65%	↓
1970	2.91%	↓	2.31%	↓	0.60%	↓
1971	2.84%	↓	2.26%	↓	0.58%	↓
1972	2.83%	↓	2.25%	↓	0.58%	↓
1973	2.76%	↓	2.21%	↓	0.55%	↓
1974	2.77%	↑	2.21%	↑	0.56%	↑
1975	2.73%	↓	2.15%	↓	0.58%	↑
1976	2.73%	↓	2.16%	↑	0.56%	↓
1977	2.70%	↓	2.15%	↓	0.55%	↓
1978	2.67%	↓	2.14%	↓	0.53%	↓
1979	2.67%	↓	2.14%	↓	0.53%	↑
1980	2.66%	↓	2.13%	↓	0.53%	↓
1981	2.64%	↓	2.11%	↓	0.53%	↓
1982	2.66%	↑	2.16%	↑	0.51%	↓
1983	2.65%	↓	2.14%	↓	0.50%	↓
1984	2.59%	↓	2.11%	↓	0.48%	↓
1985	2.60%	↑	2.11%	↑	0.48%	↑
1986	2.62%	↑	2.13%	↑	0.48%	↓
1987	2.60%	↓	2.13%	↑	0.47%	↓
1988	2.52%	↓	2.06%	↓	0.46%	↓
1989	2.50%	↓	2.05%	↓	0.45%	↓
1990	2.47%	↓	2.04%	↓	0.43%	↓
1991	2.47%	↑	2.05%	↑	0.43%	↓
1992	2.41%	↓	2.00%	↓	0.42%	↓
1993	2.42%	↑	2.01%	↑	0.41%	↓
1994	2.48%	↑	2.08%	↑	0.40%	↓
1995	2.43%	↓	2.03%	↓	0.40%	↓
1996	2.52%	↑	2.12%	↑	0.40%	↓
1997	2.49%	↓	2.09%	↓	0.40%	↓
1998	2.50%	↑	2.11%	↑	0.39%	↓
1999	2.57%	↑	2.17%	↑	0.40%	↑
2000	2.56%	↓	2.17%	↑	0.39%	↓
2001	2.58%	↑	2.19%	↑	0.39%	↑
2002	2.57%	↓	2.19%	↑	0.38%	↓
2003	2.52%	↓	2.15%	↓	0.37%	↓
2004	2.49%	↓	2.12%	↓	0.37%	↓
2005	2.52%	↑	2.14%	↑	0.38%	↑
2006	2.49%	↓	2.13%	↓	0.36%	↓
2007	2.50%	↑	2.14%	↑	0.36%	↓
2008	2.40%	↓	2.05%	↓	0.35%	↓
2009	2.38%	↓	2.04%	↓	0.34%	↓

Details in the above table may not compute to the numbers shown due to rounding.

in the level of priority members place on their church giving, giving as a percent of income is the more useful category.

Giving as a percent of income is, of course, based on the dollars given, set in the context of dollars available as income. Within the category of dollars given, there are two approaches: (1) current dollars; and (2) inflation-adjusted dollars.

Current dollars refers to the value that the dollar had in the year it was donated. However, inflation affects the value of dollars. A dollar in 2009 bought fewer goods or services than it did in 1968. In order to account for this factor, a deflator is applied to the current dollar values, to translate the dollars into the value they would have in a standard year, thereby neutralizing the economic impact of inflation.

Giving as a Percent of Income, 1968-2009. The first approach to considering giving is giving as a portion of income. Unlike dollars, there is no distinction between current or inflation-adjusted when one is considering giving as a percent of income. So long as one compares current dollar giving to current dollar income when calculating the percent of income—or inflation-adjusted giving to inflation-adjusted income—the percent will be the same.

In Table 1, giving as a percent of income is presented for per member Total Contributions, and the two subcategories of Congregational Finances and Benevolences. The arrows indicate whether the percent of income in that category increased or decreased from the previous year. Inasmuch as the percent figures are rounded to the second decimal place, the arrows indicate the direction of a slight increase or decrease, including for those values in which the percent provided appears to be the same numerical figure as the previous year.

A review of Table 1 yields the following information.

Overall, per member giving to Total Contributions as a percent of income decreased from 3.11% in 1968 to 2.38% in 2009, a decline of 23% in the portion of income donated to the church. Giving to Total Contributions as a percent of income decreased 28 of a possible 41 times, or 70% of the time, between 1968 and 2009.

Unlike measuring only the dollars given, considering giving as a percent of income takes into account changes in the resources available to the donor as well. U.S. per capita DPI serves as an average income figure for the broad spectrum of church members included in the composite denominations data set.

U.S. per capita DPI was $3,112 in current dollars in 1968. When that figure was calculated in inflation-adjusted 2005 dollars, U.S. per capita DPI in 1968 was $14,148.

The current-dollar DPI figure for 2009 was $35,888. When inflation was factored out, 2009 U.S. per capita DPI was $32,742.

Thus, after-tax per capita income in inflation-adjusted dollars increased by $18,594, an increase of 131% from 1968 to 2009. During the same period, per member Total Contributions increased 77% in inflation-adjusted dollars. This difference explains how church member contributions could be increasing in inflation-adjusted dollars in most of the years from 1968 to 2009, and yet decreasing as a percent of income in most of the years from 1968 to 2009.

As a percent of income, giving to Congregational Finances, the amount spent to maintain the operations of the local congregation, decreased from one year to the next 60% of the time in the 1968-2009 period. Congregational Finances declined from 2.45% in 1968 to 2.04% in 2009, a percent change of -17% from the 1968 base in giving as a percent of income. It may be noted that giving to Congregational Finances as a percent of income declined in more years than it increased between 1968 and 1993. In 1993, an intermittent increase in this category began, with giving to Congregational Finances as a percent of income increasing in more years than it declined in 1993 through 2009. By 2009, Congregational Finances as a portion of income had nevertheless declined to the level of 1990.

As a percent of income, giving to Benevolences, church members' investment in the larger mission of the church, declined from 0.66% of income in 1968 to 0.34% in 2009, a decline of 48% as a portion of income. In the 1968-2009 period, the portion of income that went to Benevolences declined 85% of the time, from one year to the next. The decline in giving to Benevolences as a percent of income was fairly steady in the 1968 to 2009 period, never increasing more than two years in a row (see 1974 and 1975). The level of giving to Benevolences as a percent of income in 2009 was at its lowest level in the 1968-2009 period.

An increase may be noted in giving to Benevolences as a percent of income in 2005. This increase appears to have been a function of the disaster response opportunities that year. The year 2005 included the Indian Ocean earthquake and related tsunami that occurred the day after Christmas in 2004, Hurricanes Katrina, Rita and Wilma, and the Pakistani earthquake, all presented as opportunities for compassionate response in churches. The declines in this category from 2006 through

2009, when giving to Benevolences as a percent of income reached the lowest point in the 1968-2009 period, suggests that the 2005 giving was crisis-oriented, and did not represent a change in the pattern of long-term decline.

Giving in Current Dollars, 1968-2009.

Table 2 presents per member contributions in current dollars for the composite denominations data set. Per member giving is presented as Total Contributions, and the two subcategories of Congregational Finances and Benevolences. U.S. per capita DPI is also included. The last column includes the Benevolences dollar figures divided by the DPI, yielding Benevolences as a percent of income, which is also presented in Table 1.

Table 2: Per Member Giving to Total Contributions, Congregational Finances and Benevolences, U.S. Per Capita DPI, Current Dollars, and Per Member Giving to Benevolences as a Percent of Income, 1968-2009

| | Current Dollars | | | | |
| | Per Full or Confirmed Member Giving | | | U.S. Per Capita Disposable Personal Income | Per Member Giving to Benevolences as % of Income |
Year	Total Contrib.	Cong. Finances	Benevol.		
1968	$96.79	$76.35	$20.44	$3,112	0.66%
1969	$100.82	$79.34	$21.47	$3,324	0.65%
1970	$104.36	$82.87	$21.49	$3,586	0.60%
1971	$109.55	$87.08	$22.48	$3,859	0.58%
1972	$116.97	$93.16	$23.81	$4,140	0.58%
1973	$127.37	$102.01	$25.36	$4,615	0.55%
1974	$138.87	$110.79	$28.08	$5,010	0.56%
1975	$150.19	$118.45	$31.73	$5,497	0.58%
1976	$162.87	$129.15	$33.72	$5,972	0.56%
1977	$175.82	$140.23	$35.60	$6,514	0.55%
1978	$193.05	$154.74	$38.31	$7,220	0.53%
1979	$212.42	$170.17	$42.25	$7,956	0.53%
1980	$233.57	$186.90	$46.67	$8,794	0.53%
1981	$256.59	$205.15	$51.44	$9,726	0.53%
1982	$276.72	$223.93	$52.79	$10,390	0.51%
1983	$293.52	$237.68	$55.83	$11,095	0.50%
1984	$316.25	$257.63	$58.62	$12,232	0.48%
1985	$335.43	$272.95	$62.48	$12,911	0.48%
1986	$354.20	$288.73	$65.47	$13,540	0.48%
1987	$367.87	$301.73	$66.14	$14,146	0.47%
1988	$382.54	$313.15	$69.40	$15,206	0.46%
1989	$403.23	$331.06	$72.16	$16,134	0.45%
1990	$419.65	$346.48	$73.17	$17,004	0.43%
1991	$433.57	$358.67	$74.90	$17,532	0.43%
1992	$445.00	$368.28	$76.72	$18,436	0.42%
1993	$457.47	$380.54	$76.94	$18,909	0.41%
1994	$488.83	$409.35	$79.48	$19,678	0.40%
1995	$497.71	$416.00	$81.71	$20,470	0.40%
1996	$538.39	$453.34	$85.05	$21,355	0.40%
1997	$554.59	$466.07	$88.52	$22,255	0.40%
1998	$587.90	$495.56	$92.34	$23,534	0.39%
1999	$624.81	$527.99	$96.82	$24,356	0.40%
2000	$664.25	$563.52	$100.72	$25,944	0.39%
2001	$690.79	$586.58	$104.22	$26,805	0.39%
2002	$714.79	$609.46	$105.33	$27,799	0.38%
2003	$724.64	$618.85	$105.80	$28,805	0.37%
2004	$754.08	$643.18	$110.90	$30,287	0.37%
2005	$788.78	$671.11	$117.67	$31,318	0.38%
2006	$825.25	$705.13	$120.12	$33,157	0.36%
2007	$863.81	$739.93	$123.88	$34,512	0.36%
2008	$861.43	$736.92	$124.51	$35,931	0.35%
2009	$854.25	$732.11	$122.14	$35,888	0.34%

Details in the above table may not compute to the numbers shown due to rounding.

As can be seen in Table 2, the per member amount given to Total Contributions, Congregational Finances, and Benevolences increased in current dollars between 1968 and 2009.

Overall, from 1968 to 2009, Total Contributions to the church in current dollars increased $757.46 on a per member basis. That amounted to an increase of 783% from the 1968 base.

Of this amount, $655.76 was allocated to Congregational Finances, for the benefit of members within the congregation, an increase of 859% for this category from its 1968 base.

Benevolences, or outreach activities of the congregation, increased by $101.70, an increase of 498% over the 1968 base level for the category. Meanwhile, U.S. per capita DPI increased from $3,112 in 1968, to $35,888 in 2009, an increase of 1053% from the 1968 base. Therefore, Benevolences shrank 48% as a portion of income.

In 2008, per member giving to Total Contributions decreased in current dollars for the first time in the 1968-2009 period. It declined again in 2009 as well.

While a congregation or denomination might accurately state that members gave more current dollars from one year to the next, the reality of inflation's impact should be taken into account, to understand the buying power of those dollars given.

Giving in Inflation-Adjusted Dollars, 1968-2009. The U.S. Bureau of Economic Analysis (BEA) publishes the deflator series that is used to factor out inflation. This deflator series allows dollar figures to be compared more precisely across years. The current year of base comparison in the U.S. BEA series is 2005. By applying the Implicit Price Deflator for Gross National Product to the current-dollar church member giving data, the data can be reviewed across years with the effects of inflation factored out.

Table 3 presents per member giving in inflation-adjusted dollars, as well as U.S. per capita DPI, also in inflation-adjusted dollars. The arrows next to the three inflation-adjusted giving category columns are included to provide a quick reference as to whether giving increased or decreased from one year to the next.

When the effects of inflation were removed, one may note that per member giving decreased in a number of years. Per member giving to Total Contributions did increase overall from 1968 to 2009. However, when inflation was factored out, the percent increase was smaller than in current dollars. Per member giving to Total Contributions in inflation-adjusted dollars increased from $440.03 in 1968 to $779.36 in 2009, an increase of 77% from the 1968 base.

Congregational Finances also increased in inflation-adjusted 2005 dollars from 1968 to 2009. Overall, per member giving to Congregational Finances increased from $347.12 in inflation-adjusted dollars to $667.93 in 2009, an increase of $320.81, or 92%.

Benevolences also increased from 1968 to 2009 when adjusted for inflation, although proportionately less than Congregational Finances.

Table 3: **Per Member Giving to Total Contributions, Congregational Finances and Benovelences, U.S. Per Capita DPI, Inflation-Adjusted 2005 Dollars, and Per Member Giving to Benevolences as a Percent of Income, 1968-2009**

| | Inflation-Adjusted 2005 Dollars | | | | | | U.S. Per Capita Disposable Personal Income | Per Member Giving to Benevolences as % of Income |
| | Per Full or Confirmed Member Giving | | | | | | | |
Year	Total Contrib.	↑↓	Cong. Finances	↑↓	Benevol.	↑↓		
1968	$440.03	—	$347.12	—	$92.91	—	$14,148	0.66%
1969	$436.79	↓	$343.76	↓	$93.04	↑	$14,401	0.65%
1970	$429.50	↓	$341.05	↓	$88.44	↓	$14,758	0.60%
1971	$429.37	↓	$341.27	↑	$88.09	↓	$15,124	0.58%
1972	$439.47	↑	$350.02	↑	$89.45	↑	$15,554	0.58%
1973	$453.31	↑	$363.05	↑	$90.26	↑	$16,425	0.55%
1974	$453.18	↓	$361.55	↓	$91.63	↑	$16,350	0.56%
1975	$447.77	↓	$353.16	↓	$94.61	↑	$16,389	0.58%
1976	$459.15	↑	$364.08	↑	$95.07	↑	$16,836	0.56%
1977	$465.94	↑	$371.61	↑	$94.34	↓	$17,262	0.55%
1978	$478.02	↑	$383.17	↑	$94.85	↑	$17,878	0.53%
1979	$485.58	↑	$388.99	↑	$96.58	↑	$18,187	0.53%
1980	$489.38	↑	$391.60	↑	$97.77	↑	$18,425	0.53%
1981	$491.50	↑	$392.97	↑	$98.53	↑	$18,630	0.53%
1982	$499.57	↑	$404.27	↑	$95.30	↓	$18,758	0.51%
1983	$509.70	↑	$412.75	↑	$96.95	↑	$19,267	0.50%
1984	$529.29	↑	$431.18	↑	$98.11	↑	$20,472	0.48%
1985	$544.87	↑	$443.37	↑	$101.50	↑	$20,972	0.48%
1986	$562.93	↑	$458.89	↑	$104.05	↑	$21,519	0.48%
1987	$568.15	↑	$466.00	↑	$102.15	↓	$21,847	0.47%
1988	$571.18	↑	$467.56	↑	$103.62	↑	$22,704	0.46%
1989	$580.09	↑	$476.28	↑	$103.81	↑	$23,211	0.45%
1990	$581.24	↑	$479.89	↑	$101.34	↓	$23,552	0.43%
1991	$579.99	↓	$479.79	↓	$100.20	↓	$23,453	0.43%
1992	$581.54	↑	$481.28	↑	$100.26	↑	$24,093	0.42%
1993	$584.82	↑	$486.47	↑	$98.35	↓	$24,173	0.41%
1994	$612.00	↑	$512.50	↑	$99.51	↑	$24,636	0.40%
1995	$610.37	↓	$510.16	↓	$100.20	↑	$25,104	0.40%
1996	$647.91	↑	$545.56	↑	$102.35	↑	$25,699	0.40%
1997	$655.87	↑	$551.19	↑	$104.69	↑	$26,319	0.40%
1998	$687.53	↑	$579.54	↑	$107.99	↑	$27,522	0.39%
1999	$720.10	↑	$608.52	↑	$111.59	↑	$28,071	0.40%
2000	$749.33	↑	$635.71	↑	$113.62	↑	$29,267	0.39%
2001	$762.06	↑	$647.09	↑	$114.97	↑	$29,570	0.39%
2002	$775.99	↑	$661.64	↑	$114.35	↓	$30,179	0.38%
2003	$770.11	↓	$657.68	↓	$112.44	↓	$30,612	0.37%
2004	$779.28	↑	$664.67	↑	$114.61	↑	$31,299	0.37%
2005	$788.78	↑	$671.11	↑	$117.67	↑	$31,318	0.38%
2006	$799.20	↑	$682.87	↑	$116.32	↓	$32,110	0.36%
2007	$812.62	↑	$696.08	↑	$116.54	↑	$32,467	0.36%
2008	$793.02	↓	$678.40	↓	$114.62	↓	$33,078	0.35%
2009	$779.36	↓	$667.93	↓	$111.43	↓	$32,742	0.34%

Details in the above table may not compute to the numbers shown due to rounding.

From 1968 to 2009, per member giving to Benevolences in inflation-adjusted dollars increased $18.52, an increase of 20% from the 1968 base.

U.S. per capita DPI, considered in inflation-adjusted dollars, increased from $14,148 in 1968, to $32,742 in 2009, an increase of 131%.

Per member giving to Benevolences as a percent of income is again included in Table 3. The figures for this category are the same in both Tables 2 and 3. Because the same deflator is applied to both the giving dollars and the income dollars, per member giving to Benevolences as a percent of income is proportionally the same, whether the information is considered as current or inflation-adjusted dollars. As long as current dollar giving is compared to current dollar income, or inflation-adjusted giving is compared to inflation-adjusted income, giving as a percent of income will be the same for both series.

One may observe the consequences of the fact that U.S. per capita DPI increased 131% in inflation-adjusted dollars from 1968 to 2009, while per member giving to Benevolences increased 20%. The result was the overall decline of 48% to Benevolences in the portion of income given, from the 1968 base.

Giving in Inflation-adjusted Dollars, 1968 and 2009. The first report, which served as the basis for the present series on church member giving, considered data for the denominations in the composite data set for the years 1968 and 1985. With data now available through 2009, a broader trend can be reviewed for the period under discussion, the 42-year range of 1968 through 2009.

Table 4 presents per member gifts to Total Contributions, Congregational Finances, and Benevolences in inflation-adjusted 2005 dollars for the years 1968 and 2009.

The per member amount donated to Total Contributions in inflation-adjusted 2005 dollars was $339.33 greater in 2009 than it was in 1968 for the denominations in the composite data set. This amount represented an average increase of $8.28 a year in per member contributions over this 42-year period.

Gifts to Congregational Finances also increased between 1968 and 2009. Per member contributions to Congregational Finances were $347.12 in 1968, in inflation-adjusted 2005 dollars, and increased to $667.93 in 2009, a total increase of $320.81, with an average annual rate of change of $7.82.

Table 4: Per Member Giving to Total Contributions, Congregational Finances and Benevolences, Inflation-Adjusted 2005 Dollars, 1968 and 2009

Year	Per Member Giving in Inflation-Adjusted 2005 Dollars								
	Total Contributions			Congregational Finances			Benevolences		
	Per Member Giving	Difference from 1968 Base	Average Annual Diff. in $ Given	Per Member Giving	Difference from 1968 Base	Average Annual Diff. in $ Given	Per Member Giving	Difference from 1968 Base	Average Annual Diff. in $ Given
1968	$440.03			$347.12			$92.91		
2009	$779.36	$339.33	$8.28	$667.93	$320.81	$7.82	$111.43	$18.52	$0.45

Details in the above table may not compute to the numbers shown due to rounding.

In inflation-adjusted 2005 dollars, gifts to Benevolences were $92.91 in 1968 and grew to $111.43 in 2009, an increase of $18.52, with an annual average rate of change of $0.45.

Giving as a Percent of Income, 1968 and 2009. Between 1968 and 2009, Total Contributions declined from 3.11% to 2.38% as a portion of income, an absolute decline of 0.73%, a decrease of almost three-quarters of a percent of income donated to the church. The percent change in the portion of income donated to the church in the 42-year period was -23%.

Per member gifts to Congregational Finances measured 2.45% of income in 1968, and 2.04% in 2009. The absolute change in giving as a percent of income was -0.41%. The percent change in the portion of income to Congregational Finances, from the 1968 base, was -17%.

From 1968 to 2009, the portion of member income directed to Benevolences decreased from 0.66% to 0.34%, an absolute difference of -0.32%, about three-fourths of the decline in Congregational Finances, even though Benevolences began from a smaller base. The decline in the portion of income given to Benevolences translated to a percent change in giving as a percent of income of -48% from the 1968 base.

Table 5 presents per member giving to Total Contributions, Congregational Finances, and Benevolences as a percent of income in 1968 and 2009.

Table 5: **Per Member Giving to Total Contributions, Congregational Finances and Benevolences, Percent of Income, 1968 and 2009**

Year	Per Member Giving as a Percent of Income		
	Total Contributions	Congregational Finances	Benevolences
1968	3.11%	2.45%	0.66%
2009	2.38%	2.04%	0.34%
Absolute Difference in Per Member Giving as a Percent of Income from 1968 Base	-0.73%	-0.41%	-0.32%
Percent Change in Giving as a Percent of Income, Calculated from 1968 Base	-23.47%	-16.85%	-48.18%

Details in the above table may not compute to the numbers shown due to rounding.

Notes for Chapter 1

[1] In addition to the rich vein of voluntarily reported denominational data, there is also a set of Census Bureau data for 1850, 1860, 1870, and 1890, that provides "limited information on religious bodies (number of congregations and buildings, and value of edifices)." A Census of Religious Bodies was also carried out in 1906, 1916, 1926, and 1936. See: U.S. Bureau of the Census, *Historical Statistics of the United States, Colonial Times to 1970, Bicentennial Edition, Part 1* (Washington, DC, 1975), pp. 389-390. For further discussion about the Census of Religious Bodies data, see also: Benson Y. Landis, "The 1936 Census of Religious Bodies," in Landis, ed., *Yearbook of American Churches (Fifteenth Issue) (Biennial)*, 1941 Edition (Jackson Heights, NY: Yearbook of American Churches Press, 1941), particularly pp. 138-141.

[2] For a discussion of the historical data categories available in the *YACC* series, see John Ronsvalle and Sylvia Ronsvalle, "Giving Trends and the Church's Priorities," *The State of Church Giving through 2003* (Champaign, Ill., empty tomb, inc., 2005), pp. 107-111, including Table 27, p. 111. This chapter is also available at: <http://www.emptytomb.org/SCG03Priorities.pdf>.

[3] Emily Chan and Gene Takagi, "Charities Should Drink Deeply of the 'Three Cups of Tea' Scandal's Lessons," *The Chronicle of Philanthropy*, May 5, 2011, pp. 31.

[4] Adelle M. Banks, RNS; "Cash-Strapped Cities Look to Tax Churches for Road Use"; *The Christian Century*; 1/21/2011; <http://www.christiancentury.org/article/2011-01/cash-strapped-cities-look-tax-churches-road-use>; p. 1 of 7/17/2011 11:48 AM printout.

[5] The National Commission on Fiscal Responsibility and Reform; "The Moment of Truth"; The White House; December 1, 2010; <http://www.fiscalcommission.gov/sites/fiscalcommission.gov/files/documents/TheMomentofTruth12_1_2010.pdf>; page 31 of 7/22/2011 download.

[6] John D. McKinnon; "Gang of Six Plan Cuts Both Ways"; online.wsj.com; 7/21/2011; <http://online.wsj.com/article/SB10001424053111904233404576458362024552134.html?mod=googlenews_wsj>; p. 2 of 7/22/2011 3:14 PM printout.

[7] The NonProfit Times Weekly Newsletter; "Cash-Strapped Boston Going After Nonprofits"; 12/27/2010; <http://www.thenonprofittimes.com/newsletters/weekly/nptimesweeklydec272010.html#sub1>; p. 1-2 of 7/17/2011 11:25 AM printout.

[8] Banks, pp. 1-2.

[9] G. Jeffrey MacDonald, RNS, appearing as "Shaky Economy Imperils Church Pensions," *The Christian Century*, January 11, 2011, pp. 14-15. Also: G. Jeffrey MacDonald, RNS, with contributions by Dianna L. Cagle, Biblical Recorder assistant managing editor; appearing as, "Market Bumps Raise Church Pension Concerns"; *Biblical Recorder*; 1/4/2011; <http://www.biblicalrecorder.org/post/2011/01/04/Market-bumps-raise-church-pension-concerns.aspx>; p. 1 of 1/10/2011 7:01 PM printout.

[10] Mark Hrywna, "Evangelical Groups Avoid Legislation, For Now," *The NonProfit Times*, February 1, 2011, pp. 1, 8.

[11] Matt Branaugh, "Self-Policing Pastors," *Christianity Today*, March 2011, p. 13.

[12] The total number of child deaths in 2009 was 8,087,000 per David Anthony, editor, *The State of the World's Children, 2011* (New York: UNICEF, 2011), p. 91. An estimate of $5.1 billion a year, through 2015, could prevent two-thirds of the under-five child deaths, per Jennifer Bryce, et al.; "Can the World Afford to Save the Lives of 6 Million Children Each Year?"; *The Lancet*, vol. 365; 6/25/2005; p. 2193; <http://www.thelancet.com/journals/lancet/article/PIIS014065667773/fulltext>; p. 1 of 1/11/2006 printout. Dividing the cost of $5.1 billion by two-thirds of the child deaths, or 5,391,333, yielded the $945.96 figure.

[13] No adjustment was made in the composite data for missing denominational data in the 1968-2009 analysis. The 2009 composite data set membership represented 98.5% of the benchmark 1985 membership of the composite data set.

[14] John Ronsvalle and Sylvia Ronsvalle, *A Comparison of the Growth in Church Contributions with United States Per Capita Income* (Champaign, IL: empty tomb, inc., 1988).

[15] Two of the original 31 denominations merged in 1987, bringing the total number of denominations in the original data set to 30. As of 1991, one denomination reported that it no longer had the staff to collect national financial data, resulting in a maximum of 29 denominations from the original set, which could provide data for 1991 through 2009. Of these 29 denominations, one reported data for 1968 through 1997, but did not have financial data for 1998 through 2009. A second denomination merged with another communion not included in the original composite set but that has since been added; having merged, this new denomination has not collected financial data for 2001-2009 from its congregations, although it did do a survey of congregations for one year. A third denomination indicated that the national office would no longer provide data after 2006 in order to focus on other priorities. For 2009 data, one denomination did not provide 2008 or 2009 data. Therefore, the composite data for 2009 includes information from 25 communions in the data set. Throughout this report, what was an original set of 31 denominations in 1985 will be referred to as the composite denominations. Data for 31 denominations will be included for 1968 and 1985, as well as for intervening years, as available.

[16] For 1986 through 2009, annual denominational data has been obtained which represented for any given year at least 98.5% (the 2008 and 2009 percent) of the 1985 Full or Confirmed Membership of the denominations included in the 1968-1985 study. For 1986 through 2009, the number of denominations for which data

was available varied from a low of 25 denominations of a possible 30 in 2008 and 2009 to a high of 29 in 1987 through 1997. For the years 1969 through 1984, the number of denominations varied from a low of 28 denominations of a possible 31 in 1971-1972 and 1974-1975 to 31 in 1983, representing at least 99.59% of the membership in the data set. No computation was made to adjust the series for missing data. The denominational giving data considered in this analysis was obtained either from the *YACC* series, or directly in correspondence with a denominational office. For a full listing of the data used in this analysis, including the sources, see Appendix B-1.

chapter 2

Church Member Giving for 42 Denominations, 2008 to 2009

Overview of Giving for 42 Denominations, 2008-2009

The composite denominations data set considered in chapter 1 was expanded to include seventeen additional denominations for which 2008 and 2009 data was also available.

In the composite set, from 2008 to 2009, per member giving as a portion of income, as well as in both current and inflation -adjusted dollars, decreased to Total Contributions, and the subcategories of Congregational Finances, and Benevolences.

When the data set was enlarged to a total of 42 denominations, from 2008 to 2009, per member giving as a portion of income, as well as in current and inflation-adjusted dollars, also decreased to Total Contributions, and the subcategories of Congregational Finances and Benevolences.

Details of Giving for 42 Denominations, 2008-2009

The 1968-2009 analysis in chapter 1 considers data for a group of denominations that published their membership and financial information for 1968 and 1985 in the *Yearbook of American and Canadian Churches (YACC)* series. That initial set of communions, considered in the first report on which the present series on church giving is based, has served as a denominational composite set analyzed for subsequent data years.

The goal of chapter 1 is to provide a comprehensive estimate of giving over the years from 1968 through the latest year with available data, for example 2009, in the composite set of denominations. Therefore, each year's data includes all the denominations that reported that year in the composite set. For the two most recent years, the composite set included 25 denominations that reported data for both 2008 and 2009.

Data for both 2008 and 2009 for an additional seventeen denominations was either published in the relevant editions of the *YACC* series, or obtained directly from denominational offices. By adding the data for these 17 denominations to that of the composite group for these two years, giving patterns in an expanded set of 42 communions can be considered.

In this enlarged comparison, the number of 2009 Full or Confirmed Members increased from 27.9 million in the composite set to 38,114,487 in the expanded set, a 37% increase in the number of members considered. The number of denominations increased from 25 to 42. The larger group of denominations included both The United Methodist Church and The Episcopal Church, which were not included in the original 1968-1985 analysis because of the unavailability of confirmed 1968 data at the time of that study. A list of the denominations included in the present analysis is contained in Appendix A.

Table 6 presents the data for the 42 denominations in tabular form, including per member giving in current and inflation-adjusted 2005 dollars, and giving as a percent of income.

Table 6: Per Member Giving in 42 Denominations, Current Dollars, Inflation-Adjusted 2005 Dollars, and as a Percent of Income, 2008 and 2009

Year	Total Contributions			Congregational Finances			Benevolences		
	$ Given in Current $	$ Given in Inflation-Adj. '05 $	Giving as % of Income	$ Given in Current $	$ Given in Inflation-Adj. '05 $	Giving as % of Income	$ Given in Current $	$ Given in Inflation-Adj. '05 $	Giving as % of Income
2008	$899.59	$828.16	2.50%	$760.62	$700.22	2.12%	$138.97	$127.93	0.39%
2009	$891.45	$813.30	2.48%	$755.06	$688.86	2.10%	$136.40	$124.44	0.38%
Difference from the 2008 Base	-$8.14	-$14.85	-0.02%	-$5.57	-$11.36	-0.01%	-$2.57	-$3.50	-0.01%
% Change in Giving as % of Income from the 2008 Base			-0.8%			-0.6%			-1.7%

Details in the above table may not compute to the numbers shown due to rounding.

Per Member Giving as a Percent of Income. In the composite denominations set considered in chapter 1, from 2008 to 2009, giving as a percent of income decreased to Total Contributions, and to the subcategories of Congregational Finances and Benevolences.

The percent given to Total Contributions decreased from 2.40% in 2008 to 2.38% in 2009, a percent change of -0.7% in giving as a percent of income from the 2008 base.

Congregational Finances decreased from 2.05% in 2008 to 2.04% in 2009, a percent change of -0.5% from the 2008 base.

Benevolences measured 0.35% in 2008 and 0.34% in 2009. The percent change was a change of -1.8% from the 2008 base.

In the expanded group of 42 denominations, a decline to Total Contributions and the subcategories of Congregational Finances and Benevolences in giving as a percent of income was also observed. It may be noted that the percent of income given in the expanded set was higher than the composite set. The levels of decline were similar to those of the composite set.

In the expanded set, presented in Table 6, the percent of income given on a per member basis to Total Contributions measured 2.50% in 2008 and 2.48% in 2009, a percent change of -0.8% in giving as a percent of income from the 2008 base.

Congregational Finances was 2.12% in 2008 and decreased to 2.10% in 2009, a change of -0.6% from the 2008 base.

Benevolences measured 0.39% in 2008 and 0.38% in 2009, resulting in a change of -1.7% from the 2008 base.

Giving in Dollars. In both the composite set of denominations, and the expanded group of 42, per member giving declined from 2008 to 2009, in both current and inflation-adjusted dollars.

In the composite set, per member giving to Total Contributions in current dollars, declined from $861.43 in 2008 to $854.25 in 2009, a decrease of $7.18 per member. Per member giving to Congregational Finances decreased from $736.92 to $732.11, a decline of $4.81. Per member giving to Benevolences decreased from $124.51 to $122.14, a decline of $2.37.

From 2008 to 2009 was the first time, in the composite set of denominations, that per member giving in current dollars declined from one year to the next to the three categories of Total Contributions, Congregational Finances, and Benevolences, in the 1968 to 2009 period.

When the 2008 and 2009 per member giving numbers for the composite set were converted to inflation-adjusted dollars, the resulting figures showed declines as well.

In the expanded set of 42 denominations, as shown in Table 6, per member giving in current dollars also declined from 2008 to 2009 to Total Contributions, and to the two subcategories of Congregational Finances and Benevolences.

When the per member contributions were converted to inflation-adjusted dollars, again, declines were observed to Total Contributions, Congregational Finances, and Benevolences.

Summary. When the composite denominations set considered in chapter 1 of this volume was expanded to include 17 additional denominations, the number of church members in the giving analysis increased by 37%. The same pattern of decline in giving as a percent of income, as well as in per member giving in current and inflation-adjusted dollars, was evident from 2008 to 2009 in both the composite denominations set and the expanded set of 42 denominations.

chapter 3

Church Member Giving in Denominations Defined by Organizational Affiliation, 1968, 1985, and 2009

Overview of Giving by Organizational Affiliation, 1968, 1985, and 2009

The communions included in the composite denominations data set considered in chapter 1 of this volume span the theological spectrum. Reviewing data for defined subsets within the composite group allows for additional analysis.

For example, the theory that evangelical Protestants donate more money to their churches than do members of mainline Protestant denominations can be tested by comparing giving patterns in two subgroups of communions within the composite denominations data set.

Of course, there is diversity of opinion within any denomination, as well as in multi-communion groupings. For purposes of the present analysis, however, two groups may serve as general standards for comparison, since they have been characterized as representing certain types of denominations. Specifically, the National Association of Evangelicals (NAE) has, by choice of its title, defined its denominational constituency. And traditionally, the National Council of the Churches of Christ in the U.S.A. (NCC) has counted mainline denominations among its members.

Recognizing that there are limitations in defining a denomination's theological perspectives merely by membership in one of these two organizations, a review of giving patterns of the two subsets of denominations may nevertheless provide some insight into how widely spread current giving patterns may be. Therefore, an analysis of giving patterns in 1968, 1985, and 2009 was completed for the two subsets of those denominations that were affiliated with one of these two interdenominational organizations.

Figure 4: Per Member Giving to Total Contributions, Congregational Finances and Benevolences as a Percent of income, Eight NAE and Eight NCC Denominations, 1968, 1985, and 2009

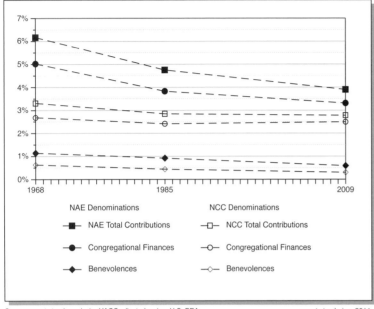

Source: empty tomb analysis; *YACC* adjusted series; U.S. BEA — empty tomb, inc. 2011

Figure 5: Per Member Giving to Total Contributions, Congregational Finances and Benevolences, Eight NAE and Eight NCC Member Denominations, Inflation-Adjusted 2005 Dollars, 1968, 1985, and 2009

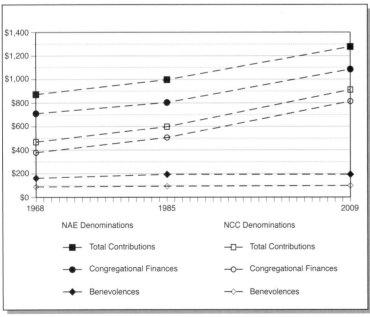

Source: empty tomb analysis; *YACC* adjusted series; U.S. BEA — empty tomb, inc. 2011

During the 1968-2009 period, members of evangelical Protestant denominations gave larger portions of income to their churches than did members of mainline Protestant denominations.

In spite of this fact, the 1968-2009 decline in giving as a portion of income to Total Contributions was greater among the members of the evangelical denominations than it was among the members of the mainline denominations.

While giving as a portion of income to Congregational Finances declined among the NAE-affiliated denominations from 1968 to 1985, and again to 2009, the level of giving to Congregational Finances in the NCC-affiliated denominations increased from 1985 to 2009.

Per member giving as a portion of income to Benevolences declined in both the evangelical and the mainline communions from 1968 to 1985, and again to 2009.

Figure 4 presents data for giving as a percent of income to Total Contributions, Congregational Finances and Benevolences for both the NAE- and NCC-affiliated denominations in graphic form for the years 1968, 1985, and 2009.

In the NAE-affiliated denominations, per member giving in inflation-adjusted dollars increased to all three categories in 1985. In 2009, per member giving in these communions increased to Total Contributions and Congregational Finances, but declined to Benevolences. In the NCC-affiliated denominations, per member giving in inflation-adjusted dollars increased to all three categories in 1985 and again in 2009. Figure 5 presents the data for per member contributions in inflation-adjusted 2005 dollars in graphic form for the years 1968, 1985, and 2009 for both the NAE-affiliated and NCC-affiliated denominations.

Membership in the evangelical denominations grew between 1968 and 2009, in contrast to the mainline denominations, which decreased in membership. Therefore, although evangelicals were receiving a smaller portion of income per member in 2009 than was donated in 1968, aggregate donations in inflation-adjusted dollars were higher in 2009 than in 1968 for this group.

Among the mainline denominations, membership decreased from 1968 to 2009. This fact, in combination with the increase in inflation-adjusted dollars being directed to Congregational Finances, may account for the finding that aggregate Benevolences donations in inflation-adjusted dollars were 35 percent smaller in 2009 than in 1968 for these communions.

Details of Giving by Organizational Affiliation, 1968-2009

In the composite group, membership and financial data is available for 1968, 1985 and 2009 for eight communions affiliated with the National Association of Evangelicals (NAE).

Eight communions affiliated with the National Council of the Churches of Christ in the U.S.A. (NCC) also had membership and financial data available for 1968, 1985, and 2009.

Using 1985 data as the reference point, the eight denominations affiliated with the NAE in the present analysis represented 18% of the total number of NAE-member denominations listed in the *Yearbook of American and Canadian Churches* (*YACC*) series. These eight denominations represented 21% of the total number of NAE-member denominations with membership data listed in the *YACC*, and approximately 21% of the total membership of those NAE-member denominations that provided membership data in the *YACC*.[1]

Data for 2009 was also available for eight NCC-member denominations. In 1985, these eight denominations represented 24% of the total number of NCC constituent bodies listed in the *YACC*; 29% of the NCC constituent bodies with membership data listed in the *YACC*; and approximately 27% of the total membership of those NCC constituent bodies with membership data listed in the *YACC*.[2]

Per Member Giving to Total Contributions, 1968, 1985, and 2009.
Per member giving as a percent of income to Total Contributions for a composite of those eight NAE-member denominations was 6.17% in 1968. That year, per member giving as a percent of income to Total Contributions was 3.31% for a composite of these eight NCC-member denominations.

In 1985, the NAE denominations' per member giving as a percent of income level was 4.75%, while the NCC level was 2.85%.

The data shows the NAE-member denominations received a larger portion of their members' incomes than did NCC-affiliated denominations in both 1968 and 1985. This information supports the assumption that denominations identifying with an evangelical perspective received a higher level of support than denominations that may be termed mainline.

Table 7: **Per Member Giving to Total Contributions as a Percent of Income, Eight NAE and Eight NCC Denominations, 1968, 1985, and 2009**

	Total Contributions									
	NAE Denominations					NCC Denominations				
Year	Number of Denom. Analyzed	Total Contrib. Per Member as % of Income	Diff. in Total Contrib. as % of Income from Previous Base	Percent Change in Total Contrib. as % of Income Figured from Previous Base	Avg. Annual Percent Change in Total Contrib. as % of Income	Number of Denom. Analyzed	Total Contrib. Per Member as % of Income	Diff. in Total Contrib. as % of Income from Previous Base	Percent Change in Total Contrib. as % of Income Figured from Previous Base	Avg. Annual Percent Change in Total Contrib. as % of Income
1968	8	6.17%				8	3.31%			
1985	8	4.75%	-1.41%	-22.93% from '68	-1.35%	8	2.85%	-0.45%	-13.73% from '68	-0.81%
2009	8	3.90%	-0.85%	-14%% from '85	-0.58%	8	2.78%	-0.07%	-2% from '85	-0.09%

Details in the above table may not compute to the numbers shown due to rounding.

The analysis also indicates that the decline in levels of giving observed in the larger composite denominations set was evident among both the NAE-member denominations and the NCC-member denominations. While giving levels decreased for both sets of denominations between 1968 and 1985, the decrease in Total Contributions was more pronounced in the NAE-affiliated communions. The percent change in the percent of income donated in the NAE-member denominations, in comparison to the 1968 base, was -23% between 1968 and 1985, while the percent change in percent of income given to the NCC-member denominations was -14%.

As shown in Table 7, a decline in giving as a percent of income continued among the eight NAE-member denominations during the 1985-2009 period. By 2009, per member giving as a percent of income to Total Contributions had declined from the 1985 level of 4.75% to 3.90%, a percentage change of -14% in the portion of members' incomes donated over that 25-year period.

The eight NCC-affiliated denominations also declined in giving as a percent of income to Total Contributions during 1985-2009, from the 1985 level of 2.85% to 2.78% in 2009. The percent decrease from the 1985 base was -2%.

In 2009 the difference in per member giving as a percent of income between the NAE-affiliated denominations and the NCC-affiliated denominations was not as large as it had been in 1968. Comparing the two rates in giving as a percent of income to Total Contributions between the NAE-member denominations and the NCC-member denominations in this analysis, the NCC-affiliated denominations received 54% as much of per member income as the NAE-member denominations did in 1968, 60% as much in 1985, and 71% in 2009.

For the NAE-affiliated denominations, during the 1985 to 2009 period, the rate of decrease in the average annual percent change in per member giving as a percent of income to Total Contributions slowed in comparison to the 1968-1985 annual percent change from the 1968 base. The 1968-1985 average annual percent change was -1.35%. The annual rate of change for 1985-2009 was -0.58%.

In the NCC-member denominations, during the 1968-1985 period, average annual percent change from the 1968 base in giving as a percent of income was -0.81%. Between 1985 and 2009, the average annual change from 1985 was -0.09%.

Per Member Giving to Congregational Finances and Benevolences, 1968, 1985 and 2009.

Were there any markedly different patterns between the two subsets of denominations defined by affiliation with the NAE and the NCC in regards to the distribution of Total Contributions between the subcategories of Congregational Finances and Benevolences?

In the subcategory of Congregational Finances, a difference was observable. The NCC-related denominations posted a decrease from 1968 to 1985, but an increase in 2009 from the 1985 level in the portion of income directed to this category. In the NAE-related denominations, the portion of income declined from 1968 to 1985, and again to 2009. Table 8 presents the Congregational Finances giving data for the NAE and NCC denominations in 1968, 1985, and 2009.

In the subcategory of Benevolences, both groups posted declines in the portion of income directed to that category. Table 9 presents the Benevolences giving data for the NAE and NCC denominations in 1968, 1985, and 2009.

Table 8: Per Member Giving to Congregational Finances as a Percent of Income, Eight NAE and Eight NCC Denominations, 1968, 1985, and 2009

| | Congregational Finances | | | | | | | | | |
| | NAE Denominations | | | | | NCC Denominations | | | | |
Year	Number of Denom. Analyzed	Cong. Finances Per Member as % of Income	Diff. in Cong. Finances as % of Income from Previous Base	Percent Change in Cong. Finances as % of Income Figured from Previous Base	Avg. Annual Percent Change in Cong. Finances as % of Income	Number of Denom. Analyzed	Cong. Finances Per Member as % of Income	Diff. in Cong. Finances as % of Income from Previous Base	Percent Change in Cong. Finances as % of Income Figured from Previous Base	Avg. Annual Percent Change in Cong. Finances as % of Income
1968	8	5.02%				8	2.68%			
1985	8	3.83%	-1.19%	-23.71% from '68	-1.39%	8	2.41%	-0.27%	-10.05% from '68	-0.59%
2009	8	3.31%	-0.52%	-10% from '85	-0.43%	8	2.49%	0.08%	3% from '85	0.12%

Details in the above table may not compute to the numbers shown due to rounding.

Table 9: Per Member Giving to Benevolences as a Percent of Income, Eight NAE and Eight NCC Denominations, 1968, 1985, and 2009

| | Benevolences | | | | | | | | | |
| | NAE Denominations | | | | | NCC Denominations | | | | |
Year	Number of Denom. Analyzed	Benevol. Per Member as % of Income	Diff. in Benevol. as % of Income from Previous Base	Percent Change in Benevol. as % of Income Figured from Previous Base	Avg. Annual Percent Change in Benevol. as % of Income	Number of Denom. Analyzed	Benevol. Per Member as % of Income	Diff. in Benevol. as % of Income from Previous Base	Percent Change in Benevol. as % of Income Figured from Previous Base	Avg. Annual Percent Change in Benevol. as % of Income
1968	8	1.14%				8	0.63%			
1985	8	0.92%	-0.22%	-19.51% from '68	-1.15%	8	0.44%	-0.18%	-29.36% from '68	-1.73%
2009	8	0.59%	-0.33%	-29% from '85	-1.21%	8	0.30%	-0.15%	-23% from '85	-0.96%

Details in the above table may not compute to the numbers shown due to rounding.

In 1968, the NAE-affiliated members were giving 6.17% of their incomes to their churches. Of that, 5.02% went to Congregational Finances, while 1.14% went to Benevolences. In 1985, of the 4.75% of income donated to Total Contributions, 3.83% was directed to Congregational Finances. This represented a percent change in the portion of income going to Congregational Finances of -24% from the 1968 base. Per member contributions to Benevolences among these NAE-member denominations declined from 1.14% in 1968 to 0.92% in 1985, representing a percent change of -20% from the 1968 base in the portion of income donated to Benevolences.

In 2009, the 3.90% of income donated by the NAE-member denominations to their churches was divided between Congregational Finances and Benevolences at the 3.31% and 0.59% levels, respectively. The percent change between 1985 and 2009 in contributions to Congregational Finances as a percent of income was a decline of -10%. In contrast, the percent change in contributions to Benevolences as a percent of income was a decline of -29% over the same 25-year period. The annual rate in the percent change in giving as a percent of income to Benevolences increased, from -1.15% from 1968 to 1985 to -1.21% from 1985 to 2009.

In 1968, the NCC-member denominations were giving 3.31% of their incomes to their churches. Of that, 2.68% went to Congregational Finances. In 1985, of the 2.85% of income donated to these communions, 2.41% went to Congregational Finances. This represented a percent change from the 1968 base in the portion of income going to Congregational Finances of -10%. In contrast, per member contributions as a percent of income to Benevolences among these same NCC-affiliated denominations had declined from 0.63% in 1968 to 0.44% in 1985, representing a percent change of -29% from the 1968 base in the portion of income donated to Benevolences.

In 2009, the 2.78% of income donated by the NCC-affiliated members to their churches was divided between Congregational Finances and Benevolences at the 2.49% and 0.30% levels, respectively. Even though the portion of income donated by members to Total Contributions decreased between 1985 and 2009, Congregational Finances increased from 2.41% in 1985 to 2.49% in 2009. The 2009 percent change in contributions to Congregational Finances as a percent of income from 1985 was an increase of 3%.

The portion of income directed to Benevolences by these NCC-member denominations declined from 1968 to 1985, and continued to decline from 1985 to 2009. The percent change in contributions to Benevolences as a percent of income declined from 0.44% in 1985 to the 2009 level of 0.30%, a decline of 23% over this 25-year period. The annual percent change from the 1985 base in giving as a percent of income to Benevolences indicated a lower rate of decline at -0.96% between 1985 and 2009, compared to the 1968-1985 annual rate of -1.73%.

Changes in Per Member Giving, 1968 to 2009. Table 10 presents the 1968 to 2009 percent change in per member giving as a percent of income to Total Contributions, Congregational Finances and Benevolences in both the NAE- and NCC-affiliated communions.

For the NAE-affiliated denominations, per member giving as a percent of income to Congregational Finances declined from 5.02% in 1968 to 3.31% in 2009, a change of -34% from the 1968 base. In Benevolences, the -49% change reflected a decline from 1.14% in 1968 to 0.59% in 2009.

For the NCC-affiliated denominations, in the subcategory of Congregational Finances, per member giving as a percent of income was 2.68% in 1968, and 2.49% in 2009, a decline of 7%. In the subcategory of Benevolences, the level of giving decreased from 0.63% in 1968 to 0.30% in 2009, a 52% decline in the portion of income donated to this subcategory.

Table 10: Percent Change in Per Member Giving as a Percent of income, Eight NAE and Eight NCC Denominations, 1968 to 2009

Year	NAE Denominations				NCC Denominations			
	Number of Denom. Analyzed	Total Contrib.	Cong. Finances	Benevol.	Number of Denom. Analyzed	Total Contrib.	Cong. Finances	Benevol.
1968	8	6.17%	5.02%	1.14%	8	3.31%	2.68%	0.63%
2009	8	3.90%	3.31%	0.59%	8	2.78%	2.49%	0.30%
% Chg. 1968-'09	8	-37%	-34%	-49%	8	-16%	-7%	-52%

Details in the above table may not compute to the numbers shown due to rounding.

Per Member Giving in Inflation-Adjusted 2005 Dollars. Table 11 below presents the levels of per member giving to Total Contributions, Congregational Finances and Benevolences, in inflation-adjusted 2005 dollars, and the percentage of Total Contributions that went to Benevolences in 1968, 1985, and 2009, for both sets of denominations. In addition, the percent change from 1968 to 2009, from the 1968 base, in per member inflation-adjusted 2005 dollar contributions is noted.

The NAE-affiliated group's level of per member support to Total Contributions in inflation-adjusted 2005 dollars was $872.54 in 1968. This increased to $996.84 in 1985, and by 2009 increased to $1,277.48.

For the NAE-affiliated denominations, per member contributions in inflation-adjusted 2005 dollars to the subcategory of Congregational Finances increased from 1968 to 1985, and again from 1985 to 2009. Per member contributions in inflation-adjusted 2005 dollars to Benevolences increased between 1968 and 1985, and decreased between 1985 and 2009. Of the increased per member giving in inflation-adjusted dollars between 1968 and 2009, 92% went to Congregational Finances.

Table 11: Per Member Giving in Eight NAE and Eight NCC Denominations, Inflation-Adjusted 2005 Dollars, 1968, 1985, and 2009

Year	NAE Denominations					NCC Denominations				
	Number of Denom. Analyzed	Total Contrib.	Cong. Finances	Benevol.	Benevol. as % of Total Contrib.	Number of Denom. Analyzed	Total Contrib.	Cong. Finances	Benevol.	Benevol. as % of Total Contrib.
1968	8	$872.54	$710.67	$161.88	19%	8	$468.17	$379.11	$89.06	19%
1985	8	$996.84	$803.70	$193.15	19%	8	$598.73	$505.48	$93.26	16%
2009	8	$1,277.48	$1,084.81	$192.67	15%	8	$911.80	$813.75	$98.05	11%
$ Diff. '68-'09		$404.93	$374.14	$30.79			$443.63	$434.64	$8.99	
% Chg. '68-'09		46%	53%	19%			95%	115%	10%	

Details in the above table may not compute to the numbers shown due to rounding.

The NCC-affiliated group also experienced an increase in inflation-adjusted per member Total Contributions between 1968 and 2009. The 1968 NCC level of per member support in inflation-adjusted 2005 dollars was $468.17. In 1985, this had increased to $598.73, and in 2009 the figure was $911.80.

The NCC-member denominations experienced an increase in inflation-adjusted per member donations to Congregational Finances in both 1985 and 2009 as well. Although 98% of the increase between 1968 and 2009 was directed to Congregational Finances, gifts to Benevolences also increased in inflation-adjusted 2005 dollars between 1968 and 1985, and again between 1985 and 2009.

As a portion of Total Contributions, the NAE-member denominations directed 19% of their per member gifts to Benevolences in 1968, 19% in 1985, and 15% in 2009. The NCC-member denominations directed 19% of their per member gifts to Benevolences in 1968, 16% in 1985, and 11% in 2009.

Aggregate Dollar Donations, 1968 and 2009. The NCC-member denominations and the NAE-member denominations differed in terms of changes in membership. The impact of this difference was evident at the aggregate dollar level.

Table 12 considers aggregate giving data for the eight NAE-member denominations included in this analysis. Membership in these eight NAE-member denominations increased 59% from 1968-2009.

Table 12: Aggregate Giving, Eight NAE Denominations, Current and Inflation-Adjusted 2005 Dollars, 1968 and 2009

Year	Number of Denom. Analyzed	Membership	Current Dollars			Inflation-Adjusted 2005 Dollars		
			Total Contributions	Congregational Finances	Benevolences	Total Contributions	Congregational Finances	Benevolences
1968	8	535,865	$102,845,802	$83,765,677	$19,080,125	$467,565,930	$380,822,318	$86,743,612
2009	8	852,744	$1,194,039,395	$1,013,957,653	$180,081,742	$1,089,362,548	$925,067,880	$164,294,667
% Chg.		59%	1061%	1110%	844%	133%	143%	89%

Details in the above table may not compute to the numbers shown due to rounding.

As measured in current aggregate dollars, giving in each of the three categories of Total Contributions, Congregational Finances and Benevolences was greater in 2009 than in 1968 for the NAE-member denominations. This was true even though per member giving as a portion of income declined to all three categories during this period.

The same can be said for the three aggregate categories when inflation was factored out by converting the current dollars to inflation-adjusted 2005 dollars. These denominations have been compensated for a decline in giving as a percent of income to all three categories by the increase in total membership. As long as these denominations continue to grow in membership, their national and regional programs may not be affected in the immediate future by the decline in the portion of income donated.

Table 13 considers aggregate data for the eight NCC-member denominations. The NCC-related denominations experienced a membership decline of 41% between 1968 and 2009. The increase in current dollar donations was sufficient to result in an increase in aggregate current dollars in each of the three categories of Total Contributions, Congregational Finances and Benevolences.

However, the inflation-adjusted 2005 dollar figures account for the acknowledged financial difficulties in many of these communions, particularly in the category of Benevolences. The impact of the decline in membership was evident at the aggregate dollar level. The increase in giving to Congregational Finances as a portion of income noted above was tempered by a loss of members. Between 1968 and 2009, while the NCC-related communions experienced an increase of 95% in per member giving to Total Contributions in inflation-adjusted 2005 dollars—from $468.17 in 1968 to $911.80 in 2009—aggregate Total Contributions in 2009 to these eight denominations measured 15% larger in inflation-adjusted 2005 dollars in 2009 than in 1968, about one-sixth of the size of the per capita percent increase.

Further, Congregational Finances absorbed all of the increased giving at the aggregate level, with aggregate dollars to Congregational Finances increasing 27%. The resulting 35% decline in aggregate Benevolences receipts in inflation-adjusted 2005 dollars between 1968 and 2009 provides insight into the basis for any cutbacks at the denominational level.

Table 13: Aggregate Giving, Eight NCC Denominations, Current and Inflation-Adjusted 2005 Dollars, 1968 and 2009

Year	Number of Denom. Analyzed	Membership	Current Dollars			Inflation-Adjusted 2005 Dollars		
			Total Contributions	Congregational Finances	Benevolences	Total Contributions	Congregational Finances	Benevolences
1968	8	12,876,821	$1,326,045,714	$1,073,798,710	$252,247,004	$6,028,576,623	$4,881,790,826	$1,146,785,797
2009	8	7,617,042	$7,612,608,672	$6,794,000,958	$818,607,714	$6,945,240,511	$6,198,396,991	$746,843,520
% Chg.		-41%	474%	533%	225%	15%	27%	-35%

Details in the above table may not compute to the numbers shown due to rounding.

Notes for Chapter 3

[1] The 1985 total church membership estimate of 3,388,414 represented by NAE denominations includes *YACC* 1985 membership data for each denomination where available or, if 1985 membership data was not available, membership data for the most recent year prior to 1985. Full or Confirmed membership data was used except in those instances where this figure was not available, in which case Inclusive Membership was used.

[2] The 1985 total church membership estimate of 39,621,950 represented by NCC denominations includes *YACC* 1985 membership data for each denomination where available or, if 1985 membership data was not available, membership data for the most recent year prior to 1985. Full or Confirmed membership data was used except in those instances where this figure was not available, in which case Inclusive Membership was used.

chapter 4

Church Member Giving and Membership in 11 Denominations, 1921-2009

Overview of Giving and Membership, 1921-2009

A continuing feature in this ongoing series on church member giving is an analysis of available giving data beginning in 1921. Because of the fixed nature of the data source, the analysis remains fairly static. However, the data can now be updated to include information through 2009. This data makes use of the U.S. Bureau of Economic Analysis (BEA) per capita Disposable (after-tax) Personal Income (DPI) series, with the benchmark year being 2005 to adjust current dollars for inflation.

For the period 1921 through 2009, the preferable approach would be to analyze the entire composite denominations data set considered in chapter 1 of this volume. Unfortunately, comparable data since 1921 is not readily available for these communions. However, data over an extended period of time is available in the *Yearbook of American and Canadian Churches* (*YACC*) series for a group of 11 Protestant communions, or their historical antecedents. This set includes ten mainline Protestant communions and the Southern Baptist Convention.

The available data has been reported fairly consistently over the time span of 1921 to 2009.[1] The value of the multiyear comparison is that it provides a historical time line over which to observe giving patterns.

A review of per member giving as a portion of income during the 1921 through 2009 period found that the portion of income given was above three percent during two multiyear periods. From 1922 through 1933 and then again from 1958 through 1962, per member giving as a percent of income was at or above 3%. This relatively high level of giving is particularly interesting because per capita DPI was also increasing from 1922-1927 (with the exception of 1925) and from 1959 through 1962. However, unlike after 1933, when the country was experiencing the Great

Depression followed by World War II, no major national catastrophes explain the drop below 3% after 1962.

Per member giving as a percent of income was at a low point during World War II, recovered during the 1950s, and then declined fairly steadily during the 1960s. The decline in giving as a percent of income that began after the peak in 1960 continued with little interruption until 1980, when giving began to alternate increases with decreases. Giving as a portion of income then hit a low point of 2.31% in 1992, the lowest level since 1948. An intermittent upward trend in giving was again visible beginning in 1993. By 2009, the level of giving as a percent of income was at 2.35%, lower than 1994 through 2008. However, the 2009 level was higher than the levels from 1977 through 1980, from 1988 through 1990, and in 1992.

Figure 6: Per Member Giving in 11 Denominations as a Percent of Income, and U.S. Per Capita DPI in Inflation-Adjusted 2005 Dollars, 1921-2009

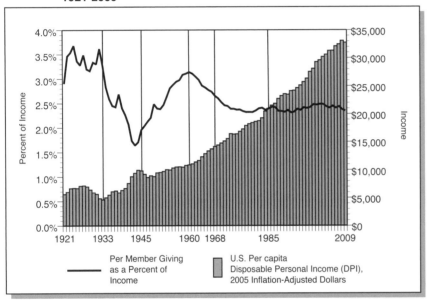

Source: empty tomb analysis; *YACC* adjusted series; U.S. BEA

empty tomb, inc. 2011

Figure 6 contrasts per member giving as a percent of income for a group of eleven Protestant denominations, with U.S. per capita DPI in inflation-adjusted 2005 dollars, for the period 1921 through 2009.

By 2009, U.S. per capita DPI had increased 482% since 1921 in inflation-adjusted 2005 dollars, and 604% since 1933—the depth of the Great Depression.

Meanwhile, by 2009, per member giving in inflation-adjusted 2005 dollars had increased 371% since 1921, and 406% since the depth of the Great Depression.

Consequently, per member giving as a percent of income was lower in 2009 than in either 1921 or 1933. In 1921, per member giving as a percent of income was 2.9%. In 1933, it was 3.3%. In 2009, per member giving as a percent of income was 2.3% for the group of the eleven denominations considered in this section. The percent change in the per member portion of income donated to the church had declined by 19% from the 1921 base, from 2.9% in 1921 to 2.3% in 2009, and by 28% from the 1933 base, from 3.3% in 1933 to 2.3% in 2009.

Membership in absolute numbers increased for the group of 11 denominations on a fairly regular basis from 1921 until 1968, when it peaked. However, as a portion of U.S. population, the group's peak was earlier, in 1961, when membership in the 11 denominations represented 20% of the U.S. population. The decline in membership as a percent of U.S. population that began in 1962 continued through 2009.

It is of some interest to note that the first decline in membership as a percent of U.S. population in the set of 11 denominations occurred in 1962, one year after the decline in giving as a percent of income occurred in 1961. While giving as a portion of income displayed a pattern of increase in some years and decline in others, the decline in membership as a percent of U.S. population continued uninterrupted through the year 2009.

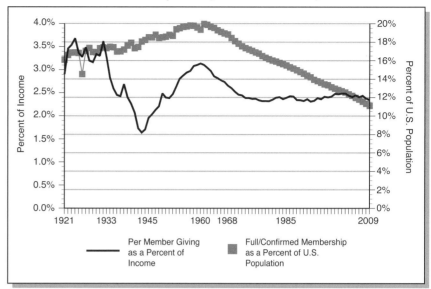

Figure 7   Per Member Giving as a Percent of Income and Membership as a Percent of U.S. Population, 11 Denominations, 1921-2009

Source: empty tomb analysis; *YACC* adjusted series; U.S. BEA   empty tomb, inc. 2011

Figure 7 presents both per member giving as a percent of income and membership as a percent of U.S. population, for the group of eleven Protestant denominations, from 1921 through 2009.

Details of Giving and Membership, 1921-2009

Giving as a Percent of Income. The period under consideration in this section of the report began in 1921. At that point, per member giving as a percent of income was 2.9%. In current dollars, U.S. per capita DPI was $555, and per member giving was $16.10. When inflation was factored out by converting both income and giving to 2005 dollars, per capita income in 1921 measured $5,622 and per member giving was $163.18.

From 1922 through 1933, giving as a percent of income stayed above the 3% level. The high was 3.7% in 1924, followed closely by the amount in 1932, when per member giving measured 3.6% of per capita income. This trend is of particular interest inasmuch as per capita income was generally increasing in inflation-adjusted dollars between 1921 and 1927, with the exception of 1925. Even as people were increasing in personal affluence, they also continued to maintain a giving level of more than 3% to their churches. Even after income began to decline, including the economic reverses in the early years of the Great Depression, giving measured above 3% from 1929 through 1933.

The year 1933 was the depth of the Great Depression. Per capita income was at the lowest point it would reach between 1921 and 2009, whether measured in current or inflation-adjusted dollars. Yet per member giving as a percent of income was 3.3%. Income had decreased by 17% between 1921 and 1933 in inflation-adjusted 2005 dollars, from $5,622 to $4,654. Meanwhile, per member giving had decreased 7%, from $163.18 in 1921 to $151.94 in 1933, in inflation-adjusted dollars. Therefore, giving as a percent of income actually increased from 2.9% in 1921 to 3.3% in 1933, an increase of 12% in the portion of income contributed to the church.

Giving in inflation-adjusted 2005 dollars declined from 1933 to 1934, although income began to recover in 1934. Giving then began to increase again in 1935. In inflation-adjusted dollars, giving did not surpass the 1927 level of $250.46 until 1953, when giving grew from $240.06 in 1952 to $264.27 in 1953.

During World War II, incomes improved rapidly. Meanwhile, church member giving increased only modestly in current dollars. When inflation was factored out, per member giving was at $157.18 in 1941, the year the United States entered the war. It declined to $152.35 in 1942, increased in 1943 to $154.24, and then to $169.79 in 1944. However, income in inflation-adjusted dollars grew from $7,589 in 1941 to $8,799 in 1942, $9,403 in 1943, and reached a high for this period of $9,946 in 1944, an income level that would not be surpassed again until 1953. Thus, giving as a percent of income reached a low point during the three full calendar years of formal U.S. involvement in World War II, at levels of 1.73% in 1942, 1.64% in 1943, and 1.71% in 1944.

In 1945, the last year of the war, U.S. per capita income was $9,833 in inflation-adjusted dollars. Giving in inflation-adjusted dollars increased from $169.79 in 1944, to $192.41 in 1945, the highest inflation-adjusted dollar amount it had been since 1930. Although per member giving increased 27% between 1933 and 1945, per capita income had increased 111%. Giving as a percent of income therefore declined from the 3.3% level in 1933, to 2.0% in 1945.

The unusually high level of per capita income slumped after the war but had recovered to war levels by the early 1950s. By 1960, U.S. per capita income was 11% higher in inflation-adjusted 2005 dollars than it had been in 1945, increasing from $9,833 in 1945 to $10,874 in 1960. Meanwhile, per member giving in inflation-adjusted dollars had increased 77%, from $192.41 in 1945 to $341.04 in 1960. Giving as a portion of income recovered to the level it had been from 1922 through 1933, and stayed above 3% from 1958 through 1962. Giving as a percent of income reached a postwar high of 3.14% in 1960, and then began to decline.

For the second time in the century, giving levels were growing to, or maintaining a level above, three percent of income even while incomes were also expanding. From 1921-1928, incomes expanded 24%. During this time giving grew to above 3% and stayed there. From 1950-1962, incomes grew 20%. Again, giving grew to above 3% in 1958 and stayed there through 1962. In both cases, church members increased or maintained their giving levels even as their incomes increased.

In the 1920s, the economic expansion was interrupted by the Great Depression, followed by World War II.

In contrast to the economic upheaval earlier in the century, however, the economy continued to expand through the 1960s. Yet the portion of income given was not sustained above 3%. By 1968, giving as a percent of income had declined to 2.7% for this group of 11 communions. U.S. per capita income increased 30% in inflation-adjusted 2005 dollars between 1960 and 1968, from $10,874 in 1960 to $14,148 in 1968. In comparison, per member giving increased 10% in inflation-adjusted dollars, from the 1960 level of $341.04 to the 1968 level of $375.40.

For the second time in the century, giving levels were growing to, or maintaining a level above, three percent of income even while incomes were also expanding.

By 1985, per member giving had increased 34% in inflation-adjusted 2005 dollars, from $375.40 in 1968 to $501.97 in 1985. U.S. per capita income measured $20,972 in 1985, an increase of 48% over the 1968 level of $14,148. Giving as a percent of income, therefore, measured 2.4% in 1985, representing a 10% decline from the 1968 level of 2.7%.

The year 2009 was the latest year for which data was available for the eleven denominations considered in this section. In that year, per member giving as a percent of income rounded to 2.3%, a 2% decrease from the 1985 level. Per member giving increased 53% in inflation-adjusted 2005 dollars, from $501.97 in 1985 to $769.10 in 2009. U.S. per capita income increased 56% during this period, from the 1985 level of $20,972 to the 2009 level of $32,742.

Membership and Giving, 1921-2009. Membership was changing for this group of 11 denominations during the 1921-2009 period as well.

Between 1921 and 1961, the portion of U.S. population that this group of 11 denominations represented grew from 16.1% of the U.S. population to 20%, or one-fifth of the United States.

In that same year of 1961, the first decline in giving as a percent of income occurred since 1951.

The next year, in 1962, a decline in membership as a percent of U.S. population began for this group that would continue through the year 2009. Membership growth slowed and then the number of members declined between 1968 and 1969, from 37,785,048 to 37,382,659. Meanwhile, U.S. population continued to expand. Therefore, while this group represented 20% of U.S. population in 1961, by the year 2009, this group represented 11.1% of U.S. population.

During the 1961-2009 period, the Southern Baptist Convention grew from 9,978,139 to 16,160,088. Meanwhile, the other ten denominations, all of which might be termed mainline Protestant, declined in membership as a group, from 26,683,648 in 1961 to 17,970,907 in 2009.

The growth in the number of members in the Southern Baptist Convention offset the mainline Protestant membership loss to some degree. Nevertheless, the group's membership of the combined group of 11 denominations declined, measuring 36,661,788 in 1961 and 34,130,995 in 2009. U.S. population increased from 183,742,000 in 1961, when the group of 11 denominations represented 20% of the U.S. population, to 307,483,000 in 2009, when the 11 denominations represented 11.1% of the U.S. population.

Although the decrease in giving as a percent of income that began in 1961 resulted in giving levels varying between 2.34% and 2.32% during 1977 through 1980, the level of giving as a portion of income recovered to 2.41% by 1983 and was at 2.43% in 1986 and 2.42% 1987. The level of giving as a percent of income went up and down until it reached a low of 2.31% in 1992. An intermittent increase occurred through 2001 and 2002, when the percent given was 2.48%. The level of income declined by 2009 to 2.35%.

Meanwhile, U.S. population continued to expand. Therefore, while this group represented 20% of U.S. population in 1961, by the year 2009, this group represented 11.1% of U.S. population.

In contrast, membership as a percent of population for the 11 denominations as a group began a decline in 1962 that continued uninterrupted through the year 2009.

Change in Per Member Giving and Total Membership. In Table 14, giving as a percent of U.S. per capita DPI is presented for the first and last year in the period noted. The difference between giving in these two years was calculated and then divided by the number of annual intervals in the period to produce the Average Annual Change.

When considered as a portion of income in Table 14, the period of 1950-1955 posted the highest Average Annual Change in giving as a percent of income, followed by the 1955-1960 period. Giving grew to 3.1% in 1958, and a level above 3% was maintained through 1962. However, the 1960-1964 period also was the period within which giving as a portion of income began to decline. It is clear from the Average Annual Change column that giving as a portion of income began a downward trend in the 1960-1964 period that continued through the 1975-1980 period. Reversing in the 1980-1985 period, the average annual change was again negative in the 1985-1990 period. During the 1990-1995 and 1995-2000 periods, positive change was measured, but the increases did not recover to the 1950-1960 Average Annual Change levels. The Average Annual Change for the 2000-2005 rounded to 0.00%. The 2005-2009 period was again negative.

Meanwhile, during the 1950-2009 period, the group of eleven denominations shrank as a portion of U.S. population. The 1950-1955 period posted an average annual increase of 0.21% in the portion of U.S. population that these denominations represented. The 1955-1960 period posted a decline. The group of 11 denominations nevertheless peaked in 1961 at 20% of U.S. population. Although the 1960-1964

Table 14: Average Annual Change in Per Member Giving as a Portion of U.S. DPI and in Membership as a Percent of U.S. Population, 11 Denominations, 1950-2009

Time Period	Per Member Giving as % of Income			Membership as % of U.S. Population		
	First Year in Period	Last Year in Period	Average Annual Change	First Year in Period	Last Year in Period	Average Annual Change
1950-1955	2.40%	2.88%	0.10%	18.58%	19.64%	0.21%
1955-1960	2.88%	3.14%	0.05%	19.64%	19.34%	-0.06%
1960-1964 [2]	3.14%	2.86%	-0.07%	19.34%	19.53%	0.05%
1964-1970 [2]	2.86%	2.52%	-0.06%	19.53%	18.10%	-0.24%
1970-1975	2.52%	2.37%	-0.03%	18.10%	17.05%	-0.21%
1975-1980	2.37%	2.32%	-0.01%	17.05%	16.16%	-0.18%
1980-1985	2.32%	2.39%	0.01%	16.16%	15.48%	-0.14%
1985-1990	2.39%	2.32%	-0.01%	15.48%	14.59%	-0.18%
1990-1995	2.32%	2.36%	0.01%	14.59%	13.59%	-0.20%
1995-2000	2.36%	2.47%	0.02%	13.59%	12.81%	-0.16%
2000-2005	2.47%	2.45%	-0.00%	12.81%	11.96%	-0.14%
2005-2009	2.45%	2.35%	-0.02%	11.96%	11.10%	-0.21%

Details in the above table may not compute to the numbers shown due to rounding.

period posted an increase, the average annual level was less than the previous five years' rate of decline. In 1964-1970, a period of decline began that continued through 2009.

Change in Per Member Giving and U.S. Per Capita Disposable Personal Income, in Inflation-adjusted 2005 Dollars. For this group of 11 communions, per member giving in inflation-adjusted 2005 dollars increased half the time during the 1921-1947 period. Per member giving in inflation-adjusted dollars decreased from 1924 to 1925. While it increased from 1925 to 1926 and again in 1927, giving began a seven-year decline in 1928. This seven-year period, from 1928 to 1934, included some of the worst years of the Great Depression. Giving increased again in 1935. Declines in 1939, 1940, 1942, 1946 and 1947 alternated with increases in the other years.

Then, from 1948 through 1968,[3] the members in these 11 communions increased per member giving in inflation-adjusted 2005 dollars each year. During the first 12 years of this period, 1948-1960, per member giving averaged an increase of $11.93 a year. Although giving continued to increase for the next few years, it was at the slower rate of $4.29 per year. Overall, in inflation-adjusted 2005 dollars, income grew 58% from 1948 to 1968, while per member giving increased 90%, resulting in the recovery of giving levels to 3% or more in the late 1950s and early 1960s.

Per member giving in inflation-adjusted dollars declined in 1969, 1970 and 1971, followed by two years of increase and two of decline.

The longest sustained period of average annual increases in per member giving in inflation-adjusted dollars during the 89-year period occurred during the 27 years that include 1976 through 2002. During this time, income increased an average of $513.21 annually in inflation-adjusted 2005 dollars. Meanwhile, per member giving increased $13.47 on average each year, a higher overall rate than during the 21 years including 1948 through 1968, when the annual increase was $8.88. However, while giving increased 88% from 1976 to 2002, it increased 90% from 1948-1968. U.S. per capita income increased 79% from 1976 to 2002. Because giving increased at a faster rate than income during the 1976 to 2002 period, giving as a percent of income was 2.37% in 1976 and 2.48% in 2002.

By reviewing this data in smaller increments of years from 1950 to 2009, the time period in which giving began to decline markedly can be identified. In Table 15, data for the first and last year in each period is presented. The difference between these two years was calculated and then divided by the number of annual intervals in the period. The Average Annual Change in Giving as a Percent of the Average Annual Change in Income column presents the Per Member Giving Average Annual Change divided by the U.S. Per Capita Income Average Annual Change.

During the 1950 to 2009 period, the highest increase in the average annual change in per member giving measured in inflation-adjusted 2005 dollars occurred from 1995-2000. However, when the average annual change in per member giving was considered as a portion of the average annual change in per capita income, the largest increase occurred in the 1955-1960 period, followed by the 1950-1955 period.

The longest sustained period of average annual increases in per member giving in inflation-adjusted dollars during the 89-year period occurred during the 27 years that include 1976 through 2002.

Table 15: **Average Annual Change in U.S. Per Capita DPI and Per Member Giving, in 11 Denominations, Inflation-adjusted 2005 Dollars, 1950-2009**

Time Period	U.S. Per Capita Income			Per Member Giving			Avg. Ann. Chg. Giv. as % Avg. Annual Chg. in Income
	First Year in Period	Last Year in Period	Average Annual Change	First Year in Period	Last Year in Period	Average Annual Change	
1950-1955	$9,463	$10,339	$175.32	$226.79	$297.59	$14.16	8.08%
1955-1960	$10,339	$10,874	$106.89	$297.59	$341.04	$8.69	8.13%
1960-1964 [2]	$10,874	$12,320	$361.50	$341.04	$352.45	$2.85	0.79%
1964-1970 [2]	$12,320	$14,758	$406.36	$352.45	$372.31	$3.31	0.81%
1970-1975	$14,758	$16,389	$326.22	$372.31	$388.35	$3.21	0.98%
1975-1980	$16,389	$18,425	$407.27	$388.35	$427.41	$7.81	1.92%
1980-1985	$18,425	$20,972	$509.42	$427.41	$501.97	$14.91	2.93%
1985-1990	$20,972	$23,552	$515.84	$501.97	$547.43	$9.09	1.76%
1990-1995	$23,552	$25,104	$310.41	$547.43	$593.09	$9.13	2.94%
1995-2000	$25,104	$29,267	$832.73	$593.09	$723.04	$25.99	3.12%
2000-2005	$29,267	$31,318	$410.14	$723.04	$766.21	$8.63	2.11%
2005-2009	$31,318	$32,742	$355.96	$766.21	$769.10	$0.72	0.20%

Details in the above table may not compute to the numbers shown due to rounding.

In 1995-2000, the annual dollar increase in giving of $25.99 represented 3% of the average annual increase in U.S. per capita income, compared to the 8% represented by the increased dollars given during 1950-1955 and 1955-1960.

Between 1960 and 1964 in these communions, the average annual change in per member giving declined markedly from the previous five years. While income was increasing at an annual rate of $361.50 in this four-year period, 238% greater than in the 1955-1960 period, the average annual increase in per member contributions in inflation-adjusted 2005 dollars was $2.85 in 1960-1964, only a third of the $8.69 annual rate of increase in the 1955-1960 period, as indicated in Table 15.

The 1960-1964 period predates many of the controversial issues often cited as reasons for declining giving as a percent of income. Also, it was in the 1960-1964 period when membership as a percent of population began to decrease in mainline denominations, ten of which are included in this group. Therefore, additional exploration of that period of time might be merited.

Increases in per member giving were consistently low from 1960-1975, compared to all but the most recent segment in the 1950-2009 period. The annual rates of increase of $2.85 per year from 1960 to 1964, $3.31 from 1964 to 1970, and $3.21 from 1970 to 1975, were the lowest in the 1950 to 2005 period. From 1960 to 1975, the increase in dollars given represented less than one percent of the average annual increase in per capita income.

In the 1975-1980 period, the average annual increase in giving grew to $7.81, representing 1.92% of the average annual increase in per capita income.

From 1980 to 1985, the average annual increase in giving of $14.91 represented 2.93% of the average annual increase in income during this period. As a portion of the increase in per capita income, the 2.93% of the 1980 to 1985 period ranked fifth among the eleven periods from 1950 to 2009.

The annual average change in giving as a percent of the average annual income increase during 1985 to 1990 fell from the 1980 to 1985 period. The 1990-1995 Average Annual change in Giving as a Percent of the Average Annual Change in Income increased from the 1985-1990 figure, although the Average Annual Change in Per Member Giving was comparable in the two periods. The slower growth in income during the 1990-1995 period resulted in the increase in dollars given representing a larger portion of the increase in income.

In the 1995-2000, the average annual change in giving as a percent of the average annual change in income increased from the 1990-1995 period. The average annual change in the number of dollars given on a per member basis was more than double that of the previous period. However, during the 1995-2000 segment, income was increasing at the fastest rate in the 1950-2009 period, in terms of per capita inflation-adjusted dollars. Thus the rate of growth in giving was less than half the rate during the 1950-1960 period, when considered as a portion of the income increases.

For the period 2000-2005, the average annual change in dollars given as a percent of the annual change in income was an increase of 2.11%.

Of the 12 periods under review within the years from 1950 through 2009, the 2005-2009 period posted the fifth lowest annual increase in U.S. per capita income in inflation-adjusted dollars. However, the 2005-2009 period posted the lowest annual average increase in church member giving during the 1950-2009 period. Giving increased an average of 72¢ a year in inflation-adjusted dollars, the only time the average annual increase measured less than $1 among the 12 time segments under consideration.

The annual per member giving change measured $6.90 from 2005 to 2006, and $18.23 from 2006 to 2007. During the economic downturn from December 2007 to mid-2009, giving decreased in both 2008 and 2009. From 2007 to 2008, per member giving in inflation-adjusted dollars declined $5.13, and from 2008 to 2009 giving again declined, this time by $17.12. For the 2005-2009 period, the total overall increase measured $2.89, increasing from $766.21 in 2005 to $769.10 in 2009. As a result, the annual average increase was $0.72 a year for this period.

Giving in recession years during the 1968 through 2009 period, as well as the 1921-1967 period, is considered in chapter 5.

Appendix A contains a listing of the denominations contained in the 1921-2009 analysis in this chapter.

Notes for Chapter 4

[1] Data for the period 1965-1967 was not available in a form that could be readily analyzed for the present purposes, and therefore data for these three years was estimated by dividing the change in per member current dollar contributions from 1964 to 1968 by four, the number of years in this

interval, and cumulatively adding the result to the base year of 1964 data and subsequently to the calculated data for the succeeding years of 1965 and 1966 in order to obtain estimates for the years 1965-1967.

[2] Use of the intervals 1960-1964 and 1964-1970 allows for the use of years for which there is known data, avoiding the use of the 1965 through 1967 years for which estimated data is used in this chapter.

[3] For the years 1965 through 1967, estimated data is used. See Note 1 above.

chapter 5

Church Member Giving and Membership Trends Based on 1968-2009 Data

Overview of Church Member Giving and Membership Trends, 1968-2009

Information as a Tool. The rich historical data series in the *Yearbook of American and Canadian Churches (YACC)* has, in this volume, been supplemented with and revised by additional denominational data for the 1968-2009 period.

Analysis of this data has been presented in the *State of Church Giving* series since the early 1990s. When first published, the finding that giving as a portion of income was shrinking was received with some surprise and intense interest in many quarters.

Now the series has continued for a number of years. The trends identified in earlier analyses impact current activities. Various denominations continue to face decisions about staff cuts and, in some cases, whether to decrease missionary forces. The emphasis on local internal operations indicated by the trend in giving to Congregational Finances has, in fact, resulted in changed dynamics between local congregations and national church offices. The numbers did not cause such changes to occur. The numbers only described symptoms of priorities. These priorities produced behaviors resulting in the changed relationships.

It is generally acknowledged that most individuals do not decide how much to give based on academic information such as that contained in these analyses. However, it is possible for institutional leaders at all levels of the church, local as well as national, to make use of trend information to formulate strategies in response to the findings. For example, the data indicated that giving to Congregational Finances began to increase as a portion of income in 1993, and continued a general trend in an upward direction through 2002. It is possible that local church leadership had recognized a negative general trend and took steps to address it. The fact that the upturn in giving that began in 1993 essentially benefited local expenses, with only a slowing of the decline to Benevolences, indicates that church leadership may yet be operating with a limited vision of whole-life stewardship. Since 2003, an overall pattern of decline in giving as a percent of income to Congregational Finances was observed. On the one hand, the decline could reflect the December 2007 to mid-2009 recession. On the other, the decline in donations for Congregational Finances that began to reoccur in 2003 may suggest support for the internal operations of the congregation will not remain robust over time if not accompanied by a broader vision reflected in support for Benevolences. In either case, the uptick from 1993 through 2002 also indicates that the direction of trends can change.

Facts and figures may be useful to those responsible for promoting the health of the church. The analyses in this chapter are presented in an effort to expand the available information base.

The Meaning of Trends. Projections produced by statistical regression models are a tool to help leaders plan in response to reported data. Experts evaluate trends in weather to plan strategies that will safeguard agriculture. Demographers map out population change trends to help government at local, national, and international levels plan for needs in education, aging, and trade.

Statistical techniques can also be used to suggest both consequences and possibilities regarding church giving and membership patterns. Of course, trend data only indicates future directions. Data does not dictate what will happen. Available information, including trend analysis, can help formulate intelligent responses to identified factors. Church leaders and members can help decide, through action or inaction, what the future will look like.

Trend analysis was first included in this series partly in response to developments in national church offices. After talking with a number of denominational officials who were making painful decisions about which programs to cut, in light of decreased Benevolences dollars being received, it seemed useful to see where the present patterns of giving might lead if effective means were not found to alter present behavior. Were current patterns likely to prove a temporary setback, or did the data suggest longer-term implications?

The data for both Benevolences and Congregational Finances can be projected using linear and exponential regression analysis. Linear regression is sometimes called a "straight-line" projection. An exponential regression is also labeled a "decay" model. To determine which type of analysis more accurately describes the data in a category's giving pattern, the data for 1968-1985 was projected using both techniques. Then, the actual data for 1986 through 2009 was plotted. The more accurate projection was judged to be the procedure that produced the trend line most closely resembling the actual 1986-2009 data.

General Trends in Church Member Giving. As noted in earlier chapters, the category of Total Contributions from church members is divided into the two general categories of Congregational Finances and Benevolences. In the category of Congregational Finances, giving as a portion of income declined overall between

...support for the internal operations of the congregation will not remain robust over time if not accompanied by a broader vision reflected in support for Benevolences.

1968 and 2009 for the composite denominations. Yet a trend toward increase in the level of giving to this category was observed beginning in 1993. These intermittent increases from one year to the next were in contrast to the decline indicated by an exponential projection through 2009, based on 1968-1985 giving data. However, since 2002, the actual data for giving as a percent of income for this category decreased in more years than it increased. Giving in 2008 and 2009 declined to the 1989-1990 levels. Although giving to this category exceeded levels suggested by either the linear or exponential trends, the recent declines suggest the data bears monitoring.

The continued decline in actual data for giving to Benevolences as a portion of income throughout the 1968-2009 period in the composite denominations initially followed the linear trend. In 1993, the rate of decline began to slow, although the level of giving remained closer to the linear trend. In 1999, the actual data moved above the exponential trend. Although Benevolences may be expected to be above either trend line, if the pattern of decline observed in the 1968-2009 period continues, Benevolences may represent a substantially reduced portion of income throughout the current century.

General Trends in Church Membership. Membership trends across the theological spectrum point to a decline when membership was considered as a percent of U.S. population.

Eleven mainline Protestant denominations represented 13.2% of the population in 1968, and 5.9% in 2009, a decline of 56% from the 1968 base.

The composite data set communions analyzed in earlier chapters of this volume measured 14.1% of U.S. population in 1968 and 9.6% in 2009, down 32% as a portion of U.S. population from the 1968 base.

A set of fifteen evangelical denominations grew 48% in the number of members between 1968 and 2009, but posted a 3% decline as a portion of U.S. population, since U.S. population expanded at a faster rate. The growth as a percent of population for this group peaked in the mid-1980s, and then began a slow decline, reaching its lowest point of the period in 2009.

Membership in a set of 36 Protestant denominations, including some of the fastest growing denominations in the U.S., and the Roman Catholic Church represented 45% of U.S. population in 1968, and 36% in 2009, a decline of 20% from the 1968 base. A trend line for this set of denominations suggests that the group will represent only one-quarter or less of the U.S. population by 2100, and 15% in 2200, if current patterns continue.

Church Member Giving in Recessions. An analysis was done of church member giving in inflation-adjusted 2005 dollars during recession years occurring during the 1968-2009 period. No clear pattern was found between recessions and church member giving. That is, giving increased in some recession years and not others, and also decreased in some non-recession years. As discussed later in this chapter, data year 2009 was the second year of the 2007-2009 recession, and per member giving declined.

No clear pattern was found between recessions and church member giving.

A review of per member giving for the 11 denominations considered in chapter 4 also found no clear pattern between church member giving in this set of denominations and economic contractions in the 1921-1967 period.

New Religious Construction. When considered as a portion of income, spending on new construction of religious buildings was higher in 1965 than in 2009. Per capita spending on new religious construction in 1965 was also higher than in 2009, when considered in inflation-adjusted dollars. Again in inflation-adjusted dollars, the aggregate billions spent in 2001 were the highest annual amount spent in the 1964-2009 period.

Details of Church Giving and Membership Trends, 1968-2009

The Current Trends in Church Giving. The first chapter in this report indicates that per member giving as a percent of income decreased between 1968 and 2009. Further, contributions to the category of Benevolences were declining proportionately faster than those to Congregational Finances between 1968 and 2009.

The data for the composite denominations analyzed for 1968 through 2009 has been projected in the *State of Church Giving* series, beginning with the edition that included 1991 data.[1] The most recent projection is based on data from 1968 through 2009.

The Trend in Congregational Finances. The 1968-2009 church giving data contained in this report indicates that giving for Congregational Finances as a percent of income declined from 2.45% in 1968, to 2.04% in 2009, a decline of 17%.

Both linear and exponential regression were used to analyze the data for giving to Congregational Finances as a percent of income for the 17-year interval of 1968 through 1985. Then the actual data for 1986 through 2009 was plotted. The actual data for 1986-1992 declined but still exceeded the exponential curve. In 1993, giving to Congregational Finances as a percent of income began to increase in some years, unlike either projection. However starting in 2003, annual declines in the giving level appeared more frequently than in the 1993-2002 period of general increase. Although the actual data remained above the projected data of the exponential curve, the decreases in 2008 and 2009 returned giving to the levels of 1989-1991. The results are shown in Figure 8.

Figure 8: Projected Trends for Composite Denominations, Giving to Congregational Finances as a Percent of Income, Using Linear and Exponential Regression Based on Data for 1968-1985, with Actual Data for 1986-2009

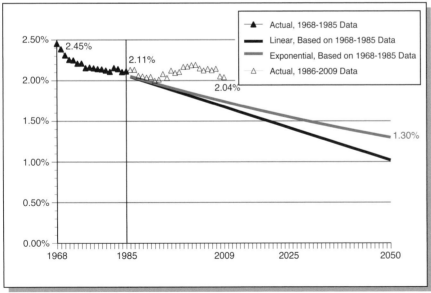

The upturn in giving as a percent of income to Congregational Finances between 1993 and 2002 posted more annual increases than decreases. This pattern differed from the 1968 through 1992 period, when annual declines were more likely. This 1993 through 2002 period of increase was followed by more frequent annual declines in giving as a portion of income to Congregational Finances. By 2009, there was an overall decline from the 1968 base. The 1993-2002 decade of general increase was not robust enough to sustain a positive trend. The 2008 and 2009 decreases in giving to Congregational Finances may reflect economic challenges faced by church members during the 2007-2009 recession. However, declines in giving as a percent of income to this category began to appear in 2003, before the recession years of 2008 and 2009. Another hypothesis is that an increase to the internal operations of the church will not be maintained over time if there is not also a broader vision attracting church member support for the category of Benevolences as well. Data for additional years could help to demonstrate whether the downturn in giving as a portion of income to Congregational Finances that began in 2003 was an interruption in the 1993-2002 pattern of increase, or if the 1993-2002 trend of increase was a temporary reversal in an overall pattern of decline in giving to this category.

The Trend in Benevolences. Per member contributions to Benevolences as a percent of income decreased from 0.66% in 1968 to 0.34% in 2009, a percent decrease in giving as a percent of income of 48% from the 1968 base, the lowest point in the 1968-2009 period.

The data for giving to Benevolences as a percent of income for the 17-year interval of 1968 through 1985 was also projected using both linear and exponential regression. The actual data for 1986 through 2009 was then plotted. The results are shown in Figure 9.

Reported per member giving to Benevolences as a percent of income was near or below the projected value of the linear regression for 1989 through 1993. In 1994, the rate of decline slowed to the point that the actual data was above, but still closer to, the linear trend line. However, from 1999-2009, giving to Benevolences as a percent of income moved above the exponential line, suggesting that, although the negative trend continued, the rate of decline slowed even further. In 2009, per member giving as a portion of income to Benevolences reached its

Figure 9:   Projected Trends for Composite Denominations, Giving to Benevolences as a Percent of Income, Using Linear and Exponential Regression Based on Data for 1968-1985, with Actual Data for 1986-2009

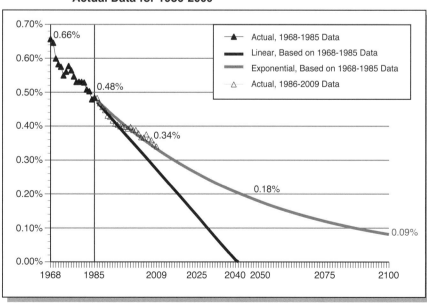

Source: empty tomb analysis; *YACC*, adjusted series; U.S. BEA   empty tomb, inc. 2011

lowest point in the 1968-2009 period. As discussed in chapter 1, it appears that the external factors of tsunami and hurricane relief efforts contributed to the increase observed in this category in 2005, since data for 2006, 2007, 2008, and 2009 again posted declines.

In summary, although giving to Benevolences as a portion of income between 1968 and 2009 continued to decline, the rate slowed toward the end of that period.

In addition to the 1968-1985 projection, shown in Figure 9, a second analysis was done on the entire period from 1968-2009. A linear trend based on the entire period of 1968-2009 data indicated that per member giving as a portion of income to the category of Benevolences would reach 0.04% of income in the year A.D. 2050, based on the 1968-2009 numbers. The exponential curve based on 1968-2009 data indicated that giving in 2050 would be 0.18%, down 46% from the 0.34% level in 2009.[2] Extending the exponential trend to 2100, Benevolences would represent 0.09% of income in that year.

These trend lines may be more useful to predict the general level of giving, rather than precise numbers. However, the overall direction suggests that by 2050 the amount of income going to support Benevolences, including denominational structures, would be severely reduced, if the overall pattern of the last 42 years continues.

However, the overall direction suggests that by 2050 the amount of income going to support Benevolences, including denominational structures, would be severely reduced, if the overall pattern of the last 42 years continues.

Trends in Church Membership as a Percent of U.S. Population, 1968-2009.[3] Membership data for various church groupings is available for review for the years 1968 through 2009. When the reported data is considered as a percent of U.S. population, the membership data is placed in the larger context of the changing environment in which the church exists. This measurement is similar to giving as a percent of income, which reflects how much a financial donation represents of the resources available to the donor. In a similar way, measuring membership as a percent of U.S. population takes into account the fact that the potential population for church membership also changed as a result of growth in the number of people in the U.S.

The State of Church Giving through 1993 included a chapter entitled, "A Unified Theory of Giving and Membership."[4] The hypothesis explored in that discussion is that there is a relationship between a decline in church member giving and membership patterns. One proposal considered in that chapter is that a denomination that is able to involve its members in a larger vision, such as mission outreach, as evidenced in levels of giving to support that idea, will also be attracting additional members.

In the present chapter, discussion will focus on patterns and trends in membership as a percent of U.S. population.

Membership in the Composite Denominations, 1968-2009. The composite denominations, which span the theological spectrum, included 28,213,589 Full or Confirmed Members in 1968. By 2009, these communions included 29,443,504 members, an increase of 4%.[5] However, during the same 41-year interval, U.S. population increased from 200,745,000 to 307,483,000, an increase of 53%. Therefore, while this church member grouping represented 14.1% of the U.S. population in 1968, it included 9.6% in 2009, a decline of 32% from the 1968 base. Figure 10 presents membership as a percent of U.S. population, and giving as a percent of income, for the composite denominations, 1968-2009.

Membership Trends in Three Church Groups. Membership data for three subgroups within the historically Christian church in the U.S. is available. Data was analyzed for eleven Protestant mainline denominations, fifteen Protestant evangelical denominations, and the Roman Catholic Church.

Figure 11 presents the membership trends for the three groups. A declining trend is noticed most markedly in the mainline Protestant communions. Full or Confirmed Membership in eleven mainline Protestant denominations affiliated with the National Council of the Churches of Christ in the U.S.A. (NCC)[6] decreased as a percent of U.S. population between 1968 and 2009. In 1968, this group included 26,508,288, or 13.2% of U.S. population. In 2009, the 11 denominations included 18,006,209, or 5.9% of U.S. population, a decline of 56% from the 1968 base, as a portion of U.S. population.

Figure 10: Membership as a Percent of U.S. Population and Giving as a Percent of U.S. Per Capita DPI, Composite Denominations, 1968-2009

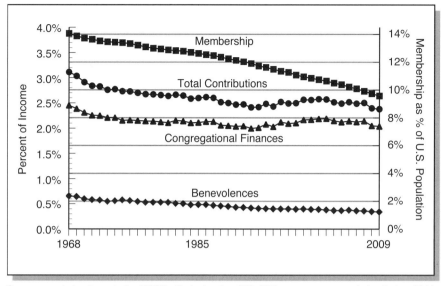

Source: empty tomb analysis; *YACC* adjusted series; U.S. BEA   empty tomb, inc. 2011

Figure 11: Membership as a Percent of U.S. Population, Fifteen Evangelical Denominations, Eleven Mainline Denominations, and the Roman Catholic Church, 1968-2009

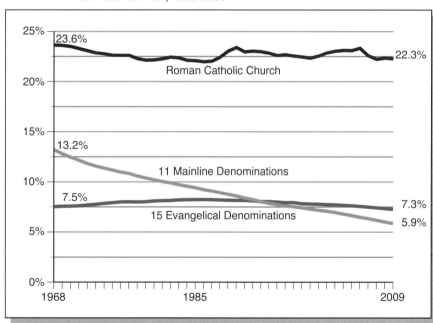

Source: empty tomb analysis; *YACC* adjusted series; US BEA   empty tomb, inc. 2011

Data is also available for a group of fifteen denominations that might be classified on the evangelical end of the theological spectrum.[7] Although one or more of the communions in this grouping might prefer the term "conservative" to "evangelical" as a description, the latter term in its current sociological usage may be useful. These communions included some of the fastest growing denominations in the United States.

This group grew 48% in membership, from 15,101,542 in 1968 to 22,345,993, in 2009, while U.S. population grew 53%. As a result, this group measured 7.52% of U.S. population in 1968, and 7.27% in 2009, a decline of 3% in the portion of the U.S. represented by these communions. In the mid-1980s, the group peaked at 8.23% as a portion of U.S. population, and then declined to 7.27% by 2009, a decline of 12% as a portion of U.S. population from the 1986 peak. In 1993, these fifteen evangelical communions surpassed the 11 mainline communions in the portion of U.S. population that they represented.

The Roman Catholic Church included 47,468,333 members in 1968, or 24% of U.S. population. Although the church's membership grew 44%, to 68,503,456 in 2009, it decreased to 22% as a portion of the faster-growing U.S. population, a decline of 6%.

Projected Membership Trends in Eleven Mainline Denominations. As with giving to Congregational Finances and Benevolences as a percent of income, trend lines using both linear and exponential regression were developed for the eleven mainline Protestant communions discussed above, using their 1968-1985 membership data. As shown in Figure 12, the actual 1986 through 2009 data was also plotted. The actual 1986-2008 data was slightly above the exponential curve for these denominations. In 2009, the actual membership was slightly below the exponential trend figure.

An exponential curve based on the entire 1968-2009 reported data series suggested that these denominations would represent 2.8% of the U.S. population in 2050, if the present rate of decline continues.

Figure 12: Trend in Membership as a Percent of U.S. Population, Eleven Mainline Protestant Denominations, Linear and Exponential Regression Based on Data for 1968-1985, with Actual Data 1986-2009

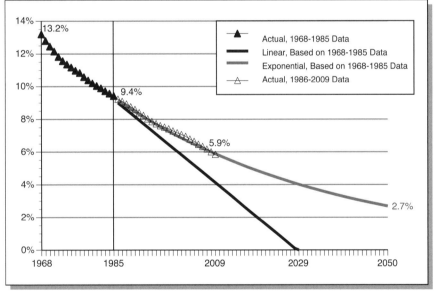

Source: empty tomb analysis; *YACC*, adjusted series; U.S. BEA   empty tomb, inc. 2011

Projected Membership Trends in the Composite Denominations. Nine of the eleven mainline Protestant denominations discussed above are also included in the composite set of denominations that have been considered in earlier chapters of this report. Regression analysis was carried out on the 1968-1985 membership data for the composite denominations to determine if the trends in the larger grouping differed from the mainline denomination subset. The results were then compared to the actual 1986 through 2009 membership data for the composite data set.

The composite denominations represented 14.1% of the U.S. population in 1968, and 12.6% in 1985. Linear trend analysis of the 1968-1985 data suggested that this grouping would have represented 10.7% of U.S. population in 2009, while exponential regression suggested it would have included 10.9%. In fact, this composite grouping of communions represented 9.6% of the U.S. population in 2009, a smaller figure than that indicated by linear regression, suggesting the trend is closer to that predicted by linear regression than the exponential curve. By 2050, these composite denominations would represent 7.5% of the U.S. population if a linear trend remains the more accurate analysis. Figure 13 presents this information in graphic form.

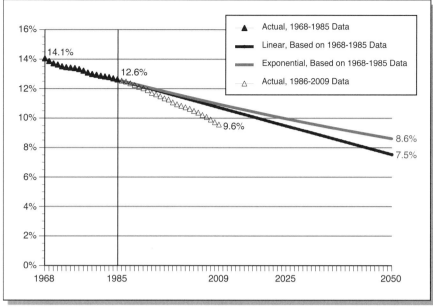

Figure 13: Trend in Membership as a Percent of U.S. Population, Composite Denominations, Linear and Exponential Regression Based on Data for 1968-1985, with Actual Data 1986-2009

Source: empty tomb analysis; *YACC* adjusted series; U.S. BEA   empty tomb, inc. 2011

Membership and Projected Membership Trends in 37 Communions. In 1968, a set of 36 Protestant denominations and the Roman Catholic Church included a total of 90,209,857 members. The Protestant churches included a broad representation of the theological spectrum, and also included some of the fastest growing denominations in the U.S. With the U.S. population at 200,745,000, these Christians constituted 45% of the 1968 U.S. population. By 2009, the group had grown to 110,844,828 members. However, with U.S. population having grown to 307,483,000 in 2009, these Christians comprised 36.0% of the American population, a percent change of -20% from the 1968 base.

As shown in Figure 14, because of the broad nature of the sampling of these historically Christian communions, a projection was extended to 2200, based on membership data for the entire period of 1968

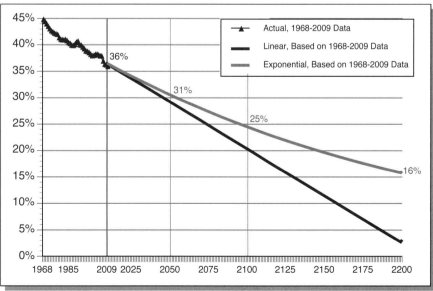

Figure 14: Trend in Membership as a Percent of U.S. Population, 37 Denominations, Linear and Exponential Regression Based on Data for 1968-2009

Source: empty tomb analysis; *YACC* adjusted series; U.S. BEA   empty tomb, inc., 2011

through 2009. The purpose was to forecast, based on past patterns, the role this group of denominations would play at the end of the next century. By 2050, the linear projection suggested the group will have declined from representing 36% of the U.S. population in 2009 to include 29%. The exponential projection forecasted 31% in 2050. By the year 2100, the linear trend projected 20% while the exponential trend projected 25% of the U.S. population will be affiliated with these 37 communions. If the trends continue long term, in 2200 this group of communions would represent 15.8% of U.S. population, according to the exponential curve, or 2.7%, if the linear trend proves more accurate.

Trends in One Denomination. The quality of trend data will be affected by the measurements taken. An example from one denomination may illustrate the point.

The United Methodist Church resulted from the merger of The Methodist Church and The Evangelical United Brethren in 1968. In 2008, the last year with data available for the following analysis,[8] The United Methodist Church was the second largest Protestant denomination, and third largest communion overall in the U.S. While The Methodist Church reported data for 1968 in the 1970 *YACC* edition, the Evangelical United Brethren did not. Therefore, data for The United Methodist Church, including both The Methodist Church and the Evangelical United Brethren, was not available in 1968, and as a result this communion was not included in the composite denominations.

Two years after the merger, in 1971, The United Methodist Church changed its reporting methodology for its information published in the *YACC* series. Specifically, the category of "Connectional Clergy Support" was switched from Congregational Finances to Benevolences. UMC Connectional Clergy Support included district superintendents and Episcopal salaries, which would standardly be included in Benevolences for other communions as well. However, UMC Connectional Clergy Support also included pastor pension and benefits, including health insurance, and a category of Equitable Salary Funds, which would be included in Congregational Finances in most denominations.

Figure 15: **The United Methodist Church, Per member Giving to Congregational Finances and Benevolences as a Portion of Income, with Connectional Clergy Support in Benevolences, 1971-2008, and in Congregational Finances, 1969-2008**

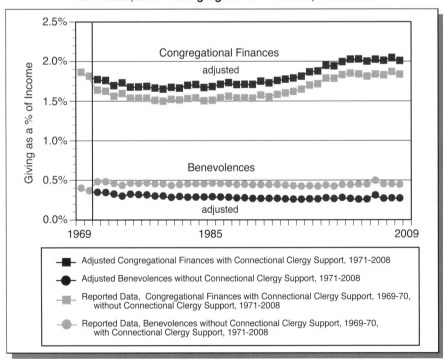

Source: empty tomb analysis; *YACC* adjusted series; UMC; U.S. BEA   empty tomb, inc. 2011

58

UMC Connectional Clergy Support increased fairly rapidly between 1969 and 2008. When UMC Connectional Clergy Support was included in per member giving to the UMC Benevolences series as a percent of income, Benevolences increased from 0.40% in 1969 to 0.44% in 2008, an 11% increase from the 1969 base. However, when UMC Connectional Clergy Support was taken out of the UMC Benevolences series for 1971 to 2008, giving to Benevolences as a portion of income in the United Methodist Church declined from 0.40% in 1969 to 0.27% in 2008, a decrease of 32%.

Per member giving as a portion of income to the single category of UMC Connectional Clergy Support increased 38% from 1969 to 2008.

Figure 15 illustrates the two trends in Benevolences giving, based on whether the category includes Connectional Clergy Support or not.

The two different trends in UMC Benevolences illustrate the point that definitions of the categories being measured are important.

If the traditional definition of Benevolences is used, which would place pastor health insurance and other benefits in Congregational Finances, then Benevolences giving in The United Methodist Church declined as a portion of income in a noticeable fashion between 1969 and 2008. If, however, a category that was initially included in Congregational Finances is transferred to Benevolences, the UMC Benevolences giving as a portion of income increased between 1969-2008.

The former definition of Benevolences, that excludes those congregationally-based expenses, provides a more specific measurement of member support for the larger mission of the church. The latter definition, which includes pastor health insurance and other benefits with broader church activities, weighted the measurement toward the funding of institutional operations.

The denominational leadership needs to be clear about its primary goal, whether it is focused on maintaining an institution or mobilizing church members to increased mission outreach through denominational channels. When that priority has been identified, the denomination can choose the most accurate definition to measure progress toward the goal.

Church Member Giving and Recessions. Does church member giving go down during recessions?

Church Member Giving and Recessions, 1968-2009. Figure 16 presents an analysis of church member giving to Total Contributions in recession years in the 1968-2009 period, based on the composite data set. The analysis presents per member church giving in inflation-adjusted 2005 dollars.

Between 1968 and 2009, seven recessions occurred. For purposes of the present analysis, a "recession year" was defined as a calendar year during the 1968-2009 period with at least one month of economic contraction during a recession, as delineated by the National Bureau of Economic Research (NBER).[9]

In four of the seven recessions, church member giving to Total Contributions declined, while in three it did not.

Between 1968 and 2009, twelve calendar years displayed one or more months of economic contraction during a recession. Church member giving to Total

In four of the seven recessions, church member giving to Total Contributions declined, while in three it did not.

Figure 16: **Church Member Giving to Total Contributions, Inflation-Adjusted 2005 Dollars, and Recession Years, 1968-2009**

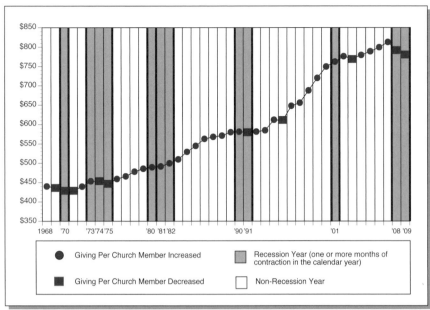

Source: empty tomb analysis; *YACC* adjusted series; U.S. BEA; NBER   empty tomb, inc., 2011

Contributions declined in six of those twelve years, that is, 1970, 1974, 1975, 1991, 2008, and 2009. Four of those six years were the second or third year of a multiyear recession.

Figure 16 also indicates that church member giving to Total Contributions declined in four non-recession years during the period of 1968 through 2009.

It may be observed, therefore, that church member giving does not necessarily decline in a recession.

It may also be noted that church member giving in two of the three single years with contraction, 1970, 1980, and 2001, giving to Total Contributions increased. In three of the first years of the four multiyear contractions in the 1968 to 2009 period under consideration, giving also increased.

An economic peak occurred in December 1969, meaning that a contraction began in January 1970. Church member giving declined in 1970, but also in 1969, before the contraction began, and in 1971, the year after the trough had been declared and economic expansion was determined to have begun again. Other factors may have influenced church giving in this period. For example, a Gallup poll found that in 1970, only 14% of respondents felt that religion was increasing in influence in American life, while 75% felt it was losing influence. These findings showed a decline from 1957, when 69% thought religion was increasing in influence. By 1974, the percent who felt religion was increasing in influence had recovered to 31%.[10] The 1970 poll results may have reflected cultural controversies that occurred in the late 1960s and early 1970s, suggesting the possibility that other factors, in addition to recession, may have influenced church member giving in the early 1970s.

The next decline in church member giving to Total Contributions took place in 1974 and 1975, the second and third years of a recession. During the recession of 1980, and the recession of 1981-1982, church member giving to Total Contributions increased each year. Church member giving declined in 1991, the second year of the 1990-1991 recession. Church member giving did not decline in the recession year of 2001. Church member giving did decline in both recession years of 2008 and 2009, after the peak in December 2007.

Table 16 indicates the specific dates of the peaks and troughs in recessions for the 1968-2009 period. A peak marks the end of a period of economic expansion and the

Table 16: Giving Per Church Member to Total Contributions, Congregational Finances, and Benevolences, Inflation-Adjusted 2005 Dollars, and Recession Years, 1968-2009

Year	Per Full or Confirmed Church Member Giving						National Bureau of Economic Research Recession Dates	Months of Contraction
	Total Contrib.	↑↓	Cong. Finances	↑↓	Benevol.	↑↓		
1968	$440.03	—	$347.12	—	$92.91	—		
1969	$436.79	↓	$343.76	↓	$93.04	↑	Peak December 1969	0
1970	$429.50	↓	$341.05	↓	$88.44	↓	Trough November 1970	11
1971	$429.37	↓	$341.27	↑	$88.09	↓		
1972	$439.47	↑	$350.02	↑	$89.45	↑		
1973	$453.31	↑	$363.05	↑	$90.26	↑	Peak November 1973	1
1974	$453.18	↓	$361.55	↓	$91.63	↑	Twelve months 1974	12
1975	$447.77	↓	$353.16	↓	$94.61	↑	Trough March 1975	3
1976	$459.15	↑	$364.08	↑	$95.07	↑		
1977	$465.94	↑	$371.61	↑	$94.34	↓		
1978	$478.02	↑	$383.17	↑	$94.85	↑		
1979	$485.58	↑	$388.99	↑	$96.58	↑		
1980	$489.38	↑	$391.60	↑	$97.77	↑	January-July 1980	6
1981	$491.50	↑	$392.97	↑	$98.53	↑	Peak July 1981	5
1982	$499.57	↑	$404.27	↑	$95.30	↓	Trough November 1982	11
1983	$509.70	↑	$412.75	↑	$96.95	↑		
1984	$529.29	↑	$431.18	↑	$98.11	↑		
1985	$544.87	↑	$443.37	↑	$101.50	↑		
1986	$562.93	↑	$458.89	↑	$104.05	↑		
1987	$568.15	↑	$466.00	↑	$102.15	↓		
1988	$571.18	↑	$467.56	↑	$103.62	↑		
1989	$580.09	↑	$476.28	↑	$103.81	↑		
1990	$581.24	↑	$479.89	↑	$101.34	↓	Peak July 1990	5
1991	$579.99	↓	$479.79	↓	$100.20	↓	Trough March 1991	3
1992	$581.54	↑	$481.28	↑	$100.26	↑		
1993	$584.82	↑	$486.47	↑	$98.35	↓		
1994	$612.00	↑	$512.50	↑	$99.51	↑		
1995	$610.37	↓	$510.16	↓	$100.20	↑		
1996	$647.91	↑	$545.56	↑	$102.35	↑		
1997	$655.87	↑	$551.19	↑	$104.69	↑		
1998	$687.53	↑	$579.54	↑	$107.99	↑		
1999	$720.10	↑	$608.52	↑	$111.59	↑		
2000	$749.33	↑	$635.71	↑	$113.62	↑		
2001	$762.06	↑	$647.09	↑	$114.97	↑	March-November 2001	8
2002	$775.99	↑	$661.64	↑	$114.35	↓		
2003	$770.11	↓	$657.68	↓	$112.44	↓		
2004	$779.28	↑	$664.67	↑	$114.61	↑		
2005	$788.78	↑	$671.11	↑	$117.67	↑		
2006	$799.20	↑	$682.87	↑	$116.32	↓		
2007	$812.62	↑	$696.08	↑	$116.54	↑	Peak December 2007	0
2008	$793.02	↓	$678.40	↓	$114.62	↓	Twelve months 2008	12
2009	$779.36	↓	$667.93	↓	$111.43	↓	Trough June 2009	6

Source: empty tomb analysis;*YACC* adjusted series; U.S.BEA, NBER

empty tomb, inc., 2011

beginning of recession. The peak is followed by months of contractions, or economic declines.[11]

Church member giving data, published in the *YACC* series, is available on an annual basis. This data collection was adjusted and supplemented by empty tomb, inc., with additional annual data obtained directly from denominational offices. In contrast to the annual reporting of church member giving data, underlying recession data is published on monthly and quarterly bases. To be able to compare church member giving and recession data within a single calendar year, it was necessary to develop a working definition of a recession calendar year. Thus, a working definition of a recession year was developed: a calendar year with at least one month of economic contraction. As indicated in Table 16, the length of economic contraction in any given "recession year" varied from one month to 12 months.

Table 16 presents giving per full or confirmed church member in inflation-adjusted 2005 dollars. Giving is presented for the category of Total Contributions, as well as the subcategories of Congregational Finances and Benevolences. The arrows indicate whether church member giving increased or decreased from the previous year. The peak and trough—start and end—dates of recessions during the 1968 through 2009 period are presented. The last column presents the number of months of economic contraction that occurred in any given recession calendar year.

A few observations can be made about giving to Congregational Finances and Benevolences. For example, as noted in chapter 1, per member giving to Benevolences in inflation-adjusted 2005 dollars declined in 13 years in the 1968-2009 period. As can be seen in Table 16, six of these 13 declines occurred in recession years. In other words, giving to Benevolences was as likely to occur in non-recession years as in recession years. In contrast, of the nine times that per member giving to Congregational Finances declined in the 1968-2009 period, six of the nine occurred during recession years.

While giving to Congregational Finances declined during two of the three years of the 1973-1975 recession, giving to Benevolences did not decline during these three years.

The data does indicate a decline in church member giving in inflation-adjusted dollars to their congregations in 2008 and 2009. The 2007-2009 recession was the longest since World War II.[12] A discussion of 2008 and 2009 giving to religion, compared to other charitable categories, is presented in chapter 7.

The declines in per member giving to congregations evident in 2008 and 2009 may have been aggravated by the recession. It is also possible that these declines were coincident with a long-term trend during the 1968-2009 period, evident in the ongoing decline in church member giving as a percent of income, as discussed in chapter 1.

Overall, from the review of giving per church member and recession years in the 1968 through 2009 period, one does not observe a predictable pattern between the level of church member giving and recession years.

... six of these 13 declines occurred in recession years. In other words, giving to Benevolences was as likely to occur in non-recession years as in recession years.

Church Member Giving and Recessions, 1921-1967. As noted in chapter 4, church member giving data to Total Contributions is available for a set of 11 denominations for the period 1921 through 2009.[13]

A review of the 1921-1967 church member giving data for these 11 denominations provided 46 two-year potential change-in-giving intervals, starting with the 1921-1922 interval. This series can be compared to data for economic contractions during the years 1922-1967.

Nine of the 11 denominations[14] are also included in the composite set of denominations analyzed above for 1968 through 2009. For the 1968 through 2009 period, the per member giving in inflation-adjusted 2005 dollars reflected the same direction of increase or decrease in the 11 denominations as in the composite set, with two exceptions. For the 11 denominations, giving increased in both 1991, a recession year, and in 1995, a non-recession year, compared to declines in both years for the composite denominations. These differences in two of the 41 changes in per member giving from the previous year in the 1968-2009 period means that the pattern of the 11 denominations matched the direction of giving of the composite denominations 95% of the time. Therefore, a review of information for the 11 denominations from 1921 through 1967 may be useful as a supplement to the composite denomination information for 1968 through 2009.

Beginning in 1923, there were eight recessions in the period under review, in addition to the major, extended contraction from August 1929 through March 1933.[15]

For purposes of this analysis, the "exceptional decline in economic activity" from 1929 through March 1933 will be referred to as the Great Depression, although that term is also extended by some to include the years through 1940 or 1941, when "economic activity had returned to approximately normal levels."[16]

The eight recessions under consideration, in addition to the Great Depression, in the 1921 through 1967 period, for which church giving was also analyzed, occurred with the following peaks and troughs.

- May 1923 through July 1924
- October 1926 through November 1927
- May 1937 through June 1938
- February through October 1945
- November 1948 through October 1949
- July 1953 through May 1954
- August 1957 through April 1958
- April 1960 through February 1961

The current data set begins in 1921, and therefore does not indicate whether church member giving in these 11 denominations increased or declined from 1920 to 1921. Therefore, the present discussion did not consider the January 1920 through July 1921 recession.

During the eight recessions that were considered, per member giving in inflation-adjusted 2005 dollars increased from the previous year in every recession year.

During the eight recessions that were considered, per member giving in inflation-adjusted 2005 dollars increased from the previous year in every recession year.

Table 17: **Giving Per Church Member to Total Contributions, 11 Denominations, Inflation-Adjusted 2005 Dollars, and Recession Years, 1921-1967**

Year	Per Full or Confirmed Church Member Giving — Total Contrib.	↑↓	National Bureau of Economic Research Recession Dates	Months of Contraction
1921	$163.18	—	Trough July 1921	7
1922	$208.94	↑		
1923	$237.22	↑	Peak May 1923	7
1924	$248.47	↑	Trough July 1924	7
1925	$225.53	↓		
1926	$233.61	↑	Peak October 1926	2
1927	$250.46	↑	Trough November 1927	11
1928	$223.57	↓		
1929	$203.93	↓	Peak August 1929	4
1930	$197.75	↓		12
1931	$186.54	↓		12
1932	$175.97	↓		12
1933	$151.94	↓	Trough March 1933	3
1934	$142.07	↓		
1935	$142.30	↑		
1936	$150.39	↑		
1937	$151.92	↑	Peak May 1937	7
1938	$158.78	↑	Trough June 1938	6
1939	$152.70	↓		
1940	$151.50	↓		
1941	$157.18	↑		
1942	$152.35	↓		
1943	$154.24	↑		
1944	$169.79	↑		
1945	$192.41	↑	Peak Feb. - Trough Oct. 1945	8
1946	$187.74	↓		
1947	$184.09	↓		
1948	$197.83	↑	Peak November 1948	1
1949	$219.02	↑	Trough October 1949	10
1950	$226.79	↑		
1951	$227.53	↑		
1952	$240.06	↑		
1953	$264.27	↑	Peak July 1953	5
1954	$280.48	↑	Trough May 1954	5
1955	$297.59	↑		
1956	$308.94	↑		
1957	$313.48	↑	Peak August 1957	4
1958	$323.02	↑	Trough April 1958	4
1959	$334.88	↑		
1960	$341.04	↑	Peak April 1960	8
1961	$343.40	↑	Trough February 1961	2
1962	$346.86	↑		
1963	$347.36	↑		
1964	$352.45	↑		
1965	*$363.31*	↑		
1966	*$369.98*	↑		
1967	*$375.16*	↑		

Source: empty tomb, inc. analysis; *YACC* adjusted series; U.S. BEA, NBER
empty tomb, inc., 2011

Per member giving in these 11 denominations, in inflation-adjusted dollars, declined in 1928, the year before the Great Depression began, and continued to decline through 1934, the year after that economic downturn ended.

Per member giving declined in 1925, the year between two recessions. Giving also declined in 1939 and 1940, after the 1937-1938 recession, and declined again in 1942.

In the 1921-1967 period, the last time per member giving declined in these 11 denominations was in 1946 and 1947, between the 1945 and 1948-1949 recessions.

Per member giving in these 11 denominations increased every year from 1948 through 1967, when four of the recessions in this period occurred.

The annual declines in per member giving in inflation-adjusted 2005 dollars in each year immediately preceding and following, as well as the years during, the Great Depression, from 1928 through 1934, may be related to the exceptional economic circumstances of those years.

Comparing Church Member Giving and Recessions, Composite Set, 1968-2009, and 11 Denominations, 1921-1967 and 1968-2009. The composite set data for 1968 through 2009 can be compared with the 11 denominations, both for 1921-1967, and also for 1968-2009.

Comparing the Composite Set for 1968-2009 with the 11 Denominations for 1921-1967. The composite denominations posted declines in giving in six of 11 recession years (a calendar year with at least one month of contraction) during 1968 through 2009. Per member giving in the 11 denominations declined in economic contraction years only during the Great Depression years of 1929 through 1933. It may be noted that per member giving in the 11 denominations increased in each of the other 15 recession years that occurred from 1922 through 1967.

The composite denominations posted four declines from any given year to the next in per member giving in four non-recession years in the 1968 through 2009 41-year interval. Per member giving in the 11 denominations declined from one year to the next in eight non-recession years in the 1921-1967 46-year interval. Of these eight years, six were adjacent to an economic contraction (immediately before and/or after).

Comparing the Composite Set and the 11 Denominations for 1968-2009. Within the 1968-2009 period, a comparison of the composite denominations and the 11 denominations found that per member giving in inflation-adjusted 2005 dollars in the 11 denominations changed in the same direction as the composite denominations in 11 of 12 recession years, or 92% of the time.

In the composite denominations, per member giving declined six times, and increased six times, in years when an economic contraction occurred during the 1968-2009 period. Data for the 11 denominations indicated per member giving declined five times, and increased seven times, in contraction years during the 1968-2009 period.

In the composite denominations, per member giving declined in four non-contraction years in the 1968-2009 period. During the same period, per member giving in the 11 denominations declined three times in non-recession years.

New Religious Construction. How does 2009 construction activity among churches in the U.S. compare to other years?

Census Bureau data provides information on the new construction of religious buildings.[17] According to the data, current dollar aggregate construction of religious buildings was $1.04 billion dollars in 1964, compared to $6.19 billion in 2009. On a current-dollar aggregate level, more building was going on in 2009 than in the mid-1960s.

However, as has been emphasized in previous chapters of this volume, aggregate numbers considered apart from inflation, or that do not take into account changes in population and income, do not give a complete picture.

When inflation was factored out, the data indicated that the aggregate sum of new religious building construction for the five-year period of 2005-2009 was $34.6 billion in inflation-adjusted 2005 dollars, which was higher than the 1964-1968 period spending of $28.0 billion. The highest single year inflation-adjusted amount in the 1964-2009 period was the 2001 level of $9.3 billion. The 1965 level of $6.3 billion had been the highest amount of aggregate, inflation-adjusted dollars spent on the construction of new religious buildings from 1964 through 1996. In 1997, aggregate inflation-adjusted spending passed the 1965 level, and religious building expenditures continued to increase through 2001. Expenditures were at or above $9 billion a year in inflation-adjusted 2005 dollars from 2000 through 2003, and decreased to $5.6 billion in 2009.

Yet, to obtain the most realistic picture about building patterns, changes in population and income also need to be factored into the evaluation. For example, taking population changes into account, in 1965 the per capita expenditure in the U.S. on religious buildings was $33 dollars per person in inflation-adjusted 2005 dollars. In 2009, it was $18 dollars.

The period 1964 through 1968 posted an average per capita expenditure on new religious buildings of $29. The period 2005-2009 was $23, suggesting that construction of new religious buildings was higher in the earlier period, when changes in population were taken into account.

Of course, a smaller portion of the entire U.S. population may have been investing in religious buildings in the late 1990s through 2009 than in the mid-1960s. To have the most meaningful comparison, changes in membership as a portion of population would have to be taken into account. Data considered above suggests that membership in historically Christian churches declined as a portion of the U.S. population between 1964 and 2009. However, other religions were added to the religious milieu of the United States during this period. The Census data includes all religious construction, not just Christian churches. So the rough estimate may be fairly useful as a first approximation.

Even comparing per capita inflation-adjusted dollars spent is of limited use because it does not account for the difference in incomes in the two periods. To review, the $33 per capita spent on religious buildings in 1965 represented a different portion of income than the $18 spent in 2009. In fact, as a portion of income, Americans spent 0.25% on the construction of new religious buildings in 1965, compared to 0.06% in 2009.

One must conclude, therefore, that the population was investing a higher portion of available resources in religious buildings in the mid-1960s than at the beginning

Figure 17:   Construction of Religious Buildings in the U.S., Aggregate Inflation-Adjusted 2005 Dollars, Per Capita Inflation-Adjusted 2005 Dollars, and Percent of U.S. Per Capita DPI, 1964-2009

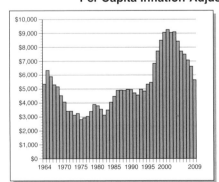
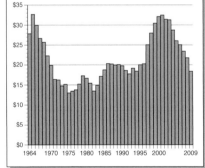
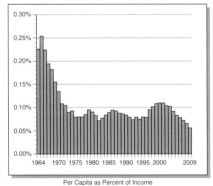

Aggregate Millions of Inflation-Adjusted Dollars | Per Capita in Inflation-Ajusted Dollars | Per Capita as Percent of Income

Source: empty tomb analysis, U.S. Census Bureau; U.S. BEA

empty tomb, inc., 2011

of this century. The building activity occurring in the late 1990s through 2009 has to be evaluated in the context of the general affluence produced by decades of economic expansion in the U.S., in order to make an intelligent evaluation of whether religious construction has in fact increased over the mid-1960s level. This fact is clear from the three charts in Figure 17. These charts contrast the annual aggregate inflation-adjusted 2005 dollar value of new religious building construction with, (1) the per capita expenditures in inflation-adjusted 2005 dollars, and (2) the per capita expenditure as a portion of U.S. per capita income, for the 1964-2009 period. One can observe that the picture is very different when the per person cost of the building is set in the context of the income available to the people paying for the building.

The Response to the Trends. As in other sectors, trend lines in church giving and membership are designed to provide an additional source of information. Planning, evaluation and creative thinking are some of the types of constructive responses that can be made in light of projections. The information on church member giving and membership trends is offered as a possible planning tool.[18] The trend lines are not considered to be dictating what must happen, but rather are seen as providing important indicators of what might happen if present conditions continue in an uninterrupted fashion. Trends in church giving and membership, if used wisely, may be of assistance in addressing conditions present in the body of Christ in the United States.

Notes for Chapter 5

[1] John Ronsvalle and Sylvia Ronsvalle, *The State of Church Giving through 1991* (Champaign, IL: empty tomb, inc., 1993), and subsequent editions in the series. The edition with data through 1991 provides a discussion of the choice to use giving as a percent of income as a basis for considering future giving patterns.

[2] In the linear regression for the 1968-2009 data, the value for the correlation coefficient, or r_{XY}, for the Benevolences data is -.98. The strength of the linear relationship in the present set of 1968-2009 data, that is, the proportion of variance accounted for by linear regression, is represented by the coefficient of determination, or r^2_{XY}, of .96 for Benevolences. In the exponential regression, the value for r_{XY}, for the Benevolences data is -.99, while the strength of the exponential relationship is .98. The Benevolences F-observed values of 954.45 for the linear, and 1,789.86 for the curvilinear, regression are substantially greater than the F-critical value of 7.31 for 1 and 40 degrees of freedom for a single-tailed test with an Alpha value of 0.01. Therefore, the regression equation is useful at the level suggested by the r^2_{XY} figure in predicting giving as a percent of income.

[3] The denominations analyzed in this section include the composite data set whose financial patterns were analyzed in earlier chapters. The data for the composite communions is supplemented by the data of eight denominations included in an analysis of church membership and U.S. population by Roozen and Hadaway in David A. Roozen and Kirk C. Hadaway, eds., *Church and Denominational Growth* (Nashville: Abingdon Press, 1993), 393-395.

[4] This article is available on the Internet at: <http://www.emptytomb.org/UnifiedTheory.pdf>.

[5] See Appendix B-1 for details of the composite denomination data included in these analyses. Consult Appendix B-4 for the total Full or Confirmed Membership numbers used for the American Baptist Churches in the U.S.A. See Appendix B-3.3 and Appendix B-4 for the membership data of the other denominations included in subsequent analyses in this chapter that are not one of the composite denominations.

[6] These eleven denominations include nine of the communions in the composite set of denominations as well as The Episcopal Church and The United Methodist Church.

[7] A list of the communions in this set is presented in Appendix A.

[8] In correspondence dated March 14, 2011, a denominational representative indicated that data for the category of United Methodist Church Connectional Clergy Support was no longer collected as of 2009.

[9] National Bureau of Economic Research; "Business Cycle Expansions and Contractions"; 9/20/2010; <http://www.nber.org/cycles/cyclesmain.html>; pp. 1 of 9/20/10 10:26 AM.

[10] George Gallup, Jr., Executive Director, *Religion in America 1990* (Princeton, NJ: The Princeton Religion Research Center, 1990), p. 60.

[11] See, for example: National Bureau of Economic Research; "Determination of the December 2007 Peak in Economic Activity"; 12/11/2008; <http://www.nber.org/dec2008.pdf>; p. 1 of 8/26/2009 printout.

[12] National Bureau of Economic Research, 9/20/2010, p. 1.

[13] See Appendix A for a list of the denominations included in this analysis. Data for the period 1965-1967 was not available in a form that could be readily analyzed for the present purposes, and therefore data for these three years was estimated by dividing the change in per member current dollar contributions from 1964 to 1968 by four, the number of years in this interval, and cumulatively adding the result to the base year of 1964 data and subsequently to the calculated data for the succeeding years of 1965 and 1966 in order to obtain estimates for the years 1965-1967. In Table xx, the calculated values for these three years are italicized.

[14] The Episcopal Church and The United Methodist Church were not included in the original 1968 and 1985 analysis of the composite data set due to lack of available 1968 data.

[15] National Bureau of Economic Research; "U.S. Business Cycle Expansions and Contractions"; 7/24/2011; <http://www.nber.org/cycles.html>; p. 1 of 7/24/2011 12:45 PM printout.

[16] National Bureau of Economic Research; "The NBER's Business Cycle Dating Procedure: Frequently Asked Questions"; 7/24/2011; <http://www.nber.org/cycles/recessions_faq.html>; p. 3 of 7/24/2011 2:26 PM printout.

[17] For a series beginning in 1964 titled "Annual Value of Construction Put in Place," the Census Bureau defined its Religious category as follows: "*Religious* includes houses of worship and other religious buildings. Certain buildings, although owned by religious organizations, are not included in this category. These include education or charitable institutions, hospitals, and publishing houses." (U.S. Census Bureau, Current Construction Reports, C30/01-5, *Value of Construction Put in Place*: May 2001, U.S. Government Printing Office, Washington, DC 20402, Appendix A, "Definitions," p. A-2). A 2003 revision of this series presented the definitions as follows: "Religious: Certain buildings, although owned by religious organizations, are not included in this category. These include educational or charitable institutions, hospitals, and publishing houses. House of worship: Includes churches, chapels, mosques, synagogues, tabernacles, and temples. Other religious: In addition to the types of facilities listed below, it also includes sanctuaries, abbeys, convents, novitiates, rectories, monasteries, missions, seminaries, and parish houses. Auxiliary building—includes fellowship halls, life centers, camps and retreats, and Sunday schools." (U.S. Census Bureau; "Definitions of Construction"; July 30, 2003; <http://www.census.gov/const/C30/definitions.pdf>; 8/17/2003 PM printout.

Although documentation for the revised series stated that the 1993 through 2001 data was not comparable to the earlier 1964-2000 data, a comparison of the two series found that there was an average of 0.1% difference between the estimated millions of dollars spent on construction of religious buildings from 1993-2000. For the purposes of the present discussion, the difference in the two series was not deemed sufficient to impact the multi-decade review to the degree that discussion would not be useful. The aggregate current dollar data is shown in Table 18:

Table 18: New Religious Construction, Aggregate Millions $, 1964-2009

Year	Millions of Current $	Year	Millions of Current $	Year	Millions of Current $	Year	Millions of Current $	Year	Millions of Current $
1964	$1,044	1974	$993	1984	$2,418	1994	$3,871	2004	$8,153
1965	$1,263	1975	$941	1985	$2,751	1995	$4,348	2005	$7,715
1966	$1,205	1976	$1,040	1986	$3,076	1996	$4,537	2006	$7,740
1967	$1,118	1977	$1,144	1987	$3,178	1997	$5,782	2007	$7,522
1968	$1,135	1978	$1,367	1988	$3,271	1998	$6,604	2008	$7,197
1969	$1,044	1979	$1,701	1989	$3,449	1999	$7,371	2009	$6,190
1970	$988	1980	$1,811	1990	$3,566	2000	$8,030		
1971	$867	1981	$1,853	1991	$3,521	2001	$8,393		
1972	$907	1982	$1,730	1992	$3,485	2002	$8,335		
1973	$877	1983	$2,009	1993	$3,894	2003	$8,559		

The source for the religious construction data is:
- U.S. Census Bureau; Table 1: Annual Value of Construction Put in Place in the U.S.: [Year-Year], p. 1: Current $s & Constant (1996) $s; last revised July 1, 2002;
  1964: 1964-1968; <http://www.census.gov/pub/const/C30/tab168.txt>
  1965-1969: 1965-1969; <http://www.census.gov/pub/const/C30/tab169.txt>
  1970-1974: 1970-1974; <http://www.census.gov/pub/const/C30/tab174.txt>
  1975-1979: 1975-1979; <http://www.census.gov/pub/const/C30/tab179.txt>
  1980-1984: 1980-1984; <http://www.census.gov/pub/const/C30/tab184.txt>
  1985-1989: 1985-1989; <http://www.census.gov/pub/const/C30/tab189.txt>
  1990: 1990; <http://www.census.gov/pub/const/C30/tab190.txt>
  1991-1992: 1991-1995; <http://www.census.gov/pub/const/C30/tab195.txt>
- 1993-2001: U.S. Census Bureau; Annual Value of Construction Put in Place in the U.S.: 1993-2002, p. 1: Current $s & Constant (1996) $s; July 29, 2003; <http://www.census.gov/const/C30/Private.pdf>
- 2002-2010: U.S. Census Bureau; Annual: Annual Value of Construction Put in Place in the U.S.: 1993-2010, p. 1 Current $s; March 30, 2011; <http://www.census.gov/const/C30/total.pdf>

[18] For additional discussion of the implications of the trends, see Ronsvalle, *The State of Church Giving through 1991*, pp. 61-67.

Chapter 6

The Potential of the Church

In Matthew 25:31-46, Jesus describes an interaction between the King and the sheep and goats. The relevance of this parable for 21ˢᵗ century Christians in the U.S. is explored in chapter 8.

One aspect of the interaction will be considered in this chapter. The King in the parable is judging whether the needs of "the least" were met by those standing before the throne. There is a clear expectation that the needs could have been met.

This chapter will explore whether Christians in the U.S. indeed have the financial potential to impact, on a significant level, the needs Jesus describes in the Matthew 25 parable.

Overview of the Potential of the Church

The analyses in this chapter compare present levels of church member giving with a few standards of potential giving.

In chapter 1 of this volume, a brief discussion was presented of one standard of potential giving—the resources that would have been available if church members in 2009 gave the same portion of income as church members gave in 1968. If church members had given the same portion of income in 2009 as was given in 1968, an additional $3.1 billion would have been available for the church to spend on the larger mission of the church through Benevolences. In this case, this level of potential giving would have required church members not to increase their giving, but rather not to let it decline.

One standard of increased giving, by which giving can be evaluated, is the classic tithe, or giving ten percent of income.[1] Calculating that difference between current giving levels and a congregationwide average of 10%, the result suggests that there would have been an additional $174 billion available for the work of the church in 2009, if historically Christian church members had given 10% of income, instead of the 2.38% that was donated. If church members had chosen to allocate 60% of this additional giving to global word and deed need, there would have been an additional $104 billion available, an amount substantially greater than estimates of the most urgent global word and deed need costs. If 20% had been directed to domestic need in the U.S., an additional $35 billion would have been available to address domestic needs including poverty, with an equal amount available for costs related to the increased international and domestic activity.

The parable in Matthew 25:31-46 is included in the "obedience" component in the Great Commission—Jesus telling his followers to go into all the world, baptizing and teaching new converts to obey the tenets of the faith (see Matthew 28:18-20 and Acts 1:8). This assignment sits in the context of the Great Commandment—to love God and therefore love the neighbor (see Mark 12:28-31). The Matthew 25 parable provides specific substance of the larger principle. Reaching out to others, often summarized by the phrase "the church's mission," seems to be a core responsibility that Jesus passed on to the church.

Reaching out
to others, often
summarized
by the phrase
"the church's
mission," seems
to be a core
responsibility that
Jesus passed on
to the church.

One measure of the church's commitment to mission is the level of spending on international missions. In response to a survey sent out by empty tomb, inc., a set of denominations, for which 2003 through 2009 Total Contributions data was available, also provided Overseas Missions Income data for the years 2003 through 2009. The weighted average in 2009 for the group was 2.1 % of Total Contributions being directed to denominational overseas ministries. Stated another way, of every dollar donated to a congregation, about two cents was spent on denominational overseas missions. In 2009, one communion within the group of 32 gave more than 10¢ of each dollar to overseas missions, while seven denominations each gave about 1¢ or less.

In general, the level of support for denominational overseas missions was lower in 2009 than in the 1920s.

Analysis resulted in an estimate that an additional $1 billion a year could have a significant impact on the goal of meeting global evangelism needs. The cost would be only cents per day for various groups of church members.

If the goal were expanded to include not only evangelization, but also the cost of helping to stop, in Jesus' name, global child deaths, providing primary education for all children around the world, and providing additional funds for addressing poverty in the U.S., then the bottom line would increase and yet still only require less than a quarter per day per every church member in the U.S. If wealthy church members donated half the costs, then the daily cost would decrease for the other church members.

A potential giving number was calculated for nine Roman Catholic archdioceses in the U.S. led by cardinals as of *The Official Catholic Directory (OCD) 2005*, or subsequently. The calculation indicated an increased level of giving among Catholics in these nine archdioceses would have resulted in a combined total of billions of additional dollars that could be applied to international needs, as well as domestically, for example, to inner-city Catholic schools.

A 2011 report highlighted an estimate for the amount of money that flowed out of the U.S. to other countries. A review of the data suggested that foreign-born residents of the U.S. were about one-fourth the number of the native-born church member population in the U.S., and yet sent over six times the amount of money internationally than did the native-born church members.

Details of the Potential of the Church

Potential Giving at 10% of Income in 2009. If members of historically Christian churches had chosen to give 10% to their congregations in 2009, rather than the 2.38% given that year, there would have been an additional $174 billion available for work through the church.[2]

Further, if those members had specified that 60% of their increased giving were to be given to international missions, there would have been an additional $104 billion available for the international work of the church. That would have left an additional $35 billion for domestic missions, including poverty conditions in the U.S., and an equal amount for costs related to the increased missions activity.[3]

This level of giving could have made a major impact on global need. One estimate is that an additional $70 to $80 billion a year could address the basic needs of the poorest people around the world.[4] Basic primary education for all children around the globe would cost $7 billion a year.[5] Of the estimated 8.8 million children under five dying around the globe each year,[6] about two-thirds are dying from causes that could be addressed through low-cost solutions, according to one international study. The report stated: "Our findings show that about two-thirds of child deaths could be prevented by interventions that are available today and are feasible for implementation in low-income countries at high levels of population coverage."[7] The cost for these interventions might be about $5 billion a year for the portion focused specifically on the children.[8] An annual estimate of $1 billion to cover the costs of global evangelization is discussed below.

Figure 18 displays the potential giving levels, and issues of global need that could be addressed by the increased giving.

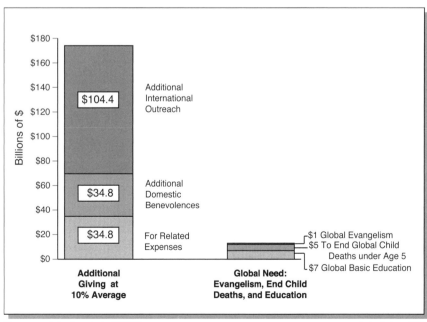

Figure 18: Potential Additional Church Giving at a 2009 Average of 10%, and Illustrations of Global Need That Could Be Addressed

Billions of $

$104.4 — Additional International Outreach

$34.8 — Additional Domestic Benevolences

$34.8 — For Related Expenses

Additional Giving at 10% Average

Global Need: Evangelism, End Child Deaths, and Education

$1 Global Evangelism
$5 To End Global Child Deaths under Age 5
$7 Global Basic Education

Source: empty tomb analysis; UNICEF

empty tomb, inc., 2011

Per Capita Giving to International Missions. A survey of a group of Protestant denominations found that, on average, about two cents of each dollar donated to their affiliated congregations in 2009 funded international missions through the denominations.

The goal of the empty tomb, inc. research survey form was to discern how much of Overseas Missions Income came from living member giving. "Overseas Missions Income" was used in the title of the survey form, and "overseas ministries income" was used in the text of the questions on the survey form. In this volume, the two terms, "overseas missions" and "overseas ministry," are used interchangeably. The following questions were asked on the denominational Overseas Missions Income survey form for those denominations that had reported 2003, 2004, 2005, 2006, 2007, and 2008 data in previous years.

1. What was the amount of income raised in the U.S. during the calendar or fiscal year 2009 for overseas ministries?

2. How many dollars of the total amount on Line 1. came from endowment, foundation, and other investment income?

3. Of the total amount on Line 1., what is the dollar value of government grants, either in dollars or in-kind goods for distribution?

4. Balance of overseas ministries income: Line 1. minus Lines 2. and 3.

The form sent to denominations that had provided data in previous years included six columns labeled "Reported 2003," "Reported 2004," "Reported 2005," "Reported 2006," "Reported 2007," and "Reported 2008." These columns presented on each line the data previously reported by that denomination. A column to the right of these six columns was labeled "Newly Requested 2009" and included blank cells for each of the four lines.

A total of 32 denominations had complete data available for 2009.[9] The 32 denominations included a combined total of 37.1 million Full or Confirmed members, attending 144 thousand congregations, in 2009.

Data for 34 denominations, including Overseas Missions Income and Total Contributions, is presented in Tables 19 through 25, for the years 2003, 2004, 2005, 2006, and 2007, respectively, for 33 denominations in 2008, and for 32 denominations for the year 2009.

The following observations can be drawn from Tables 19-25 data.

The overall weighted average of Overseas Missions Income as a percent of Total Contributions to the denominations in 2009 was 2.1%. That is, for each dollar of Total Contributions donated to a congregation, about 2¢ was spent on denominational overseas missions.

Information in the endnotes to Tables 19 through 25 indicates that several of the denominations noted in survey correspondence that the dollar figure for international mission activity provided was only for activities funded through the national denominational office, and did not include overseas missions funded directly by the congregations. That is, some of the national denominational offices were of the opinion that congregations may be doing international mission activity in addition to any

That is, for each dollar of Total Contributions donated to a congregation, about 2¢ was spent on denominational overseas missions.

Table 19: Overseas Missions Income, Excluding Any Investment or Government Income, as a Percent of Total Contributions to Congregations, 34 Denominations, 2003

Denomination	2003 Overseas Missions Income (Line 4)	2003 Total Contributions	Overseas Missions Income as % of Total Contributions	Cents of Each Dollar for Overseas Ministries
Allegheny Wesleyan Methodist Connection	$262,260	$5,216,941	5.0%	5¢
American Baptist Churches in the U.S.A.	$8,513,838	$452,422,019	1.9%	2¢
Associate Reformed Presbyterian Church (General Synod)	$3,332,992	$44,279,992	7.5%	8¢
Brethren in Christ Church	$1,606,911	$36,309,353	4.4%	4¢
Christian Church (Disciples of Christ)	$4,079,019	$501,756,492	0.8%	1¢
Christian and Missionary Alliance [10]	$43,160,960	$381,439,326	11.3%	11¢
Church of the Brethren [11]	$1,563,623	$93,876,819	1.7%	2¢
Church of God General Conference (Oregon, Ill., and Morrow, Ga.)	$67,193	$4,297,394	1.6%	2¢
Church of the Lutheran Confession	$155,156	$5,855,961	2.6%	3¢
Church of the Nazarene	$45,640,480	$728,931,987	6.3%	6¢
Churches of God General Conference [12]	$899,679	$27,444,027	3.3%	3¢
Conservative Congregational Christian Conference [13]	$147,805	$52,572,753	0.3%	0.3¢
Cumberland Presbyterian Church	$290,764	$49,168,885	0.6%	1¢
The Episcopal Church [14]	$13,193,855	$2,133,772,253	0.6%	1¢
Evangelical Congregational Church	$1,045,237	$19,628,647	5.3%	5¢
Evangelical Covenant Church	$7,913,682	$247,440,270	3.2%	3¢
Evangelical Lutheran Church in America	$19,637,381	$2,517,027,671	0.8%	1¢
Evangelical Lutheran Synod [15]	$246,587	$13,013,890	1.9%	2¢
Fellowship of Evangelical Churches	$912,689	$14,138,539	6.5%	6¢
Free Methodist Church of North America	$9,121,599	$137,005,736	6.7%	7¢
General Association of General Baptists	$1,858,866	$35,428,127	5.2%	5¢
Lutheran Church-Missouri Synod [16]	$13,079,041	$1,256,382,217	1.0%	1¢
Moravian Church in America, Northern Province [17]	$467,570	$17,864,570	2.6%	3¢
The Orthodox Presbyterian Church [18]	$1,214,449	$36,644,100	3.3%	3¢
Presbyterian Church in America	$24,070,885	$529,220,570	4.5%	5¢
Presbyterian Church (U.S.A.) [19]	$23,255,000	$2,743,637,755	0.8%	1¢
Primitive Methodist Church in the U.S.A. [20]	$536,903	$4,771,104	11.3%	11¢
Reformed Church in America	$7,852,464	$275,354,238	2.9%	3¢
Seventh-day Adventists, North Am. Div. [21]	$48,225,234	$1,088,682,947	4.4%	4¢
Southern Baptist Convention	$239,663,000	$9,648,530,640	2.5%	2¢
United Church of Christ	$8,373,084	$878,974,911	1.0%	1¢
The United Methodist Church [22]	$82,000,000	$5,376,057,236	1.5%	2¢
The Wesleyan Church	$8,507,914	$260,315,979	3.3%	3¢
Wisconsin Evangelical Lutheran Synod	$10,779,164	$278,209,035	3.9%	4¢
Total/Average for 34 Denominations	$631,675,283	$29,895,672,384	2.1%	2¢

Source: empty tomb, inc. analysis 2011. See data notes at the end of the chapter. See Appendix B-5 for detail.

Table 20: Overseas Missions Income, Excluding Any Investment or Government Income, as a Percent of Total Contributions to Congregations, 34 Denominations, 2004

Denomination	2004 Overseas Missions Income (Line 4)	2004 Total Contributions	Overseas Missions Income as % of Total Contributions	Cents of Each Dollar for Overseas Ministries
Allegheny Wesleyan Methodist Connection	$266,299	$5,638,852	4.7%	5¢
American Baptist Churches in the U.S.A.	$9,491,848	$432,734,941	2.2%	2¢
Associate Reformed Presbyterian Church (General Synod)	$3,954,575	$49,290,082	8.0%	8¢
Brethren in Christ Church	$1,800,963	$32,235,440	5.6%	6¢
Christian Church (Disciples of Christ)	$3,832,092	$493,377,355	0.8%	1¢
Christian and Missionary Alliance [10]	$43,534,066	$401,702,995	10.8%	11¢
Church of the Brethren [11]	$1,558,320	$90,440,250	1.7%	2¢
Church of God General Conference (Oregon, Ill., and Morrow, Ga.)	$113,497	$4,445,000	2.6%	3¢
Church of the Lutheran Confession	$206,896	$6,187,297	3.3%	3¢
Church of the Nazarene	$48,173,085	$743,526,726	6.5%	6¢
Churches of God General Conference [12]	$1,047,148	$28,360,228	3.7%	4¢
Conservative Congregational Christian Conference [13]	$149,299	$59,795,058	0.2%	0.2¢
Cumberland Presbyterian Church	$323,340	$49,800,171	0.6%	1¢
The Episcopal Church [14]	$14,781,000	$2,132,774,534	0.7%	1¢
Evangelical Congregational Church	$941,409	$22,831,988	4.1%	4¢
Evangelical Covenant Church	$8,591,574	$267,267,027	3.2%	3¢
Evangelical Lutheran Church in America	$23,431,081	$2,568,013,806	0.9%	1¢
Evangelical Lutheran Synod [15]	$266,241	$12,926,484	2.1%	2¢
Fellowship of Evangelical Churches	$847,526	$16,525,789	5.1%	5¢
Free Methodist Church of North America	$10,186,619	$147,016,945	6.9%	7¢
General Association of General Baptists	$1,768,537	$33,771,637	5.2%	5¢
Lutheran Church-Missouri Synod [16]	$13,177,379	$1,307,764,010	1.0%	1¢
Moravian Church in America, Northern Province [17]	$528,733	$18,514,925	2.9%	3¢
The Orthodox Presbyterian Church [18]	$1,374,254	$38,660,300	3.6%	4¢
Presbyterian Church in America	$24,319,185	$544,857,944	4.5%	4¢
Presbyterian Church (U.S.A.) [19]	$24,588,000	$2,774,907,848	0.9%	1¢
Primitive Methodist Church in the U.S.A. [20]	$526,640	$5,565,638	9.5%	9¢
Reformed Church in America	$7,284,560	$296,856,834	2.5%	2¢
Seventh-day Adventists, North Am. Div. [21]	$46,752,585	$1,121,549,712	4.2%	4¢
Southern Baptist Convention	$242,140,000	$10,171,197,048	2.4%	2¢
United Church of Christ	$7,935,678	$895,654,110	0.9%	1¢
The United Methodist Church [22]	$91,200,000	$5,541,540,536	1.6%	2¢
The Wesleyan Church	$8,881,386	$259,011,346	3.4%	3¢
Wisconsin Evangelical Lutheran Synod	$10,304,863	$296,791,013	3.5%	3¢
Total/Average for 34 Denominations	$654,278,678	$30,871,533,869	2.1%	2¢

Source: empty tomb, inc. analysis 2011. See data notes at the end of the chapter. See Appendix B-5 for detail.

Table 21: Overseas Missions Income, Excluding Any Investment or Government Income, as a Percent of Total Contributions to Congregations, 34 Denominations, 2005

Denomination	2005 Overseas Missions Income (Line 4)	2005 Total Contributions	Overseas Missions Income as % of Total Contributions	Cents of Each Dollar for Overseas Ministries
Allegheny Wesleyan Methodist Connection	$399,514	$5,383,333	7.4%	7¢
American Baptist Churches in the U.S.A.	$11,096,481	$336,894,843	3.3%	3¢
Associate Reformed Presbyterian Church (General Synod)	$4,516,302	$50,921,233	8.9%	9¢
Brethren in Christ Church	$1,920,000	$39,800,056	4.8%	5¢
Christian Church (Disciples of Christ)	$4,222,777	$503,045,398	0.8%	1¢
Christian and Missionary Alliance [10]	$54,267,422	$442,917,566	12.3%	12¢
Church of the Brethren [11]	$2,270,134	$97,940,974	2.3%	2¢
Church of God General Conference (Oregon, Ill., and Morrow, Ga.)	$80,000	$4,496,822	1.8%	2¢
Church of the Lutheran Confession	$309,823	$6,551,799	4.7%	5¢
Church of the Nazarene	$52,753,682	$765,434,742	6.9%	7¢
Churches of God General Conference [12]	$1,130,100	$32,249,551	3.5%	4¢
Conservative Congregational Christian Conference [13]	$166,875	$59,346,227	0.3%	0.3¢
Cumberland Presbyterian Church	$293,346	$54,148,837	0.5%	1¢
The Episcopal Church [14]	$15,371,967	$2,180,974,503	0.7%	1¢
Evangelical Congregational Church	$725,089	$21,408,687	3.4%	3¢
Evangelical Covenant Church	$9,008,719	$291,847,011	3.1%	3¢
Evangelical Lutheran Church in America	$26,084,001	$2,604,798,005	1.0%	1¢
Evangelical Lutheran Synod [15]	$222,204	$13,831,771	1.6%	2¢
Fellowship of Evangelical Churches	$785,676	$18,426,832	4.3%	4¢
Free Methodist Church of North America	$10,720,240	$154,525,029	6.9%	7¢
General Association of General Baptists	$1,924,508	$40,146,583	4.8%	5¢
Lutheran Church-Missouri Synod [16]	$17,175,578	$1,296,818,738	1.3%	1¢
Moravian Church in America, Northern Province [17]	$482,157	$17,835,255	2.7%	3¢
The Orthodox Presbyterian Church [18]	$1,856,529	$40,736,400	4.6%	5¢
Presbyterian Church in America	$25,890,591	$586,824,356	4.4%	4¢
Presbyterian Church (U.S.A.) [19]	$31,618,000	$2,814,271,023	1.1%	1¢
Primitive Methodist Church in the U.S.A. [20]	$497,845	$5,541,336	9.0%	9¢
Reformed Church in America	$10,727,347	$310,909,691	3.5%	3¢
Seventh-day Adventists, North Am. Div. [21]	$52,130,967	$1,273,399,341	4.1%	4¢
Southern Baptist Convention	$259,394,000	$10,721,544,568	2.4%	2¢
United Church of Christ	$7,652,371	$908,726,794	0.8%	1¢
The United Methodist Church [22]	$127,600,000	$5,861,722,397	2.2%	2¢
The Wesleyan Church	$9,769,938	$280,214,570	3.5%	3¢
Wisconsin Evangelical Lutheran Synod	$8,794,293	$299,324,485	2.9%	3¢
Total/Average for 34 Denominations	$751,858,476	$32,142,958,756	2.3%	2¢

Source: empty tomb, inc. analysis 2011. See data notes at the end of the chapter. See Appendix B-5 for detail.

Table 22: Overseas Missions Income, Excluding Any Investment or Government Income, as a Percent of Total Contributions to Congregations, 34 Denominations, 2006

Denomination	2006 Overseas Missions Income (Line 4)	2006 Total Contributions	Overseas Missions Income as % of Total Contributions	Cents of Each Dollar for Overseas Ministries
Allegheny Wesleyan Methodist Connection	$286,781	$4,891,827	5.9%	6¢
American Baptist Churches in the U.S.A.	$8,779,170	$312,485,013	2.8%	3¢
Associate Reformed Presbyterian Church (General Synod)	$3,821,297	$48,592,174	7.9%	8¢
Brethren in Christ Church	$2,117,594	*$42,357,718*	5.0%	5¢
Christian Church (Disciples of Christ)	$4,421,669	$539,112,457	0.8%	1¢
Christian and Missionary Alliance [10]	$52,505,044	$458,063,183	11.5%	11¢
Church of the Brethren [11]	$1,887,202	$92,834,308	2.0%	2¢
Church of God General Conference (Oregon, Ill., and Morrow, Ga.)	$63,355	$4,421,793	1.4%	1¢
Church of the Lutheran Confession	$188,817	$6,965,144	2.7%	3¢
Church of the Nazarene	$50,969,965	$792,831,191	6.4%	6¢
Churches of God General Conference [12]	$1,233,843	$33,061,351	3.7%	4¢
Conservative Congregational Christian Conference [13]	$123,509	$65,417,224	0.2%	0.2¢
Cumberland Presbyterian Church	$290,307	$54,727,911	0.5%	1¢
The Episcopal Church [14]	$14,806,793	$2,187,308,798	0.7%	1¢
Evangelical Congregational Church	$1,326,393	$22,174,004	6.0%	6¢
Evangelical Covenant Church	$8,530,245	$313,771,228	2.7%	3¢
Evangelical Lutheran Church in America	$21,541,809	$2,664,147,210	0.8%	1¢
Evangelical Lutheran Synod [15]	$330,651	$16,412,280	2.0%	2¢
Fellowship of Evangelical Churches	$700,159	$19,031,219	3.7%	4¢
Free Methodist Church of North America	$11,878,875	$158,820,542	7.5%	7¢
General Association of General Baptists	$2,048,570	$35,905,960	5.7%	6¢
Lutheran Church-Missouri Synod [16]	$13,432,946	$1,355,458,558	1.0%	1¢
Moravian Church in America, Northern Province [17]	$512,828	$17,780,604	2.9%	3¢
The Orthodox Presbyterian Church [18]	$1,706,292	$45,883,300	3.7%	4¢
Presbyterian Church in America	$27,627,770	$650,091,428	4.2%	4¢
Presbyterian Church (U.S.A.) [19]	$20,964,000	$2,854,719,850	0.7%	1¢
Primitive Methodist Church in the U.S.A. [20]	$566,116	$5,080,485	11.1%	11¢
Reformed Church in America	$7,486,527	$328,793,517	2.3%	2¢
Seventh-day Adventists, North Am. Div. [21]	$48,905,616	$1,290,321,473	3.8%	4¢
Southern Baptist Convention	$275,747,000	$11,372,608,393	2.4%	2¢
United Church of Christ	$7,539,124	$920,094,107	0.8%	1¢
The United Methodist Church [22]	$83,100,000	$6,012,378,898	1.4%	1¢
The Wesleyan Church	$13,105,882	$292,826,250	4.5%	4¢
Wisconsin Evangelical Lutheran Synod	$10,468,560	$314,016,686	3.3%	3¢
Total/Average for 34 Denominations	$699,014,709	$33,333,386,084	2.1%	2¢

Source: empty tomb, inc. analysis 2011. See data notes at the end of the chapter. See Appendix B-5 for detail.

Table 23: Overseas Missions Income, Excluding Any Investment or Government Income, as a Percent of Total Contributions to Congregations, 34 Denominations, 2007

Denomination	2007 Overseas Missions Income (Line 4)	2007 Total Contributions	Overseas Missions Income as % of Total Contributions	Cents of Each Dollar for Overseas Ministries
Allegheny Wesleyan Methodist Connection	$332,511	$4,973,589	6.7%	7¢
American Baptist Churches in the U.S.A.	$9,866,010	$325,941,205	3.0%	3¢
Associate Reformed Presbyterian Church (General Synod)	$4,819,622	$49,424,200	9.8%	10¢
Brethren in Christ Church	$2,171,822	*$43,936,567*	4.9%	5¢
Christian Church (Disciples of Christ)	$4,774,004	$519,082,964	0.9%	1¢
Christian and Missionary Alliance [10]	$55,964,407	$467,812,148	12.0%	12¢
Church of the Brethren [11]	$1,736,654	$88,668,503	2.0%	2¢
Church of God General Conference (Oregon, Ill., and Morrow, Ga.)	$103,495	$4,378,745	2.4%	2¢
Church of the Lutheran Confession	$277,600	$7,207,712	3.9%	4¢
Church of the Nazarene	$50,591,155	$817,722,230	6.2%	6¢
Churches of God General Conference [12]	$1,118,921	$35,106,856	3.2%	3¢
Conservative Congregational Christian Conference [13]	$169,508	$74,467,155	0.2%	0.2¢
Cumberland Presbyterian Church	$352,644	$57,766,770	0.6%	1¢
The Episcopal Church [14]	$15,028,559	$2,221,167,438	0.7%	1¢
Evangelical Congregational Church	$1,464,523	$17,180,755	8.5%	9¢
Evangelical Covenant Church	$7,954,834	$323,916,976	2.5%	2¢
Evangelical Lutheran Church in America	$21,747,378	$2,725,349,028	0.8%	1¢
Evangelical Lutheran Synod [15]	$504,018	$16,104,636	3.1%	3¢
Fellowship of Evangelical Churches	$700,590	$19,031,219	3.7%	4¢
Free Methodist Church of North America	$12,478,468	$158,820,542	7.9%	8¢
General Association of General Baptists	$2,179,048	$31,385,133	6.9%	7¢
Lutheran Church-Missouri Synod [16]	$13,186,920	$1,399,774,702	0.9%	1¢
Moravian Church in America, Northern Province [17]	$524,149	$19,021,572	2.8%	3¢
The Orthodox Presbyterian Church [18]	$1,824,389	$45,730,400	4.0%	4¢
Presbyterian Church in America	$28,456,453	$686,331,677	4.1%	4¢
Presbyterian Church (U.S.A.) [19]	$40,366,000	$2,916,788,414	1.4%	1¢
Primitive Methodist Church in the U.S.A. [20]	$566,810	$4,632,031	12.2%	12¢
Reformed Church in America	$7,611,613	$338,446,877	2.2%	2¢
Seventh-day Adventists, North Am. Div. [21]	$52,038,112	$1,259,280,736	4.1%	4¢
Southern Baptist Convention	$278,313,000	$12,107,096,858	2.3%	2¢
United Church of Christ	$7,307,090	$936,862,062	0.8%	1¢
The United Methodist Church [22]	$79,500,000	$6,295,942,455	1.3%	1¢
The Wesleyan Church	$13,554,996	$321,461,982	4.2%	4¢
Wisconsin Evangelical Lutheran Synod	$10,672,195	$323,082,651	3.3%	3¢
Total/Average for 34 Denominations	$728,257,498	$34,663,896,788	2.1%	2¢

Source: empty tomb, inc. analysis 2011. See data notes at the end of the chapter. See Appendix B-5 for detail.

Table 24: Overseas Missions Income, Excluding Any Investment or Government Income, as a Percent of Total Contributions to Congregations, 33 Denominations, 2008

Denomination	2008 Overseas Missions Income (Line 4)	2008 Total Contributions	Overseas Missions Income as % of Total Contributions	Cents of Each Dollar for Overseas Ministries
Allegheny Wesleyan Methodist Connection	$306,946	$4,756,409	6.5%	6¢
American Baptist Churches in the U.S.A.	$9,846,000	$317,338,230	3.1%	3¢
Associate Reformed Presbyterian Church (General Synod)	$5,838,994	$46,948,089	12.4%	12¢
Brethren in Christ Church	*$2,452,498*	*$44,671,975*	*5.5%*	*5¢*
Christian Church (Disciples of Christ)	$4,527,471	$524,213,682	0.9%	1¢
Christian and Missionary Alliance [10]	$52,012,830	$466,388,400	11.2%	11¢
Church of the Brethren [11]	$1,748,520	$87,494,968	2.0%	2¢
Church of God General Conference (Oregon, Ill., and Morrow, Ga.)	$101,028	$4,056,759	2.5%	2¢
Church of the Lutheran Confession	$360,323	$7,073,530	5.1%	5¢
Church of the Nazarene	$53,761,093	$829,801,861	6.5%	6¢
Churches of God General Conference [12]	$1,187,253	$33,239,825	3.6%	4¢
Conservative Congregational Christian Conference [13]	$84,460	$72,677,645	0.1%	0.1¢
Cumberland Presbyterian Church	$301,245	$57,646,214	0.5%	1¢
The Episcopal Church [14]	$14,599,354	$2,294,941,221	0.6%	1¢
Evangelical Congregational Church	$1,583,478	$18,736,646	8.5%	8¢
Evangelical Covenant Church	NA	NA	NA	NA
Evangelical Lutheran Church in America	$24,160,174	$2,764,009,721	0.9%	1¢
Evangelical Lutheran Synod [15]	$619,754	$15,635,281	4.0%	4¢
Fellowship of Evangelical Churches	$724,626	$24,446,883	3.0%	3¢
Free Methodist Church of North America	$13,244,864	$171,677,077	7.7%	8¢
General Association of General Baptists	$2,105,841	$33,520,716	6.3%	6¢
Lutheran Church-Missouri Synod [16]	$14,505,811	$1,343,086,275	1.1%	1¢
Moravian Church in America, Northern Province [17]	$473,520	$18,268,105	2.6%	3¢
The Orthodox Presbyterian Church [18]	$1,800,305	$46,035,988	3.9%	4¢
Presbyterian Church in America	$29,173,722	$714,356,133	4.1%	4¢
Presbyterian Church (U.S.A.) [19]	$19,919,000	$2,921,571,493	0.7%	1¢
Primitive Methodist Church in the U.S.A. [20]	$542,438	*$4,827,828*	*11.2%*	11¢
Reformed Church in America	$7,642,569	$329,904,049	2.3%	2¢
Seventh-day Adventists, North Am. Div. [21]	$51,501,480	$1,195,419,795	4.3%	4¢
Southern Baptist Convention	$254,860,000	$12,121,220,925	2.1%	2¢
United Church of Christ	$7,244,977	$941,553,540	0.8%	1¢
The United Methodist Church [22]	$114,500,000	$6,300,722,381	1.8%	2¢
The Wesleyan Church	$13,669,461	$333,767,545	4.1%	4¢
Wisconsin Evangelical Lutheran Synod	$11,635,379	$319,988,294	3.6%	4¢
Total/Average for 33 Denominations	$717,035,415	$34,409,997,483	2.1%	2¢

Source: empty tomb, inc. analysis 2011. See data notes at the end of the chapter. See Appendix B-5 for detail.

Table 25: Overseas Missions Income, Excluding Any Investment or Government Income, as a Percent of Total Contributions to Congregations, 32 Denominations, 2009

Denomination	2009 Overseas Missions Income (Line 4)	2009 Total Contributions	Overseas Missions Income as % of Total Contributions	Cents of Each Dollar for Overseas Ministries
Allegheny Wesleyan Methodist Connection	$275,139	$5,053,282	5.4%	5¢
American Baptist Churches in the U.S.A.	$9,585,000	$288,839,340	3.3%	3¢
Associate Reformed Presbyterian Church (General Synod)	$4,234,871	$54,800,721	7.7%	8¢
Brethren in Christ Church	$2,473,594	$40,370,797	6.1%	6¢
Christian Church (Disciples of Christ)	$3,978,592	$495,988,245	0.8%	1¢
Christian and Missionary Alliance [10]	$52,888,984	$464,694,407	11.4%	11¢
Church of the Brethren [11]	$1,904,137	$89,631,907	2.1%	2¢
Church of God General Conference (Oregon, Ill., and Morrow, Ga.)	$166,433	$4,013,750	4.1%	4¢
Church of the Lutheran Confession	$402,162	$6,974,801	5.8%	6¢
Church of the Nazarene	$43,370,879	$823,915,528	5.3%	5¢
Churches of God General Conference [12]	$1,335,598	$35,331,543	3.8%	4¢
Conservative Congregational Christian Conference [13]	$18,397	$70,496,255	0.0%	0.03¢
Cumberland Presbyterian Church	$277,412	$56,383,201	0.5%	0.5¢
The Episcopal Church [14]	$15,611,043	$2,182,330,459	0.7%	1¢
Evangelical Congregational Church	$1,462,048	$19,594,243	7.5%	7¢
Evangelical Covenant Church	NA	NA	NA	NA
Evangelical Lutheran Church in America	$24,665,494	$2,716,085,854	0.9%	1¢
Evangelical Lutheran Synod [15]	$1,144,111	$15,919,860	7.2%	7¢
Fellowship of Evangelical Churches	$804,057	$24,323,500	3.3%	3¢
Free Methodist Church of North America	$11,720,519	$173,629,647	6.8%	7¢
General Association of General Baptists	$1,946,149	$38,261,252	5.1%	5¢
Lutheran Church-Missouri Synod [16]	NA	NA	NA	NA
Moravian Church in America, Northern Province [17]	$503,817	$18,241,950	2.8%	3¢
The Orthodox Presbyterian Church [18]	$1,979,044	$46,575,856	4.2%	4¢
Presbyterian Church in America	$27,219,278	$696,680,887	3.9%	4¢
Presbyterian Church (U.S.A.) [19]	$21,986,831	$2,773,343,691	0.8%	1¢
Primitive Methodist Church in the U.S.A. [20]	$429,530	$4,664,330	9.2%	9¢
Reformed Church in America	$8,187,860	$301,838,760	2.7%	3¢
Seventh-day Adventists, North Am. Div. [21]	$49,538,644	$1,275,496,054	3.9%	4¢
Southern Baptist Convention	$255,427,000	$11,912,179,313	2.1%	2¢
United Church of Christ	$6,213,752	$928,638,925	0.7%	1¢
The United Methodist Church [22]	$96,920,000	$6,218,009,630	1.6%	2¢
The Wesleyan Church	$14,139,092	$323,061,444	4.4%	4¢
Wisconsin Evangelical Lutheran Synod	$11,030,819	$314,982,519	3.5%	4¢
Total/Average for 32 Denominations	$671,840,286	$32,420,351,951	2.1%	2¢

Source: empty tomb, inc. analysis 2011. See data notes at the end of the chapter. See Appendix B-5 for detail.

Table 26: Overseas Missions Income, Excluding Any Investment or Government Income, as a Percent of Total Contributions to Congregations and Membership, 32 Denominations, Ranked by Cents per Dollar, 2009 [23]

Rank	Deonomination	Cents of Each Dollar for Overseas Ministries	Number of Full/Conf Members
1	Christian and Missionary Alliance [23]	11¢	197,653
2	Primitive Methodist Church in the U.S.A. [23]	9¢	3,430
3	Associate Reformed Presbyterian Church (General Synod)	8¢	34,977
4	Evangelical Congregational Church	7¢	17,834
5	Evangelical Lutheran Synod [23]	7¢	15,672
6	Free Methodist Church of North America	7¢	67,472
7	Brethren in Christ Church	6¢	23,014
8	Church of the Lutheran Confession	6¢	6,217
9	Allegheny Wesleyan Methodist Connection	5¢	1,334
10	Church of the Nazarene	5¢	639,182
11	General Association of General Baptists	5¢	54,088
12	The Wesleyan Church	4¢	122,359
13	The Orthodox Presbyterian Church [23]	4¢	21,608
14	Church of God General Conference (Oregon, Ill., and Morrow, Ga.)	4¢	3,010
15	Presbyterian Church in America	4¢	272,323
16	Seventh-day Adventists [23]	4¢	1,043,606
17	Churches of God General Conference [23]	4¢	32,691
18	Wisconsin Evangelical Lutheran Synod	4¢	306,881
19	American Baptist Churches in the U.S.A.	3¢	1,310,505
20	Fellowship of Evangelical Churches	3¢	7,137
21	Moravian Church in America, Northern Province [23]	3¢	16,352
22	Reformed Church in America	3¢	154,977
23	Southern Baptist Convention	2¢	16,160,088
24	Church of the Brethren [23]	2¢	121,781
25	The United Methodist Church [23]	2¢	7,724,821
26	Evangelical Lutheran Church in America	1¢	3,444,041
27	Christian Church (Disciples of Christ)	1¢	417,068
28	Presbyterian Church (U.S.A.) [23]	1¢	2,077,138
29	The Episcopal Church [23]	1¢	1,624,025
30	United Church of Christ	1¢	1,080,199
31	Cumberland Presbyterian Church	0.5¢	77,811
32	Conservative Congregational Christian Conference [23]	0.03¢	42,296

Source: empty tomb, inc. analysis, 2011. See data notes at the end of the chapter. See Appendix B-5 for detail.

contributions sent to their offices. In at least two instances, dialogue with the denominational offices resulted in the finding that the national office sends a congregation statistics report form to affiliated congregations, and that this report form does not ask the congregation to distinguish that portion of Benevolences that was spent for international mission activity other than through the national denominational office. One denomination indicated that the national office obtains information from the congregations about missions done both directly by the congregation, and also through the denomination.

Congregational forms, sent by denominations to their congregations to obtain annual reports, could routinely, but apparently often do not, include details of congregational global missions expenditures that are not conducted through the denomination. The denominational structures presumably monitor other congregational expenditures, such as staff compensation and payments for pastor health insurance and pension benefits, as well as the general unified budget assessments requested from the congregations.

Table 26 lists the 32 denominations with complete 2009 data in order of the level of unrounded cents per dollar donated to the congregation that was directed to denominational overseas missions. The membership for each denomination is also listed.

Figure 19 presents, in graphic form, the 2009 cents per dollar donated to the congregation that were directed to denominational overseas missions in 32 denominations in the U.S., reporting data for 2009. One additional denomination that reported data through 2008, and another through 2007, are also included in the figure. The gray shading marks a potential standard of giving for overseas missions at 60¢ per dollar. As noted earlier in this chapter, this goal could be achieved if church members increased giving to a congregationwide average of ten percent and earmarked the major portion of the increase to international missions.

Figure 19: Cents Directed to Denominational Overseas Missions, Per Dollar Donated to the Congregation, 32 Denominations in the U.S., 2009, One Denomination, 2008, and One Denomination, 2007

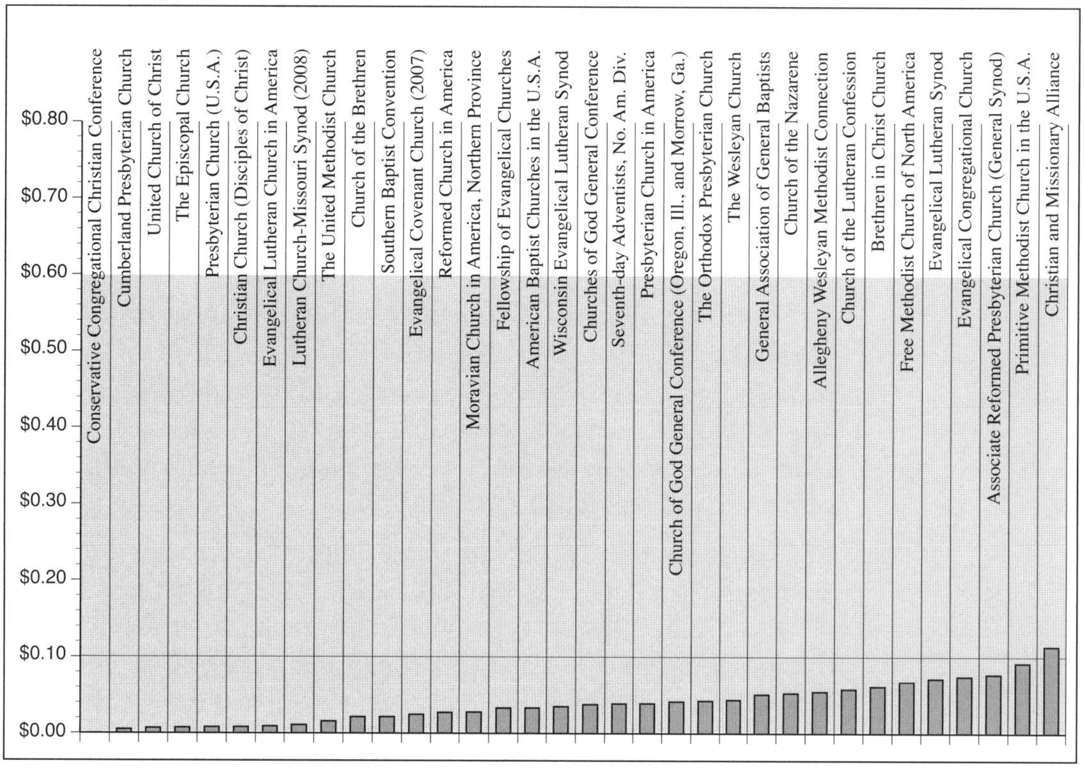

Source: empty tomb analysis

empty tomb, inc., 2011

Appendix B-5 lists the four lines of data for the denominations for data years 2003 through 2009.

A Comparison of Per Member Giving to Overseas Missions in Three Denominations. In the discussion immediately above, aggregate overseas missions income is set in the context of Total Contributions for each denomination.

One can also consider contributions to overseas missions income on a per member basis. A review of three denominations provided the following results.

The three denominations were selected as follows. The Church of the Nazarene, with 639,182 Full or Confirmed Members in 2009 was the largest denomination with membership in the National Association of Evangelicals that provided data. The Southern Baptist Convention, with 16,160,088 Full or Confirmed Members in 2009, was the largest Protestant denomination in the U.S. The United Methodist Church, with 7,724,821 Full or Confirmed Members in 2009, was the largest denomination with membership in the National Council of the Churches of Christ in the U.S.A. that provided data.

Dividing the amount of overseas missions income by the number of reported members resulted in a per member dollar giving level for each denomination. Since the data is for the year 2009 for all three denominations, current dollars can be effectively used in the comparison.

The dollar figure for per member giving to denominational overseas missions for the Church of the Nazarene was $68 in 2009.

The dollar figure for per member giving to denominational overseas missions for the Southern Baptist Convention was $16 in 2009.

The dollar figure for per member giving to denominational overseas missions for The United Methodist Church was $13 in 2009.

Further analysis of factors that might have contributed to the difference in the level of support for denominational overseas missions may yield insight about how denominational structures and priorities affect the level of overseas missions support.

Denominational Overseas Missions Income, 1916-1927. The *Yearbook of American and Canadian Churches (YACC)* series began with the 1916 *Federal Council Year Book*. The second edition, published in 1917, and continuing through the 1927 edition, presented detailed denominational "foreign missions" information. Income as well as geographical placement and type of missionaries were presented on multi-page tables.

Changes in the level of mission support also led a group of denominations to commission a report, published in 1929, about levels of missions giving. As found in Table 27, the 1929 study provided "per capita" (per member) giving to Foreign Missions, Benevolences, and Total Contributions for 11 denominations.[24] With this information, it was possible to calculate per capita Foreign Missions as a percent of per capita Benevolences, and per capita Foreign Missions as a percent of per capita Total Contributions.

During the 1916-1927 period, for the group of 11 denominations, Foreign Missions Income represented about 30% of all Benevolences. The 1929 study was commissioned in response to the concern of members of the Foreign Missions Conference of North America that giving to foreign missions was declining. As seen in Table 27, per capita Foreign Missions Income had decreased to 6.54% of Total Contributions in 1927.

By 2009, some 80 years later, per capita Foreign Missions Income had decreased further, to 2.1% of Total Contributions for a set of 32 Protestant denominations.

The overall average of per capita Foreign Missions Income as a percent of Total Contributions for 11 denominations for the 1916 through 1927 period was

Table 27: Foreign Missions, Benevolences, and Total Contributions, 11 Denominations, 1916-1927, Current Dollars

Year	Per Capita Foreign Missions Income from Living Donors	Per Capita Benevolences	Per Capita Foreign Missions as a Percent of Per Capita Benevolences (Calculated)	Per Capita Total Contributions	Per Capita Foreign Missions as a Percent of Per Capita Total Contributions (Calculated)
1916	$0.73	$2.24	32.59%	$10.11	7.22%
1917	$0.74	$2.52	29.37%	$10.75	6.88%
1918	$0.86	$2.89	29.76%	$11.44	7.52%
1919	$1.18	$3.89	30.33%	$12.90	9.15%
1920	$1.66	$5.75	28.87%	$16.45	10.09%
1921	$1.70	$5.51	30.85%	$17.20	9.88%
1922	$1.46	$5.18	28.19%	$17.19	8.49%
1923	$1.44	$5.12	28.13%	$17.69	8.14%
1924	$1.32	$4.97	26.56%	$18.44	7.16%
1925	$1.27	$4.59	27.67%	$18.74	6.78%
1926	$1.32	$4.49	29.40%	$18.94	6.97%
1927	$1.24	$4.17	29.74%	$18.95	6.54%

Source: empty tomb analysis; Charles H. Fahs, *Trends in Protestant Giving* (1929), Tables XVIII and XXIX.

7.9%, compared to 2.1% for 32 denominations in 2009. The average U.S. per capita Disposable Personal Income (DPI) during the 1916-1927 period was $6,349, in inflation-adjusted 2005 dollars. That average income figure compares to the inflation-adjusted U.S. per capita DPI figure of $32,742 in 2009. Since per capita income was over five times the average in the 1916-1927 period, Americans had 415% more after-tax income in 2009 than in the earlier period. The data indicates that overseas missions support was not as high a priority in 2009 as it was in the 1920s, in spite of improved communication about global needs and a higher level of member income in 2009 compared to the 1916-1927 period.

Calculating the Cost of Missions. One area that is exclusively within the realm of the church is the cost of global evangelization. Interestingly, there have been few if any firm cost estimates for insuring that people around the globe have the opportunity to make an informed choice about responding to the Christian message. This has been true even though the accessibility to information about Christianity can be regarded as a justice issue. As a report from one international organization observed:

> There is also a tragic coincidence that most of the world's poor have not heard the Good News of the Gospel of Jesus Christ; or they could not receive it, because it was not recognized as Good News in the way in which it was brought. This is a double injustice: they are victims of oppression of an unjust economic order or an unjust political distribution of power, and at the same time they are deprived of the knowledge of God's special care for them. To announce the Good News to the poor is to begin to render the justice due to them.[25]

One term that is often used to describe the population most excluded from accessibility to the Christian message is "unreached people group" although the term "least-reached" may also be used. The Joshua Project offered a definition that reads:

> A people group among which there is no indigenous community of believing Christians with adequate numbers and resources to evangelize this people group.[26]

Various factors make it complicated to define an exact number of the "unreached" people groups. In discussing these issues, the Joshua Project Web site also cites another definition:

> The Lausanne 1982 people group definition says "For evangelization purposes, a people group is the largest group within which the Gospel can spread as a church planting movement without encountering barriers of understanding or acceptance."[27]

In 2011, the Joshua Project suggested there were almost 7,000 such unreached people groups.[28]

One denomination that is on record as having a particular concern about unreached people groups is the Southern Baptist Convention. The Southern Baptist Convention (SBC) is the second largest communion, and the largest Protestant denomination, in the United States. As noted on the Web site of the SBC Executive Committee Director, Dr. Morris Chapman, "In 1845, a network of churches was organized into the Southern Baptist Convention for the purpose of evangelizing the world…."[29] The SBC International Mission Board (IMB) is the group within the Convention that is currently charged with supervising the continuing task of global evangelization.

One area that is exclusively within the realm of the church is the cost of global evangelization.

In 2010, the Executive Committee of the SBC asked its international mission arm, the IMB, about additional needed resources to "reach all of the unreached people groups." The IMB replied that $200 million a year would field the needed additional 3,000 missionaries.[30] The figure of $200 million a year, therefore, may serve as one estimate of the additional word evangelism resources that are needed.

Another model can be developed for mission costs that could be pursued by the broad spectrum of the church.

For example, other communions are also actively pursuing the engagement of unreached people groups. Some groups opt to send cross-cultural missionaries, and others choose to work through missionaries born in the region in which the unreached people groups are located.

Two groups that build their outreach through native-born missionaries are Christian Aid Mission and Gospel for Asia.

Christian Aid Mission coordinates with native workers in various countries to "establish a witness for Christ in every unreached nation." Its Web site stated, "Approximately 100,000 of these [native missionaries] have no regular support..." The average monthly support number cited is $50 a month.[31] At $600 a year per missionary, the cost to fund the 100,000 missionaries would be $60,000,000 a year.

Gospel for Asia also trains and coordinates a network of native missionaries through Asian countries. To reach a goal of supporting 100,000 missionaries,[32] Gospel for Asia would need to support an additional 83,500 missionaries over the current number of 16,500.[33] The costs for Gospel for Asia missionaries range from $90 to $150 a month.[34] Taking an average cost of $120 a month, the annual cost of $1,440 was multiplied by the 83,500 figure for the number of additional missionaries needed, yielding a total need of $120,240,000 a year.

The estimate for Christian Aid Mission and Gospel for Asia additional missionaries would total $180,240,000 a year.

Other communions and para-denominational groups in the U.S. are also focused on the goal of engaging the unreached. If the cost of those efforts were on a par with the estimate for the SBC, the cost would be $182,000,000.

Combining these amounts, the four sets of numbers equal $580,240,000.

If the total cost of evangelization were to be estimated, including not only expanded but also ongoing work, the increased total might not exceed $1 billion a year.[35]

Various groups could accept the challenge of funding the cost of this expanded budget for global evangelization. Table 28 indicates the daily and annual costs based on the population of each group.[36]

Of course, the Great Commission, in the context of the Great Commandment, would present the good news of Jesus Christ in both word and deed. Christians generally agree about God's concern for the children of the world. In 2009, about 22,000 children under the age of five died each day around the globe.[37] With about two-thirds, or 14,700, of these children dying from preventable poverty conditions for which there are low-cost immediate solutions, the church should recognize both the

> Some groups opt to send cross-cultural missionaries, and others choose to work through missionaries born in the region in which the unreached people groups are located.

Table 28: Great Commandment and Great Commission Outreach Estimated Costs, Calculated Per Member for Selected Church Populations, 2009

	A. Engage Unreached People Estimate (SBC) $200,000,000	B. Combined Estimate for Global Evangelization $580,240,000	C. High Estimate for Global Evangelization $1,000,000,000	D. Stopping, in Jesus' Name Global Under-5 Child Deaths $5,000,000,000	C. + D. + Global Elementary Education + Domestic Poverty $15,000,000,000
Love Expressed in Great Commission Outreach					
Engage Unreached People Estimate (So. Baptist Conv.)	$200,000,000				
Combined Estimate for Global Evangelization		$580,240,000			
High Estimate for Global Evangelization			$1,000,000,000		$1,000,000,000
Stopping in Jesus' Name Under-Five Child Deaths				$5,000,000,000	$5,000,000,000
Global Elementary Education					$7,000,000,000
Domestic U.S. Poverty Need					$2,000,000,000
Total Per Year	$200,000,000	$580,240,000	$1,000,000,000	$5,000,000,000	$15,000,000,000
Historically Christian Church Members (59.45% US Pop. = 182,392,600)					
Annual Amount per Historically Christian Ch. Member	$1	$3	$5	$27	$82
Daily Amount per Historically Christian Church Member	Less than $0.01	$0.01	$0.02	$0.08	$0.23
Evangelical Christians (7% US Pop. = 21,476,000)					
Annual Amount per Evangelical Christian	$9	$27	$47	$233	$698
Daily Amount per Evangelical Christian	$0.03	$0.07	$0.13	$0.64	$1.91
Born Again Christians (40% US Pop. = 122,720,000)					
Annual Amount per Born Again Christian	$2	$5	$8	$41	$122
Daily Amount per Born Again Christian	Less than $0.01	$0.01	$0.02	$0.11	$0.33
National Council of the Churches of Christ in the U.S.A. Inclusive Members (= 39,838,369)					
Annual Amount per NCCC Member	$5	$15	$25	$126	$377
Daily Amount per NCCC Member	$0.01	$0.04	$0.07	$0.34	$1.03
Roman Catholic Members (= 68,503,456)					
Annual Amount per Roman Catholic Member	$3	$8	$15	$73	$219
Daily Amount per Roman Catholic Member	$0.01	$0.02	$0.04	$0.20	$0.60
Southern Baptist Members (= 16,160,088)					
Annual Amount per Southern Baptist Member	$12	$36	$62	$309	$928
Daily Amount per Southern Baptist Member	$0.03	$0.10	$0.17	$0.85	$2.54
United Methodist Members (= 7,724,821)					
Annual Amount per United Methodist Member	$26	$75	$129	$647	$1,942
Daily Amount per United Methodist Member	$0.07	$0.21	$0.35	$1.77	$5.32

Note: The annual and daily numbers in the above table would be divided by two if wealthy Christians in that grouping provided half in the form of matching funds.
Source: empty tomb analysis 2011

possibility and the responsibility inherent in this challenge. Table 28 also considers the annual and daily costs for various groups if members should choose to prevent more deaths among children under five around the globe.

However, the choice need not be between global evangelization *or* helping to stop, in Jesus' name, global child deaths, *or* primary education, *or*

Table 29: Great Commandment and Great Commission Outreach Estimated Costs, Calculated Per Household for Populations with Selected Levels of Net Worth apart from Primary Residence, 2009

	A. Engage Unreached People Estimate (SBC) $200,000,000	B. Combined Estimate for Global Evangelization $580,240,000	C. High Estimate for Global Evangelization $1,000,000,000	D. Stopping, in Jesus' Name Global Under-5 Child Deaths $5,000,000,000	C. + D. + Global Elementary Education + Domestic Poverty $15,000,000,000
Love Expressed in Great Commission Outreach					
Engage Unreached People Estimate (So. Baptist Conv.)	$200,000,000				
Combined Estimate for Global Evangelization		$580,240,000			
High Estimate for Global Evangelization			$1,000,000,000		$1,000,000,000
Stopping in Jesus' Name Under-Five Child Deaths				$5,000,000,000	$5,000,000,000
Global Elementary Education					$7,000,000,000
Domestic U.S. Poverty Need					$2,000,000,000
Total Per Year	$200,000,000	$580,240,000	$1,000,000,000	$5,000,000,000	$15,000,000,000
Historically Christian Church Households					
Greater than or Equal to $5 million (= 582,610)					
Annual Amount per Historically Christian Ch. Household	$343	$996	$1,716	$8,582	$25,746
Daily Amount per Historically Christian Church Hshld.	$0.94	$2.73	$4.70	$23.51	$70.54
Greater than or Equal to $1 million (= 4,637,100)					
Annual Amount per Historically Christian Ch. Household	$43	$125	$216	$1,078	$3,235
Daily Amount per Historically Christian Church Hshld.	$0.12	$0.34	$0.59	$2.95	$8.86
Greater than or Equal to $500,000 (= 7,550,150)					
Annual Amount per Historically Christian Ch. Household	$26	$77	$132	$662	$1,987
Daily Amount per Historically Christian Church Hshld.	$0.07	$0.21	$0.36	$1.81	$5.44
Evangelical Christian Households					
Greater than or Equal to $5 million (= 68,600)					
Annual Amount per Evangelical Christian Household	$2,915	$8,458	$14,577	$72,886	$218,659
Daily Amount per Evangelical Christian Household	$7.99	$23.17	$39.94	$199.69	$599.07
Greater than or Equal to $1 million (= 546,000)					
Annual Amount per Evangelical Christian Household	$366	$1,063	$1,832	$9,158	$27,473
Daily Amount per Evangelical Christian Household	$1.00	$2.91	$5.02	$25.09	$75.27
Greater than or Equal to $500,000 (=889,000)					
Annual Amount per Evangelical Christian Household	$225	$653	$1,125	$5,624	$16,873
Daily Amount per Evangelical Christian Household	$0.62	$1.79	$3.08	$15.41	$46.23
Born Again Christian Households					
Greater than or Equal to $5 million (= 392,000)					
Annual Amount per Born Again Christian Household	$510	$1,480	$2,551	$12,755	$38,265
Daily Amount per Born Again Christian Household	$1.40	$4.06	$6.99	$34.95	$104.84
Greater than or Equal to $1 million (= 3,120,000)					
Annual Amount per Born Again Christian Household	$64	$186	$321	$1,603	$4,808
Daily Amount per Born Again Christian Household	$0.18	$0.51	$0.88	$4.39	$13.17
Greater than or Equal to $500,000 (= 5,080,000)					
Annual Amount per Born Again Christian Household	$39	$114	$197	$984	$2,953
Daily Amount per Born Again Christian Household	$0.11	$0.31	$0.54	$2.70	$8.09
NCCCUSA Households					
Greater than or Equal to $5 million (= 127,254)					
Annual Amount per NCCC Household	$1,572	$4,560	$7,858	$39,291	$117,874
Daily Amount per NCCC Household	$4.31	$12.49	$21.53	$107.65	$322.94
Greater than or Equal to $1 million (= 1,012,840)					
Annual Amount per NCCC Household	$197	$573	$987	$4,937	$14,810
Daily Amount per NCCC Household	$0.54	$1.57	$2.70	$13.52	$40.57
Greater than or Equal to $500,000 (= 1,649,111)					
Annual Amount per NCCC Household	$121	$352	$606	$3,032	$9,096
Daily Amount per NCCC Household	$0.33	$0.96	$1.66	$8.31	$24.92

Note: The annual and daily numbers in the above table would be divided by two if the general church population provided half the money in response to matching funds offered by wealthy church members.
Source: empty tomb analysis, 2011

addressing poverty within the United States. When Jesus Christ came to announce God's love for the world in a physical body, he combined the power of the spoken word with healing, feeding, clothing, and freeing those he encountered. Given the resources and the broad base of the church, the current body of Jesus Christ, Christians in the early 21st century have the power to follow Jesus' example of loving the whole person in need. The higher cost for combining evangelization, addressing global child deaths, providing primary education, and having $2 billion a year additional to address domestic poverty needs within the U.S. in Jesus' name was estimated at $15 billion a year. Table 28 also displays the annual and daily costs for various groupings of Christians to engage all of these needs simultaneously.

If creative church leadership were displayed, wealthy Christians might be found who would provide matching funds for donations from the general church population for these needs. In that case, the annual and daily costs presented in Table 28 would be divided by two.

Table 29 considers the same word and deed needs from a slightly different perspective. In this table, the size of the population with varying degrees of wealth was calculated for four sets of church groups. Annual and daily costs to meet the outlined needs are presented for households with $5 million net worth, $1 million net worth, and $500,000 net worth, apart from primary residence.[38] Again, if the general church population were to provide half the funds needed to address these needs, the numbers in the table would be divided by two.

Potential Roman Catholic Giving.

Potential Roman Catholic Giving. The Roman Catholic Church is the largest single religious body in the United States. Unfortunately, that communion has opted not to publish financial giving data on a regular basis. Therefore, any estimates of giving among this major part of the body of Christ must be only approximations. Given the size of the Catholic Church, however, such an approximation is worth exploring.

There has been some discussion in Catholic circles about the practice of the tithe in recent years.[39]

To explore what might result from Catholics giving an average of ten percent of income, a review of potential giving levels at an average of 10% per member was conducted for nine archdioceses that were led by a cardinal as of the *OCD 2005,* or subsequently. Each archdiocese comprises certain U.S. counties. As a result, the total population[40] and the U.S. per capita DPI could be obtained for each archdiocese.[41] A general estimate of 1.2% of income was used as the current level of Catholic giving.[42]

Two observations may be made in regard to the estimate of 1.2% of per capita DPI. First, although the estimate is lower than estimates of Protestant giving, as a previous analysis in the *State of Church Giving* series demonstrated, there are certain efficiencies in the way that Catholic parishes are organized. These efficiencies allow Catholics to maintain basic operations on a par with Protestants, with a smaller per member contribution.[43]

Second, preliminary calculations based on a 2010 survey of Catholic parishes suggest that the per member contribution for "average weekly offering in U.S. parishes" was about 0.3% of income. A 1.2% estimate, for per Catholic giving as a

Given the resources and the broad base of the church, the current body of Jesus Christ, Christians in the early 21st century have the power to follow Jesus' example of loving the whole person in need.

percent of income, therefore takes into account the possibility of additional charitable contributions, including those to second collections, that are three times the amount of weekly offerings.[44]

The nine archdioceses combined had a present estimated giving level of $9.3 billion. If Catholics in these archdioceses increased from the current 1.2% of income given to 10% of income, the additional total would have been $68.1 billion in 2009. The increased amounts varied from $2 billion in the Archdiocese of Baltimore, to $14 billion in the Archdioceses of Los Angeles and New York.

The results of the calculations are shown in Table 30.

Table 30: Potential Additional Giving at 10% of Income, Nine Roman Catholic Archdioceses in the U.S., 2009

Area Name	Total U.S. BEA Personal Income for Counties in Archdioceses ($)	% Catholic of Total Population in Area	Calculated U.S. BEA Personal Income Available to Catholics ($)	Estimated Current Catholic Giving at 1.2% of Income ($)	Estimated Potential Additional Catholic Giving at 10% of Income ($)
Archdiocese of Baltimore	$146,198,255,000	16.1%	$23,610,948,134	$283,331,378	$2,077,763,436
Archdiocese of Boston	$225,333,322,288	45.7%	$102,891,069,386	$1,234,692,833	$9,054,414,106
Archdiocese of Chicago	$281,273,237,000	39.0%	$109,700,987,099	$1,316,411,845	$9,653,686,865
Archdiocese of Detroit	$164,933,580,000	32.3%	$53,316,138,466	$639,793,662	$4,691,820,185
Archdiocese of Galveston-Houston	$271,599,243,000	19.7%	$53,605,026,422	$643,260,317	$4,717,242,325
Archdiocese of Los Angeles	$458,276,779,000	35.8%	$164,190,395,635	$1,970,284,748	$14,448,754,816
Archdiocese of New York	$358,290,962,000	45.0%	$161,230,905,083	$1,934,770,861	$14,188,319,647
Archdiocese of Philadelphia	$191,619,984,000	37.6%	$72,121,635,284	$865,459,623	$6,346,703,905
Archdiocese of Washington	$153,087,817,000	22.0%	$33,679,314,058	$404,151,769	$2,963,779,637
Total: 9 Archdioceses with Cardinals	$2,250,613,179,288		$774,346,419,567	$9,292,157,035	$68,142,484,922

Source: empty tomb analysis, 2011

The application of this potential giving could make an impact on international need, as discussed in chapter 8. This additional giving could address domestic needs as well. For example, Catholic schools have been closing across the U.S. Many of these schools were located in inner cities. A *New York Times* article focused on the 2011 closing of Rice High School in Harlem, after the graduation of its 70th commencement class. The article noted, "With a student body that is 98 percent black or Hispanic, with 80 percent of its students requiring financial aid, virtually every graduating senior was bound for college." One observer was quoted in the article as follows:

"Given all the money that's been raised for charter schools — from the Gates Foundation, from Eli Broad, from hedge fund managers — I find it perplexing that Catholics can't raise money for their own schools that have a track record of success," Mr. Gecan said. "I don't think they've tried hard enough. They've lost focus on their core mission."[45]

A 2008 Associated Press news report on the closing of Catholic schools noted, "High school enrollment has remained roughly the same and schools are opening in suburbs, particularly in the West and Southwest. The Northeast and Midwest have been hit hardest." The same article quoted Sister Dale McDonald, the National Catholic Education Association director: "The church has always had a strong sense of mission, particularly to the poor... As it becomes more and more difficult, not only on the poor but on middle-income people, we're not really fulfilling the mission of the church to serve all if we only can afford to serve the people who can afford the big bucks."[46]

As proposed earlier in this chapter, increased giving at the ten percent level could be allocated so that 60 percent is directed to international ministries and 20 percent to domestic needs. That distribution could direct billions of additional dollars to inner-city Catholic schools in these nine archdioceses, even while providing critical resources for missions that address international need.

However, as shown earlier in Table 28, Catholics, as well as all other Christians, could make a dramatic impact on global word and deed need for much less than the cost of increasing giving to the classic tithe.

Putting Potential into Perspective. A 2011 report introduced an additional estimate on the amount of money being sent from the United States to other countries. *The Index of Global Philanthropy and Remittances 2011 (Index)* is the sixth in a series from the Hudson Institute.[47]

The ambitious project seeks to bring a broad and fresh perspective to the growing area of global philanthropy. The report is not limited to the traditional boundaries of the area, instead including, for example, "private capital flows," representing investment on market terms by for-profit businesses in developing countries, and remittances by foreign-born residents to their home countries into the mix.

The focus of the discussion in the current chapter is on the potential of religious giving. Some preliminary calculations, based on the text descriptions that are presented, suggest that the *Index*'s $7.2 billion may be a somewhat low estimate for religious philanthropy directed to other countries. That is, in order not to double-count $6.3 billion in congregational donations to U.S.-based relief and development organizations, the *Index* included that $6.3 billion in the Private Voluntary Organization category, and subtracted that amount from its survey findings of international assistance provided by congregations. However, in the present discussion of Religion giving to international ministry, there is no basis for excluding that $6.3 billion. When that amount is added to the *Index*'s Religion figure of $7.2 billion, a revised total of $13.5 billion donated internationally by people in the U.S. can be described as given as a function of Religion.

Two observations about the *Index*'s numbers as they are presented can be made. One observation considers the potential to stop child deaths in light of total assistance to developing countries, and the second compares religious philanthropy to remittances.

Total Assistance to Developing Countries and Child Deaths. The "Total U.S. Economic Engagement with Developing Countries, 2009" was estimated to be $226.2 billion.[48]

As noted earlier in this chapter, a figure of $5 billion a year has been calculated as the amount needed to stop the deaths of two-thirds of the 8.1 million children under five being killed each year by preventable causes that could be addressed with available, low-cost solutions.

Catholics, as well as all other Christians, could make a dramatic impact on global word and deed need for much less than the cost of increasing giving to the classic tithe.

A comparison of the $226.2 billion economic engagement with developing countries, and the $5 billion needed to stop most of the child deaths in those countries, leads to a question of priorities. Why have the leaders responsible for the billions of dollars transmitted to developing countries not focused 2% of that total on the strategies available to prevent these child deaths? Or alternatively, why have the leaders not organized to increase the total slightly, with the targeted goal of applying the increase to addressing these child deaths?

Church Giving to Global Need Compared to Immigrant Remittances. The *Index*'s estimate of private religious philanthropy to developing countries figure was $7.2 billion in 2009. As noted above, this figure of $7.2 billion has been adjusted to $13.5 billion, to compare a maximum estimate of religious giving in the U.S. to international causes for the present analysis. An estimate of 159,616,902 native-born members in historically Christian churches in the U.S. in 2009 was used in the comparison.[49] For purposes of the present discussion, one may attribute all of the $13.5 billion in private religious assistance to these native-born church members.

Yet, those foreign-born inhabitants sent over six times the amount of assistance to developing countries than did the native-born church members.

That figure of $13.5 billion from native-born church members in the U.S. can be compared to the $90.7 billion figure of "U.S. Remittances."[50] The category represents assistance "…from individuals, families, and hometown associations in the United States going to developing countries…" provided by "…immigrants and migrant workers."[51] The aid sent home was observed to decrease in 2009 from the 2008 level of $96.8 billion. The developing countries that received the largest amount of these remittances sent from the U.S. were Mexico, other countries in Latin America and the Caribbean, the Philippines, India, and China.[52]

A comparison of these numbers leads to questions of both potential and priorities. There were an estimated 159,616,902 native-born church members, which was three times greater than the 38,517,234 foreign-born people living in the U.S.[53] Yet, those foreign-born inhabitants sent over six times the amount of assistance to developing countries than did the native-born church members. Given the list of recipient countries, one might hypothesize that the foreign-born people living in the U.S. and sending remittances to developing countries are from varying economic backgrounds, and not necessarily wealthier than native-born church members. These foreign-born inhabitants have to obtain housing, food, and clothing to maintain themselves while living in the U.S., as do the native-born church members.

If the total remittances sent by foreign-born people in the United States figure is divided by the foreign-born population in the U.S., the amount is calculated to be $2,355. Following a similar procedure for the native-born church members, it is estimated that the per member contribution to international ministries in 2009 was $85. If native-born church members in the U.S. were to donate to international ministries on the same level as foreign-born people in the U.S., the additional donations would total $362 billion more.

The numbers are another demonstration of the potential of church members in the U.S. to increase contributions, in this instance to approach the level of foreign-born people's remittances, in order to impact global needs. The numbers also point out the disparity of priorities between the foreign-born inhabitants and the church members. The first is presumably sending assistance to family and hometowns.

The second is directed by Jesus Christ to send assistance to Jesus himself via "the least of these" (per Matthew 25:31-46). The question may be posed, in light of the available resources, if native-born church members will honor Jesus' wishes to the same degree that foreign-born people living in the U.S. honor their families still living in their home countries.

Making Missions Giving a Priority in order to Act on the Potential.

The numbers in this chapter document the potential for church members in the U.S. to increase giving, and outline some of the impact on global word and deed need, as well as domestic need, that could be made as a result.

Various comparisons in this chapter demonstrate that the issue of meeting global and domestic need is not one of resources, but of priorities and intentions. The Biblical mandate, as well as various methodologies, are in place to lay the groundwork for impacting global word and deed need in Jesus' name. Chapter 8 considers the implications of the potential in light of the need.

Notes for Chapter 6

[1] See Jesus' statement in Matthew 23:23. For a discussion of various views of the tithe, see John and Sylvia Ronsvalle, *Behind the Stained Glass Windows: Money Dynamics in the Church* (Grand Rapids, MI: Baker Book House, 1996), pp. 187-193.

[2] The basis for the calculations of potential giving by historically Christian churches in the U.S. in 2009 is as follows. In chapter seven of this volume titled "Why and How Much Do Americans Give?" a 2009 figure of total giving to religion was presented in the "Denomination-Based series Keyed to 1974 Filer Estimate." That figure was $73.7 billion. A figure of 73.8% was multiplied by the 2009 figure for giving to religion of $73.7 billion to determine what amount was given by those who identify with the historically Christian church. The result was $54.4 billion. In 2009, if giving had increased to an average of 10% from the actual level of 2.38% given, instead of $54.4 billion, an amount of $228 billion would have been donated to historically Christian churches. The difference between the $54.4 billion given and the potential of $228 billion is $174 billion, the additional money that would have been available at an average of 10% giving. The above figure of 73.8% was based on an empty tomb, inc. analysis of data published in Barry A. Kosmin and Ariela Keysar; American Religious Identification Survey [ARIS 2009] Summary Report; Hartford, Conn.: Trinity College, March 2009; p. 5 of 7/4/2009 printout, and referred to that portion of the U.S. population that identifies with the historically Christian church—those communions and traditions, such as Roman Catholic, Orthodox, evangelical and mainline Protestant, Pentecostal, and Anabaptist, that profess a commitment to the historic tenets of the faith.

[3] It may be noted that the estimate of an additional $174 billion that would be available if average giving were at 10% is at the lower end. Rather than using the calculation detailed in the previous endnote, two other estimates of $602 billion and $760 billion for 2009 were obtained based on alternate assumptions. An alternative estimate of $602 billion was derived based on the assumption that: (1) 59.45% of Americans are members of historically Christian churches, with aggregate after-tax income of $6.6 trillion; (2) religious giving was $73.7 billion in 2009; and (3) 73.8% of religious giving was from self-identifying Christians (estimate based on ARIS 2009). The results indicated that the giving level among self-identifying Christians was 0.83% of historically Christian church member after-tax income in 2009, rather than the 2.38% noted in the previous endnote. In that case, the difference between 2009 giving at 0.83% and 10% would have been $602 billion. Alternatively, one could base the potential giving level calculation on the assumptions that: (1) 73.8% of Americans identify with the historically Christian church, whether

or not they are members (estimate based on ARIS 2009); (2) this portion of Americans had an aggregate after-tax income of $8.1 trillion; and (3) the calculation considered contributions as possibly available from this 73.8% of U.S. population. Giving levels would then have been at the 0.67% of income level. In that case, the difference between self-identified Christian giving in 2009 at the 0.67% level and a potential 10% level would have yielded an additional $760 billion in 2009. The estimate of 59.45% church member figure was an empty tomb, inc. calculation based on Gallup, *Religion in America 2002*, pp. 28, 40. The 2009 aggregate Disposable Personal Income figure of $11.0349 trillion that was multiplied by the church member population figures in the two alternative calculations contained in this endnote above was obtained from U.S. Bureau of Economic Analysis National Income and Product Accounts, Table 2.1, Personal Income and Its Disposition, line 26, data published 3/25/2011.

[4] Carol Bellamy, *The State of the World's Children 2000* (New York: UNICEF, 2000), p. 37.

[5] Carol Bellamy, *The State of the World's Children 1999* (New York: UNICEF, 1999), p. 85.

[6] United Nations Children's Fund (UNICEF), *The State of the World's Children, Special Edition, Statistical Tables* (New York: UNICEF, November 2009), p. 11.

[7] Gareth Jones, et al.; "How Many Child Deaths Can We Prevent This Year?"; *The Lancet*, vol. 362; 7/5/2003; <http://www.thelancet.com/journal/vol1362/iss9377/full/llan.362.9377.child_survival.26292.1>; p. 6 of 7/7/03 2:06 PM printout.

[8] James Grant, *The State of the World's Children 1990* (New York: Oxford University Press, 1990), p. 16, estimated that $2.5 billion a year would be needed by the late 1990s to stop preventable child deaths. An updated figure of $5.1 billion was cited in Jennifer Bryce, et al.; "Can the World Afford to Save the Lives of 6 Million Children Each Year?"; *The Lancet*, vol. 365; 6/25/2005; p. 2193; <http://www.thelancet.com/journals/lancet/article/PIIS0140656677773/fulltext>; p. 1 of 1/11/2006 printout.

[9] Two additional denominations provided Overseas Missions Income for 2003 through 2009, but indicated that they were not able to provide Total Contributions for 2003 through 2009. Those denominations and their data are listed in a table in Appendix B-5. It should be noted that in 2004, Friends United Meeting changed fiscal years to end June 30, 2004, and so only six months of data was available for 2004. Data for Tables 19-25, and the two denominations, is presented in Appendix B-5.

[10] Christian and Missionary Alliance: "Since both domestic and overseas works are budgeted through the same source (our 'Great Commission Fund'), the amount on lines 1 and 4 are actual amounts spent on overseas missions."

[11] Church of the Brethren: "This amount is national denominational mission and service, i.e., direct staffing and mission support, and does not include other projects funded directly by congregations or districts, or independent missionaries sponsored by congregations and individuals that would not be part of the denominational effort."

[12] Churches of God General Conference: "[Data Year] 2008 line 2 represents a net loss in investment income included in line 1. By adding this net loss amount back, line 4 represents the amount received in contributions from donors."

[13] Conservative Congregational Christian Conference: The structure of this communion limits the national office coordination of overseas ministries activity. By design, congregations are to conduct missions directly, through agencies of their choice. The national office does not survey congregations about these activities. The one common emphasis of affiliated congregations is a focus on Micronesia, represented by the reported numbers. 2009: "The amount raised is down because we didn't have any missionary that we sent overseas."

[14] The Episcopal Church: "The Episcopal Church USA Domestic and Foreign Missionary Society does not specifically raise money to support our non-domestic ministries. Many of the activities included in our budget are, however, involved, directly or indirectly with providing worldwide mission...Many other expenditures (e.g., for ecumenical and interfaith relations; for military chaplaincies; for management's participation in activities of the worldwide Anglican Communion) contain an overseas component; but we do not separately track or report domestic vs. overseas expenses in those categories."

[15] Evangelical Lutheran Synod: "[Data Year 2009] Line 1 includes an estate of [$]690,764 given in '09."

[16] Lutheran Church-Missouri Synod: "LCMS World Mission is the global Gospel outreach of The Lutheran Church-Missouri Synod (LCMS), a confessional Lutheran church with more than 6,000 congregations and 2.5 million members in North America. Ministry work is focused in three areas: International Mission, National Mission, and Ministry to the Armed Forces. The information provided in this report solely represents the *international component* of LCMS World Mission work. Annual budget income; above budget income; administrative incomes; and the special, multi-year, mission funding campaign, called *Fan into Flame,* income is included in the overseas income data. The majority of LCMS World Mission funding comes from direct gifts from individuals, congregations, and organizations.

"Note, information from LCMS World Relief and Human Care, another official LCMS entity involved in international and national ministry, is not included in the statistics provided here.

"In more recent years, the 35 districts of the LCMS and a number of congregations and Lutheran mission societies began sponsoring various mission fields and projects directly—with funds not flowing through the two national LCMS entities for world mission and world relief and human care. More information regarding the international work of the 35 LCMS districts can be found at <www.lcmsdistricts.org> and the 75-plus members of Association of Lutheran Mission Agencies at <www.alma-online.org>. Therefore, millions of dollars of additional support from LCMS members is raised and spent for international ministry each year. But, since these funds are not sent through the LCMS accounting department—and not required to be—the financial totals are not verifiable."

For the 2009 data: "In July of 2010 the Lutheran Church - Missouri Synod met in regular convention and adopted a new structure for the management of all programmatic activities being performed at the national and international mission level, including the creation of a new national mission board and new international mission board. A restructuring work group was formed following the convention and delivered recommendations to the President's Office in February, 2011. The final organization structure is planned to take effect in July, 2011 at which time financial reporting functions and processes will be established."

[17] Moravian Church, Northern Province: "Data provided by the Board of World Mission, an interprovincial agency of the North American Moravian Church." The Overseas Missions Income figure was estimated for the Northern Province by the Board of World Mission of the Moravian Church. The Northern Province is the only one of the three Moravian Provinces that reports Total Contributions to the *Yearbook of American and Canadian Churches* series.

[18] Orthodox Presbyterian Church: "These figures, as in past years, reflect only what was given through our denominational committee. Local churches and individuals also give directly to a variety of overseas missions causes."

[19] Presbyterian Church (U.S.A.): For Data Year 2005: "Nos. 1 & 4 Year 2005: Higher for Asian Tsunami Relief."

[20] Primitive Methodist Church in the U.S.A.: "This only includes monies passing through our Denominational Mission Board (International). Many churches send money directly to a mission field."

[21] Seventh-day Adventist, North American Division: This estimate, prepared by the General Conference Treasury Department, is for the U.S. portion of the total donated by congregations in both Canada and the U.S.

[22] The United Methodist Church: "The above represents total income received by the General Board of Global Ministries, The United Methodist Church."

[23] See notes for Tables 19 through 25.

[24] Charles H. Fahs, *Trends in Protestant Giving* (New York: Institute of Social and Religious Research, 1929), pp. 26, 29, 53. The eleven denominations included in the 1916-1927 figures are: Congregational; Methodist Episcopal; Methodist Episcopal, South; Northern Baptist Convention; Presbyterian Church in the U.S.; Presbyterian Church in the U.S.A.; Reformed Church in the United States; Reformed Church in America; Southern Baptist Convention; United Brethren; and United Presbyterian. For a more detailed discussion of the Fahs study, and a comparison of church member giving in the 1920s and 2003, see John and Sylvia Ronsvalle, *The State of Church Giving through 2003* (Champaign, IL: empty tomb, inc., 2005), pp. 55-60. The chapter is also available at <http://www.emptytomb.org/scg03missions.pdf>.

[25] Commission on World Mission and Evangelism of the World Council of Churches, "Mission and Evangelism—An Ecumenical Affirmation, *International Review of Mission*, vol. LXXI, no. 284 (October, 1982), p. 440.

[26] "Definitions and Terms Related to the Great Commission"; Joshua Project; n.d.; <http://www.joshuaproject. net/definitions.php?term=24>; p. 1 of 7/25/2011 4:28 PM printout.

[27] "How Many People Groups Are There?"; The Joshua Project; n.d.; <http://www.joshuaproject.net/how-many-people-groups.php>; p. 1 of 7/31/2011 10:48 AM printout.

[28] In July 2011, the Joshua Project posted a number 6,933 ("Unreached Peoples of the World"; <http://www. joshuaproject.net>; p. 1 of 7/25/2011 3:25 PM printout.

[29] Morris Chapman; "The Conversation is Changing"; published July 1, 2006; <http://www.morrischapman. com/article.asp?is=57>; p. 1 of 8/6/06 4:48 PM printout.

[30] Bob Rodgers, Southern Baptist Convention Executive Committee vice president for Cooperative Program & stewardship; "Analysis: Are We Serious About Penetrating Lostness?"; Baptist Press; 5/28/2010; <http://www. bpnews.net/printerfriendly.asp?ID=33027>; p. 1 of 5/29/2010 10:54 AM printout.

[31] "Frequently Asked Questions"; Christian Aid Mission; n.d.; <http://www.christianaid.org/About/FAQ.aspx>; pp. 1-2 of 6/10/2008 1:58 PM printout.

[32] "F.A.Q.'s"; Gospel for Asia; <http://www.gfa.org/gfa/faqs>; p. 2 of 8/23/2005 8:48 AM printout.

[33] "Frequently Asked Questions"; Gospel for Asia; 2008; <http://www.gfa.org/faqs#q13>; p. 1 of 6/10/2008 2:42 PM printout.

[34] "Sponsorship FAQ's"; Gospel for Asia; 2008; <http://www.gfa.org/sponsore-faqs>; p. 1 of 6/10/2008 3:36 PM printout.

[35] John Ronsvalle and Sylvia Ronsvalle, *The State of Church Giving through 2005: Abolition of the Institutional Enslavement of Overseas Missions* (Champaign, IL: empty tomb, inc., 2008), pp. 66-67.

[36] Membership data for specific denominations is provided in Appendix B. The Evangelical and Born Again population percents are taken from "The Barna Update: Barna Survey Reveals Significant growth in Born Again Population"; The Barna Group; <http://www.barna.org/FlexPage/aspx?Page=BarnaUpdate&BarnaUpdate ID=271>; p. 2 of 7/9/2007 9:22 AM printout. The NCC inclusive membership figure was obtained from Eileen W. Lindner, ed., *YACC 2011* (Nashville: Abingdon, 2011); pp. 374-75.

[37] UNICEF estimated there were 8,087,000 under-five child deaths in 2009: "Statistical Tables: Table 1," *The State of the World's Children 2011*, (New York: UNICEF, February 2011), p. 91. Dividing that number by 365 days in 2009 yields the estimate of 22,156 children a day.

[38] Deb West; "Spectrem Group Reports That Millionaires Are On The Rise Again!"; luxist.com; 3/12/2010 7:01 PM; <http://www.luxist.com/2010/03/12/spectrem-group-reports-that-millionaires-are-on-the-rise-again/print/>; p. 1 of 6/27/2010 11:49 AM printout.

[39] For a brief review of this topic, see John Ronsvalle and Sylvia Ronsvalle, *The State of Church Giving through 2002* (Champaign, IL: empty tomb, inc., 2004), pp. 65-66. Also available at <http://www.emptytomb.org/ scg036Potential.php>.

[40] The percent Catholic for each diocese was derived by dividing "Total Catholic Population" by "Total Population" as found in the *OCD*, P.J. Kenedy & Sons, New Providence, NJ, 2010, subtitled, "Giving Status of the Catholic Church as of January 1, 2010." The population data for the Archdioceses under consideration was found in the *OCD* as follows: Baltimore (p. 74), Boston (p. 133), Chicago (p. 253), Detroit (p. 384), Galveston-Houston (p. 488), Los Angeles (p. 707-08), New York (pp. 881-82), Philadelphia (p. 1016), and Washington (p. 1471).

The *OCD* 2009 (New Providence, NJ: P.J. Kenedy & Sons with National Register Publishing, 2009, p. 249) listed the Data Year (DY) 2008 "Total Catholic Population" of the Archdiocese of Chicago as 2,338,000 as of 1/1/2009. The *OCD* 2010, p. 253, also listed the DY 2009 "Total Catholic Population" of the Archdiocese of Chicago as 2,338,000 as of 1/1/2010. On an empty tomb, inc., data request form titled, "Data Years 2008 & 2009: Requesting Population Information for the Archdiocese of Chicago," dated April 28, 2011, a representative of the Archdiocese of Chicago office supplied a revised 2009 "Total Catholic Population" figure for the Archdiocese of Chicago of 2,336,000.

The Official Catholic Directory 2009 (New Providence, NJ: P.J. Kenedy & Sons with National Register Publishing, 2009, p. 384) listed the Data Year (DY) 2008 "Total Catholic Population" of the Archdiocese of Detroit as 1,434,622, and the "Total Population" in the Archdiocese as 4,438,006, as of 1/1/2009. The Official Catholic Directory 2010, p. 386, also listed the DY 2009 "Total Catholic Population" of the Archdiocese of Detroit as 1,434,622, and the "Total Population" in the Archdiocese of Detroit as 4,438,006, as of 1/1/2010. On an empty tomb, inc., data request form titled, "Data Years 2008 & 2009: Requesting Information for Archdiocese of Detroit," dated April 29, 2011, a representative of the Archdiocese of Detroit office confirmed the same numbers for Data Years 2008 and 2009.

The percent Catholic calculated for each diocese was used to obtain an estimate of U.S. BEA Personal Income for Catholics in each Archdiocesan county. An alternative approach would have been to employ data from Dale E. Jones et al., *Religious Congregations & Membership in the United States (RCMUS), 2000* (Nashville: Glenmary Research Center, 2002). The *RCMUS* provided "Total Adherents" as a "% of Total Pop." data for Catholics as well as other denominations and religions for each county. A cursory review in 2005 of this data for selected counties suggested that this latter approach using somewhat older data would have resulted in marginal differences.

[41] Total 2009 U.S. BEA Personal Income for Counties in Archdioceses ($s) County level U.S. BEA Personal Income data for 2009, the latest year listed, was accessed on 5/16/2011 via <http://www.bea.gov/regional/reis/drill.cfm>. The Archdiocese of Boston was adjusted for Archdiocesan "excepting the towns of Marion, Mattapoisetts and Wareham" from Plymouth County, MA. This involved using the 2009 population of the five Archdiocesan counties and the aforementioned three excepted towns. Population for these entities were derived from <http://www.bea.gov/bea/regional/bearfacts/> and <www.city-data.com> or cached versions thereof, respectively.

[42] The source for the estimate employed for current Catholic giving as 1.2% of income is as follows: " '...[W]e know that the national statistics are that Catholics give to the church about 1.2 percent of their income...' [Tim Dockery, director of development services for the Chicago archdiocese] said" (Cathleen Falsani, Religion Reporter, "Archdiocese May Ask for 10%: Cardinal George Considers Program That Includes Tithing," *Chicago Sun-Times*, Sunday, February 1, 2004, pp. 1A, and 6A).

[43] John Ronsvalle and Sylvia Ronsvalle, "An Exploration of Roman Catholic Giving Patterns," *The State of Church Giving through 1993* (Champaign, Ill.: empty tomb, inc., 1995), pp. 59-78. The article is also available at: < http://www.emptytomb.org/cathgiv.html>.

[44] A 2010 survey was conducted by the Center for Applied Research in the Apostolate (CARA), as a collaborative "work of five Catholic national ministerial organizations," (Mark M. Gray, Mary L. Gautier, and Melissa Cidade; "The Changing Face of U.S. Catholic Parishes"; National Association of May Ministry (Washington, D.C.); 2011; <www.emergingmodels.org/doc/Emerging Models Phase One report.pdf>; pp. 1, 2, 6 of 7/28/2011 printout). The survey found the "total average weekly offering in U.S. parishes" was $9,200. Multiplying that number by the 2010 number of parishes, 17,784, yielded a total annual offering calculation of $8,507,865,600. Using the most recent *OCD* figure for membership, which was 68,503,456 in 2009 (see Appendix B-4), a per member total average weekly offering calculation of $124.20. The estimated 2010 U.S. per capita DPI figure was $36,697 (see Appendix C). The $124.20 per member total average weekly offering amount represented 0.3% of 2010 income.

[45] Samuel G. Freedman; "As Catholic Schools Close in Major Cities, the Need Only Grows"; The New York Times; June 3, 2011; <http://www.nytimes.com/201/06/04/us/04religion.html>; pp. 2, 3 of 7/25/2011 4:42 PM printout.

[46] Associated Press; "More Catholic Schools Closing Across U.S."; msnbc; 4/12/2008; <http://www.msnbc.msn.com/id/24082482/ns/us_news-pope_in_america/t/more-catholic-schools-closing-across-us/>; p. 1, 2 of 7/25/2011 4:42 PM printout.

[47] *The Index of Global Philanthropy and Remittances 2011;* Hudson Institute Center for Global Prosperity; created 4/13/2011 6:04:54 AM and modified 5/9/2011 10:12:38 AM: printed 6/13/2011; <http://www.

hudson.org/files/documents/2011%20Index%20of%20Global%20Philanthropy%20and%20Remittances%20 downloadable%20version.pdf>; p. 9 of 6/13/2011 printout.

[48] *The Index of Global Philanthropy and Remittances 2011*, p. 9.

[49] The native-born church member figure was calculated by multiplying the native-born population figure of 268,489,322 by 59.45%, the estimated percent of the U.S. population that has membership in historically Christian churches. The result was 159,616,902. The 268,489,322 figure for the native-born population was from U.S. Census Bureau; 2009 American Community Survey, Data Set: 2009 American Community Survey 1-Year Estimates: Selected Social Characteristics in the United States: 2009; Accessed 6/14/2011; <http:// factfinder.census.gov/servlet/ADPTable?_bm=y&-geo_id=01000US&-qr_name=ACS_2009_1YR_G00_DP2&- ds_name=ACS_2009_1YR_G00&-_lang=en&-_caller=geoselect&-redoLog=false&-format=>; p. 3 of 6/14/11 4:27 PM printout. The figure of 59.45% is an empty tomb analysis of data in George H. Gallup, Jr., *Religion in America 2002*, pp. 28, 40.

[50] *The Index of Global Philanthropy and Remittances 2011*, p. 19.

[51] *The Index of Global Philanthropy and Remittances 2011*, pp. 9, 10, 16.

[52] *The Index of Global Philanthropy and Remittances 2011*, pp. 3, 20.

[53] U.S. Census Bureau; 2009 American Community Survey; p. 3.

chapter 7

Why and How Much Do Americans Give?

Overview of Why and How Much Americans Give

Why Do Americans Give? The reasons for donating money vary by individual, and for the individual, may vary by circumstance.

Even so, some evidence exists regarding the broad motivation for the active participation among Americans in the practice of donating to charity.

A key source of information is the United States Government Department of Labor, Bureau of Labor Statistics (BLS) that takes a regular survey of Americans' spending patterns. In the Consumer Expenditure Survey (CE), the respondents are asked to categorize their "cash contributions" among four categories relevant to the present inquiry: (1) "charities and other organizations"; (2) "church, religious organizations"; (3) "educational institutions"; (4) "gifts to non-CU [consumer unit] members of stocks, bonds, and mutual funds."

In 2009, the category of gifts to "church, religious organizations" represented 74 percent of the charitable donations reported by Americans.

This percentage differs from other sources that report a lower percent directed to the category of "religion." A major difference may be due to the fact that, in other surveys, the frame of reference has been defined by the professional practitioners interested in certain end-use categories, rather than either by the perception of the donors, or by the self-understanding and governance of the recipient organizations themselves.

Various well-known surveys of giving emphasize the end-use of the contributions. The much higher percent of giving categorized as "church, religious organizations" by donors in the CE is therefore of interest in that it may provide insight as to the motivation of donors. For example, while practitioner surveys might categorize a gift to Catholic Social Services or the Salvation Army under "human services," the donor may view the contribution as a gift to "church, religious organizations." Again, professional fundraiser surveys may label gifts to Lutheran World Relief and World Vision as "international" while donors would identify the gifts as being directed to "church, religious organizations." The net effect is that the category of "religion" is underreported in many surveys of charitable giving.

As can be seen from the analysis of CE data that follows, donors in every age group, every income group, and every region of the country identified gifts to "church, religious organizations" as the primary focus of their charitable activity.

Consider the analysis by Age. The Under-25 group gave the smallest portion of income to charity. However, of the amount given, 85% was categorized as gifts to "church, religious organizations." This observation suggests that young people learn their philanthropic values first in religious settings. As can be seen from Table 34, the categories of "charities and other organizations" and "educational institutions" were added as people aged, although gifts to "church, religious organizations" remained a large portion of total giving.

> This observation suggests that young people learn their philanthropic values first in religious settings.

If, as observed in earlier chapters of this volume, giving to church is weakening, over time the observed trends could have a negative impact on the entire charitable sector in the U.S. An accurate understanding of the role of religion in the practice of philanthropy in the U.S. could benefit academics, practitioners, and the general population in the U.S., as well.

One suggestion for improving this categorization process is a revision of the nonprofit Form 990 reporting document. Before selecting one of the ten core definition categories, the reporting nonprofit organization could first indicate its form of governance as either "faith-based" or "secular."

How Much Do Americans Give? Various surveys provide different answers to the question of how much Americans give. The source that serves as a benchmark is the Consumer Expenditure Survey.

The Consumer Expenditure Survey. The U.S. Government BLS CE is a sophisticated research instrument that affects many aspects of American life through the Consumer Price Index (CPI).

The CE serves as a benchmark for understanding charitable giving patterns. The data series provides information about Americans' giving patterns by age, region of residence, and income levels.

In 2009, the CE figure for charitable giving by living individuals was $975.86 per household. Given that there were 120.847 million households in the U.S. in 2009, the aggregate amount of charitable giving from living individuals in 2009 was calculated to be $117.93 billion.

Other Sources of Giving Estimates. Another source of information about charitable giving is found in the U.S. Internal Revenue Service (IRS) Form 990. The Form 990 series must be filled out by charitable organizations with at least $25,000 in income, and by foundations. Data for the Form 990 series was obtained for the period 1989 through 2007, the latest year for which data for Form 990 was listed on the IRS Web site.

A third major source of philanthropic information is the *Giving USA* series. A major component of this series is based on deductions claimed on IRS Individual Tax returns. The series is "researched and written" on behalf of professional fundraisers by a university-based philanthropy center.

By adjusting both the Form 990 and the *Giving USA* series to yield cash contributions by living donors, the CE, the Form 990, and the *Giving USA* series were compared for 1989 through 2007. The resulting estimates of these two sources differed by as much as $54 billion from the CE.

Details of How Much Americans Give

Details of the Consumer Expenditure Survey, 2009. The U.S. Department of Labor BLS CE provides a benchmark measure of Americans' charitable cash contributions. The CE provides the U.S. Government data designed to measure Americans' charitable contributions.

The CE presents data per "consumer unit." The definition reads:

A consumer unit consists of any of the following: (1) All members of a particular household who are related by blood, marriage, adoption, or other legal arrangements; (2) a person living alone or sharing a household with others or living as a roomer in a private home or lodging house or in permanent living quarters in a hotel or motel, but who is financially independent; or (3) two or more persons living together who use their incomes to make joint expenditure decisions. Financial independence is determined by spending behavior with regard to the three major expense categories: Housing, food, and other living expenses. To be considered financially independent, the respondent must provide at least two of the three major expenditure categories, either entirely or in part.

The terms consumer unit, family, and household are often used interchangeably for convenience. However, the proper technical term for purposes of the Consumer Expenditure Survey is consumer unit.[1]

The CE data for 2009 was aggregated, conflated, and analyzed by empty tomb, inc. The result found that Americans gave $117.93 billion in cash contributions to charitable causes in 2009, the latest year for which data was available.

The CE categories include "Cash contributions to: charities and other organizations; church, religious organizations; and educational institutions" as well as "Gifts to non-CU [Consumer Unit] members of stocks, bonds, and mutual funds."[2] An analysis of the CE data resulted in the finding

Table 31: U.S. BLS CE, Cash Contributions: Americans' Charitable Giving (Aggregated), 2009

Item	Average Annual Expenditures Multiplied by 120.847 million Consumer Units: Aggregated (billions $)	Item as % of Total
Annual Expenditures **Cash Contributions for Charitable Giving** Cash contributions to:		
charities and other organizations	$25.16	21.3%
church, religious organizations	87.57	74.3%
educational institutions	3.69	3.1%
Gifts to non-CU members of stocks, bonds, and mutual funds	1.52	1.3%
Total	$117.93	100.0%

Details in the above table may not compute to the numbers shown due to rounding.
Source: empty tomb, inc. 2011 analysis of U.S. BLS CE, 2009

that Americans contributed 74% of their charitable contributions to "church, religious organizations" in 2009.

Further detail regarding this analysis of U.S. Department of Labor BLS CE charitable giving data is presented in Table 31.[3]

Cash Contributions by Income Level, 2009. The CE measured Americans' cash contributions to charitable causes by income levels, as displayed in Tables 32 and 33.[4]

Table 32: U.S. BLS CE, Cash Contributions for Charitable Giving by Income Level, 2009

Item	All consumer units	$5,000 to $9,999	$10,000 to $14,999	$15,000 to $19,999	$20,000 to $29,999	$30,000 to $39,999	$40,000 to $49,999	$50,000 to $69,999
Number of consumer units (in thousands)	120,847	5,203	7,726	7,669	15,022	13,053	11,444	17,799
Consumer unit characteristics:								
Income after taxes	$60,753	$8,163	$12,749	$17,699	$25,089	$34,432	$43,940	$57,610
Average Annual Expenditures								
Cash Contributions for Charitable Giving								
Cash contributions to:								
charities and other organizations	$208.20	$22.47	$52.68	$63.31	$59.33	$112.94	$104.51	$158.01
church, religious organizations	724.60	224.60	203.53	298.53	352.60	532.71	602.52	795.76
educational institutions	30.52	2.42	1.86	19.21	8.13	5.29	5.23	8.64
Gifts to non-CU members of stocks, bonds, and mutual funds	12.54	No Data	2.04	0.05	3.43	3.88	1.52	13.49
Total (calculated)	$975.86	$249.49	$260.11	$381.10	$423.49	$654.82	$713.78	$975.90
Calculated:								
% of Income after Taxes								
Cash contributions to:								
charities and other organizations	0.34%	0.28%	0.41%	0.36%	0.24%	0.33%	0.24%	0.27%
church, religious organizations	1.19%	2.75%	1.60%	1.69%	1.41%	1.55%	1.37%	1.38%
educational institutions	0.05%	0.03%	0.01%	0.11%	0.03%	0.02%	0.01%	0.01%
Gifts to non-CU members of stocks, bonds, and mutual funds	0.02%	No Data	0.02%	0.00%	0.01%	0.01%	0.00%	0.02%
Total	1.6%	3.1%	2.0%	2.2%	1.7%	1.9%	1.6%	1.7%

Details in the above table may not compute to the numbers shown due to rounding.
Source: empty tomb, inc. 2011 analysis of U.S. BLS CE, 2009

An analysis was conducted for 12 income levels, ranging from "$5,000 to $9,999" up to both "$120,000 to $149,999" and the highest category of "$150,000 and more," with the average "Income after taxes" for the income levels ranging from $8,163 to $127,030, and $222,535, respectively.[5]

A comparison of cash contributions among different income brackets may be of interest.

However, it should be noted that CE lower income brackets, which for purposes of this analysis ranged from $5,000 through $39,999, reported higher expenses than income before taxes. The CE observes:

Data users may notice that average annual expenditures presented in the income tables sometimes exceed income before taxes for the lower income groups. The primary reason for that is believed to be the underreporting of income by respondents, a problem common to most household surveys…

There are other reasons why expenditures exceed income for the lower income groups. Consumer units whose members experience a spell of unemployment may draw on their savings to maintain their expenditures. Self-employed consumers may experience business losses that result in low or even negative incomes, but are able to maintain their expenditures by borrowing or relying on savings. Students may get by on loans while they are in school, and retirees may rely on savings and investments.[6]

To the extent that income is proportionately underreported across all income levels, but is more evident in lower income brackets, then comparisons across income brackets may be informative on an exploratory basis.

Table 33: U.S. BLS CE, Cash Contributions for Charitable Giving by Higher Income Level, 2009

Item	All consumer units	$70,000 to $79,999	$80,000 to $99,999	$100,000 to $119,999	$120,000 to $149,999	$150,000 and more
Number of consumer units (in thousands)	120,847	6,640	9,951	7,260	5,882	8,447
Consumer unit characteristics:						
Income after taxes	$60,753	$72,124	$86,130	$104,701	$127,030	$222,535
Average Annual Expenditures						
Cash Contributions for Charitable Giving						
Cash contributions to:						
charities and other organizations	$208.20	$149.80	$231.49	$246.34	$320.05	$1,258.90
church, religious organizations	724.60	804.84	1,119.15	1,072.50	1,502.35	1,786.01
educational institutions	30.52	15.13	12.43	24.48	24.97	288.24
Gifts to non-CU members of						
stocks, bonds, and mutual funds	12.54	14.98	18.45	25.76	35.47	54.34
Total (calculated)	$975.86	$984.75	$1,381.52	$1,369.08	$1,882.84	$3,387.49
Calculated						
% of Income after Taxes						
Cash contributions to:						
charities and other organizations	0.34%	0.21%	0.27%	0.24%	0.25%	0.57%
church, religious organizations	1.19%	1.12%	1.30%	1.02%	1.18%	0.80%
educational institutions	0.05%	0.02%	0.01%	0.02%	0.02%	0.13%
Gifts to non-CU members of						
stocks, bonds, and mutual funds	0.02%	0.02%	0.02%	0.02%	0.03%	0.02%
Total	1.6%	1.4%	1.6%	1.3%	1.5%	1.5%

Details in the above table may not compute to the numbers shown due to rounding.
Source: empty tomb, inc. 2011 analysis of U.S. BLS CE, 2009

Having noted this caveat, it is still of interest to observe that Consumer Units (CU) in the "$5,000 to $9,999" through the "$20,000 to $29,999" income brackets reported charitable cash contributions that represented a higher portion of after-tax income than any of the other higher income brackets.

It may be observed that 2009 giving as a percent of income after taxes to "church, religious organizations" was higher in each of the twelve income levels, than to either "charities and other organizations," "educational institutions," or "Gifts to non-CU members of stocks, bonds, and mutual funds."

In the twelve brackets, "charities and other organizations" received the second largest dollar donation per CU, after "church, religious organizations" and before "educational institutions."

In each income bracket, the dollars given to "church, religious organizations" was greater than the sum of the dollars given to "charities and other organizations" and "educational institutions."

Cash Contributions by Age, 2009. The CE also measured Americans' cash contributions to charitable causes by age of contributor.[7] Table 34 presents the data in tabular form.

The seven age categories under consideration started with the "Under 25 years" grouping, proceeded with "25-34 years" as the first of five 10-year periods, and culminated with the "75 years and older" cohort.

In 2009, giving as a percent of income after taxes to "church, religious organizations" grew as a portion of income in each bracket as age advanced. The 55-64 years bracket posted a lower income than the 45-54 years group did, and yet gave more dollars to "church, religious organizations," and "charities and other organizations." As a result, the portion of income given to those categories increased from the previous bracket.

Income for the 65-74 years bracket was 38% less than the 55-64 years cohort. Yet, the dollars given to "church, religious organizations" remained about the same, and the difference in dollars given to "charities and other organizations" between the two brackets was the largest for that category between any two groups. Again, the dynamic of decreased income and increased giving resulted in an increase in the percent of income given from the previous bracket.

Although the 75 years and older cohort had the lowest dollar income, giving to the category of church, religious organizations was highest in this bracket, both in the number of dollars given, and as a portion of income.

Contributions to "educational institutions" as a portion of income were highest in the 75 years and older age bracket. The second highest level of donations was posted by those in the 35-44 age bracket.

Table 34: U.S. BLS CE, Cash Contributions for Charitable Giving by Age, 2009

Item	All consumer units	Under 25 years	25-34 years	35-44 years	45-54 years	55-64 years	65-74 years	75 years and older
Number of consumer units (in thousands)	120,847	7,875	20,044	22,199	25,440	20,731	12,848	11,709
Consumer unit characteristics:								
Income after taxes	$60,753	$25,522	$57,239	$74,900	$77,460	$67,586	$46,147	$31,272
Average Annual Expenditures								
Cash Contributions for Charitable Giving								
Cash contributions to:								
charities and other organizations	$208.20	$27.22	$62.86	$105.85	$218.47	$296.15	$534.59	$236.58
church, religious organizations	724.60	154.84	456.56	663.66	821.52	886.27	887.73	1,006.32
educational institutions	30.52	0.27	6.61	49.37	36.10	28.34	19.84	59.53
Gifts to non-CU members of								
stocks, bonds, and mutual funds	12.54	No Data	8.28	5.73	21.35	17.28	13.66	12.38
Total (calculated)	$975.86	$182.33	$534.31	$824.61	$1,097.44	$1,228.04	$1,455.82	$1,314.81
Calculated								
% of Income after Taxes								
Cash contributions to:								
charities and other organizations	0.34%	0.11%	0.11%	0.14%	0.28%	0.44%	1.16%	0.76%
church, religious organizations	1.19%	0.61%	0.80%	0.89%	1.06%	1.31%	1.92%	3.22%
educational institutions	0.05%	0.00%	0.01%	0.07%	0.05%	0.04%	0.04%	0.19%
Gifts to non-CU members of								
stocks, bonds, and mutual funds	0.02%	No Data	0.01%	0.01%	0.03%	0.03%	0.03%	0.04%
Total	1.6%	0.7%	0.9%	1.1%	1.4%	1.8%	3.2%	4.2%

Details in the above table may not compute to the numbers shown due to rounding.
Source: empty tomb, inc. 2011 analysis of U.S. BLS CE, 2009

Contributions to "charities, and other organizations" as a portion of income increased through the 65-74 years cohort.

The fact that members of the "Under 25 years" directed 85% of their giving as a percent of after-tax income to the "church, religious organizations" category provides support for the view that religion serves as the seedbed of philanthropic giving in America. The portion of income given to that category among this group was considerably higher at 0.61% than to "charities and other organizations" at 0.11%. There was no measurable contribution to "educational institutions" in this age bracket.

The age bracket in which total charitable giving as a portion of income was highest was the 75 years and older cohort.

One factor that all age brackets had in common was that giving as a portion of income to "church, religious organizations" was the largest category. Further, in all cohorts, giving to "church, religious organizations" as a portion of income was greater than the sum of the two categories of "charities and other organizations" plus "educational institutions."

Cash Contributions by Region, 2009. In addition, as shown in Table 35, the CE also measured Americans' cash contributions to charitable causes by region.[8]

The four region categories for which information was presented in the CE data were Northeast, Midwest, South, and West. Regional charitable giving data and regional income figures were available for the comparison.

Analysis of the 2009 data showed that contributions to charitable causes were highest in the South and West, at 1.8% of income after taxes, with the South slightly higher in the unrounded percentage. The Midwest followed at 1.7%, with the Northeast at 1.0%.

In each of the four regions, contributions to "church, religious organizations" were higher than the sum of contributions to "charities and other organizations" and "educational institutions."

The differences in 2009 between the Northeast and the larger gift levels in each of the other three regions for the category of "church, religious organizations" were significant at the 0.05 level. The differences between the larger amount of donations to "total giving"

Table 35: U.S. BLS CE, Cash Contributions for Charitable Giving by Region of Residence, 2009

Item	All consumer units	Northeast	Midwest	South	West
Number of consumer units (in thousands)	120,847	22,411	27,536	43,819	27,080
Consumer unit characteristics:					
Income after taxes	$60,753	$68,986	$57,866	$56,795	$63,279
Average Annual Expenditures Cash Contributions for Charitable Giving					
Cash contributions to:					
charities and other organizations	$208.20	$268.48	$154.70	$198.75	$228.00
church, religious organizations	724.60	395.75	759.11	794.42	848.66
educational institutions	30.52	15.36	32.80	31.96	38.42
Gifts to non-CU members of stocks, bonds, and mutual funds	12.54	22.91	11.29	2.80	20.98
Total (calculated)	$975.86	$702.50	$957.90	$1,027.93	$1,136.06
Calculated % of Income after Taxes					
Cash contributions to:					
charities and other organizations	0.34%	0.39%	0.27%	0.35%	0.36%
church, religious organizations	1.19%	0.57%	1.31%	1.40%	1.34%
educational institutions	0.05%	0.02%	0.06%	0.06%	0.06%
Gifts to non-CU members of stocks, bonds, and mutual funds	0.02%	0.03%	0.02%	0.00%	0.03%
Total	1.6%	1.0%	1.7%	1.8%	1.8%

Details in the above table may not compute to the numbers shown due to rounding.
Source: empty tomb, inc. 2011 analysis of U.S. BLS CE, 2009

in the Midwest compared to the Northeast, and also in the South compared to the Northeast, were significant at the 0.05 level. The larger size of contributions to "educational institutions" in the Midwest, and in the West, compared to the Northeast, were significant at the 0.05 level as well.[9]

The charitable giving patterns, particularly to "church, religious organizations" correspond to the results of a 2009 Gallup poll that found states in the Northeast were "least religious" while those in the South were "most religious."[10] The title of an Associated Press article on church initiatives in the Northeast referred to the area as "spiritually cold."[11] Given the implications of charitable giving in the Under-25 years bracket with giving to "church, religious organizations" — that young people first learn philanthropy in the context of religion — the reported lack of religious fervor in the Northeast could be associated with the level of charitable giving.

Records were available back to 1987 from the BLS CE. The specific category of "Gifts to non-CU members of stocks, bonds, and mutual funds," however, was not available before the second quarter of 2001. Therefore, in the historical series for 1987-2009, comparing Charitable Giving as a portion of after-tax income, Charitable Giving included the three categories of "charities and other organizations," "church, religious organizations," and "educational institutions." Consequently, the 2009 numbers in Table 36, which does not include the category of "Gifts to non-CU members of stocks, bonds, and mutual funds," differ slightly from the figures in Table 35, which does include that category.

As can be seen in Table 36, the regional pattern indicates the South had the highest average percent of after-tax income in the "cash contributions for charitable giving" category in the 1987-2009 period. The Midwest and the West were next, and then the Northeast.

The South's overall average was 1.7% of income given to charity during the 1987-2009 period. The Northeast posted the lowest portion of income donated for charitable purposes consistently throughout the 1987 through 2009 period, with the exception of 1994, when the Northeast was third and the West was the lowest in the comparison. In unrounded numbers, the Midwest's 1987-2009 average of 1.62% was slightly larger than the West's average of 1.61%.

The question may be asked whether regional differences in spending on other expenditures categories influence or limit charitable giving levels in the four regions. Table 37 presents expenditure data by region of residence for 2009.[12] The category of "Cash Contributions for Charitable Giving" was subtracted from the expenditures total. The reason for this

Table 36: U.S. BLS CE, Expenditures for Charitable Giving by Region of Residence, 1987-2009

Year	All consumer units	Northeast	Midwest	South	West
1987	1.46%	0.86%	1.53%	1.76%	1.56%
1988	1.40%	0.83%	1.43%	1.68%	1.52%
1989	1.56%	1.04%	1.55%	2.01%	1.47%
1990	1.43%	1.03%	1.40%	1.69%	1.50%
1991	1.58%	1.11%	1.69%	1.74%	1.72%
1992	1.58%	1.26%	1.78%	1.78%	1.42%
1993	1.46%	0.98%	1.57%	1.57%	1.68%
1994	1.44%	1.30%	1.42%	1.73%	1.20%
1995	1.50%	1.06%	1.41%	1.66%	1.79%
1996	1.42%	0.93%	1.57%	1.75%	1.23%
1997	1.39%	0.88%	1.41%	1.70%	1.41%
1998	1.41%	0.89%	1.42%	1.68%	1.50%
1999	1.58%	1.03%	1.59%	1.83%	1.75%
2000	1.46%	0.95%	1.93%	1.42%	1.50%
2001	1.53%	1.14%	1.66%	1.72%	1.48%
2002	1.55%	1.14%	1.69%	1.64%	1.65%
2003	1.57%	0.99%	1.75%	1.82%	1.57%
2004	1.47%	0.84%	1.93%	1.53%	1.52%
2005	1.68%	1.13%	1.94%	1.99%	1.49%
2006	1.82%	1.19%	1.91%	1.81%	2.28%
2007	1.66%	1.02%	1.60%	1.67%	2.25%
2008	1.55%	1.00%	1.55%	1.71%	1.81%
2009	1.59%	0.99%	1.64%	1.80%	1.76%
Average for the 1987-2009 Period	1.5%	1.0%	1.6%	1.7%	1.6%

Source: empty tomb, inc. 2011 analysis of U.S. BLS CE, 1987-2009

adjustment was to calculate the portion of income remaining after expenditures other than those for charitable giving. The adjusted total expenditures figure was then divided by the region's after-tax income. The resulting percentage is shown in Table 37.

It was instructive to note that variations in giving to charity by region did not seem to be a function of regional expenditures in comparison to regional income differentials. The West had the highest expenditures as a percent of after-tax

Table 37: U.S. BLS CE, Expenditures as a Percent of Income after Taxes, by Region of Residence, 2009

Item	All consumer units	Northeast	Midwest	South	West
Number of consumer units (in thousands)	120,847	22,411	27,536	43,819	27,080
Consumer unit characteristics:					
Income after taxes	$60,753	$68,986	$57,866	$56,795	$63,279
Average Annual Expenditures Seven Major Categories					
Food	$6,371.89	$6,974.90	$6,030.89	$5,943.84	$6,903.48
Housing	16,895.11	19,342.71	15,108.96	15,386.59	19,127.09
Apparel and services	1,725.11	1,781.90	1,461.38	1,786.00	1,843.83
Transportation	7,658.25	8,107.78	7,648.75	7,400.09	7,710.87
Health care	3,126.09	3,132.17	3,271.65	3,030.49	3,127.86
Entertainment	2,692.66	2,767.10	2,627.31	2,466.98	3,061.60
Personal insurance and pensions	5,471.07	6,012.51	5,339.70	5,015.12	5,894.36
Other Expenses*	5,127.05	5,749.03	5,062.04	4,719.93	5,335.60
Total Expenditures (calculated)	$49,067.23	$53,868.10	$46,550.68	$45,749.04	$53,004.69
Charitable Giving	$975.86	$702.50	$957.90	$1,027.93	$1,136.06
Total Expenditures Less Charitable Giving	$48,091.34	$53,165.61	$45,592.77	$44,721.11	$51,868.61
Calculated: Average Annual Expenditures Less Charitable Giving as % Income after Taxes	79%	77%	79%	79%	82%

Details in the above table may not compute to the numbers shown due to rounding.
*Other expenses include: "Alcoholic beverages; Personal care products and services; Reading; Education; Tobacco products and smoking supplies; Miscellaneous; Cash contributions."
"Cash contributions" includes: "Support for college students; Alimony expenditures; Child support expenditures; 'Charitable giving' (Cash contributions to charities and other organizations; Cash contributions to church, religious organizations; Cash contributions to educational institutions; Gift to non-CU members of stocks, bonds, and mutual funds); Cash contribution to political organizations."
Source: empty tomb, inc. 2011 analysis of U.S. BLS CE, 2009

income, and the second highest level of charitable giving as a percent of income in 2009. The Northeast had both the highest income and the highest level of expenditures, in terms of dollars. However, expenditures as a portion of income measured fourth out of the four regions. Meanwhile, the Northeast posted the lowest percent of income spent for cash contributions in 2009.

CE Charitable Giving and the Recession of 2007 through 2009. The first month of contraction in the declared recession of 2007-2009 was in January 2008. Available data now permits a review of the change in Americans' charitable giving from 2007 to 2008, and from 2008 to 2009.

The U.S. BLS CE series found that giving to "church, religious organizations" increased from 2007 to 2008 in inflation-adjusted 2005 dollars, while giving to the other CE categories of "charities and other organizations" and "education" declined.

The CE data presented in Table 38 indicated there was a decline, in inflation-adjusted dollars, to "church, religious organizations" from 2008 to 2009, while gifts to "charities and other organizations" increased. Gifts to "education" again declined. However, the increase to "charities and other organizations" from 2008 to 2009 was not as large as the decrease from 2007 to 2008. Further, the decline in giving to "church, religious organizations" from 2008 to 2009 was smaller than the increase from 2007 to 2008 in that category.[13]

Table 38: U.S. BLS CE, Cash Contributions for Charitable Giving, Inflation-Adjusted 2005 Dollars, 2007 through 2009

Item	Average Annual Expenditure: All Consumer Units 2007 Inflation-Adj. 2005 $	Average Annual Expenditure: All Consumer Units 2008 Inflation-Adj. 2005 $	Difference 2008-2007	Average Annual Expenditure: All Consumer Units 2009 Inflation-Adj. 2005 $	Difference 2009-2008
"Cash contributions to charities and other organizations"	$259.59	$155.42	-$104.16	$189.95	$34.52
"Cash contributions to church, religious organizations"	$644.18	$685.40	$41.22	$661.08	-$24.32
"Cash contributions to educational institutions"	$48.07	$41.91	-$6.17	$27.84	-$14.06
"Gifts to non-CU members of stocks, bonds, and mutual funds"	$58.56	$19.72	-$38.84	$11.44	-$8.28
Total	$1,010.40	$902.45	-$107.95	$890.31	-$12.13

Details in the above table may not compute to the numbers shown due to rounding.
Source: empty tomb, inc. 2011 analysis of U.S. BLS CE, 2007, 2008 and 2009.

The CE data shown in Table 38 may suggest that there was an increase in giving to other religious organizations, given the decline in church member giving in 2008 noted in Table 3 in chapter 1. For example, the Salvation Army Red Kettle campaign set new records in both 2008 and 2009.[14] Surveys by *Christianity Today* and the Evangelical Council for Financial Accountability both found that many Christian nonprofits did not report giving declines in the fourth quarter of 2008.[15] However, various reports indicated that the sustained nature of the recession took a toll on both churches and charitable organizations.[16]

General Information regarding the Consumer Expenditure Survey. One benefit of the CE is its unbiased data. The Mission Statement of the U.S. Department of Labor BLS reads:

> The **Bureau of Labor Statistics (BLS)** is the principal fact-finding agency for the Federal Government in the broad field of labor economics and statistics. The BLS is an independent national statistical agency that collects, processes, analyzes, and disseminates essential statistical data to the American public, the U.S. Congress, other Federal agencies, State and local governments, business, and labor. The BLS also serves as a statistical resource to the Department of Labor.

> BLS data must satisfy a number of criteria, including relevance to current social and economic issues, timeliness in reflecting today's rapidly changing economic conditions, accuracy and consistently high statistical quality, and impartiality in both subject matter and presentation.[17]

The BLS, among its various activities, is the source for the following indexes:

Producer price index (PPI)—This index, dating from 1890, is the oldest continuous statistical series published by BLS. It is designed to measure average changes in prices received by producers of all commodities, at all stages of processing, produced in the United States...

Consumer price indexes (CPI)—The CPI is a measure of the average change in prices over time in a "market basket" of goods and services purchased either by urban wage earners and clerical workers or by all urban consumers. In 1919, BLS began to publish complete indexes at semiannual intervals, using a weighting structure based on data collected in the expenditure survey of wage-earner and clerical-worker families in 1917-19 (BLS Bulletin 357, 1924)...

International price indexes—The BLS International Price Program produces export and import price indexes for nonmilitary goods traded between the United States and the rest of the world.[18]

Among the numerous applications of the BLS CE, the Survey is used for periodic revision of the CPI. Following are excerpted comments from a "Brief Description of the Consumer Expenditure Survey."

> The current CE program was begun in 1980. Its principal objective is to collect information on the buying habits of U.S. consumers. Consumer expenditure data are used in a variety of research endeavors by government, business, labor, and academic analysts. In addition, the data are required for periodic revision of the CPI.

> The survey, which is conducted by the U.S. Census Bureau for the Bureau of Labor Statistics, consists of two components: A diary or recordkeeping, survey…and an interview survey, in which expenditures of consumer units are obtained in five interviews conducted at 3-month intervals…

> Each component of the survey queries an independent sample of consumer units that is representative of the U.S. population…The Interview sample, selected on a rotating panel basis, surveys about 7,500 consumer units each quarter. Each consumer unit is interviewed once per quarter, for 5 consecutive quarters. Data are collected on an ongoing basis in 105 areas of the United States.[19]

The BLS, in commenting on the various functions of the CE, observed that, "Researchers use the data in a variety of studies, including those that focus on the spending behavior of different family types, trends in expenditures on various expenditure components including new types of goods and services, gift-giving behavior, consumption studies, and historical spending trends."[20]

Writing in the mid-1980s with reference to the then forthcoming CE-based revisions in the CPI, eminent business columnist Sylvia Porter remarked that the CPI is "the most closely watched, widely publicized and influential government statistic we have…"[21]

> ... business columnist Sylvia Porter remarked that the CPI is "the most closely watched, widely publicized and influential government statistic we have…"

In addition to the fact that the "CPI is used to adjust federal tax brackets for inflation,"[22] a glimpse into the wide-ranging, CE-based network of CPI usage in American culture is gained from the following information:

> The CPI is the most widely used measure of inflation and is sometimes viewed as an indicator of the effectiveness of government economic policy. It provides information about price changes in the Nation's economy to government, business, labor, and private citizens and is used by them as a guide to making economic decisions. In addition, the President, Congress, and the Federal Reserve Board use trends in the CPI to aid in formulating fiscal and monetary policies.

> The CPI and its components are used to adjust other economic series for price changes and to translate these series into inflation-free dollars. Examples of series adjusted by the CPI include retail sales, hourly and weekly earnings, and components of the National Income and Product Accounts…

> The CPI is often used to adjust consumers' income payments (for example, Social Security) to adjust income eligibility levels for government assistance and to automatically provide cost-of-living wage adjustments to millions of American

Table 39: **Giving to Religion, Based on the Commission on Private Philanthropy and Public Needs (Filer Commission) Benchmark Data for the Year of 1974, and Annual Changes in the Composite Denomination-Based Series, Aggregate Billions of Dollars and Per Capita Dollars as Percent of DPI,1968-2009**

Year	Denomination-Based Series Keyed to 1974 Filer Estimate	
	Billions, Dollars	Per Capita Dollars as % of DPI
1968	8.04	1.29%
1969	8.35	1.24%
1970	8.68	1.18%
1971	9.14	1.14%
1972	9.79	1.13%
1973	10.72	1.10%
1974	11.70	1.09%
1975	12.74	1.07%
1976	13.86	1.06%
1977	15.00	1.05%
1978	16.38	1.02%
1979	18.11	1.01%
1980	20.06	1.00%
1981	22.11	0.99%
1982	23.96	0.99%
1983	25.62	0.99%
1984	27.73	0.96%
1985	29.43	0.96%
1986	31.14	0.96%
1987	32.35	0.94%
1988	33.59	0.90%
1989	35.38	0.89%
1990	36.85	0.87%
1991	38.26	0.86%
1992	39.32	0.83%
1993	40.38	0.82%
1994	43.31	0.84%
1995	44.12	0.81%
1996	47.62	0.83%
1997	49.35	0.81%
1998	52.21	0.80%
1999	55.00	0.81%
2000	59.23	0.81%
2001	61.74	0.81%
2002	63.78	0.80%
2003	64.48	0.77%
2004	66.84	0.75%
2005	69.26	0.75%
2006	72.13	0.73%
2007	75.02	0.72%
2008	74.88	0.68%
2009	73.68	0.67%

Source: empty tomb, inc. analysis 2011;
Commission on Private Philanthropy and
Public Needs; *YACC*, adjusted series; U.S. BEA

workers. As a result of statutory action the CPI affects the income of about 80 million persons: the 51.6 million Social Security beneficiaries, about 21.3 million food stamp recipients, and about 4.6 million military and Federal Civil Service retirees and survivors. Changes in the CPI also affect the cost of lunches for 28.4 million children who eat lunch at school, while collective bargaining agreements that tie wages to the CPI cover over 2 million workers. Another example of how dollar values may be adjusted is the use of the CPI to adjust the Federal income tax structure. These adjustments prevent inflation-induced increases in tax rates, an effect called *bracket creep...*

Data from the Consumer Expenditure Survey conducted in 2001 and 2002, involving a national sample of more than 30,000 information families, provided detailed information on respondents' spending habits. This enabled BLS to construct the CPI market basket of goods and services and to assign each item in the market basket a weight, or importance, based on total family expenditures...[23]

How Much Do Americans Give? An Estimate of Aggregate Giving to Religion, 1968-2009.

An estimate of Americans' giving to religion was calculated for the 1968 to 2009 period. This estimate employed a 1974 benchmark estimate of $11.7 billion for giving to religion provided by the watershed Commission on Private Philanthropy and Public Needs of the 1970s, commonly referred to as the Filer Commission.[24]

The amount of change from year to year, calculated for 1968 to 1973 and also 1975 to 2009, was the annual percent change in the composite denomination set analyzed in other chapters of this report.[25] This calculation yielded a total of $8.04 billion given to religion in 1968, and $73.68 billion in 2009. Table 39 presents this data both in aggregate form, and as adjusted for population and income.

A Comparison of Three Sources.

Estimates of charitable giving vary by substantial margins. Three sources of information can be described and compared in an attempt to develop an overview of aggregate charitable giving patterns among Americans.

Consumer Expenditure Survey, 2009. As noted earlier, the U.S. Government BLS CE is a sophisticated research instrument that affects many aspects of American life. The CE is used to inform the CPI which, in turn, is used, among other purposes, to adjust federal tax brackets, Social Security benefits, and military retirement benefits for inflation. The CE's figure for charitable giving serves as a benchmark for the level of philanthropy in the U.S.

Table 40 presents CE data for the year 2009 in both "consumer unit" and aggregate values.[26] The CE data included the categories of: "Cash contributions to charities and other organizations"; "Cash contributions to church, religious organizations"; "Cash contributions to educational institutions"; and "Gifts to non-CU [Consumer Unit] members of stocks, bonds, and

Table 40: Living Individual Charitable Giving in the United States, U.S. BLS CE, 2009

Item	Average Annual Expenditure: All Consumer Units	Average Annual Expenditures Multiplied by 120,847 Consumer Units in 000's: Aggregated 000's of $	Item as % of Total
"Cash contributions to charities and other organizations"	$208.20	$25,160,345	21.3%
"Cash contributions to church, religious organizations"	$724.60	$87,565,736	74.3%
"Cash contributions to educational institutions"	$30.52	$3,688,250	3.1%
"Gifts to non-CU members of stocks, bonds, and mutual funds"	$12.54	$1,515,421	1.3%
Total	$975.86	$117,929,753	100%

Details in the above table may not compute to the numbers shown due to rounding.
Source: empty tomb, inc. 2011 analysis of U.S. BLS CE, 2009.

mutual funds." The annual average expenditure for the four categories in 2009 was $975.86 per CU. In 2009, there were 120.847 million CUs in the United States. The average annual expenditure amount of $975.86 multiplied by the number of consumer units, resulted in a 2009 estimate of total charitable giving of $117.9 billion.

Form 990 Series. A second source of information about charitable giving is found in the U.S. IRS Form 990 series. The Form 990 series must be filled out by charitable organizations with at least $25,000 in income, and by foundations. Form 990 data was obtained for the years 1989-2007, the latest year listed on the IRS Web site.[27]

Table 41 presents Form 990 data for the year 2007. As can be seen in that table, nonprofit charitable organizations in the United States reported on Form 990 that they received $157.3 billion in Direct Public Support in 2007, and another $31 billion from Indirect Public Support. The category of Indirect Public Support includes receipts from parent charitable organizations or groups like the United Way. A third category introduced in the 2007 Form 990 was support from Donor-Advised Funds, which totaled $10.9 billion in 2007. These three sources of support totaled $199.3 billion. Organizations with at least $25,000 but less than $100,000 in gross receipts were able to use Form 990-EZ to report receipts of $1.5 billion in 2007, for a Form 990 and Form 990-EZ contributions total of $201 billion.

A figure of $37.4 billion was added to the Public Support figure to account for giving in 2007 to private foundations.[28] Private foundations are required to file the IRS Form 990-PF. An adjusted total for giving to foundations was published in *Giving USA 2011*.

Based on the Form 990 series data, the combined total of $238.2 billion is the amount that charitable organizations received in 2007.

Form 990 could, but does not, request data for cash contributions by living individuals. One recommendation to improve the usefulness of information in the

Form 990 is that charitable organizations be required to report cash contributions from living individuals on a separate line of the form.

In order to compare the Form 990 series data with the CE data for cash contributions from living individuals for a 1989 to 2007 series, the Form 990 series information was adjusted. To obtain a figure for contributions from living individuals, estimates for giving by corporations and foundations, and receipts from bequests,[29] were subtracted from the "Gifts to charities and foundations" figure in Table 41. Giving by Living Individuals was thus estimated to be $161 billion in 2007.

The Form 990 data also includes "Other than cash contributions." Therefore, the value of "Other than cash contributions" was subtracted from the Form 990 data to allow a comparison of charitable cash contributions. As shown in Table 41, the IRS estimated that Americans deducted $58.7 billion in "Other than cash contributions" in 2007.[30] This amount was subtracted from the Giving by Living Individuals figure of $161 billion, resulting in a subtotal of $102 billion in 2007.

To develop an estimate of Form 990 organizational receipts that could be compared with the CE figure of what people gave required one additional step. Churches are not required to file Form 990. The CE estimate, however, included a measure for charitable contributions to churches and religious organizations. The following procedure was followed to develop an estimate for church giving to be added to the Form 990 Living Individuals contributions figure. The CE figure for 2007 "Cash contributions to church, religious organizations" was $82.3 billion. The present analysis employs a working estimate that giving to church represents about 90% of giving to religion, based in part on the work of two publications in this area.[31] Charitable organizations that combine religion with international or human services activities would be expected to file Form 990, and therefore these figures would already be included in the 2007 Form 990 Living Individual figure of $102.0 billion. Subtracting 10% from the 2007 CE figure for "church, religious organizations" of $82.3 billion resulted in an estimate of $74.1 billion given to churches in 2007. When this "giving to church" estimate was added to the estimated 2007 Form 990 "Living Individual Giving in cash, not including giving to church" figure of $102 billion, Total Cash Giving by Living Donors was calculated to be $176.1 billion in 2007, based on the Form 990 series information.

Table 41 presents the procedure and results in tabular form for 2007. A similar

Table 41: Living Individual Charitable Giving in the United States, Form 990 Series, 2007

	000's of $
Form 990	
Donor-Advised Funds	$10,902,610
Direct Public Support	$157,337,807
Indirect Public Support	+ $31,074,073
Total Public Support	$199,314,490
Form 990-EZ contributions	+ $1,465,577
Form 990 and 990-EZ contributions	$200,780,067
Gifts to foundations	+ $37,430,000
Gifts to charities and foundations	$238,210,067
Less gifts from other than Living Individuals	
Giving by Corporations	- $14,240,000
Giving by Foundations	- $40,000,000
Giving by Bequests	- $23,220,000
Giving by Living Individuals	$160,750,067
Less Individual "Other than cash contributions"	- $58,747,438
Living Individuals Giving in cash, not including giving to church	$102,002,629
Church: Individual Giving to church, adjusted for religious organizations included in Form 990	+ $74,059,465
Total Cash Giving by Living Donors	$176,062,094

Data may not compute to the numbers shown due to rounding.
Soorce: empty tomb, inc. 2011 analysis, IRS Form 990 series data, 2007, U.S. BLS CE 2007, Giving USA 2011

procedure was followed to calculate the Form 990 series figures for 1989-2006,[32] to compare with the CE series for those years.

Giving USA *Series.* A third source of charitable giving information, which is the most widely reported in the popular media, is from *Giving USA*, a series begun in the 1950s as an industry information compilation by a former vice president for public relations of a major professional fundraising firm.[33] The series has continued, and is currently prepared by a university-based philanthropy program, with active oversight by professional fundraisers. A major component of this series is based on deductions claimed on the IRS Individual Tax Returns. The *Giving USA 2011* Editorial Review Board was comprised of 11 principals or representatives of fundraising firms, nine of whom are affiliated with "member firms" of the 35 companies that make up the "Giving Institute: Leading Consultants to Non-Profits."[34] This report is acknowledged as a fundraising tool for those in the profession,[35] and the publication's most recent estimates of philanthropy are built on the pre-academic measurements in the historical series.

In order to compare a *Giving USA* estimate for individual giving with the CE data for the 1989-2007 period, the category of "Other than cash contributions" was subtracted from the *Giving USA* numbers. For the 2007 data, for example, the IRS $58.7 billion figure for "Other than cash contributions" that was subtracted from the Form 990 series data in the analysis above also was subtracted from the *Giving USA* figure. The *Giving USA* estimate for individual giving in 2007 was $233.1 billion.[36] When the $58.7 billion figure for "Other than cash contributions" was subtracted from that number, the result was a Total Individual Cash Giving figure of $174.4 billion.

Table 42: Living Individual Charitable Cash Giving in the United States, *Giving USA*, 2007

Data Year 2007	000's of $
Giving by Individuals	$233,110,000
Less Individual "Other than cash contributions"	- $58,747,438
Total Individual Cash Giving	$174,362,562

Source: empty tomb, inc. analysis 2011, Giving USA 2011, IRS

Table 42 presents the development of the *Giving USA* figure for 2007 to be used in a comparison with the CE and Form 990 series data. A similar procedure was used to calculate comparable *Giving USA* figures for 1989 through 2006.

A Comparison of Three Charitable Giving Estimates, 1989-2007. The CE charitable giving series is also available for the 1989-2007 period. However, the CE category of "Gifts to non-CU members of stocks, bonds, and mutual funds" was not available before the year 2000. Also, both the Form 990 series and the *Giving USA* series were adjusted to remove noncash donations; that category includes gifts of stocks, bonds and mutual funds. Therefore, the CE series for 1989-2007 used in Table 43 below does not include the category of "Gifts to non-CU members of stocks, bonds, and mutual funds." In contrast, the category of "Gifts to non-CU members of stocks, bonds, and mutual funds" is included in the discussion of 2009 CE charitable giving data elsewhere in this chapter.

As can be observed in Table 43, two of the sources of information on Total Charitable Giving in the U.S. differed from the CE by up to $54 billion in 2007. For example, the CE measurement for Total Individual Contributions in 2007 was calculated to be $122 billion dollars. Data from the Form 990 series reports filed

Table 43: Living Individual Charitable Cash Giving in the United States, A Comparison of the Consumer Expenditure Survey, Form 990 Series, and *Giving USA*, 1989-2007

Year	U.S. Bureau of Labor Statistics, Consumer Expenditure Survey (Calculated) millions of $	Form 990 Series (Adjusted) millions of $	*Giving USA* (Adjusted) millions of $
1989	$42,631	$49,875	$71,899
1990	$40,052	$52,558	$73,546
1991	$47,601	$55,614	$74,588
1992	$48,721	$56,842	$78,067
1993	$46,695	$57,680	$79,721
1994	$48,593	$56,032	$77,781
1995	$52,239	$77,101	$81,838
1996	$51,674	$75,578	$86,261
1997	$53,747	$70,895	$96,239
1998	$57,864	$89,687	$109,094
1999	$69,861	$92,783	$116,343
2000	$66,217	$85,833	$127,254
2001	$75,330	$104,296	$135,362
2002	$81,652	$101,547	$140,147
2003	$88,159	$116,413	$143,929
2004	$89,384	$120,779	$159,597
2005	$110,846	$142,049	$173,933
2006	$125,659	$171,725	$172,129
2007	$121,589	$176,062	$174,363

Source: empty tomb, inc. 2011 analysis

by recipient organizations, with an estimate of giving to religion added and other-than-cash contributions subtracted, resulted in a calculation of $176 billion received by nonprofits and foundations in 2007. Meanwhile, a *Giving USA* number for financial giving by living individuals in 2007, with other-than-cash contributions subtracted, was $174 billion, exceeding the benchmark CE figure by 43 percent.

The CE is a detailed U.S. BLS survey carried out on a quarterly basis.

The Form 990 series reports are completed by charitable organizations and foundations, based on their accounting records. Because the Form 990 does not presently ask for cash contributions from living individuals, only a calculated estimate for cash contributions by living individuals can be developed. If for any reason the estimates for giving by corporations, foundations, or bequests—the categories that are used to calculate a figure for Form 990 cash donations from living individuals—are not sound, that degree of error will impact the calculation. In this regard, it may be of interest to note that in 2007 the *Akron Beacon Journal* posted a short item with the lead sentence: "Warning: Analyzing trends in corporate philanthropy is far from a perfect science." Citing The Foundation Center, the Committee Encouraging Corporate Philanthropy, and *Giving USA*, the article noted corporate philanthropy in 2006 either increased 2.7% or 4.7%, or decreased 7.6%.[37]

The *Giving USA* series is based largely on deductions taken by Americans on their IRS Individual Income Tax Returns.

A CNN report on an annual poll conducted by the IRS Oversight Board found the number of Americans who indicated they cheated on their taxes had increased from 2008 to 2009, to 13% who thought it was acceptable, and to four percent for those who cheat "as much as possible." "Inflating the value of charitable donations and claiming personal expenses as business expenses" were both regarded as "common cheating tactics."[38]

A discussion of problems of noncash contributions estimates was presented in some detail in a previous edition in the *State of Church Giving* series.[39] Two comments may be relevant.

When he was Internal Revenue Service Commissioner, Mark W. Everson, in written testimony submitted to a Congressional hearing, in a section titled "Overstated Deductions" wrote that, "A common problem occurs when a taxpayer takes an improper or overstated charitable contribution deduction. This happens most frequently when the donation is of something other than cash or readily marketable securities."[40] In a *Chronicle of Philanthropy* article, Mr. Everson was quoted as suggesting that noncash deductions may be overstated by as much as $15 to $18 billion a year.[41]

The problems observed by Mark Everson apparently have not been resolved. A 2009 *Chronicle of Philanthropy* item reported:

> The misuse of nonprofit organizations to shield income or provide fake tax breaks has once again appeared on the Internal Revenue service's "dirty dozen," the agency's annual list of the top 12 tax scams in the United States. Most of the abuse stems from people giving money or property to charities but retaining too much control over the donations, or from people overestimating the value of donated property. In addition, the IRS says that an old scam—claiming private tuition payments as charitable donations—continues to grow.[42]

Scott Burns, business writer for *The Dallas Morning News* and Universal Press Syndicate columnist, considered the topic of "over-statement" of deductions in a 2009 column. A reader wrote in to say that a consultant had told the reader how he "can claim up to 10 percent of the total income as a write-off without proof or receipts." The reader wrote that he was pleased to be getting money back from the IRS, instead of paying taxes. He went on, "Our total income for 2005 was $101,083. My consultant has entered $9,224 for charities, $12,253 for job expenses and certain miscellaneous deductions, and $3,825 for meals and entertainment. I can tell you, those figures are exaggerated. But is it legal?"

Scott Burns began his reply with the comment, "Excuse me if I sound like a close relative of Goody Two Shoes, but do you really want to be a lying freeloader just because others are?" Burns also noted that, "The IRS has estimated unpaid taxes exceed $290 billion a year. The Treasury inspector general for tax administration thinks the IRS is low-balling the number." Burns advised the man to keep good records and deduct appropriately.[43]

The exchange in Scott Burns' column highlights some of the difficulties with using deductions from IRS Individual Income Tax Returns as a basis for calculating charitable giving in the U.S.

The results of this comparison of three estimates of individual giving suggest that the area of philanthropy measurement needs quality attention.

Recommendations for Improving the Measurements. Past editions in the *State of Church Giving* series have presented recommendations for improving the measurement of philanthropy in the United States.[44]

A Standing Commission on Nonprofits. One recent development has the potential for contributing to the objective reporting of philanthropy measurement. A 2010 news article indicated proposed legislation "…would create a bi-partisan, 16-member U.S. Council on Nonprofit Organizations and Community Solutions, headed up by an executive director, as well as the Interagency Working Group on Nonprofit Organizations and the Federal Government." According to a news report on the legislation, in addition to providing the means to improve communication between the nonprofit sector and the Federal Government regarding policies affecting the sector, the proposed bill provides that an "existing federal agency would be tasked to compile data on nonprofits and develop metrics for performance, establish reporting requirements, and expand information to better inform Congress on the impacts of nonprofit organizations."[45] This proposal hearkens back to the 1975 Filer Commission report, which recommended that the original United States Commission on Private Philanthropy and Public Needs become a standing commission.[46] Such a commission could, among other activities, help improve the measurement and reporting of philanthropic data.

Consumer Expenditure Survey as a Benchmark. Presently, the CE data has become an important source of information on the giving patterns of Americans. The CE, by reporting only cash contributions, avoids the problems inherent in using tax records, including cash and noncash deductions. It is recommended that the U.S. Department of Labor BLS CE be utilized as the unbiased, broad-gauge benchmark of living Americans' aggregate cash giving to charity, until such time as the U.S. IRS makes summary Form 990 living individual giving data available on an annual basis.

Form 990 Living Donor Category. With some adjustments, the Form 990 information could also provide a sound basis on which to answer the question of how much Americans give. The Form 990 would be improved by obtaining a measure of giving by living donors. As can be seen in Table 41, currently a variety of adjustments need to be made in order to obtain a working estimate of this number.

Faith-based or Secular Governance Choice. An important refinement would provide a more complete picture of philanthropy in America. Before selecting one of the ten core definition categories, the nonprofit organization could first indicate its form of governance as either "faith-based" or "secular." This identification could provide valuable information to help clarify the role of religion in the area of giving. Form 990 could also require that the organization define itself, first by selecting either faith-based or secular as the category of governance, and then the specific activity described by one or more of the National Taxonomy of Exempt Organizations core codes.

The importance of being able to classify giving by both faith-based or secular categories, as well as by specific activity codes can be seen from an observation in *Giving USA 1990*'s discussion of "Giving to Religion." That issue of *Giving USA*, edited by Nathan Weber, noted, "Further, among many religious groups, giving to religion is considered identical with giving to human services, health care, etc., when such services are administered by organizations founded by the religious groups" (p. 187). An analysis of the

Figure 20: Account Classification Application with Faith-based/ Secular Governance Option Included

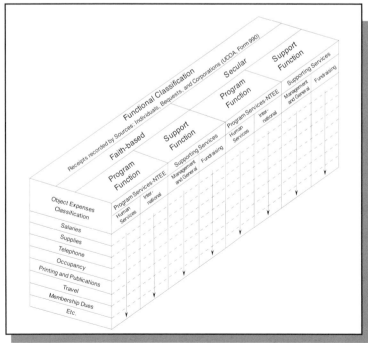

Source: Adaptation of graphic in Sumariwalla and Levis   empty tomb, inc. graphic 2001

CE data for 2009 found that donors identified 74% of their charitable donations as given to churches and religious organizations. That figure compares to an estimate of *Giving USA 2011* 2009 giving to religion as a percent of individual giving of 48%.[47] The extent of this variation suggests that the definitions of what constitutes a religious organization differ broadly among the charitable giving estimate sources.

In their book on the Unified Chart of Accounts, Russy D. Sumariwalla and Wilson C. Levis reproduced a graphic originally prepared by United Way of America that depicts how the account classification would appear in practical application.[48] For purposes of the present discussion, that graphic was adapted to include a statement about receipts classification, and to describe at what point the choice of faith-based or secular governance would be included in the accounting hierarchy (see Figure 20).

Associated Press Reports on Philanthropy. The power of the press in influencing the opinions of Americans was noted as a factor in a discussion of the "illusion of potential" in a 2010 book, *The Invisible Gorilla, And Other Ways Our Intuitions Deceive Us*. The authors, Christopher Chabris and Daniel Simons, state that the "*illusion of potential* leads us to think that vast reservoirs of untapped mental ability exists in our brains, just waiting to be accessed."[49] They give two examples of myths that became quickly accepted by the general public enamored with the illusion of potential. The media's role in popularizing myths was considered, and the following observation was made: "The media gives tremendous weight and coverage to the *first* study published on a research question, and essentially ignores all of those that come later"[50] (emphasis in original).

Consider that other researchers could not reproduce the initial finding that listening to certain types of music makes one more intelligent, popularly known as the "Mozart Effect." Wide media reports of the initial research helped establish the legend, but less attention was given to the follow-up studies that contradicted the initial findings. Further, although the research was conducted on adult subjects, the idea that music could affect infants was also reported in the media. Chabris and Simons note, "Until we each had our first child, we didn't realize the extent to which the Mozart-for-babies myth has permeated the child-care industry. Intelligent, highly educated friends sent us toys that included—as a matter of routine, not a special feature—a 'Mozart' setting that played classical music."[51]

Chabris and Simons also regard as a myth subliminal messages on movie screens impacting concessions purchases. They use as an example an "experiment" in the 1950s. The researcher reported that flashing subliminal messages in a movie theater increased popcorn and soft drink sales, helping to establish in the public's mind the idea of subliminal marketing. However, years later the "researcher" confessed that the "research" was fabricated as a way to increase business for his advertising firm. Yet a survey by Chabris and Simons found that 76 percent of respondents believed in subliminal marketing.[52]

These examples indicate that the media's presentation of information to the public can have an important role in how the public views an issue. The examples also demonstrate the media's initial treatment of a topic may define that topic for the public, independent of the relevant facts.

"The media gives tremendous weight and coverage to the *first* study published on a research question, and essentially ignores all of those that come later."

Aspects of the Associated Press' presentation of philanthropy giving in the United States may be regarded as an example.

The Associated Press (AP) routinely leads with the gross aggregate total of the annual *Giving USA* report. This aggregate number includes not only giving by individuals, but also includes corporate donations, bequests from dead people, and gifts to foundations. The AP then routinely notes the change in this aggregate number from the previous year. However, this comparison across years does not take into account changes in either population or income.

Rarely does the media provide numbers to the public without placing those numbers in a larger context of population and/or the economy. Consider that the press routinely reports the crime rate, the unemployment rate, the savings rate, the poverty rate, the on-time flight rate, the unpaid mortgage rate, and the Consumer Confidence Index. In each case, numbers are not reported as aggregates, but rather are put into context of the larger population so that the reader has some basis to evaluate the meaning. For example, a major factor in the economic recovery is the creation of new jobs. When discussing job creation and the economic recovery, the media has routinely connected the number of jobs needed to changes of the population, as indicated by the formulation that it takes 125,000 new jobs a month to keep up with growth in the work force.[53]

Researchers considering the status of religion in the world offered another example of the importance of changes in population:

> An interesting overall comment is that virtually all activities of Christian churches, missions, denominations, and communions are growing numerically and expanding. This is usually interpreted as showing the success of church programs. In fact, however, everybody's programs are all expanding fast because since AD 1800 populations everywhere have been expanding rapidly and now stand at 372,000 births a day.

> In fact, the key to understanding religious trends is the ability to compare growth rates of religious variables with secular ones. This is the only way to know if a religion is growing faster or slower than the general population.[54]

Good reporting seems to include the responsibility of placing numbers in the larger context so the reader will understand the importance of the figures being quoted.

Yet the media emphasize aggregate charitable giving numbers that are independent of either population or the economy.

For example, once again in 2011, the AP article that appeared on the release of the new *Giving USA* report reflected the *Giving USA* press release focus on the aggregate billions of dollars raised. Further, the lead emphasized the percent change in those aggregate billions of dollars from the previous year: "Total contributions from individuals, corporations and foundations were estimated at $290.9 billion, up from $280.3 billion in 2009, the Giving USA Foundation reported. That represented growth of 3.8 percent in current dollars and 2.1 percent in inflation-adjusted dollars."[55]

In fact, when population and changes in the economy were taken into account, individual giving as a percent of DPI declined 0.4% and total giving as a percent of the Gross Domestic Product (GDP) declined 0.1%.

However, this comparison across years does not take into account changes in either population or income.

Nevertheless, other media, such as *The Washington Post*, *The New York Times*, and *The Wall Street Journal* also popularized the idea that charitable giving had increased, by leading their stories with the report on aggregate giving. *The Washington Post* suggested the increase was a sign of economic rebound.[56]

With the exception of coverage in 2008, different AP reporters' lead focus did not adjust the announced aggregate data for population and economy changes. As a result, the articles announced, in 2002 through 2007, an increase in aggregate current dollars, even though a decrease has occurred when population and the economy are taken into account. For 2009 and 2010, the lead focus was on aggregate decrease. The focus again returned to aggregate increase in the 2011 news report.

Consider that the change from 2003-2004 in total contributions was reported as an increase of 5.0 percent. When those billions of dollars were adjusted to a percent of GDP, there was actually a decline of 1.6%. Individual giving that year, as a percent of Disposable (after-tax) Personal Income (DPI), also declined 1.6%

The change in total contributions aggregate billions of dollars from 2007-2008 was reported as -2%. When those billions were adjusted to a percent of GDP, the decline was -5.2%. Individual giving that year, adjusted to a percent of DPI, was -7%.

The change from 2008-2009 was reported as a decline of 3.6%. When adjusted for GDP, the decline in total contributions was actually less, at 2.3%, and also less in individual giving adjusted for DPI, at 1.4%.

According to the Urban Institute, the nonprofit sector accounts for "5 percent of GDP, 8 percent of the economy's wages, and nearly 10 percent of jobs."[57]

Yet reporting about philanthropy in the U.S. is not put into context of the giving rate, but rather is left as the total amount of aggregate dollars.

The American people have a right to know how their charitable giving rates are changing from year to year. The measure that validly conveys that information is the category of individual giving as a percent of income, which adjusts the aggregate numbers for changes in both population and income. As illustrated in earlier chapters in this volume, church giving appears different when considered in aggregate form, and when giving is considered per member and as a portion of an after-tax income.

Tables and Chart regarding the Disparity between Associated Press Reports on Aggregate Charitable Giving Levels, and Giving Adjusted for Population and Income. As pointed out above, the AP charitable giving articles' lead routinely with an emphasis on the generally upbeat tone of the *Giving USA* press releases in terms of aggregate billions of dollars raised, unadjusted for population and income.

As shown in Table 44, an analysis of AP reporting of *Giving USA* releases for the past ten years found the following. In seven years, 2002, 2003, 2004, 2005, 2006, 2007, and 2011, the AP article released nationally and internationally led with a percent change that indicated an increase in total charitable giving from the previous year. Yet, when a basic adjustment for changes in U.S. population and economic growth was made to the *Giving USA* aggregate numbers, individual giving as a percent of DPI declined rather than increased in six of the seven years, and total giving as a percent of U.S. GDP declined in all seven years.

The American people have a right to know how their charitable giving rates are changing from year to year.

Table 44: **Associated Press Reported Aggregate Changes, Americans' Individual Giving Changes as a Percent of DPI, and Total Giving Changes as a Percent of GDP, 2000-2009, from Previous Year's Base: Data from *Giving USA* 2002, 2003, 2004, 2005, 2006, 2007, 2008, 2009, 2010, and 2011 Editions**

Giving USA Edition	*Giving USA* Data Year Interval	AP: First Percent Change from Previous Year Listed in AP Story: Aggregate Bil. $[58]	Per Capita Individual Giving as % of Per Capita DPI: % Change from Base Year[59]	Total Giving as % of GDP: % Change from Base Year[60]	AP Headline and AP First Mention of Percent Change	AP Byline and AP Dateline
2002	2000-01	0.5%	-2.6%	-2.8%	"2001 Charitable Giving Same As 2000" "Total giving by individuals, corporations and other groups amounted to $212 billion, up 0.5 percent from 2000 before inflation is figured in…"	Helena Payne, Associated Press Writer, New York
2003	2001-02	1.0%	-4.7%	-2.5%	"Donations Held Steady in 2002" "Giving rose 1 percent last year to $240.92 billion from $238.46 billion in 2001…"	Mark Jewell, The Associated Press, Indianapolis
2004	2002-03	2.8%	-2.0%	-1.9%	"Charitable Giving Rises in 2003" "…the survey showed a 2.8 percent increase over 2002, when giving amounted to $234.1 billion"	Kendra Locke, The Associated Press, New York
2005	2003-04	5.0%	-1.6%	-1.6%	"Charitable Giving Among Americans Rises" "Americans increased donations to charity by 5 percent in 2004…"	Adam Geller, AP Business Writer, New York
2006	2004-05	6.1%	2.0%	-0.3%	"Charitable Giving in U.S. Nears Record Set at End of Tech Boom" "The report released Monday by the Giving USA foundation estimates that in 2005 Americans gave $260.28 billion, a rise of 6.1 percent…"	Vinnee Tong, AP Business Writer, New York
2007	2005-06	1.0%	-0.9%	-2.0%	"Americans Give Nearly $300 Billion to Charities in 2006, Set a New Record" "Donors contributed an estimated $295.02 billion in 2006, a 1 percent increase when adjusted for inflation, up from $283.05 billion in 2005."	Vinnee Tong, AP Business Writer, New York
2008	2006-07	"remained at…" [0.0% implied]	-2.8%	-1.0%	"Americans Are Steady in Donations to Charity" "Donations by Americans to charities remained at 2.2 percent of gross domestic product in 2007…"	Vinnee Tong, AP Business Writer, New York
2009	2007-08	-2.0%	-7.0%	-5.2%	"Amid Meltdown, Charitable Gifts in US Fell in 2008" "Charitable giving by Americans fell by 2 percent in 2008 as the recession took root…"	David Crary, AP National Writer [AP National Reporting Team: Family and Relationships], New York
2010	2008-09	-3.6%	-1.4%	-2.3%	"2009 Charitable Giving Falls 3.6 Percent in US" "Charitable giving fell by 3.6 percent last year as Americans continued to struggle with the recession…"	Caryn Rousseau, Associated Press Writer, Chicago
2011	2009-10	3.8%	-0.4%	-0.1%	"Charitable giving in US rebounds a bit after drop" "That represented growth of 3.8 percent in current dollars and 2.1 percent in inflation-adjusted dollars."	David Crary, AP National Writer, New York

Source: Associated Press, USBEA, *Giving USA*, empty tomb, inc. analysis 2011

Table 45: *Giving USA* **Executive Statement or Foreword First Mention of Percent Change and** *Giving USA* **Attribution**

Giving USA Executive Statement or Foreword First Mention of Percent Change	*Giving USA* Attribution
"The 0.5 percent increase in giving for 2001 is more attributable to the economy than to crisis."	(Indianapolis, Ind.: AAFRC Trust for Philanthropy, 2002), p. 1 Executive Statements: Statement of Chair, AAFRC Trust for Philanthropy: Leo P. Arnoult, CFRE, Chair, AAFRC Trust for Philanthropy
"Giving in 2002 is estimated to be $240.92 billion, growing one percent over the new estimate for 2001 of $238.46 billion."	(Indianapolis, Ind.: AAFRC Trust for Philanthropy, 2003), p. ii Foreword: Leo P. Arnoult, CFRE, Chair, AAFRC Trust for Philanthropy John J. Glier, Chair, AAFRC Eugene R. Tempel, Ed.D., CFRE, Executive Director, The Center on Philanthropy at Indiana University
"Giving in 2003 grew 2.8 percent over the revised estimate for 2002 of $234.09 billion."	(Glenview, Ill.: AAFRC Trust for Philanthropy, 2004), p. ii Foreword: Henry (Hank) Goldstein, CFRE, Chair, *Giving USA* Foundation John J. Glier, Chair, AAFRC Eugene R. Tempel, Ed.D., CFRE, Executive Director, The Center on Philanthropy at Indiana University
"Giving grew at the highest rate since 2000, 5.0 percent over a revised estimate of $236.73 billion for 2003 (2.3 percent adjusted for inflation)."	(Glenview, Ill.: AAFRC Trust for Philanthropy, 2005), p. ii Foreword: Henry (Hank) Goldstein, CFRE, Chair, *Giving USA* Foundation™, President, The Oram Group, Inc., New York, New York C. Ray Clements, Chair, American Association of Fundraising Counsel, CEO and Managing Member, Clements Group, Salt Lake City, Utah Eugene R. Tempel, Ed.D., CFRE, Executive Director, The Center on Philanthropy at Indiana University, Indianapolis, Indiana
"The combined result is that charitable giving rose to $260.28 billion, showing growth of 6.1 percent (2.7 percent adjusted for inflation)."	(Glenview, Ill.: *Giving USA* Foundation, 2006), p. ii Foreword: Richard T. Jolly, Chair, *Giving USA* Foundation™, George C. Ruotolo, Jr., CFRE, Acting Chair, Giving Institute: Leading Consultants to Non-Profits Eugene R. Tempel, Ed.D., CFRE, Executive Director, The Center on Philanthropy at Indiana University
"In constant [*sic*] dollars, the increase was 4.2 percent over 2005; in inflation-adjusted numbers, the increase was 1.0 percent."	(Glenview, Ill.: *Giving USA* Foundation, 2007), p. ii Foreword: Richard T. Jolly, Chair, *Giving USA* Foundation™, George C. Ruotolo, Jr., CFRE, Chair, Giving Institute: Leading Consultants to Non-Profits Eugene R. Tempel, Ed.D., CFRE, Executive Director, The Center on Philanthropy at Indiana University
"The estimates for 2007 indicate that giving rose by 3.9 percent over the previous year (1 percent adjusted for inflation), to reach a record $306.39 billion."	(Glenview, Ill.: *Giving USA* Foundation, 2008), p. ii Foreword: Del Martin, CFRE, Chair, *Giving USA* Foundation™, George C. Ruotolo, Jr., CFRE, Chair, Giving Institute: Leading Consultants to Non-Profits Eugene R. Tempel, Ed.D., CFRE, Executive Director, The Center on Philanthropy at Indiana University
"This is a drop of 2 percent in current dollars (-5.7 percent adjusted for inflation), compared to 2007."	(Glenview, Ill.: *Giving USA* Foundation, 2009), p. ii Foreword: Del Martin, CFRE, Chair, *Giving USA* Foundation™, publisher of *Giving USA* Nancy L. Raybin, Chair, Giving Institute: Leading Consultants to Non-Profits Patrick M. Rooney, Ph.D., Executive Director, The Center on Philanthropy at Indiana University
"Total charitable giving fell 3.6 percent (-3.2 percent adjusted for inflation) in 2009, to an estimated $303.75 billion."	*Giving USA 2010;* Created: 6/8/10; published by *Giving USA* Foundation, Glenview, Ill.; <www.givingusa2010.org/downloads.php>; p. ii of 6/9/2010 printout. Foreword: Edith H. Falk, Chair, *Giving USA* Foundation Nancy L. Raybin, Chair, Giving Institute: Leading Consultants to Non-Profits Patrick M. Rooney, Ph.D., Executive Director, The Center on Philanthropy at Indiana University
"It is promising to see the 2010 inflation-adjusted increase of 2.1 percent after two years of such steep declines."	*Giving USA 2011;* Created: 6/20/11; published by Giving USA Foundation, Chicago, Ill.; <www.givingusareports.org/downloads.php>; p. i of 6/20/2011 printout. Foreword: Edith H. Falk, Chair, Giving USA Foundation Thomas W. Mesaros, CFRE, Chair, Giving Institute: Leading Consultants to Non-Profits Patrick M. Rooney, Ph.D., Executive Director, The Center on Philanthropy at Indiana University

Source: Associated Press, USBEA, *Giving USA*, empty tomb, inc. analysis 2011

This pattern of disparity between AP reports on aggregate billions of dollars raised, and the complete picture of changes in charitable giving patterns, can be observed in Table 44, which also includes the text from the related AP release. This AP text can be compared with the first mention of percent change included in the related editions in the *Giving USA* series, also presented in Table 45.

Figure 21 illustrates the disparity in the category of percent changes in aggregate total charitable giving reported by the AP and the same Total Contributions aggregate billions adjusted to a percent of GDP. In addition, the percent change from one year to the next for each *Giving USA* edition's Individual giving figure is presented as a portion of DPI.

The observation may be made that the Associated Press apparently chooses to highlight an industry's interpretation of its own work in a relatively uncritical fashion that de-emphasizes essential elements of the whole truth.

Total current dollar philanthropy as presented by *Giving USA*, unadjusted by population and income, has increased, that is, "set a new record" each year for 53 years from the first edition in 1955 through the 2008 edition, with qualification obtaining only for the year 1987.[61] This consistent pattern of growth is not surprising in light of the fact that both U.S. population and U.S. per capita DPI in current dollars increased each year from 1955 through 2007, the period under consideration.[62]

When correspondence was sent to then-Associated Press Vice President and Senior Managing Editor Mike Silverman, describing this topic, he responded in a May 8, 2009, letter: "You make some interesting points about how we might put these reports into better perspective for our readers." Note in Table 44 that Associated Press business writer Vinee Tong led in the 2009 article on the release of *Giving USA 2009* with the aggregate billions of charitable dollars as a percent of GDP, which accounted for changes in population. This perspective was an improvement in the reported information provided to the public, even though the percent change in Total Giving as a percent of GDP between 2006 and 2007 was actually -1.0%.

However, the 2009 AP article on the release

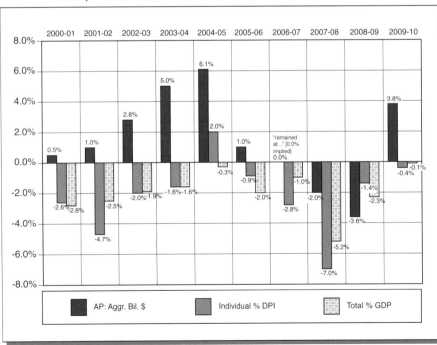

Figure 21: Associated Press Reported Aggregate Changes, Americans' Individual Giving Changes as a Percent of DPI, and Total Giving Changes as a Percent of GDP, 2000-2010, from Previous Year's Base: Data from *Giving USA* 2002, 2003, 2004, 2005, 2006, 2007, 2008, 2009, 2010, and 2011 Editions

Source: Associated Press; *Giving USA* data; U.S. BEA data; empty tomb analysis   empty tomb, inc. 2011

of *Giving USA 2009* was written by someone listed on the AP Web site as reporting on Family and Relationships, and the lead returned to the standard aggregate current dollar change. It may be reasonable that the writer focused on the decrease in aggregate current dollars of -2% as newsworthy, given that only in 1987 did such a decline also occur. In the fifteenth paragraph of a 16-paragraph story, the AP writer did note that when adjusted for inflation, aggregate total charitable giving was down 5.7%. However, in the sixteenth paragraph, when discussing individual giving, the writer again referred to aggregate dollars declining 2.7%, and did not present individual giving as a percent of DPI, which measure was down 7%. Also, there was no discussion of the fact that total charitable giving, as a percent of GDP, was down 5.2% from 2007 to 2008. Both of the latter measures would have placed the charitable giving numbers into the broader context of the economy, including changes in population, and helped the reader understand rates of giving rather than only gross amounts.

In 2010, an AP writer from Chicago emphasized a decline in aggregate dollars of -3.6% from 2008-2009, which, as noted above, was more than the decline measured when adjusted for population and changes in the economy.

...religion plays a vital role in the practice of philanthropy in the United States.

As noted, the 2011 story emphasized an aggregate increase of 3.8%, which was in fact a decline in both individual and total giving when population and change in the economy were taken into account.

The nonprofit area constitutes a large enough sector of the American economy that the philanthropy practices supporting it deserve the quality of reporting applied to other economic sectors, including adjustment for population and income to provide information about changes in the rate of giving.

Summary

Individuals give to charity for a variety of reasons. When given the opportunity to categorize their own donations in 2009, Americans indicated that 74% of their giving was to "churches, religious organizations." This finding suggests that religion plays a vital role in the practice of philanthropy in the United States.

The comparison of various estimates of giving in the U.S. suggest that the measurement of philanthropy could be improved. Currently, the U.S. Bureau of Labor Statistics Consumer Expenditure Survey serves as a benchmark in providing unbiased information about giving levels in the United States.

Notes for Chapter 7

[1] U.S. Department of Labor, Bureau of Labor Statistics; "Frequently Asked Questions"; n.d.; <http://www.bls.gov/cex/csxfaqs.htm>; p. 2 of 5/28/2005 10:32 AM printout.

[2] The above estimate of $117.93 billion is likely a high measure of charitable giving insofar as it includes all of the $1.52 billion in the category, "Gift[s] to non-CU members of stocks, bonds, and mutual funds." This attribution thus assumes that all of the $1.52 billion given in this category went to charitable organizations, although the CE does not allocate the funds of this category between charitable and non-charitable recipients.

³ Americans' charitable giving was calculated by multiplying the 120,847,000 "Number of consumer units" by each of the average annual consumer unit contributions for 2009, the components of which were $208.20 ("charities and other organizations"), $724.60 ("church, religious organizations"), $30.52 ("educational institutions"), and $12.54 ("Gifts to non-CU members of stocks, bonds, and mutual funds"). The resultant sum of the aggregated components, $975.86, yielded a total giving amount of $117.93 billion. The "Cash contributions to church, religious organizations" amount, therefore, was calculated by multiplying the number of consumer units by $724.60 yielding an amount of $87.6 billion for 2009. Religion as a percent of the total was calculated by dividing $87.6 billion by $117.93 billion, yielding 74%. "Cash contributions" items not included in the above calculations for charitable contributions were "Support for college students (Sec.19); Alimony expenditures (Sec. 19); Child support expenditures (Sec. 19); Cash contribution to political organizations; Other cash gifts." Data source: U.S. Department of Labor, Bureau of Labor Statistics, "Table 1800. Region of residence: Average annual expenditures and characteristics, Consumer Expenditure Survey, 2009" [Item detail]; StTable1800Region2009. pdf; Created 8/31/2010 7:04 AM; unnumbered pp. 1, 17 & 28 of 4/18/2011 printout.

⁴ Data sources: U.S. Department of Labor, Bureau of Labor Statistics, "Table 1202. Income before taxes: Average annual expenditures and characteristics, Consumer Expenditure Survey, 2009" [Item detail]; StTable1200Income2009.pdf; Created 8/31/2010 6:53 PM; unnumbered pp. 1, 17, & 30 of 4/18/2011 printout; and "Table 2301. Higher Income before taxes: Average annual expenditures and characteristics, Consumer Expenditure Survey, 2009" [Item detail]; StTable2301HiInc2009.pdf; Created 8/31/2010 7:23 AM; unnumbered pp. 1, 17, & 29 of 4/18/2011 printout.

⁵ Information from the outlier "Less than $5,000" bracket, while part of the "All consumer units" data, was not otherwise included in the present analysis.

⁶ Consumer Expenditure Survey "Frequently Asked Questions"; U.S. Department of Labor, Bureau of Labor Statistics, Consumer Expenditure Surveys, Branch of Information and Analysis; Last Modified Date: March 17, 2005; <http://www.bls.gov/cex/csxfaqs.htm>; p. 7 of 5/28/05 10:32 AM printout.

⁷ Data source: U.S. Department of Labor, Bureau of Labor Statistics, "Table 1300. Age of reference person: Average annual expenditures and characteristics, Consumer Expenditure Survey, 2009" [Item detail]; <StTable1300Age2009.pdf>; Created 8/31/2010 6:54AM; unnumbered pp. 1, 17 & 29 of 4/18/2011 printout.

⁸ Data source: U.S. Department of Labor, Bureau of Labor Statistics, "Table 1800, Region of residence: Average annual expenditures and characteristics, Consumer Expenditure Survey, 2009" [Item detail]; <StTable1800Region.2009.pdf>; Created 8/31/2010 7:04 AM; unnumbered pp. 1, 17 & 28 of 4/18/2011 printout.

⁹ The significance levels noted in the text reflected a z statistic having an absolute value greater than 2. In addition, it may be noted that the larger size of contribution in the West for "total contributions" compared to the Northeast had an absolute value greater than 1.96. The larger size of contributions in the West for "charities and other organizations" compared to that of the Midwest also had an absolute value greater than 1.96.

¹⁰ See Adelle M. Banks, RNS, "God Big in South, Not So Much in New England and Pacific Northwest," *Christian Century*, March 20, 2009, p. 15. Also, Jennifer Riley; "Report: Top 10 Most Religious States in America"; Christian Post; 2/2/2009; <http://www.christianpost.com/Society/Polls_reports/2009/02/report-top-10-most-religious-states-in-america-02/index.html>; pp. 1-2 of 2/3/2009 8:16 AM printout.

¹¹ An Associated Press article titled "Denominations Target Spiritually Cold Region," appearing in *Champaign (Ill.) News-Gazette*, October 30, 2009, p. B-7.

¹² Data source: U.S. Department of Labor, Bureau of Labor Statistics, "Table 1800, Region of residence: Average annual expenditures and characteristics, Consumer Expenditure Survey, 2009" [Item Detail]; unnumbered pp. 1, 5, 10, 12-14, 16-17, & 28 of 4/18/2011 printout.

¹³ Data source: 2007 Data: U.S. Department of Labor, Bureau of Labor Statistics, "Table 1800. Region of residence: Average annual expenditures and characteristics, Consumer Expenditure Survey, 2007" [Item detail]; StTable1800Region2007.pdf; Created 11/13/2008 9:12 AM; unnumbered pp. 1, 17 & 29 of 3/25/2009 printout.

2008 Data: U.S. Department of Labor, Bureau of Labor Statistics, "Table 1800. Region of residence: Average annual expenditures and characteristics, Consumer Expenditure Survey, 2008" [Item detail]; StTable1800Region2008.pdf; Created 9/1/2009 2:32 PM; unnumbered pp. 1, 17 & 29 of 4/23/2010 printout.

¹⁴ "One of the nation's largest Christian charities announced Wednesday that it broke its Red Kettle record for the sixth straight year…" Jennifer Riley; "Salvation Army Breaks Red Kettle Record with $142 Million"; Christian

Post; 2/24/2011; <http://www.christianpost.com/news/salvation-army-breaks-red-kettle-record-with-142-million-49144/>; p. 1 of 2/24/2011 8:51 AM printout.

[15] John Kennedy, "The Not-for-Profit Surge," *Christianity Today*, May 2009, pp. 22-27. Also, Aaron J. Leichman; "Survey: 7 in 10 Evangelical Ministries Report Little, No Loss in Donations"; Christian Post; 2/25/2009; <http://www.christianpost.com/Society/ngo/2009/02/survey-7-in-10-evangelical-ministries-report-little-no-loss-in-donations-25/print.html>; pp. 1-2 of 2/25/2009 7:19 PM printout.

[16] See for example: LifeWay Research; "Churches Not Yet Enjoying Economic Rebound"; Christian Post; 1/14/2010; <http://www.christianpost.com/article/20100114/churches-not-yet-enjoying-economic-rebound/print.html>; p.1-2 of 1/14/2010 2:47 PM printout. Christian Leadership Alliance; "Economic Outlook Executive Summary, The Recession's Impact on Christian Nonprofit Organizations"; Christian Leadership Alliance; June 2009; <http://www.christianleadershipalliance.org/store/inc/economic_outlook_research_executive_summary.pdf>; Printed 7/6/2009, 1:48 PM; Ben Gose, "93% of Charities Feel Effects of Recession," *The Chronicle of Philanthropy*, December 10, 2009, p. 1.

[17] "Mission Statement"; U.S. Department of Labor, Bureau of Labor Statistics; Last Modified Date: October 16, 2001; <http://www.bls.gov/bls/blsmissn.htm>; p. 1 of 8/15/05 4:59 PM printout.

[18] U.S. Census Bureau, *Statistical Abstract of the United States: 2006*, 125th edition; published 2005; <http://www.census.gov/prod/2005pubs/06statab/prices.pdf>; pp. 479, 481 of 5/31/06 printout.

[19] "Consumer Expenditures in 2004"; Report 992; U.S. Department of Labor, Bureau of Labor Statistics; April 2006; <http://www.bls.gov/cex/csxann04.pdf>; pp. 4-5 of 5/30/06 printout.

[20] Consumer Expenditure Survey "Frequently Asked Questions"; U.S. Department of Labor, Bureau of Labor Statistics, Consumer Expenditure Surveys, Branch of Information and Analysis; Last Modified Date: March 17, 2005; <http://www.bls.gov/cex/csxfaqs.htm>; p. 2 of 5/28/05 10:32 AM printout.

[21] Sylvia Porter, "Out-of-Date Consumer Price Index to Be Revised in '87," a "Money's Worth" column appearing in *Champaign (Ill.) News-Gazette,* January 9, 1985, sec. D, p. 3.

[22] "Price Index Undergoes Statistical Adjustment," an Associated Press (Washington) article appearing in the *Champaign (Ill.) News-Gazette,* April 19, 1998, sec. C, p. 1.

[23] Consumer Price Indexes "Addendum to Frequently Asked Questions"; U.S. Department of Labor, Bureau of Labor Statistics, Division of Consumer Prices and Price Indexes; Last Modified Date: March 28, 2005; <http://www.bls.gov/cpi/cpiadd.htm#2_1>; pp. 1-2 of 5/31/06 10:54 AM printout.

[24] Gabriel Rudney, "The Scope of the Private Voluntary Charitable Sector," Research Papers Sponsored by The Commission on Private Philanthropy and Public Needs, Vol. 1, History, Trends, and Current Magnitudes, (Washington, DC: Department of the Treasury, 1977), p. 136. The nature of these numbers, specifically whether they are for giving to church only or combine giving to church and religious organizations, would benefit from a review in light of the relatively recent CE introduction of the "church, religious organizations" category.

[25] For this comparison, the composite data set of denominations was adjusted for missing data.

[26] U.S. Department of Labor, Bureau of Labor Statistics; "Table 1800.Region of Residence: Average annual expenditures and characteristics, Consumer Expenditure Survey, 2009"; unnumbered pp. 1, 17 & 28.

[27] See Appendix B-6 for sources of Form 990 series detail.

[28] Giving USA Foundation (2011); *Giving USA 2011*; Created and Modified: 6/20/11 2:56:09 AM; published by Giving USA Foundation, Chicago, Ill.; <www.givingusareports.org/downloads.php>; p. 53 of 6/20/2011 printout.

[29] *Giving USA 2011*, p. 53.

[30] "Charitable contributions deduction: Other than cash contributions": "Table 3. Returns with Itemized Deductions: Itemized Deductions by Type and by Size of Adjusted Gross Income, Tax Year 2007"; download 07in03id.xls; IRS; <http://www.irs.gov/pub/irs-soi/07in03id.xls>; p. 3 of 4/28/2010 4:48 PM printout.

[31] See Appendix B-6 for 2007 CE data source. "...church represents 90% of giving to religion...": Dean R. Hoge, Charles Zech, Patrick McNamara, Michael J. Donahue, *Money Matters: Personal Giving in American Churches* (Louisville: Westminster John Knox Press, 1996), p.49; Jerry White, *The Church & the Parachurch* (Portland, OR: Multnomah Press, 1983), p.104.

[32] See Appendix B-6 for the data used and sources.

33 *Giving USA 1980 Annual Report* (New York: American Association of Fund-Raising Counsel, Inc., 1980), p. 9.

34 *Giving USA 2011*, pp. 75, 78.

35 For example, member firms of the "Giving Institute: Leading Consultants to Non-Profits" planned *Giving USA 2011* release events: (1) Presentations in Boston, Chicago, Cleveland, and Washington, DC, as well as a national webinar ("Campbell & Company Presents First Look: Giving USA 2011, The Latest Trends in Giving"; <http://www.campbellcompany.com/events/giving-usa-2011-events/>; p. 1 of 8/5/2011 3:38 PM printout). (2) A presentation in Kansas City ("Americans Gave $290.89 Billion in 2010"; <http://www.jeffreybyrneandassociates.com/giving20.html>; p. 1 of 8/5/2011 3:37 PM). (3) A webinar ("Inside This Year's *Giving USA*"; <http://www.arabellaadvisors.com/press/givingusawebinar062111.html>; p. 1 of 8/5/2011 3:38 PM).

36 *Giving USA 2011*, p. 53.

37 Paula Schleis; "Ups and Downs"; Akron Beacon Journal; posted 8/13/07; <http://www.ohio.com/business/9119806.html>; p. 1 of 8/15/07 11:45 AM printout.

38 Blake Ellis; "Are You A Tax Cheat?"; CNNMoney.com; 2/19/2010; <http://money.cnn.com/2010/02/19/news/economy/tax_cheating/>; p. 1 of 2/26/10 11:13 AM printout.

39 John Ronsvalle and Sylvia Ronsvalle, *The State of Church Giving through 2003* (Champaign, IL: empty tomb, inc., 2005), pp. 91-93. The chapter is also available at: <http://www.emptytomb.org/scg03chap7.pdf>.

40 Mark W. Everson; "Written Statement of Mark W. Everson, Commissioner of Internal Revenue, Before The Committee on Finance, United States Senate, Hearing On Exempt Organizations: Enforcement Problems, Accomplishments, and Future Direction"; April 5, 2005; <http://finance.senate.gov/hearings/testimony/2005test/metest040505.pdf>; p. 9 of 4/27/05 printout.

41 Brad Wolverton (Washington), "Taking Aim at Charity," *Chronicle of Philanthropy*, published by The Chronicle of Higher Education, Inc., Washington, D.C., April 14, 2005, p. 27.

42 Sam Kean, Peter Panepento, and Grant Williams, "Tax Watch: Write-Offs," *The Chronicle of Philanthropy*, April 3, 2008, p. 42.

43 Scott Burns, "No, It's Not OK to Lie on Return," *Champaign (Ill.) News-Gazette,* May 10, 2006, p. B-8.

44 For the complete discussion of these recommendations, see Ronsvalle and Ronsvalle, *The State of Church Giving through 2003*, pp. 93-100. The chapter is also available at: <http://www.emptytomb.org/scg03chap7.pdf>.

45 "Legislation Seeks New Federal Agency for Nonprofits"; The NonProfit Times; 7/12/2010; <http://www.nptimes.com/10July/weekly-100712.html?tr=y&auid=6612712>; p. 1 of 7/12/2010 1:27 PM printout.

46 For a brief overview of the Filer Commission recommendation, see John Ronsvalle and Sylvia Ronsvalle, *The State of Church Giving through 1999* (Champaign, IL: empty tomb, inc., 2001), p. 59.

47 *Giving USA 2011*, pp. 53, 55. Calculated by attributing 100% of 2009 Religion $99.83 billion to 2009 Individuals, $206.16 billion.

48 Russy D. Sumariwalla and Wilson C. Levis, Unified *Financial Reporting System for Not-for-Profit Organizations: A Comprehensive Guide to Unifying GAAP, IRS Form 990, and Other Financial Reports Using a Unified Chart of Accounts* (San Francisco: Jossey-Bass, 2000), p. 41.

49 Christopher Chabris and Daniel Simons, *The Invisible Gorilla, And Other Ways Our Intuitions Deceive Us*, (New York, Crown, 2010), p. 186.

50 Chabris and Simons, p. 190.

51 Chabris and Simons, pp. 186-197, especially pp. 191, 194-195.

52 Chabris and Simons, pp. 200-203.

53 An Associated Press article appearing as "Job Growth Weak in November," *The (Champaign, Ill.) News-Gazette*, December 4, 2010, p. A-4, col. 2. See also the transcript: "Dismal Unemployment Report Suggests Recovery May Be Stalling"; PBS Newshour; 7/8/2011; <http://www.pbs.org/newshour/bb/business/july-dec11/jobs_07-08.html>; p. 1 of 7/9/2011 2?35 PM printout.

54 David B. Barrett, Todd M. Johnson, and Peter F. Crossing, "Missiometrics 2008: Reality checks for Christian World Communions," *International Bulletin of Missionary Research*, Vol. 32, No. 1, January 2008, p. 27.

55 David Crary, Associated Press; "Charitable Giving in US Rebounds a Bit after Drop"; Yahoo.com; 6/20/2011; <http://news.yahoo.com/s/ap/20110620/ap_on_re_us/us_charitable_giving>; p. 1 of 6/22/2011 4:31 PM printout.

56 Annie Gowen; "Rise in Giving signals Economic Rebound"; Washington Post; 6/19/2011; <http://www.washingtonpost.com/local/rise-in-giving-signals-economic-rebound/2011/06/16/AGX8nKcH_story.html>; p. 1 of 6/20/2011 4:22 PM printout.

Stephanie Strom; "Charitable Giving Rose Last year for First Time Since 2007"; New York Times; 6/19/2011; <http://www.nytimes.com/2011/06/20/business/20charity.html?_r=1>; p. 2 of 6/20/2011 4:18 PM printout.

Melanie Grayce West; "Charitable Giving Rose Last Year, Still Below Peak"; Wall Street Journal Online; 6/19/2011; <http://online.wsj.com/article/SB10001424052702304070104576395800746718570.html>; p. 1 of 6/22/2011 4:44 PM printout.

57 The Urban Institute; "Nonprofits"; 2009; <http://www.urban.org/nonprofits/index.cfm>; p. 1 of 8/16/2009 12:56 PM printout.

58 The references for the Associated Press stories listed are as follows:

•Helena Payne, Associated Press Writer; "2001 Charitable Giving Same As 2000"; published June 20, 2002, 12:20 PM; <http://www.washingtonpost.com/ac2/wp-dyn/A17534-2002Jun20?language=printer>; p. 1 of 6/27/02 9:09 PM printout.

•Mark Jewell; "Donations Held Steady in 2002"; published June 23, 2003, 4:23 PM; <http://www.washingtonpost.com/ wp-dyn/A23604-2003Jun23.html>; p. 1 of 6/26/03 8:49 AM printout.

•Kendra Locke; "Charitable Giving Rises in 2003"; published June 21, 2004, 12:24 AM; <http://www.washingtonpost.com/wp-dyn/articles/A56830-2004Jun21.html>; p. 1 of 6/25/04 4:56 PM printout.

•Adam Geller, AP Business Writer; "Charitable Giving Among Americans Rises"; published June 14, 2005 10:16 AM; <http://www.guardian.co.uk/worldlateststory/0,1280,-5073041,00.html>; p. 1 of 6/15/2005 9:42 AM printout.

•Vinnee Tong, AP Business Writer; "Charitable Giving in U.S. Nears Record Set at End of Tech Boom"; The Associated Press, New York, published June 18, 2006 11:10 PM GMT; <http://web.lexis.com[…extended URL]>; p. 1 of 6/20/2006 8:51 AM printout.

•Vinnee Tong, AP Business Writer; "Americans Give Nearly $300 Billion to Charities in 2006, Set a New Record"; published June 25, 2007 4:58 GMT; <http://web.lexis.com…>; p. 1 of 6/25/07 5:01 PM printout.

•Vinee Tong, AP Business Write; {Americans Are Steady in Donations to Charity"; published June 23, 2008; 11:43 AM GMT; <http://web.lexis.com…>; p. 1 of 6/23/2008 5:23 PM printout.

•David Crary, AP National Writer; "Amid Meltdown, Charitable Gifts in US Fell in 2008"; published June 10, 2009; 04:01 AM GMT; <http://web.lexis.com…>; p. 1 of 6/10/2009 5:11 PM printout.

•Caryn Rousseau, Associated Press Writer; "2009 Charitable Giving Falls 3.6 Percent in US"; published June 9, 2010; 04:01 AM GMT; <http://web.lexis.com…>; p. 1 of 6/9/2010 3:56 PM printout.

•David Crary, AP National Writer, New York; "Charitable Giving in US Rebounds a Bit After Drop."

59 See Appendix C for the source of data on which the calculation of "Per Capita Individual Giving as % of Per Capita Disposable Personal Income: % Change from Base Year" figures by empty tomb, inc. was based.

60 The calculation of "Total Giving as % of Gross Domestic Product: % Change from Base Year" figures by empty tomb, inc. was based on the following data. The aggregate Total giving sources for the 2000-01, 2001-02, 2002-03, 2003-04, 2004-05, 2005-06, 2006-2007, 2007-2008, and 2008-2009 intervals were the 2002 (p. 177), 2003 (p. 194), 2004 (p. 218), 2005 (p. 194), 2006 (p. 204), 2007 (p. 212), 2008 (p. 210), 2009 (p. 210), 2010 (p. 50), and 2011 (p. 53), Giving USA editions, respectively. The source of Gross Domestic Product (GDP) data in current dollars: U.S. Bureau of Economic Analysis; "Table 1.1.5. Gross Domestic Product"; Line 1: "Gross Domestic Product"; National Income and Product Accounts Tables; Data Published on March 25, 2011; 1969-2010: Tab "10105 Ann" of Section1All_xls_1.1.9_1.1.5" downloaded as xls file "Section1All_xls.cls"; <http://www.bea.gov/national/nipaweb/DownSS2.asp>; downloaded 3/25/2011.

61 For the years 1955 through 1979, see Giving USA, 1980 Annual Report, 25th Anniversary Issue (New York: American Association of Fund-Raising Counsel, Inc., 1980), p. 22. For a revised, overlapping series covering the years 1970 through 2010, see Giving USA 2011 (p. 53).

In the 1988 edition of Giving USA: The Annual Report for the Year 1987 (New York: American Association of Fund-Raising Counsel Trust for Philanthropy, 1988), Total Contributions increased from 1986 to 1987 (p. 11). Although the 1987 figure was later revised to show a decrease from 1986 (see Giving USA 1998: The Annual

Report on Philanthropy for the Year 1997, p. 156), any media reports at the time of the release of the 1988 *Giving USA* edition would have had access only to the information that giving increased in 1987.

The 1988 edition of *Giving USA* Foreword, coauthored by Maurice G. Gurin, Chairman, AAFRC Trust for Philanthropy, and George A. Brakeley III, Chairman, American Association of Fund-Raising Counsel, opened with the following paragraph. "The stock market crash of October 19 and the loss of the charitable deduction gave rise to predictions that philanthropic giving last year would suffer significantly. Quite the opposite occurred: total giving increased significantly. Indeed it achieved an impressive new high" (p. 5).

The "State of the Philanthropic Sector, 1987" section, located a number of pages further in the same volume, opens with the heading in bold type and closing punctuation of "$93.68 Billion!" The complete first two paragraphs of that section including the ellipsis follow. "Stock market crash. End of the charitable tax deduction for non-itemizers. Decline in the economy's competitiveness. Well-publicized hijinks of televangelists using much of the money donated for 'religion' to create their own heavens on earth.... In the face of it all, estimated giving in the United States reached an all-time high in 1987—$93.68 billion.

"That amount represents an increase of 6.45 percent over the estimated amount donated a year earlier. The yearly increase marks the continuation of a decades-long trend" (p. 16). Yet, as noted above, subsequent corrections to the initial estimate so enthusiastically announced and reported on found that giving actually declined rather than increased from 1986 to 1987.

[62] See Appendix C for U.S. population, 1955 through 2007. For Gross Domestic Product, see U.S. Bureau of Economic Analysis; "Table 1.1.5.Gross Domestic Product"; Line 1 (see End Note 60 for full citation). 1969-2010: Tab "10105 Ann" of Section1All_xls_1.1.9_1.1.5" downloaded as xls file "Section1All_xls.cls."

1955-1968: Tab "10105 Ann" of "Section1All_Hist_1.1.9_1.1.5.xls" downloaded as xls file "Section1All_Hist. xls" on 3/25/2011 from <http://www.bea.gov/national/nipaweb/SS_Data/Section1All_Hist.xls>.

chapter 8

Jesus Christ, the Church in the U.S., & the 16 No-Progress-in-Child Deaths Nations, 10 Being 84% Christian

"The King will reply, 'I tell you the truth, whatever you did for one of the least of these brothers of mine, you did for me.' ... 'I tell you the truth, whatever you did not do for one of the least of these, you did not do for me.'"
—Matthew 25:40, 45, New International Version

"And the king will say to them in reply, 'Amen, I say to you, whatever you did for one of these least brothers of mine, you did for me.' ... 'Amen, I say to you, what you did not do for one of these least ones, you did not do for me.'"
—Matthew 25:40, 45, New American Bible

"And the king will answer them, 'Truly I tell you, just as you did it to one of the least of these who are members of my family, you did it to me.' ... 'Truly I tell you, just as you did not do it to one of the least of these, you did not do it to me.'"
—Matthew 25:40, 45, New Revised Standard Version

The New International Version is the best-selling Bible translation.[1] The New American Bible has been the leading Roman Catholic translation in the U.S.[2] The New Revised Standard Version is rooted in the King James and published by the National Council of the Churches of Christ in the U.S.A.[3]

All three translations of Matthew 25, verses 40 and 45, focus on the "least."

The verses above, of course, are quoted from the parable of the sheep and the goats. It is one of three parables in Matthew 25. In Matthew 26, the arrest and trial of Jesus is presented. By placing these parables in the chapter before that climax to Jesus' earthly career, Matthew may have seen them as Jesus preparing the disciples for both Jesus' impending departure and planned return.

In the current discussion, the issue is church member giving patterns, both current and potential. The previous chapters demonstrate that church member giving as a percent of income, particularly that portion spent beyond the local congregation, has been declining over four decades.

This pattern contrasts with the potential giving levels discussed in chapter 6. There, data suggests that with relatively low-level per-member contributions, significant resources could be freed up to share the good news of Jesus Christ with those who have never heard it, to help stop, in Jesus' name, global child deaths, to provide basic education, and to increase outreach in the U.S.

But those resources have not been forthcoming in the past 40 years at a scale to meet the needs.

What relationship is there between Matthew 25:40 and 45 and the trend to decrease giving to churches, which have spent an average of two cents of each dollar donated to them on denominational overseas missions?

By not helping the least, one might conclude that the church in the U.S. has not organized to help Jesus.

How is the church in the 21st century U.S. to interpret a responsibility to attend to the least in light of these verses?

However, there may be some who ask, where do we find Jesus overseas? A close reading of the verses above indicates that Jesus was talking about "these brothers of mine" and "one of these least brothers of mine" and "these who are members of my family." How is the church in the 21st century U.S. to interpret a responsibility to attend to the least in light of these verses?

John Calvin read a special emphasis, rather than exclusion, into Jesus' focus in the statement: "*So far as you have done it to one of the least of my brethren.* Believers only are expressly recommended to our notice; not that he bids us altogether despise others, but because the more nearly a man approaches to God, he ought to be the more highly esteemed by us"[4] [emphasis in original].

Likewise, John Wesley did not see an either/or proposition in the verses. His note on Matthew 25:40 reads: "Inasmuch as ye did it to one of the least of these my brethren, ye did it to me – What encouragement is here to assist the household of faith? But let us likewise remember to do good to all men."[5]

John Wesley's notes bring to mind Paul's letter to the Galatians, chapter 6, verse 10: "Therefore, as we have opportunity, let us do good to all people, especially to those who belong to the family of believers" (New International Version, NIV). On a practical level, if the person in need is not a Christian, any assistance given may provide an opportunity to express the gospel in word and deed to that individual. If the person in need is already a Christian, then as a brother or sister in the faith, the individual has a claim on assistance in the same way that a member of any family would.

Of course, the entire discussion sits in the context of Jesus' challenge to the disciples in Luke 6:32, 35: "If you love those who love you, what credit is that to you? Even 'sinners' love those who love them. ... But love your enemies, do good to them, and lend to them without expecting to get anything back" (NIV).

The Sheep, the Goats, and the Church in the U.S.

The discussion that follows considers dynamics that may produce the declines in church member giving patterns discussed throughout the earlier chapters of this volume.

Further, the discussion builds on an assumption that leaders at all levels of the church in the U.S. could be working to reverse those negative giving patterns, with an emphasis on mobilizing church members to help the "least."

Still further, another working assumption is that the least are particularly represented in the countries with high rates of under-five child deaths, especially the 16 countries identified as making no progress in reducing the number of child deaths.

In light of the fact that in ten of these 16 no-progress countries, an average of 84% of the people identify as Christians, Jesus' statement in Matthew 25:40 would leave little room other than for the church in the U.S. to understand Jesus' reference to the least as including the people in these countries.

In the discussion that follows, the first section describes some of the "least" in the no-progress countries.

The second section considers dynamics that may be producing current church member giving trends.

Finally, signs of hope in the church will be considered.

The Least. Millennium Development Goal (MDG) 4 is to reduce by two-thirds, between 1990 and 2015, the mortality rate of children under the age of five. The standards and measurements are set by the MDGs, which were goals set by "world leaders" in the year 2000. The MDGs give a framework to impact global poverty by the year 2015.[6]

Measurements suggest that MDG 4 is lagging behind progress on the other goals.[7] The implications of that fact affect real people. As indicated in Figure 22, although the goal for 2009 was a reduction to 39 under-5 child deaths per 1,000 live births,[8] the actual 2009 number was 60, well behind the goal.

If all were on track, the world would be 85% towards the goal of achieving MDG 4, with 15% farther to go by 2015. Instead, based on *The State of Church Giving through 2009* analysis of *The State of the World's Children* 1990 and 2009 data, the world was, on average, about 49% toward meeting the MDG 4 target, leaving 51% of the goal to be achieved before 2015.[9]

In 2009, because of this lack of progress, 2,837,693 children under the age of five died who would not have died if the world had kept its promises to help them. Regarding these intentions, UN Secretary-General Ban Ki-moon, at a meeting to assess progress on meeting the MDGs, planned to call on world leaders to exercise leadership "and keep their promise to translate the eight MDGs targets into a reality."[10]

If the rate evident in the 2009 reported data continues at its present pace, in 2012 there will be mothers and fathers helplessly watching an estimated 2,991,761 children under the age of five die from preventable causes, who would not have died

The discussion that follows considers dynamics that may produce the declines in church member giving patterns discussed throughout the earlier chapters of this volume.

Figure 22: Exponential Interpolation of MDG 4 Under-5 Child Deaths Per 1,000 Live Births, Based on Reported 1990 Data and 2015 Goal; Reported Data, 1995, 2000, 2005, 2007, 2008, and 2009; Projected 2012 Data

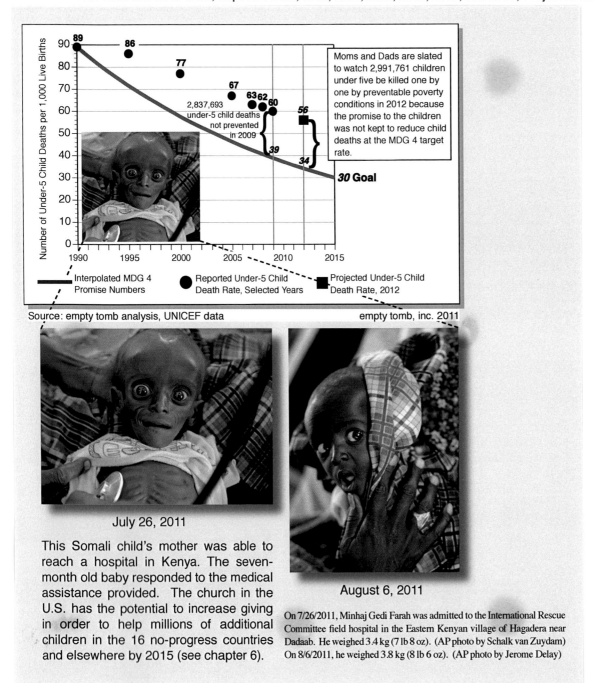

Source: empty tomb analysis, UNICEF data   empty tomb, inc. 2011

July 26, 2011

This Somali child's mother was able to reach a hospital in Kenya. The seven-month old baby responded to the medical assistance provided. The church in the U.S. has the potential to increase giving in order to help millions of additional children in the 16 no-progress countries and elsewhere by 2015 (see chapter 6).

August 6, 2011

On 7/26/2011, Minhaj Gedi Farah was admitted to the International Rescue Committee field hospital in the Eastern Kenyan village of Hagadera near Dadaab. He weighed 3.4 kg (7 lb 8 oz). (AP photo by Schalk van Zuydam) On 8/6/2011, he weighed 3.8 kg (8 lb 6 oz). (AP photo by Jerome Delay)

had world leaders kept their promise to the children to reduce child deaths at a rate that would achieve the goal by 2015, as indicated in Figure 22.

It may be noted that 19 nations of 68 countries are "on track" in their efforts to reduce child mortality levels. However, a 2010 analysis, *Countdown to 2015*, based on 2008 data, indicated that there are 16 countries that are making "no progress" toward decreasing the number of deaths among their children.[11] Table 46 lists the 16 countries, and the number of under-5 child deaths and population for each country in 2008.

It is of particular interest to note that in 10 of the 16 countries, a majority of the population is self-identified as Christian.

In his seminal work, *The World Christian Encyclopedia*, the late missiologist David Barrett referenced Matthew 10:32 and Romans 10:9 as support for the position used in defining Christian populations in the encyclopedia. Building on the 1948 *Universal Declaration of Human Rights*, he elaborated: "This fundamental right also includes the right to claim the religion of one's choice, and the right to be called a follower of that religion and to be enumerated as such."[12]

The *World Christian Encyclopedia* also provides information about what Christian faith traditions are active in the 16 countries. Four major Christian traditions present in the U.S. are noted in the *Encyclopedia's* entries for these countries. These traditions are Roman Catholic, Protestant, Anglican, and Orthodox. The Christian percent of population and the percent of adherents in each of the four traditions in mid-2000 for these 16 countries are also included in Table 46. The ten countries with a majority population self-identified as Christian, and with a weighted average of 84% Christian, are highlighted in the table as well.[13]

It is true that there are difficulties in providing assistance to some of the 16 countries. Structural and political difficulties render aid relationships with Afghanistan and the Democratic People's Republic of Korea challenging at best.

Table 46: Sixteen Countries Making "No Progress" in Reducing Under-5 Child Deaths, Number of Under-5 Child Deaths, 2008, Country Population, 2008, Christian Percent of Country, Mid-2000, and Four Christian Traditions Affiliated Adherents Percent of Country, Mid-2000

Country	Number of Under-5 Child Deaths, 2008	Population 2008	Christian Percent of Country, Mid-2000	Four Christian Traditions, Affiliated Adherents Percent of Country, Mid-2000			
				Roman Catholic	Protestant	Anglican	Orthodox
Afghanistan	311,000	27,208,000	0.0%				
Angola	*165,000*	*18,021,000*	*94.1%*	*62.1%*	*15.0%*		
Burundi	*45,000*	*8,074,000*	*91.7%*	*57.2%*	*12.0%*	*7.5%*	
Cameroon	*89,000*	*19,088,000*	*54.2%*	*26.5%*	*20.7%*		
Central African Republic	*26,000*	*4,339,000*	*67.8%*	*18.4%*	*14.4%*		
Chad	99,000	10,914,000	22.8%	6.6%	10.2%		
Congo	*16,000*	*3,615,000*	*91.2%*	*49.3%*	*17.0%*		
Democratic People's Republic of Korea	18,000	23,819,000	2.1%	0.2%			
Democratic Republic of the Congo	*554,000*	*64,257,000*	*95.4%*	*50.9%*	*20.3%*	*0.9%*	
Kenya	*189,000*	*38,765,000*	*79.3%*	*23.3%*	*21.2%*	*10.0%*	*2.5%*
Mauritania	12,000	3,215,000	0.3%	0.2%			
Somalia	76,000	8,926,000	1.4%				1.3%
South Africa	*73,000*	*49,668,000*	*83.1%*	*8.3%*	*30.7%*	*6.6%*	*0.4%*
Sudan	138,000	41,348,000	16.7%	10.7%	2.7%	7.9%	0.5%
Zambia	*77,000*	*12,620,000*	*82.4%*	*33.5%*	*29.5%*	*2.4%*	*0.1%*
Zimbabwe	*36,000*	*12,463,000*	*67.5%*	*9.6%*	*12.3%*	*2.7%*	*0.1%*
Total Under-5 Child Deaths	1,924,000						

Note: The *World Christian Encyclopedia* Christian Percent of Country figure shown reflects additional traditions present in the country and may include an adjustment for "doubly-affiliated."

Source: empty tomb Analysis; *The State of the World's Children, 2010; Countdown to 2015 Decade Report (2000-2010); World Christian Encyclopedia* (2001)

Another nation in which assistance from either secular or religious organizations is accompanied by complications is Somalia. However, it is of interest to note that, in the face of the famine of 2011, some Somalis were retreating from their country, where power structures have interfered with aid intervention, to Kenya, a country both with a high level of Christian population, and with established international relationships with aid organizations, including Christian ministries.

The news reports of the famine in Somalia provide glimpses of the scope of the tragedy.

One August 2011 Associated Press (AP) article recounted the cruel choice a mother made in leaving her collapsed four-year-old son by the road so she could continue with her one-year old toward a refugee camp. The mother later told a reporter, "Now I'm reliving the pain of abandoning my child. I wake up at night to think about him." A mental health officer for the International Rescue Committee stated that the parents caught in this dilemma will have post-traumatic stress disorder.[14]

A mental health officer for the International Rescue Committee stated that the parents caught in this dilemma will have post-traumatic stress disorder.

Meanwhile, another AP report described the response of one Kenyan police constable who gave "his entire July salary of $376" to help the Somali refugees after a television report "about a young child trying to nurse from his dead mother." The news report indicated that "ordinary Kenyans—a majority of whom live on less than $2 a day—have contributed more than $1.3 million in a little over a week."[15]

It may be noted that Kenya, accepting refugees from Somalia, is also on the list of 16 no-progress countries. In 2008, Somalia, with a population of 8.9 million, had a reported 76,000 under-5 child deaths. Meanwhile, Kenya, with a 2008 population of 38.8 million, had 189,000 under-five child deaths. A 2009 UNICEF update indicated that Kenya's child deaths had declined to 124,000, and Somalia's to 69,000. These numbers were occurring before a probable increase related to the 2011 famine. The 2008 and 2009 figures highlight the fact that a tragic number of deaths occur among the very young in the 16 countries on an ongoing basis. For example, the Democratic Republic of the Congo experienced 554,000 under-five deaths in 2008. The 2009 updated figure increased to 558,000.[16]

Dynamics Affecting the Church in the U.S. The following section considers factors that may contribute to the church in the U.S. not having organized sufficiently to impact the needs of, and solve the problems faced by, the global least.

The Tradition. In his insightful book, *The Rise of Christianity: How the Obscure, Marginal Jesus Movement Became the Dominant Religious Force in the Western World in a Few Centuries*, Rodney Stark brings a sociologist's review to ancient texts in order to explore the growth of early Christianity. He found that, "Christianity presented an exceedingly vigorous otherworldly faith, capable of generating strong commitment."[17]

A high level of commitment led to behaviors that strengthened the church from within, and led to respect from without. For example, according to Stark, Christian behavior during two devastating plagues in the first and second centuries led to a high rate of survival among Christians and those they nursed, including non-Christians. He notes that a contributing factor may have been that basic nursing, even apart from more sophisticated intervention, increases the rate of survival. Those Christians that survived would then have had a higher immune rate, freeing them to continue to nurse others. The high rate of survival would likely have appeared "miraculous" to those inside and outside the community of faith. From a purely numerical aspect, he notes, the high rate of survival among Christians changed the ratio between Christians who were still living and pagans, a higher proportion of whom died.[18]

Stark describes the difference between the pagan response to the plagues, which was generally to escape the city if they could or, in many cases, remain and die, and the Christian response, which was to choose to stay and minister to those in need, and sometimes to die. While Stark cites texts supporting the fact that the early Christians ministered to both Christians and pagans,[19] his description of the differences in the pagan and Christian worldviews emphasizes the ministry among Christians.

> What was new was the notion that more than self-interested exchange relations were possible between humans and the supernatural. The Christian teaching that God loves those who love him was alien to pagan beliefs.... Equally alien to paganism was the notion that because God loves humanity, Christians cannot please God unless they *love one another*. Indeed, as God demonstrates his love through sacrifice, humans must demonstrate their love through sacrifice on behalf of *one another*. Moreover, such responsibilities were to be extended beyond the bonds of family and tribe, indeed to "all those who in every place call on the name of our Lord Jesus Christ" (1 Cor. 1:2). These were revolutionary ideas[20] [emphasis in original].

In applying current sociological theory to records of the early church, Stark highlighted an issue that is particularly relevant to the present discussion: the theory of "attachments."

Attachments. Stark summarizes the theory of attachments as follows.

> Rather than asking why people deviate, why they break laws and norms, control theorists ask why anyone ever does conform. Their answer is posed in terms of *stakes in conformity*. People conform when they believe they have more to lose by being detected in deviance than they stand to gain from the deviant act. Some people deviate while others conform because people differ in their stakes in conformity. That is, some people simply have far less to lose than do others. A major stake in conformity lies in our attachments to other people Most of us conform in order to retain the good opinion of our friends and family. But some people lack attachments. Their rates of deviance are much higher than those of people with an abundance of attachments [emphasis in original].[21]

For the present discussion, the concept of "attachment" is particularly relevant in the parable of the sheep and the goats. As Stark has observed, the idea that God could want love, and want his followers to demonstrate that love by loving others, was in marked contrast to the pagan approach to gods based on self-interest.

Taking that idea a step farther, in the parable of the sheep and the goats, Jesus was explicitly transferring the attachment, which the disciples had to Jesus, from himself to the "least." In identifying completely with the "least" who need assistance from the disciples, Jesus expanded the disciples' sense of responsibility beyond the God-person relationship. The implications for action on the part of followers of Jesus are profound. As author and pastor Francis Chan has written, "Ask yourself this: If you actually saw Jesus starving, what would you do for Him?"[22]

...in the parable of the sheep and the goats, Jesus was explicitly transferring the attachment, which the disciples had to Jesus, from himself to the "least."

With that question as a setting event, the discussion turns to a consideration of the church in the U.S. in the 21ˢᵗ century.

Evaluation. The church member giving patterns presented in chapters 1 through 6 demonstrate a marked pattern on the part of the church in the U.S. For over 40 years, there has been a pronounced trend to turn inward on the part of congregations. That trend is shown in the steady decrease in the portion of income donated by members for the category of Benevolences, which includes expenses beyond the local congregation such as denominational and seminary support, as well as direct congregational mission outreach, both local and international. Unlike the category of Congregational Finances, the portion of donations that serves the present members, giving as a portion of income to Benevolences declined in a pronounced fashion between 1968 and 2009 (see Table 1). Further, the change in the level of missions support is evident in the comparison between the average of eight cents of every dollar donated to a congregation supporting foreign missions in the 1920s (see Table 27), compared to an average of two cents supporting denominational overseas missions from 2003-2009 (see Tables 19 to 25).

These giving patterns have been accompanied by changing conditions in the church. In Table 47, various leaders comment on what might be termed the present "lukewarm" condition among Christians in the U.S.

In chapter 6, the potential for giving among church members in the U.S. is considered. The spontaneous donation by the Kenyan police officer, noted above, hearkens back to the discussion in chapter 6 of remittances sent by foreign-born people living in the U.S. That analysis suggested that if native-born church members in the U.S. were to support overseas ministries at a level similar to those remittances, there would have been an additional $362 billion a year available to send through already established church channels to help the "least." The difference between present giving levels and that potential might be summarized as "underperformance."

Underperformance. In the nonprofit world, donors and nonprofits often discuss how to improve their impact. Two recent books on that topic raise issues that deserve consideration in the present discussion of the church in the U.S.

Thomas J. Tierney advises nonprofits and donors. Joel L. Fleishman is a Duke law and public policy professor. In their book, *Give $mart*, these two authors suggest that "underperformance" is too frequently present in the nonprofit sector. They write, "Basically, the problem is human nature. It feels good to be generous, and it's flattering to be thanked for our generosity. It doesn't feel as good to impose discipline on ourselves.… In an arena where excellence is self-imposed, we are all too inclined to set the bar low, to fall back on enticing but fuzzy definitions of success."[23]

Mario Morino, with experience as an entrepreneur, as well as in civic and business leadership, founded both a "philanthropic investment organization" and an institute to develop innovative methods to impact social needs. In his summary of the nonprofit sector performance, he notes, "We don't manage to outcomes, thus greatly diminishing our collective impact." Rather, nonprofits in general, and the

"In an arena where excellence is self-imposed, we are all too inclined to set the bar low, to fall back on enticing but fuzzy definitions of success."

Table 47: Church Leaders Comment on the Lukewarm Church in the U.S.

"If we want to see the people of God unleashed in the church, we need to start with the gospel of God in Christians. After all, putting everything in our lives on the table before God is the natural overflow of the gospel. Yet confusion abounds concerning the gospel in the church today." David Platt, author and pastor[24]
"I quickly found that the American church is a difficult place to fit in if you want to live out New Testament Christianity. The goals of American Christianity are often a nice marriage, children who don't swear, and good church attendance. Taking the words of Christ literally and seriously is rarely considered. That's for the 'radicals' who are 'unbalanced' and who go 'overboard.' Most of us want a balanced life that we can control, that is safe, and that does not involve suffering." Francis Chan, author and pastor[25]
"To say the Church offers 'therapy' is to use that term colloquially. True therapy would assist in curing diseases or disorders, including spiritual ones, such as greed or self-absorption. It would help cure the disordered heart, as God did for Augustine of Hippo, who prays: 'It pleased you to transform all that was misshapen in me.'   "The 'therapy' that today's churches offer is akin to what one gets from watching Oprah. This type of therapy might provide a morale boost, or shore up an attitude that helps someone cope. But it masks the need to reform what people want out of life. It glosses over ingrained habits of the heart, from gluttony to envy, pretending they're not as deadly as they truly are. This therapeutic function hampers the Church's mission by steering people to fulfill their lower appetites and to neglect higher mandates." G. Jeffrey MacDonald, minister, author, and journalist[26]
"…Christianity had become divided and incoherent to the average spiritual sojourner. The century-long buildup to this perfect storm had wreaked havoc on the movement of Jesus. Many spiritually curious non-Christians weren't seeing a clear expression of God's work through Christians. Instead, they were experiencing splinters of a fractured community laden with dysfunction." Author and nonprofit CEO Gabe Lyons, reflecting on his efforts to help an interested non-Christian understand the culture of the church in the U.S.[27]
"Look in the mirror. The Church, the bride of Christ, has been unfaithful. WE are at fault. We-collectively and individually-have chased after every idol the world has to offer. We have tried so hard to be relevant that we've become almost completely irrelevant. We offer no other way, there is nothing distinctive about us." Chuck Colson, founder of Prison Fellowship Ministries [emphasis in original][28]
"What it clearly says to us is that no matter how much our people profess that they love Jesus, they love their money more." Bryant Wright, president of the Southern Baptist Convention, commenting on the level of giving to missions[29]

"For to what extent do people still belong to the Church in the first place? On the one hand, they want to belong to her and do not want to lose this foundation. On the other hand, they are of course also shaped and formed interiorly by the modern way of thinking. It is the unfermented coexistence, with and alongside each other, of the basic Christian intention and a new world view, which leaves its mark on all of life. To that extent what remains is a sort of schizophrenia, a divided existence.
 	
    "We must strive to integrate the two, insofar as they are compatible with each other. Being Christian must not become a sort of archaic stratum to which I cling somehow and on which I live to a certain extent *alongside* of modernity…
 	
    "It is important for us to try to live Christianity and to think as Christians in such a way that it incorporates what is good and right about modernity—and at the same time separates and distinguishes itself from what is becoming a counter-religion." His Holiness Benedict XVI [emphasis in original][30]

church might be included in the assessment, are "navigating with little more than intuition and anecdotes."[31]

Tierney and Fleishman introduce an issue that ought to be in the purview of the church.

> What is the inescapable conclusion? Simply this: if you are truly committed to achieving as much impact as is practical with your limited philanthropic resources, you will have to demand excellence of yourself. And that means being willing to engage in the hard work of setting a high bar, and holding yourself accountable for clearing it.
>
> Pursuing outstanding results, year after year, when they are not being demanded by anyone else is not a natural act. It takes extraordinary determination and self-discipline....
>
> Self-imposed accountability is also "unnatural," in the sense that if you set a high bar, you may not clear it, and that can be embarrassing, particularly in a world that largely shuns failure. So if no one is demanding that you set a high standard and hold yourself accountable for meeting it, and if doing so is hard (and risks embarrassment), why ever would you do it?[32]

...research by the Barna Group noted that many Americans are not clear about the contributions of Christianity to society.

The type of self-discipline that rises above human nature, a necessary virtue for the effective pursuit of nonprofit goals according to Tierney and Fleishman, ought to bring the discussion to the church's doorstep. The difficulty, as noted below, is that, to a large degree, the church may no longer be sufficiently "salty" to produce the virtues required to maintain the level of excellence that will more effectively impact the needs of the "least."

Then and Now. Rodney Stark relates a number of stories about early Christians who were martyred, and the remarkable attitudes they displayed. While pagans viewed early Christians' "contempt for death" with respect, Stark notes, modern social scientists sometimes label it "psychopathological."[33]

This view is not limited to social scientists. Francis Chan described the reaction when he decided to downsize to a smaller house in order to have more to give away to missions: "Sometimes I feel like when I make decisions that are remotely biblical, people who call themselves Christians are the first to criticize and say I'm crazy, that I'm taking the Bible too literally, or that I'm not thinking about my family's well-being."[34]

Salt or No Salt? The quotes in Table 47 suggest there is concern in various quarters about the condition of the church in the U.S. The issue might be summed up as whether or not the church has lost its "saltiness," and therefore it's ability to influence culture.

The descriptions of the heart condition of Christians located in the U.S. in the 21st century give insight not only about church member giving patterns, but perhaps also about changes in society in general.

For example, a summary of recent research by the Barna Group noted that many Americans are not clear about the contributions of Christianity to society: "...contemporary Americans are hard pressed to identify any specific value added" to American culture by Christianity. "The primary obstacle is not the substance of the principles on which Christianity is based, and therefore the solution is not solely providing an increase in preaching or public relations. The most influential aspect of Christianity in America is how believers do—or do not—implement their faith in public and private."[35]

The Barna research results bring to mind the one-liner: When the man was accused of being a Christian, he was acquitted for lack of evidence.

Journalist, author, and minister G. Jeffrey MacDonald laments the marketing of the church, resulting in increasing consumerism, and the results it has produced. He notes the emergence of guidebooks to help people find "a church or even a religion that matched their values and preferences."[36] He writes, "In churches big and small, it seems, governing structures have come to mirror those of organizations that specialize in satisfying their 'best' customers (read: those with the most to offer the institution in terms of donations and professional talents). Perhaps it was bound to happen eventually in a consumer-driven marketplace, but American society will be paying spiritual costs for this shift for years to come."[37]

Said another way, if the salt loses its flavor, what happens to the stew the salt is supposed to be seasoning?

Whether or not Christian virtues are practiced can indeed impact society in general—and some would say that it already has. Consider an observation from Eliot Spitzer, the ex-Governor of New York and former New York State Attorney General turned television commentator. A filmmaker exploring the 2008 financial crisis in the U.S. and elsewhere interviewed Spitzer, apparently based on his public, rather than private, integrity. One of Spitzer's conclusions centered on the absence of what would commonly be termed a basic Christian virtue:

> What it comes down to at the end of the day is a violation of one's fiduciary obligation to one's client. That — if there's sort of an over-arching issue that under an umbrella under which all of these issues fit, that's it. And getting people to live up to that fiduciary duty, which is probably about as boring an issue as you can try to get people excited about, is really the nub of the problem. Because if people were loyal to that fiduciary duty, then most of these problems would not occur. Whether it's a loan officer to somebody whom you're marketing a loan, whether it is a bank trying to sell a security debt instrument — At every one of these points, truthfulness and loyalty to fiduciary duty would resolve the problem.[38]

Truthfulness is certainly a basic Christian virtue. So are thrift and self-denial. What can be concluded about the level at which these are practiced in a U.S. economy that has borrowed 100% of the Gross Domestic Product (GDP)? Rating agencies would prefer to see the level reduced, perhaps to 73%.[39] This level of debt increases in significance in light of one analyst identifying a relationship between the amount of debt and the impact of recessions on an economy.[40] Whether on an individual basis or a national basis, moral behavior can have practical consequences.

However, with church bond ratings being reviewed for possible downgrading,[41] the church may not be providing an alternative to the practice of debt evident in the broader society.

John M. Buchanan, editor of *Christian Century*, recognized both the absence of the values, and the need to recover them, in the financial "crisis" present in the U.S.: "If there is anything redemptive about this crisis, it is the possibility it offers

Said another way, if the salt loses its flavor, what happens to the stew the salt is supposed to be seasoning?

to learn again the virtues we may have forgotten—modesty, frugality, responsibility, community—and to learn again who we are."[42]

His Holiness Benedict XVI responded to a question about the possible broader implications for change, as a result of the sexual abuse scandal involving the priesthood, with comments that can also be applied more generally in the current discussion:

> This catharsis is for all of us, for all of society, but especially of course for the Church, a call to recognize again our fundamental values and to see the dangers that profoundly threaten not only priests but also society as a whole. Knowledge about this threat and the destruction of the moral framework of our society should be for us a call to purification. We must acknowledge again that we cannot simply live in any way we please. That freedom cannot be arbitrariness. That it is imperative to learn to exercise a freedom that is responsibility.[43]

The Pontiff's comment brings to mind the early Christian teaching contained in the apostle Paul's letter to the Galatians (chapter 5, verse 13) and, here quoted, in the first epistle of Peter (chapter 2, verse 16): "Live as free men, but do not use your freedom as a cover-up for evil; live as servants of God" (NIV).

Christian or Pagan? Rodney Stark made a distinction between the pagans, who lived only in their current world, and the early Christians, who had hope for a better future, and therefore a willingness to demonstrate sacrifice by loving one another out of love for God. This distinction raises an uncomfortable question. Given the decline in church member giving and the increasing de-emphasis in churches on serving others, as evident in the decline of Benevolences in favor of Congregational Finances—a trend that now extends over decades—to what degree is the Christian church in the U.S. moving along a spectrum from Christianity toward paganism?

That question is somewhat offensive, even as it is written. However, consider the observation of G. Jeffrey MacDonald on the "therapy" offered by the church (see Table 47). He also describes the effect produced by a "consumer" emphasis in the church: "Though the particulars of prior eras' ascetic practices often seem a bit silly to later generations, the understanding that an elevated heart stems from self-denial has endured—and still endures for many. But in the last three decades, America has witnessed a radical reformulation of the Christian ideal, in which the Church and other Christian organizations have begun repositioning the faith as a resource for satisfying primitive desires."[44]

Author and pastor David Platt encountered this redefinition of the Christian agenda when he accepted the role of pastor at a large megachurch in Birmingham, Alabama. Wanting to get up to speed with his new responsibilities, he studied the popular literature about developing a "vision" for his congregation. The literature focused on innovative worship, suggesting even the hiring of a consultant. Platt writes, "At first it seemed to make sense. But over time I found myself getting nauseated by all the vision talk. Setting and reaching goals is important, of course. But were my sights really supposed to be set on bringing a large crowd together in a cool environment where they could hear terrific music, see killer graphics, and then listen to me talk live or via video or maybe even via hologram (if only I had really innovative vision)?"

...to what degree is the Christian church in the U.S. moving along a spectrum from Christianity toward paganism?

Instead, after talking and praying with the congregation's leaders, a vision for the congregation developed that was distinct from the popular advice. "The only possible vision for the church of Jesus Christ is to make known the glory of God in all the nations. This preferred future or visual destination must drive us because this is what drives God."[45]

In considering whether the contemporary church in the U.S. has more affinity with traditional Christianity or is moving toward classical paganism, contrast these two observations.

Rodney Stark states that the Christian idea, new at that point in history, was that God not only was capable of loving interaction, but also wanted Christians to show love for God by loving one another. The pagan view also involved sacrifice, emphasizing self-interest without the idea of relationship. Stark indicated that pagans also understood "…the supernatural makes behavioral demands upon humans—the gods have always wanted sacrifices and worship…" and "…that the supernatural will respond to offerings—that the gods can be induced to exchange services for sacrifices."[46] The Christian view focused on loving God by loving others. The pagan view focused on sacrificing to a god in order to obtain a service in return.

Compare Stark's description with an observation from Francis Chan writing in the 21st century U.S.: "The irony is that while God doesn't need us but still wants us, we desperately need God but don't really want Him most of the time. He treasures us and anticipates our departure from this earth to be with Him—and we wonder, indifferently, how much we have to do for Him to get by."[47]

The end result is what Benedict XVI has described as "practical atheism."

> For many people today, practical atheism is the normal rule of life. Maybe there is something or someone, they think, who once set the world in motion eons ago, but he does not matter to us at all. If this attitude becomes a general existential position, then freedom no longer has any standards, then everything is possible and permissible. That is why it is so urgent also to bring the question about God back into the center. Of course, this does not mean a God who exists in some way or other, but rather a God who knows us, speaks to us, and approaches us—and who is then our judge also.[48]

Faith or No Faith. One may note that the parable of the sheep and goats also presents a theme of judgment (see Matt. 25:34, 41, 46). One could misread the story to imply that Jesus, just before his arrest in Matthew 26, was introducing a works theology for his followers through the consequences cited in the parable. However, there is strong evidence that such a reading would be wrong. Note that the "righteous" apparently did not do the works in anticipation of reward. The king has to explain the virtue of their actions to them. It is more likely that Jesus was building on a concept that he had talked about earlier. That is, if someone believes in Jesus, actions will naturally follow from that belief: "No good tree bears bad fruit, nor does a bad tree bear good fruit. Each tree is recognized by its own fruit" (Luke 6:43-44, NIV).

David Neff, *Christianity Today* editor in chief, came to a similar conclusion about the implications in this parable. He writes, "Both the sheep and the goats are puzzled by what the Lord says… But the relevant question is whom they served.

The Christian view focused on loving God by loving others. The pagan view focused on sacrificing to a god in order to obtain a service in return.

Did they serve themselves? Or did they serve the imprisoned, the hungry, the sick, and those trapped in poverty?"[49]

David Platt, building on Ephesians 2:10, James 2, and 1 John 3:16-18, observes, "All through the Bible we encounter an important truth, namely that the gospel that saves us *from* work also saves us *to* work." He goes on to note, "Scripture is full of examples of faith producing work."[50]

In an earlier edition of the *State of Church Giving* series, the implications of actions growing out of faith included a review of writings by Martin Luther and John Calvin on the topic of grace overflowing in works. The review concluded that the issue was one of "faith or no faith." [51]

It seems appropriate, then, to empower Christians living in the U.S. in the 21st century to produce fruit in keeping with their professed faith. Such empowerment will result from effective leadership. Current church structures have broad communication and delivery channels that could be used to lead toward mobilization of church members to help the least. To date, however, the leadership has not organized to strengthen and encourage Christians to act on their potential for helping the least at the same level they would if they really believed that they were helping Jesus himself.

Setting Goals. Denominations have announced high-commitment efforts, but they have not also organized for their members to be successful in achieving those goals.

Southern Baptist Convention. For example, the Southern Baptist Convention (SBC) introduced the idea of engaging all the remaining unreached people groups (those without any exposure to the Gospel of Jesus Christ) by the year 2010, yet no dedicated financial campaign was organized to pay for the specified number of additional missionaries needed, and the goal was not met.[52]

Leaders in the denomination also announced in 2010 that $200 million would make it possible to send enough cross-cultural missionaries in order to engage the unengaged people groups that were not reached. Yet, there was no organized effort to raise the money.[53]

The new president of the SBC International Mission Board (IMB) said at the time he was appointed in 2011, "Frankly, I think we live in a generation of students who are asking, 'Why do we keep hearing about these unreached people groups? Why don't we just go reach them?' "[54]

The president of the SBC, Bryant Wright, expressed a similar frustration in his annual address at the June 2011 Convention. Urging Southern Baptists to return to their "first love," as the church in Ephesus was urged to do in Revelation 2, Wright told the gathered messengers, "I believe the number one idol within the lives of our people and in the lives of our churches is materialism." He warned that, "If Southern Baptists do not respond to the challenge God has given us to reach the world, we risk having our lampstand removed," referring to the warning given the church in Ephesus in Revelation 2.[55]

In an earlier presentation to the Association of State Baptist Papers annual meeting, Bryant Wright was also quoted as saying, " 'If individuals would be faithful

It seems appropriate, then, to empower Christians living in the U.S. in the 21st century to produce fruit in keeping with their professed faith. Such empowerment will result from effective leadership.

to God, giving would be far beyond anything we could imagine.' But, he lamented, 'people are in bondage' to materialism."[56]

Bryant Wright's remarks may have been, in part, a response to the level of support for the annual Lottie Moon offering, sponsored by the SBC Women's Missionary Union. The Lottie Moon offering is named after an early Southern Baptist missionary, and supplements the unified budget Cooperative Program support for missionaries sent out by the SBC. The per member contribution to the Lottie Moon annual Christmas offering increased from 2008 to 2009, from $8.71 to $9.22. The per member contribution as a percent of U.S. Disposable (after-tax) Personal Income (DPI) was up slightly from 2008 to 2009, but has been shrinking since the 1960s. In 1968, on average, Southern Baptists contributed 0.48% of DPI to the annual offering. By 2009, it was 0.26%. Figure 23 shows per member giving as a percent of DPI to the Lottie Moon annual Christmas offering from 1921 through 2009.[57]

Figure 23: SBC Lottie Moon Christmas Offering, Per Member Giving as a Percent of U.S. Per Capita DPI, 1921-2009

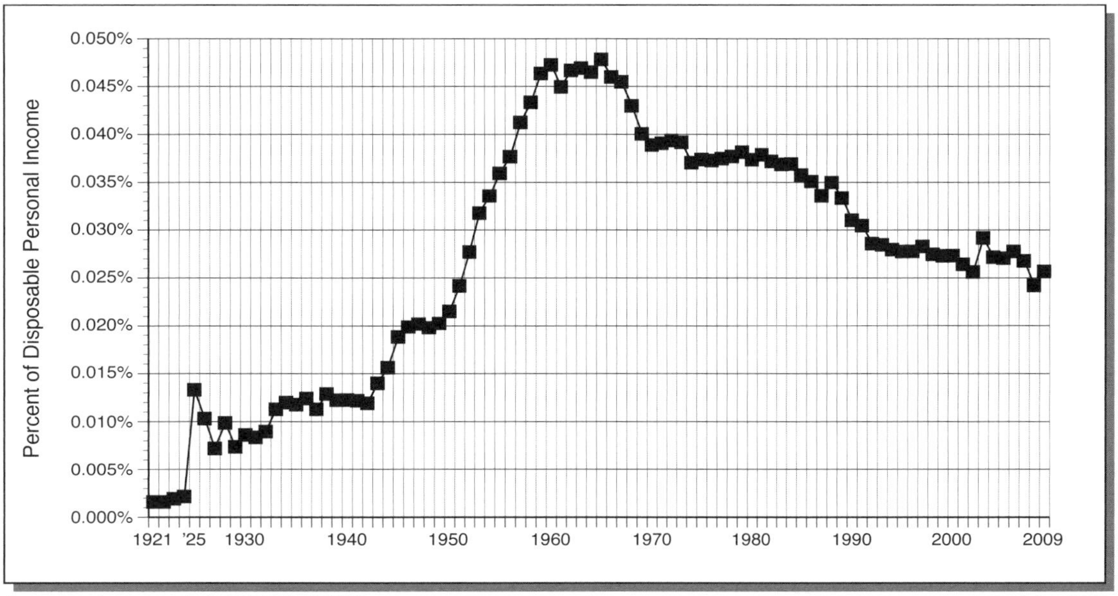

Source: empty tomb analysis, SBC IMB, US BEA   empty tomb, inc. 2011

To their credit, the SBC continues to return to the issue of unreached peoples. The latest strategy is described under the Signs of Hope section at the end of this chapter.

United Methodist Church. In 1997, the United Methodist Church announced a major initiative to address the needs of children in poverty, both in the U.S. and around the globe. As discussed in a previous edition in the *State of Church Giving*, the initiative was "discontinued" after eight years.[58]

More recently, the United Methodist Church has emphasized ending malaria in Africa by 2015. An empty tomb analysis of the *Countdown to 2015* Country Profiles for nations in Africa found that malaria caused an estimated 16% of the under-5 child deaths on that continent in 2008. An original partner in the "Nothing But Nets" campaign, the United Methodist Church has recast that effort as "Imagine No Malaria." The goal over five years is a modest $1.94 more per member per year.

Nevertheless, due to the fact that this global-need effort has a specific goal and timeframe, the Imagine No Malaria campaign is noteworthy among denominational efforts. Therefore, it is included under the Signs of Hope section at the end of this chapter.

Roman Catholic Church. Issues facing the two largest Protestant communions in the U.S. are also impacting giving and participation in the Catholic Church.

Francis Butler, president of the Foundations and Donors Interested in Catholic Activities (FADICA), observed in an interview that Catholics need to be challenged in the area of "generosity, giving and stewardship." He said that other areas of concern among the foundations associated with FADICA include support for Catholic institutions, including schools, and the level of engagement of young people "and their participation in the life of the church." When asked about the trends of Protestants as well as Catholics to emphasize maintenance in their congregations and parishes, he responded, "It's sort of counterintuitive: The more the parish is outward-oriented, the more global it is in focus, the more the vitality of the parish increases." Contrasting maintenance and vision, he went on: "When you're just talking to people about maintenance of the plant or the electric bill, you're not going to touch people's hearts. That's why the vision has to be a Catholic vision, which is a vision of universal solicitude for humanity. It is a grand vision, capable of having people give their lives for it."[59]

Caritas Internationalis, an organized global Catholic outreach, is considered in the Signs of Hope section at the end of this chapter.

Defining Success. Thomas Tierney and Joel Fleishman observe that philanthropists may find honest evaluation of their efforts somewhat difficult. To the degree that denominations see global missions outreach as one activity among many, rather than the driving force in its coalition of congregations, the following observation would apply to denominations as well as philanthropists: "All too often, philanthropists who are demonstrably lost give themselves an 'A' for their efforts, declare victory, and move on to new challenges. The only people who spot the underlying failures are those who needed help, and didn't get it."[60]

Although the least and their needs do not now have a voice that commands attention, the parable of the sheep and goats suggests that the returning king will give them one.

In the meantime, it would be difficult to identify clear common global mission goals, designed to be at a scale to solve rather than cope with problems, that have been embraced by any large segment of the church in the U.S. and therefore are being offered for church members to rally around.

Francis Chan observed, "We say things like, 'I can do all things through Christ who strengthens me,' and 'Trust in the Lord with all your heart.' Then we live and plan like we don't believe God even exists. We try to set our lives up so everything will be fine even if God doesn't come through. But true faith means holding nothing back. It means putting every hope in God's fidelity to His promises."[61]

With no agenda on a scale that is intended to solve rather than cope with desperate life-and-death conditions facing so many in the world, efforts organized by the church

"It's sort of counterintuitive: The more the parish is outward-oriented, the more global it is in focus, the more the vitality of the parish increases."

appear to be just enough to make members and leaders feel good. Yet, an A for effort may no longer be a relevant or sufficient measure, given the urgent needs of the least or the increasing difficulty of stemming declining giving and membership trends.

One may suppose that there is still an appetite for a more demanding level of Christianity. Books by Francis Chan[62] and David Platt[63] make the New York Times Best Seller List. Churches study the description of world need written by Richard Stearns, president of World Vision U.S.[64] Gabe Lyons writes about the "next Christians" who reportedly emphasize the "whole" Gospel, including creation and restoration that leads them beyond the congregation, as well as the standard message of fall and redemption.[65]

Indeed, although membership has declined, a sizeable portion of the U.S. population continues to attend church. A conservative estimate of "American church attendance rates" was "24 to 25 percent" of the population "over the past decade" through 2008.[66] That means that 74 to 77 million people are putting themselves in a position to hear what church leaders have to say on a given weekend, with those numbers presumably swelling at Christmas and Easter. Consider that in 2011 businesses paid $3 million to address 110 million Super Bowl viewers for 30 seconds[67] for a once-a-year event.

Or consider that one survey found that three in five unchurched Americans are "self-described Christians" who have often disaffiliated because of inconsistencies between what Christians say and do.[68] Further, a survey again confirmed that those who identify as "actively religious" gave more to charity than others, with the under-35 donors in that category giving five times more than non-religious donors.[69]

These statistics suggest there is still a window of opportunity to communicate with and mobilize a large percent of the population that identifies as Christian, both those presently inside congregations and those outside who need a reason to come inside, on behalf of the least. The challenge will be how to proceed in a way that actually does more than try to fill pews, but rather engages people in changing the world because of their faith.

The issue is an important one. Denominations have been engaged in marketing campaigns for years. The level of effectiveness of those campaigns is evident in the decreasing portion of income given to the church, and declines in membership as a percent of population. A completely different approach would be needed both to attract increased commitment from current attenders, and encourage others to return or join in congregational efforts.

Denominational and congregational leaders can offer present and future members the long tradition of the Christian heritage to sacrifice for the greater vision. However, it seems difficult for leaders at both levels to risk funding for their present structures as they consider whether to raise their members' sights with such ideas.

Leadership in the SBC, for example, uses every opportunity to promote their unified budget, the Cooperative Program. Concern for securing support for this general income may be why there was little organized effort to raise the $200 million needed for the number of missionaries necessary to "reach the unreached," as discussed above. This view seems likely in light of a 2011 article in a denominational

...an A for effort may no longer be a relevant or sufficient measure, given the urgent needs of the least or the increasing difficulty of stemming declining giving and membership trends.

magazine that noted the "fragile nature of the relationships" in the denominational structure: "states cannot direct the SBC, neither can the SBC direct the states." Therefore, the article asserts, it was a positive development, in 2010, that the Convention adopted the Great Commission Resurgence Report, and thus "again affirmed the interdependent relationship the SBC and the state conventions share in receiving and disbursing Cooperative Program receipts for the purposes of impacting a lost world with the Gospel of the Lord Jesus Christ."[70]

The SBC is not alone in regard to navigating the "fragile nature" between congregations and denominations. In a 1994 survey of pastors and denominational regional officials, 87% of the pastors and 89% of the regional officials agreed or strongly agreed with the statement, "Most congregations take the services which the denomination provides to them for granted." Further, 96% of the pastors and 97% of the regional officials disagreed or strongly disagreed with the statement, "Most congregations have as strong a denominational identity as they did forty years ago."[71] Benevolences giving data does not suggest that the situation has changed in the intervening years. During the 16 years from 1995 through 2009, giving as a percent of income to Benevolences, that includes denominational support, dropped from 0.40% in 1994 to 0.34% in 2009, a 16 percent decline.

These findings highlight the changing nature of the relationship between congregations and denominations. In light of these changes, it may not be reasonable to gauge expectations on how denominations should understand and promote the unified budget now based on how it was done 40 or even 100 years ago. With less established identity, denominations might have to promote a larger vision that congregations and their members can embrace. Special dedicated financial campaigns to solve rather than cope with life-and-death-and-eternity problems might become a priority interaction between the denomination and the congregations. The unified budget could continue to be raised through assessments. The unified budget then becomes subordinated to the larger goal, but the unified budget can also be promoted as a necessary expense to serve as a base from which to succeed in achieving the larger goal. Currently, while a larger goal is used to promote raising the unified budget, the subordination of the larger goal within the unified budget results in a tepid response to the unified budget.[72]

Denominations responsible for maintaining their national and middle judicatory structures may join pastors responsible for maintaining local churches in viewing a financial campaign for a larger vision as competition with payment of looming bills in order to keep basic operations going. Support of a vision can thus be seen as risking those operations. Consider another SBC interchange. The new president of the International Mission Board, Tom Elliff, was being introduced in a teleconference to the staff of several state Baptist papers. In his acceptance speech, Elliff announced a goal for SBC congregations to embrace 3,800 unengaged people groups. Elliff was urging that the process begin in June 2011 and be completed by June 2012. Referring to that goal, Jimmy Pritchard, a Texas pastor and IMB trustee chairman, made a comment during the teleconference that was recorded as follows: "And as to him [Elliff] being an interim, if you'll listen to his acceptance speech today it will be anything but interim. In fact we won't have any work to do after 2012. (laughter in the room)."[73]

Special dedicated financial campaigns to solve rather than cope with life-and-death-and-eternity problems might become a priority interaction between the denomination and the congregations.

The laughter might have inadvertently highlighted the implicit tension that exists between actually achieving the big goal, and continuing to use the big goal as a reason to fund the unified budget. Denominations appear to have a choice regarding their future direction. One choice is to continue in the direction that already seems to be in motion: assisting in areas such as health insurance, other pastor benefits, and pastor placement for the congregations, thus moving toward the trade association end of the coordination spectrum. The other direction requires more risk, as denominations could provide leadership in efforts to reverse congregations turning inward, as evidenced in Congregational Finances taking a larger portion of total congregational income. This leadership would have denominations moving toward the end of the coordination spectrum where campaigns to raise significant global missions dollars are located. This latter direction is risky for at least two reasons.

First, the denomination's emphasis on the big goal can seem self-interested, continuing the long tradition of using missions to secure the unified budget. The campaign to turn the congregation outward could be interpreted as little more than self-promotion of the denominational structure. The only way to counter this cynicism, which is perhaps rooted in past experience, would be to pursue the missions campaign with great clarity, energy, and creativity.

Second, the denomination would have to risk that the declining level of support for its maintenance activities would be accelerated if the campaign did not immediately translate into increased unified budget contributions as well.

Perhaps part of the difficulty is that denominational leaders and pastors do not demonstrate the type of hope for the future that empowered early Christians. According to Rodney Stark, a hope for a better world gave the early Christians the courage to encounter grave threats in the present one. If denominational leaders and pastors are bound to the past, their vision for changing the future could be hampered.

In this context, it may be of interest to consider observations by Harvard economist John Kenneth Galbraith. He noted that policies of countries can be wrong if they reflect past rather than current realities. If Galbraith's comments are applied to church structures and members in the U.S., rather than countries, these comments are relevant for church leadership. As Galbraith wrote in the late 1950s:

> As with individuals so with nations. And the experience of nations with well-being is exceedingly brief. Nearly all, throughout all history, have been very poor. The exception, almost insignificant in the whole span of human existence, has been the last few generations in the comparatively small corner of the world populated by Europeans. Here, and especially in the United States, there has been great and quite unprecedented affluence, which until now has been the accepted future.

> The ideas by which the people of this favored part of the world interpret their existence, and in measure guide their behavior, were not forged in a world of wealth. These ideas were the product of a world in which poverty had always been man's normal lot, and any other state was in degree unimaginable....

> These are the days when men of all social disciplines and all political faiths seek the comfortable and the accepted; when the man of controversy is looked upon as a disturbing influence; when originality is taken to be a mark of instability; and when, in minor modification of the scriptural parable, the bland lead the bland....

The other direction requires more risk, as denominations could provide leadership in efforts to reverse congregations turning inward...

Illusion is a comprehensive ill. The rich man who deludes himself into behaving like a mendicant may conserve his fortune although he will not be very happy. The affluent country which conducts its affairs in accordance with rules of another and poorer age also forgoes opportunities. And in misunderstanding itself, it will, in any time of difficulty, implacably prescribe for itself the wrong remedies.[74]

Church leaders not recognizing, understanding, and engaging the spread of affluence among Americans in the 20th century has had a major impact on its present condition. Consider this assessment by missiologist David Barrett. Citing the optimism expressed in the mission movement from 1889-1914, that embraced the theme "The Evangelization of the World in This Generation," Barrett reflects:

> The 20th century itself, however, has proved to be startlingly different from these expectations. Certainly the total of Christians has grown enormously, from 558 millions in 1900 to 1,433 millions by 1980. Certainly also, since 1900 Christianity has become massively accepted as the religion of the developing countries in the so-called Third World, Africa in particular. But no-one in 1900 expected the massive defections from Christianity that subsequently took place in Western Europe due to secularism, in Russia and later Eastern Europe due to Communism, and in the Americas due to materialism.[75]

If denominations do not develop fresh attitudes and strategies that reflect current economic realities, the past will bind them to ineffectiveness. As noted in chapter 1, U.S. per capita after-tax income increased by $18,594 in inflation-adjusted dollars, or 131%, between 1968 and 2009. Even considering the recent recession of 2008-2009, Americans had more than doubled their incomes. Business recognized the changed economic reality and marketed lifestyle improvements. Meanwhile, church leaders did not offer a vision large enough to help church members integrate their expanding resources with exciting faith goals.

If denominational leaders remain committed to a pre-affluence economic view, that will likely mean that denominational leaders will continue to strive to protect their unified budgets at all costs, not promoting global mission strategies at a scale that matches the need. The result could well be that denominations continue to move toward the role of trade associations for pastor benefits. In that case, para-denominational groups, or meta-denominational associations of congregations, that are working hard to present specific challenges to church members, may fill the void, providing specific feedback and articulate goals. The result could be a continuing decrease of commitment between congregations and denominations, as congregations find it more convenient to carry out any larger vision without the intermediation of the denomination. Further, the disintermediation effect could spread to members' relationships with their congregations, as individuals pursue larger goals directly, rather than through the congregation.

The long-term consequence could be a weakening of the church with an overflow effect on society. For example, consider the Christian values that have been taught at the congregational level, such as the practice of charity in the youth as suggested by the Consumer Expenditure by Age analysis in chapter 7. A reinterpretation of giving to the church as primarily benefiting current members, as represented in Congregational Finances, could educate young people that philanthropy has more to do with creating a comfortable environment for themselves, rather than helping

Church leaders not recognizing, understanding, and engaging the spread of affluence among Americans in the 20th century has had a major impact on its present condition.

those in need. In addition, if members decrease commitment or even leave the congregations as a result of a lack of vision on the part of the congregation and/or denomination, then, to that extent, the youth will not be present to learn any type of Christian values.

"To What End?" The church member giving and membership trends in the earlier chapters have now been sustained across at least four decades. Meanwhile, world leaders' goal to decrease child deaths lags. The prolonged nature of these trends suggests that maintaining the current direction of church leadership is a recipe for continued marginalization of the church in both the lives of members, and society in general.

Consider that a 2010 Gallup poll found that seven in ten Americans felt that "religion as a whole is losing its influence on American life," a near-record high for a survey question that has been asked for more than 50 years.[76] Although 77% of Americans identified themselves as Christian in 2008, that number is at a low point in the 1948-2008 period.[77]

The Consumer Expenditure Survey analysis in chapter 7 found that those under 25 gave the largest portion of income to "church, religious organizations," suggesting that philanthropic values are learned first in religious settings. That puts a responsibility on church leaders to develop a relationship with a generation that is "just not interested in religion."[78] Bradley Hill, in an April 2011 *Christian Century* article, cited one source that referred to the group as the first to have been raised without God. Hill noted that among the youth who *were* involved in a congregation he served, their interest was beyond the church walls.[79] A *Christianity Today* overview of organizations focused on college students found that leaders in various groups have noticed an increased response to social justice activities rather than traditional social gatherings.[80] If congregations have increasingly emphasized Congregational Finances over Benevolences for the past 40 years, as evident in the church member giving trend numbers, how will these congregations speak to a generation focused on larger issues beyond the congregation?

> If congregations have increasingly emphasized Congregational Finances over Benevolences for the past 40 years... how will these congregations speak to a generation focused on larger issues beyond the congregation?

The alternative to extending the declining giving trends would be intentional intervention to change the patterns.

G. Jeffrey MacDonald observes, "The human condition, as Protestants understand it, means that churchgoers need consistent purging and strengthening of the heart, such that they might cultivate indomitable love for God's priorities and for their neighbors' well-being." MacDonald suggests that there is a way to return to these basic priorities. However, it will include, as he describes it, "facing down the demons of consumerism."[81]

Pastors may see that move as risky. The 1994 survey cited earlier found that 40% of pastors disagreed or disagreed strongly with the statement, "Most pastors feel they would receive strong support from their denominational structure if they were to challenge perceived selfish patterns among their congregation members." Another 27% were unsure about the statement, while 33% agreed or agreed strongly. Perhaps as unsettling, only 38% of the regional officials agreed or agreed strongly with the statement, while 30% were unsure and 31% disagreed or disagreed strongly.[82]

MacDonald writes, "In the consumer-driven age, parishioners are not educated from the pulpit or elsewhere on what they ought to be demanding from the Church in terms of reordering their desires.... Unless we openly address the competitive nature of the new religious marketplace, and educate our parishioners about what they *should* be demanding of their church experiences, we can expect religious consumers to keep demanding the cost-free approach to discipleship that has come to mark and mar our generation" [emphasis in the original].[83]

According to MacDonald, one area of change needed is in the lay-clergy role. MacDonald advises that pastors would "...do well to view themselves less as consolers or performers on a stage for God and more as trainers who set high standards and help people master their desires through grace and habit."[84]

On a more hopeful note, one congregational consultant and pastor, Peter Steinke, found that introducing change that helps turn congregations outward may be less difficult than introducing other types of changes into a congregation. He states, "When I first saw a congregation making a significant change by associating that change with mission, I saw far less resistance to the change than in other congregations. And I have seen change made that had no connection to mission and was easily sabotaged or emotionally resisted. It makes sense to raise the congregation's consciousness of mission before embarking on a major shift—to put the horse (mission) before the cart (change)."[85]

Turning again to the general nonprofit sector, Mario Morino advises that nonprofits develop a "performance culture," even while Morino acknowledges that the business term might be distasteful to those who pursue more altruistic goals in the nonprofit sphere. As he uses the term, it means "...simply that the organization should have the mindset to do what it does as well as it possibly can and continually seek to do even better."[86]

> However, defining what the organization "does" is a vitally important step in developing a meaningful performance culture.

However, defining what the organization "does" is a vitally important step in developing a meaningful performance culture. Willow Creek Church in South Barrington, Illinois, set national standards for innovative worship. Only after many years did the congregational leaders discover, and to their credit also share on a national scale, that their efforts were not producing the level of discipleship that they desired among those who wanted to grow beyond the seeker stage.[87]

Mario Morino here offers a critically important insight. He observes, "The simple question that has served me best throughout my business and nonprofit careers is 'To what end?' "[88] This question might be helpful for leaders who want to reverse present church member giving trends, and the level of declining interest in the church that those trends imply.

The church in the U.S. has not successfully attracted or directed the potential of church members on behalf of the global "least" at a level sufficiently significant to change their circumstances. Perhaps that is because church members do not see increased support of their churches as a "rational choice."

Rodney Stark considers the willingness of early Christians to endure martyrdom from "rational choice theory." He introduces a proposition "fundamental to the whole of social science: *Individuals choose their actions rationally, including those actions which concern compensators.*" This choice involves "weighing the anticipated costs and benefits of actions and then seeking to act so as to maximize net benefits." Christians confident of a better world were willing to sacrifice themselves, believing *"religion generates tangible benefits that are not readily explained in secular terms"*[89][emphasis in original].

According to the *Encyclopedia of Religion and Society*, the term "compensator" may be defined as "the promise of a future reward that cannot be tested by empirical means. A major proposition is that when humans cannot achieve a desired reward, they will accept a compensator instead, and will even treat the compensator as if it were a tangible reward."[90] Thus the *promise* of eternal life made the cost of martyrdom a rational choice.

Based on declining church giving trends, church leaders have not identified either present rewards or compensators of sufficient value to church members such that members see increased giving as a rational choice. The immediate reward, for example, of counting a decrease in under-5 child deaths, or a compensator presented that decreasing these deaths would make God happy in the long-run, could have, but have not, been offered to church members in a convincing way.

Instead, although leaders at both the congregational and denominational levels feel that members *ought* to increase giving to support basic operations, including for the unified budgets of the denominations, the perceived promise of a functioning congregation or denomination has not been sufficiently attractive to a broad set of members to result in the increased giving and involvement needed to achieve those goals.

David Platt raises the issue of setting effective church priorities from another direction when he writes: "I simply and humbly want to ask the question, 'Amid all the good things we are doing and planning, are there better ways to align with God's Word, mobilize God's people, and marshal God's resources for God's glory in a world where millions of people are starving and more than a billion have never even heard of Jesus?' "[91]

As leaders evaluate efforts to engage church members, asking "to what end" may help define priorities that members could see supporting as a rational choice.

Mobilization. Once again returning to Rodney Stark, he addresses a question that is relevant for any attempt to revitalize the church in the U.S. He asks, "How do religions 'revitalize'? Primarily by effectively mobilizing people to attempt collective actions."[92]

In the parable of the sheep and the goats, Jesus introduces a priority for action: meeting the needs of the "least." Tables 48 through 49 that follow consider one of the needs that could be addressed, the child mortality rates.

In *The State of Church Giving through 2006*, the concept of global need triage was suggested. The two issues before the church, proposed as key for the least, were providing unreached people groups with an adequate presentation of the Gospel, and helping to prevent, in Jesus' name, the vast majority of under-5 child deaths.[93]

As leaders evaluate efforts to engage church members, asking "to what end" may help define priorities that members could see supporting as a rational choice.

Table 48: Country-Specific Dollar-Cost Estimates for Causes of Under-5 Child Deaths, 68 Countries, with 16 No-Progress Countries Highlighted, 2008

	Nation	Under-5 Mortality Rank	Annual no. of Under-5 Deaths (000s) 2008	Country Total as % of Total Annual No. of Under-5 Deaths (000s) 2008	Country Total $ Need, Based on $5 Billion Total Estimate
	Africa: 44 Nations		4,447	51%	$2,537,083,524
1	*Angola*	*2*	*165*	*1.88%*	*94,135,098*
2	Benin	23	39	0.45%	22,250,114
3	Botswana	83	1	0.01%	570,516
4	Burkina Faso	11	117	1.34%	66,750,342
5	*Burundi*	*12*	*45*	*0.51%*	*25,673,209*
6	*Cameroon*	*19*	*89*	*1.02%*	*50,775,901*
7	*Central African Republic*	*10*	*26*	*0.30%*	*14,833,409*
8	*Chad*	*3*	*99*	*1.13%*	*56,481,059*
9	*Congo*	*22*	*16*	*0.18%*	*9,128,252*
10	Côte d'Ivoire	25	79	0.90%	45,070,744
11	*Democratic Rep. of the Congo*	*5*	*554*	*6.32%*	*316,065,723*
12	Djibouti	39	2	0.02%	1,141,031
13	Egypt	97	45	0.51%	25,673,209
14	Equatorial Guinea	14	3	0.03%	1,711,547
15	Eritrea	56	10	0.11%	5,705,157
16	Ethiopia	27	321	3.66%	183,135,555
17	Gabon	46	3	0.03%	1,711,547
18	Gambia	30	6	0.07%	3,423,094
19	Ghana	47	55	0.63%	31,378,366
20	Guinea	16	54	0.62%	30,807,850
21	Guinea-Bissau	6	12	0.14%	6,846,189
22	*Kenya*	*21*	*189*	*2.16%*	*107,827,476*
23	Lesotho	45	5	0.06%	2,852,579
24	Liberia	17	20	0.23%	11,410,315
25	Madagascar	30	71	0.81%	40,506,618
26	Malawi	34	56	0.64%	31,948,882
27	Mali	7	100	1.14%	57,051,575
28	*Mauritania*	*24*	*12*	*0.14%*	*6,846,189*
29	Morocco	72	24	0.27%	13,692,378
30	Mozambique	20	110	1.26%	62,756,732
31	Niger	13	121	1.38%	69,032,405
32	Nigeria	9	1,077	12.29%	614,445,459
33	Rwanda	26	41	0.47%	23,391,146
34	Senegal	29	49	0.56%	27,955,272
35	Sierra Leone	7	43	0.49%	24,532,177
36	*Somalia*	*4*	*76*	*0.87%*	*43,359,197*
37	*South Africa*	*52*	*73*	*0.83%*	*41,647,649*
38	*Sudan*	*27*	*138*	*1.57%*	*78,731,173*
39	Swaziland	43	3	0.03%	1,711,547
40	Togo	35	20	0.23%	11,410,315
41	Uganda	18	190	2.17%	108,397,992
42	United Republic of Tanzania	33	175	2.00%	99,840,256
43	*Zambia*	*14*	*77*	*0.88%*	*43,929,712*
44	*Zimbabwe*	*38*	*36*	*0.41%*	*20,538,567*

Details in the above table may not compute to the numbers shown due to rounding.
Sources: empty tomb, inc. analysis, UNICEF data

empty tomb, inc., 2011

	Pneumonia	Diarrhea	Measles	Malaria	HIV/AIDS	Injuries	Other	Neonatal (Total)
Africa	$362,283,204	$436,815,381	$16,898,676	$406,789,137	$108,489,274	$54,136,239	$403,725,468	$756,846,189
1	*16,944,318*	*23,533,775*	*941,351*	*7,530,808*	*1,882,702*	*2,824,053*	*20,709,722*	*20,709,722*
2	3,115,016	2,892,515	0	5,117,526	222,501	445,002	4,005,021	6,230,032
3	39,936	39,936	0	5,705	0	28,526	165,450	290,963
4	11,347,558	12,682,565	0	13,350,068	667,503	2,002,510	12,682,565	14,685,075
5	*3,850,981*	*5,904,838*	*256,732*	*2,310,589*	*513,464*	*1,026,928*	*4,877,910*	*6,675,034*
6	*8,124,144*	*8,124,144*	*507,759*	*9,647,421*	*2,538,795*	*1,015,518*	*8,631,903*	*12,693,975*
7	*2,521,680*	*2,521,680*	*0*	*2,076,677*	*1,038,339*	*148,334*	*2,521,680*	*4,153,355*
8	*9,601,780*	*11,861,022*	*0*	*10,731,401*	*1,694,432*	*564,811*	*9,601,780*	*12,425,833*
9	*1,277,955*	*1,277,955*	*0*	*2,190,780*	*456,413*	*91,283*	*1,369,238*	*2,555,911*
10	4,957,782	5,859,197	0	9,464,856	1,802,830	450,707	5,859,197	16,676,175
11	*50,570,516*	*56,891,830*	*3,160,657*	*53,731,173*	*3,160,657*	*6,321,314*	*50,570,516*	*91,659,060*
12	182,565	205,386	0	0	68,462	22,821	216,796	433,592
13	1,797,125	1,283,660	0	0	0	1,283,660	5,904,838	15,660,657
14	171,155	154,039	154,039	479,233	51,346	17,115	188,270	496,349
15	969,877	1,198,083	114,103	0	228,206	285,258	1,198,083	1,711,547
16	21,976,267	40,289,822	0	12,819,489	5,494,067	5,494,067	29,301,689	69,591,511
17	136,924	102,693	17,115	496,349	171,155	17,115	171,155	616,157
18	376,540	445,002	34,231	787,312	34,231	102,693	479,233	1,129,621
19	2,510,269	2,824,053	627,567	8,158,375	941,351	627,567	2,824,053	12,865,130
20	3,696,942	4,005,021	924,236	7,393,884	616,157	308,079	4,005,021	9,550,434
21	1,095,390	1,300,776	136,924	1,232,314	136,924	136,924	1,163,852	1,643,085
22	*16,174,121*	*21,565,495*	*1,078,275*	*11,861,022*	*5,391,374*	*3,234,824*	*20,487,220*	*29,113,419*
23	313,784	256,732	0	0	484,938	57,052	370,835	1,369,238
24	1,597,444	1,939,754	228,206	1,825,650	342,309	114,103	1,825,650	3,651,301
25	7,696,257	8,911,456	0	1,620,265	0	810,132	8,101,324	13,772,250
26	3,514,377	3,514,377	0	5,431,310	4,472,843	638,978	4,792,332	9,904,153
27	7,987,220	10,839,799	0	11,980,831	570,516	1,141,031	8,557,736	15,974,441
28	*1,026,928*	*1,026,928*	*0*	*890,005*	*68,462*	*136,924*	*1,026,928*	*2,670,014*
29	1,232,314	1,643,085	0	0	0	410,771	1,643,085	8,763,122
30	8,158,375	6,903,241	0	8,158,375	8,785,942	1,255,135	8,785,942	21,337,289
31	13,116,157	13,806,481	0	12,425,833	690,324	1,380,648	13,116,157	15,187,129
32	92,166,819	110,600,183	0	122,889,092	18,433,364	6,144,455	92,166,819	172,044,728
33	3,274,760	5,146,052	233,911	1,403,469	233,911	935,646	4,210,406	7,952,990
34	3,634,185	3,913,738	838,658	5,311,502	559,105	559,105	4,193,291	9,225,240
35	3,925,148	4,906,435	1,226,609	3,189,183	490,644	735,965	4,415,792	5,642,401
36	*7,371,063*	*9,105,431*	*2,167,960*	*2,601,552*	*0*	*867,184*	*7,371,063*	*13,874,943*
37	*2,498,859*	*3,748,288*	*0*	*0*	*19,157,919*	*832,953*	*3,748,288*	*12,077,818*
38	*7,873,117*	*7,873,117*	*0*	*19,682,793*	*1,574,623*	*2,361,935*	*10,235,052*	*29,917,846*
39	154,039	136,924	0	0	838,658	17,115	188,270	376,540
40	1,141,031	1,255,135	0	2,966,682	684,619	228,206	1,255,135	3,993,610
41	13,007,759	17,343,679	2,167,960	23,847,558	5,419,900	4,335,920	16,259,699	26,015,518
42	12,979,233	10,982,428	0	15,974,441	8,985,623	2,995,208	13,977,636	33,945,687
43	*5,710,863*	*6,150,160*	*439,297*	*6,589,457*	*5,271,565*	*1,317,891*	*7,468,051*	*11,421,725*
44	*2,464,628*	*1,848,471*	*1,643,085*	*616,157*	*4,313,099*	*410,771*	*3,080,785*	*6,161,570*

Table 48: Country-Specific Dollar-Cost Estimates for Causes of Under-5 Child Deaths, 68 Countries, with 16 No-Progress Countries Highlighted, 2008 (continued)

	Nation	Under-5 Mortality Rank	Annual no. of Under-5 Deaths (000s) 2008	Country Total as % of Total Annual No. of Under-5 Deaths (000s) 2008	Country Total $s Need, Based on $5 Billion Total Estimate
Asia: 17 Nations			3,716	42%	$2,120,036,513
1	*Afghanistan*	*1*	*311*	*3.55%*	*177,430,397*
2	Azerbaijan	72	6	0.07%	3,423,094
3	Bangladesh	58	183	2.09%	104,404,382
4	Cambodia	41	32	0.37%	18,256,504
5	China	102	365	4.16%	208,238,247
6	*Dem. People's Rep. of Korea*	*57*	*18*	*0.21%*	*10,269,283*
7	India	49	1,830	20.88%	1,044,043,816
8	Indonesia	66	173	1.97%	98,699,224
9	Iraq	64	41	0.47%	23,391,146
10	Lao People's Dem. Republic	54	10	0.11%	5,705,157
11	Myanmar	35	98	1.12%	55,910,543
12	Nepal	60	37	0.42%	21,109,083
13	Pakistan	42	465	5.31%	265,289,822
14	Philippines	81	73	0.83%	41,647,649
15	Tajikistan	53	12	0.14%	6,846,189
16	Turkmenistan	61	5	0.06%	2,852,579
17	Yemen	49	57	0.65%	32,519,398
Latin America/Caribbean: 6 Nations			166	2%	$94,705,614
1	Bolivia	58	14	0.16%	7,987,220
2	Brazil	100	67	0.76%	38,224,555
3	Guatemala	77	15	0.17%	8,557,736
4	Haiti	48	19	0.22%	10,839,799
5	Mexico	112	36	0.41%	20,538,567
6	Peru	96	15	0.17%	8,557,736
Oceania: 1 Nation					
1	Papua New Guinea	49	14	0.16%	$7,987,220
Total for 68 Nations			8,343	95%	$4,759,812,871

	Pneumonia	Diarrhea	Measles	Malaria	HIV/AIDS	Injuries	Other	Neonatal (Total)
Asia	$280,054,770	$259,641,716	$45,259,014	$4,701,050	$11,210,634	$86,102,236	$329,238,932	$1,099,971,474
1	*40,808,991*	*49,680,511*	*1,774,304*	*0*	*0*	*7,097,216*	*40,808,991*	*35,486,079*
2	581,926	376,540	0	0	0	68,462	616,157	1,711,547
3	11,484,482	10,440,438	1,044,044	2,088,088	0	2,088,088	12,528,526	64,730,717
4	4,746,691	1,277,955	182,565	182,565	0	547,695	4,929,256	6,389,776
5	31,235,737	6,247,147	0	0	0	20,823,825	33,318,120	116,613,419
6	*1,745,778*	*1,129,621*	*0*	*0*	*0*	*205,386*	*1,848,471*	*5,237,335*
7	114,844,820	114,844,820	41,761,753	0	10,440,438	31,321,314	156,606,572	574,224,099
8	17,765,860	14,804,884	0	986,992	0	1,973,984	17,765,860	45,401,643
9	3,274,760	2,573,026	0	0	0	1,169,557	3,274,760	13,099,042
10	1,483,341	399,361	171,155	0	0	171,155	1,540,393	1,939,754
11	6,709,265	6,709,265	0	1,118,211	559,105	12,300,319	6,709,265	22,364,217
12	2,110,908	2,955,272	0	0	211,091	422,182	2,321,999	12,876,540
13	29,181,880	37,140,575	0	0	0	5,305,796	29,181,880	161,826,791
14	7,913,053	2,915,335	0	0	0	1,665,906	10,411,912	18,741,442
15	1,369,238	1,300,776	0	0	0	205,386	1,574,623	2,464,628
16	570,516	342,309	0	0	0	85,577	599,042	1,255,135
17	4,227,522	6,503,880	325,194	325,194	0	650,388	5,203,104	15,609,311

	Pneumonia	Diarrhea	Measles	Malaria	HIV/AIDS	Injuries	Other	Neonatal (Total)
LA/C	$10,856,915	$8,358,056	$0	$108,398	$884,299	$4,689,639	$27,989,503	$42,104,062
1	1,277,955	1,198,083	0	0	0	239,617	1,677,316	3,674,121
2	3,057,964	1,911,228	0	0	0	1,528,982	12,614,103	19,112,277
3	1,454,815	1,625,970	0	0	256,732	427,887	2,139,434	2,652,898
4	1,951,164	2,167,960	0	108,398	541,990	216,796	2,059,562	3,793,930
5	2,259,242	1,026,928	0	0	0	1,848,471	7,188,498	8,420,812
6	855,774	427,887	0	0	85,577	427,887	2,310,589	4,450,023

	Pneumonia	Diarrhea	Measles	Malaria	HIV/AIDS	Injuries	Other	Neonatal (Total)
Oceania								
1	$1,597,444	$399,361	$159,744	$559,105	$239,617	$239,617	$1,837,061	$3,035,144

	Pneumonia	Diarrhea	Measles	Malaria	HIV/AIDS	Injuries	Other	Neonatal (Total)
Total	$654,792,332	$705,214,514	$62,317,435	$412,157,691	$120,823,825	$145,167,732	$762,790,963	$1,901,956,869

Table 49: Country-Specific Dollar-Cost Estimates Detail for Causes of Neonatal Deaths, 68 Countries, with 16 No-Progress Countries Highlighted, 2008

	Nation	Country Total Neonatal Need ($s)	Neonatal Diarrhea ($s)	Neonatal Other ($s)	Neonatal Congential ($s)	Neonatal Tetanus ($s)	Neonatal Asphyxia ($s)	Neonatal Preterm ($s)	Neonatal Infection ($s)
	Africa: 44 Nations	$756,846,189	$17,014,776	$36,493,382	$56,513,350	$17,965,427	$196,668,188	$230,210,121	$205,677,773
1	*Angola*	*20,709,722*	*414,194*	*1,035,486*	*1,449,681*	*414,194*	*5,384,528*	*5,798,722*	*6,212,916*
2	Benin	6,230,032	62,300	249,201	560,703	124,601	1,370,607	2,180,511	1,682,109
3	Botswana	290,963	0	20,367	37,825	2,910	55,283	122,204	52,373
4	Burkina Faso	14,685,075	146,851	587,403	1,027,955	734,254	3,377,567	4,258,672	4,552,373
5	*Burundi*	*6,675,034*	*133,501*	*333,752*	*400,502*	*133,501*	*1,935,760*	*1,735,509*	*2,002,510*
6	*Cameroon*	*12,693,975*	*253,880*	*634,699*	*1,142,458*	*126,940*	*3,300,434*	*4,315,952*	*3,046,554*
7	*Central African Republic*	*4,153,355*	*83,067*	*207,668*	*290,735*	*41,534*	*1,079,872*	*1,246,006*	*1,204,473*
8	*Chad*	*12,425,833*	*248,517*	*621,292*	*621,292*	*1,118,325*	*3,603,492*	*3,106,458*	*3,106,458*
9	*Congo*	*2,555,911*	*51,118*	*127,796*	*255,591*	*0*	*587,859*	*996,805*	*536,741*
10	Côte d'Ivoire	16,676,175	333,524	667,047	1,167,332	166,762	4,002,282	5,336,376	5,002,853
11	*Democratic Rep. of the Congo*	*91,659,060*	*2,749,772*	*3,666,362*	*7,332,725*	*916,591*	*20,164,993*	*30,247,490*	*27,497,718*
12	Djibouti	433,592	8,672	17,344	69,375	4,336	99,726	125,742	108,398
13	Egypt	15,660,657	0	939,639	3,601,951	313,213	1,252,853	8,300,148	1,409,459
14	Equatorial Guinea	496,349	9,927	24,817	49,635	0	129,051	173,722	104,233
15	Eritrea	1,711,547	17,115	119,808	171,155	51,346	393,656	599,042	376,540
16	Ethiopia	69,591,511	1,391,830	3,479,576	3,479,576	2,783,660	20,877,453	16,006,047	21,573,368
17	Gabon	616,157	6,162	24,646	61,616	6,162	141,716	252,624	123,231
18	Gambia	1,129,621	11,296	45,185	79,073	22,592	259,813	384,071	316,294
19	Ghana	12,865,130	128,651	643,257	1,029,210	128,651	3,473,585	3,730,888	3,730,888
20	Guinea	9,550,434	191,009	477,522	573,026	191,009	2,483,113	2,387,608	3,342,652
21	Guinea-Bissau	1,643,085	32,862	82,154	98,585	16,431	410,771	525,787	476,495
22	*Kenya*	*29,113,419*	*582,268*	*1,455,671*	*2,037,939*	*291,134*	*8,442,891*	*8,151,757*	*7,860,623*
23	Lesotho	1,369,238	27,385	68,462	109,539	0	369,694	451,848	342,309
24	Liberia	3,651,301	73,026	182,565	219,078	36,513	949,338	1,168,416	1,058,877
25	Madagascar	13,772,250	275,445	688,613	826,335	137,723	3,580,785	4,544,843	3,718,508
26	Malawi	9,904,153	99,042	495,208	792,332	99,042	2,575,080	3,169,329	2,575,080
27	Mali	15,974,441	479,233	638,978	958,466	319,489	3,833,866	4,632,588	5,111,821
28	*Mauritania*	*2,670,014*	*53,400*	*106,801*	*186,901*	*53,400*	*640,803*	*854,404*	*774,304*
29	Morocco	8,763,122	87,631	350,525	1,226,837	175,262	2,015,518	2,804,199	2,190,780
30	Mozambique	21,337,289	426,746	1,066,864	1,493,610	426,746	5,334,322	6,187,814	6,614,560
31	Niger	15,187,129	303,743	759,356	759,356	1,063,099	3,796,782	4,708,010	3,948,654
32	Nigeria	172,044,728	5,161,342	8,602,236	12,043,131	5,161,342	49,892,971	48,172,524	44,731,629
33	Rwanda	7,952,990	159,060	397,649	556,709	79,530	2,385,897	2,067,777	2,306,367
34	Senegal	9,225,240	92,252	369,010	738,019	184,505	2,121,805	2,859,824	2,767,572
35	Sierra Leone	5,642,401	112,848	225,696	282,120	112,848	1,410,600	1,805,568	1,692,720
36	*Somalia*	*13,874,943*	*554,998*	*693,747*	*1,109,995*	*1,248,745*	*3,746,235*	*3,468,736*	*3,191,237*
37	*South Africa*	*12,077,818*	*120,778*	*1,087,004*	*966,225*	*120,778*	*2,777,898*	*4,951,906*	*2,174,007*
38	*Sudan*	*29,917,846*	*598,357*	*1,196,714*	*2,393,428*	*299,178*	*5,385,212*	*14,061,387*	*6,282,748*
39	Swaziland	376,540	3,765	26,358	41,419	3,765	75,308	139,320	86,604
40	Togo	3,993,610	39,936	199,681	319,489	79,872	958,466	1,277,955	1,118,211
41	Uganda	26,015,518	520,310	1,300,776	1,821,086	260,155	7,284,345	7,804,655	7,024,190
42	United Republic of Tanzania	33,945,687	678,914	1,697,284	2,715,655	339,457	9,844,249	9,504,792	9,165,335
43	*Zambia*	*11,421,725*	*228,435*	*571,086*	*799,521*	*114,217*	*3,198,083*	*3,312,300*	*3,312,300*
44	*Zimbabwe*	*6,161,570*	*61,616*	*308,079*	*616,157*	*61,616*	*1,663,624*	*2,279,781*	*1,170,698*

Details in the above table may not compute to the numbers shown due to rounding.
Sources: empty tomb, inc. analysis, UNICEF data

empty tomb, inc., 2011

Nation	Country Total Neonatal Need ($s)	Neonatal Diarrhea ($s)	Neonatal Other ($s)	Neonatal Congential ($s)	Neonatal Tetanus ($s)	Neonatal Asphyxia ($s)	Neonatal Preterm ($s)	Neonatal Infection ($s)
Asia: 17 Nations	$1,099,971,474	$27,331,527	$171,407,519	$61,988,704	$15,244,067	$243,109,767	$291,274,133	$287,537,939
1 *Afghanistan*	*35,486,079*	*709,722*	*1,774,304*	*2,838,886*	*1,419,443*	*9,226,381*	*7,806,937*	*11,710,406*
2 Azerbaijan	1,711,547	17,115	136,924	205,386	0	342,309	718,850	308,079
3 Bangladesh	64,730,717	1,294,614	3,236,536	3,236,536	1,294,614	18,124,601	16,829,986	20,066,522
4 Cambodia	6,389,776	127,796	319,489	383,387	63,898	1,853,035	1,980,831	1,725,240
5 China	116,613,419	1,166,134	36,150,160	8,162,939	1,166,134	33,817,891	30,319,489	6,996,805
6 *Dem. People's Rep. of Korea*	*5,237,335*	*52,373*	*209,493*	*576,107*	*0*	*1,204,587*	*2,094,934*	*1,047,467*
7 India	574,224,099	17,226,723	114,844,820	17,226,723	5,742,241	109,102,579	137,813,784	166,524,989
8 Indonesia	45,401,643	454,016	2,270,082	4,994,181	454,016	9,988,361	18,614,674	9,080,329
9 Iraq	13,099,042	130,990	523,962	1,702,875	261,981	2,750,799	5,108,626	2,750,799
10 Lao People's Dem. Republic	1,939,754	19,398	116,385	174,578	155,180	601,324	484,938	368,553
11 Myanmar	22,364,217	670,927	1,118,211	1,118,211	0	6,038,339	7,827,476	5,814,696
12 Nepal	12,876,540	257,531	643,827	772,592	257,531	3,734,197	3,476,666	3,862,962
13 Pakistan	161,826,791	4,854,804	6,473,072	16,182,679	3,236,536	38,838,430	43,693,234	50,166,305
14 Philippines	18,741,442	0	2,623,802	2,623,802	374,829	2,811,216	7,683,991	2,998,631
15 Tajikistan	2,464,628	24,646	123,231	221,817	24,646	640,803	1,010,497	443,633
16 Turkmenistan	1,255,135	12,551	62,757	163,168	12,551	288,681	502,054	238,476
17 Yemen	15,609,311	312,186	780,466	1,404,838	780,466	3,746,235	5,307,166	3,434,048
Latin America/Caribbean: 6 Nations	$42,104,062	$74,681	$5,117,812	$7,237,220	$799,293	$6,921,326	$14,927,373	$6,919,443
1 Bolivia	3,674,121	36,741	183,706	330,671	36,741	992,013	1,249,201	845,048
2 Brazil	19,112,277	0	3,440,210	3,631,333	191,123	2,675,719	6,115,929	2,866,842
3 Guatemala	2,652,898	0	106,116	265,290	132,645	344,877	1,485,623	318,348
4 Haiti	3,793,930	37,939	189,696	227,636	265,575	1,062,300	1,176,118	834,665
5 Mexico	8,420,812	0	842,081	1,936,787	84,208	1,178,914	3,031,492	1,431,538
6 Peru	4,450,023	0	356,002	845,504	89,000	667,503	1,869,010	623,003
Oceania: 1 Nation								
1 Papua New Guinea	$3,035,144	$60,703	$182,109	$242,812	$91,054	$910,543	$880,192	$698,083
Total for 68 Nations	$1,901,956,869	$44,481,686	$213,200,822	$125,982,086	$34,099,840	$447,609,824	$537,291,819	$500,833,238

The church as a whole, through its distinct and independent denominational traditions, could accept these two priorities—unreached people groups and under-5 child deaths—as the key priorities for action by their congregations. Once these priorities are embraced within and between denominations, each plan and initiative could be evaluated by asking, "To what end?" What is the purpose of each plan, each initiative, in light of the overarching goals that are guiding both leaders and lay participants to live out their Christian faith? Consensus on these basic needs would still allow for a wide variety of specific, and yet coherent, responses.

The needs of those without an adequate presentation of the Gospel were considered in the previous edition in the *State of Church Giving* series.[94]

In the present discussion, the needs of the least focus on the children under five who are dying around the globe, mostly from preventable poverty conditions.

As shown earlier in Figure 22, the progress in this area has been slow, in fact behind the progress on the other goals.[95] However, Anthony Lake, executive director of UNICEF, writes in the foreword to *The State of the World's Children 2011*, that not only is progress possible, but research shows "we can achieve that progress more quickly and cost-effectively by focusing first on the poorest children in the hardest-to-reach places."[96]

Thus, developing a strategy to assist children, and specifically those on the no-progress country list, may be not only a moral imperative, but also a practical one as well.

In chapter 6, Tables 28 and 29 presented the estimated cost for different church constituencies to address various global needs, including evangelism, preventing child deaths, and providing basic elementary education. The additional daily cost that would provide sufficient funds to address all these needs was calculated to be less than 25¢ a day per historically Christian church member in the U.S.

Tables 48 and 49 consider one of the needs that could be addressed, the child mortality rates. The 2008 data in these tables has not been updated to 2009, as one of the two information sources about global need, *Countdown to 2015 Decade Report (2000-2010)*, was not releasing an update until April 2012.[97]

The results presented in Tables 48 and 49 provide dollar-cost estimates for the causes of under-5 deaths in each of the 68 countries included in the tables.[98] The rows presenting data for the 16 no-progress countries are highlighted. The model suggests the type of information that can be developed to foster initiatives to eliminate conditions that result in needless child deaths.

Two valuable sources of information served as the basis of the analysis. The United Nations Children's Fund (UNICEF) 2010 edition of the annual *State of the World's Children* report with data for 2008 provided detailed information on "Basic Indicators," including the number of under-5 child deaths by country.[99]

The second source was the *Countdown to 2015 Decade Report (2000-2010)*.[100] This report with data for 2008 provided, for 68 countries, a percentage enumeration for eight "Causes of under-5 deaths," one of which was the summary category, "Neonatal." Additionally, detail data for seven "Causes of neonatal deaths" was provided. The number of under-5 child deaths in these 68 countries accounted for 95% of the under-5 child deaths in the world.

This model, a first approximation for estimating country-specific costs to prevent child deaths, was based on the assumption that the cost of the disease remedies was equal for each disease. A second working assumption was that the cost of a package of disease remedies per child was the same across the different countries. While this model could be refined by disease-specific and country-specific pricing factors including rate of progress, this first approximation may be useful for exploring how to address, and mobilize for meeting, specific country goals.

In Table 48, a summed dollar figure for all Neonatal causes is presented.

Table 49 presents the Neonatal detail.

The numbers in the tables suggest that addressing these needs is doable.

Further, the cost per general church member could be reduced if an effective challenge were to be presented to wealthy church members. As noted in Table 28 in

> Thus, developing a strategy to assist children, and specifically those on the no-progress country list, may be not only a moral imperative, but also a practical one as well.

chapter 6, a strategy could challenge higher-income church members to donate half the costs of addressing these needs. A review of the Forbes 400 "Rich Listers" for 2010[101] found that their locations are dispersed throughout the U.S., with the West having the most, the South second, followed by the Northeast and the Midwest. Table 50 locates those listed in the 2010 Forbes 400 list by U.S. region. Eleven of the individuals on the list live abroad.

Table 50: Forbes 400 "Rich Listers" 2009, Region of Residence Summary

Region of U.S.	Number of Rich Listers	Aggregate Wealth ($ Billions)
Northeast	96	$320
Midwest	60	$198
South	112	$339
West	121	$479
Subtotal	389	$1,336
Abroad	11	$33
Total	400	$1,369

To initiate specific goals, however, denominational officials and congregational leaders may first have to examine their own institutional choices before being able to mobilize members in special campaigns on behalf of the least, at a scale designed to solve rather than cope with the problems. It will be tempting for denominational officials to value their unified budgets so much that a focus on the least will not be seen as faithful obedience but rather as a threat to their institutional structures. On the other hand, as observed earlier by Francis Butler, denominational officials could recognize the "counterintuitive" nature of the alternative: focusing on mission could actually help the base operations. An effort to mobilize increased giving on the part of church members, specifically for ministry to the least, could actually, as a welcome side-effect, provide more stable funding for the unified budgets that would now be perceived to serve as the framework from which to reach out to those in need.

Once priorities are examined and established, mobilization could be a reasonable next step. The question, then, entails both *whether* as well as *how* to engage more Christians in common efforts that not only meet the needs of the least but also provide the Christians being mobilized with meaning and purpose.

Signs of Hope. There are signs that it may well be possible to challenge church members in the U.S. to mobilize on behalf of those in need. The power to challenge introduced by the Christian faith still is attracting people in dynamic ways in the 21st century. These signs of hope may provide models or information to help more denominations and congregations to engage more of their members effectively.

SBC Continued Focus on Unengaged People Groups. The SBC developed a new goal for addressing the need of the world's "unengaged people groups" at the 2011 Convention. Both the Convention president, Bryant Wright, and the newly appointed president of the SBC IMB, Tom Elliff, urged that SBC congregations "embrace" 3,800 "unengaged" people groups. Each congregation was challenged to take direct responsibility or combine with one or more additional congregations to engage a people group.[102] Tom Elliff stated that his hope was that all 3,800 people groups would be embraced within 12 months of the 2011 Convention, although he tempered that specific schedule with a more indefinite timetable of "one day": " 'Our goal,' Elliff added, 'is to one day have boots on the ground [among them] sharing the Gospel, and that's an exciting prospect.' "[103] At the June 2011 Convention, president Bryant Wright urged, "With all of our resources and with all 45,000 churches, there is no reason why we cannot have a sufficient number of churches to step forward and embrace every one of the unengaged and unreached people groups."[104] At the

Convention, there were 600-plus commitment cards received. Elliff indicated he saw this response as a beginning, and hoped to involve more congregations in the coming months. The IMB effort includes a Web site, <call2embrace.org> to help congregations become involved.[105] In response to the presentation at the Convention, in August 2011, the Southern Baptists of Texas Convention voted to forward $1 million of their operating reserve to the IMB to help fund present missionaries, and also urged their associated churches to embrace specific people groups.[106]

United Methodist Imagine No Malaria. According to the Web site dedicated to the effort, "Imagine No Malaria is an initiative of the people of The United Methodist Church to raise $75 million to eliminate malaria deaths in Africa by 2015."[107] The executive director of the United Methodist Board of Global Ministries, Thomas Kemper, noted that in Africa 40 percent of the health-care infrastructure is operated by religious organizations.[108] Although the additional $1.94 annual contribution per member is a modest goal for the campaign, the project states a specific goal and a specific timeframe.

Lazarus at the Gate Bible Study. An eight-week Bible study, titled "Lazarus at the Gate," was launched in 2006. The significance of the effort is that participants are challenged to decrease spending in order to free up donations to "the world's poor."[109] The study groups decide what nonprofits and projects to fund. Episcopal City Mission and the Presbyterian Hunger Program have provided financial support designed to "encourage the curriculum's use in their respective denominations."[110] The connection between simplicity and generosity gives the study an unusual and practical emphasis.

58: End Extreme Poverty. A coalition of 10 organizations addressing an array of needs has launched an effort to "end extreme poverty" in 25 years. The effort is labeled a "Christ-centered global initiative to end extreme poverty." An initial 8-minute video reviewed facts that emphasize the potential of the church to make an impact on these needs. A 75-minute film was due to be released in October 2011. On the Web site, individuals are encouraged to sign up to "live Isaiah 58" by selecting a specific project to support and encourage others to support. In a tab section titled, "Who is **58:** for," the Web site states, "**58:** is NOT for people who just want to talk about changing the world but who never take any steps to do anything. We're serious in our belief that we can end extreme poverty in our lifetime"[111] [emphasis in original].

ACT Alliance Increases Efficiency. The merging of ACT Development and ACT International into ACT Alliance was designed to combine relief and development efforts among the member church structures.[112] For example, eight national and international organizations were represented in the Democratic Republic of the Congo, where the ACT members work together, "frequently sharing information about their work, security and future programmes" and aid workers travel to "remote and dangerous places where people suffer."[113]

Caritas Internationalis Coordinates Catholic Efforts. Caritas Internationalis is coordinating the efforts of member organizations to provide an effective global response. The umbrella structure includes 162 national members, and is headquartered in the Vatican City. Together, the member organizations have 440,000 paid staff, 625,000 volunteers, and a combined worth of US $5.5 billion.[114] In 2010, Caritas launched a campaign to challenge world leaders to "live up to their anti-poverty promises" by achieving the MDGs by 2015.[115]

Wycliffe Bible Translators Progress. The Wycliffe Bible Translators campaign to begin the last Bible translation by 2025 continues. Fundraising continues toward a goal of $1.15 billion.[116] "The Last Languages Campaign will use cutting-edge translation techniques to accelerate the pace of language development and Bible translation from 125 years to 17 years." As Paul Edwards, executive director of the Last Languages Campaign, was quoted to observe, "Can you name another 2,000-year-long continuous movement that is going to have its closing in our lifetime?"[117]

World Vision's Child Health Now. World Vision "… aims to ensure that government leaders deliver on their commitments to reduce child mortality by two-thirds by 2015…"[118] The "Child Health Now" initiative, launched in late 2009 by World Vision, provides a model for an ambitious goal. The campaign includes at least three purposes. The campaign is designed to work with local communities, and urge national governments, to improve the health of children in those countries. The second component is World Vision's commitment of a total of $1.5 billion over five years to address child health needs directly as well. The third component is to "urge wealthy nations to fulfill their promises to improve conditions in the developing world." [119]

The *Radical* Approach. The Brook Hills Church in Birmingham, Alabama, is having a national impact through a best-selling book, *Radical*, written by its pastor, David Platt. The strategy emphasizes making the needs of the least a top priority. As an example, the congregation turned a growth strategy in another direction. In choosing a target for evangelism, the usual choice would be "Brook Hills Bob," a "person" in theory similar to present members. Instead, the congregation has opted to focus on "Brook Hills Baruti" who, in theory, lives in North Africa, in a village where conversion to Christ can lead to death inflicted by relatives, and where poor pay means food and water are scarce commodities.[120]

"Next Christians." Gabe Lyons, in his book *The Next Christians*, describes a movement among some believers to engage in direct action. Reflecting on the consequences of limiting authentic Christian witness to Word evangelism solely, he suggests that approach excludes many church members. "Now, put restoration back into the story. Instantly, you've created millions of jobs for all the 'unemployed' and bored Christians in the church—jobs they can get excited about. Now there is work to do for people who want to make the world a better place in the meantime. Instead of simply waiting for God to unveil the new heaven and the new earth, the rest of us can give the world a taste of what God's kingdom is all about—building up, repairing brokenness, showing mercy, reinstating hope, and generally adding value. In this expanded model, everyone plays an essential role. In this way, relearning becomes exciting and personal."[121]

Young Pentecostals Integrating Social Justice into Tradition. In a world where 25% of Christians are identified as Pentecostals, it is significant that Pentecostals in the U.S., especially those who are 30 and younger, are integrating "compassionate ministries and social change" into their practice of the faith. One leader in the movement, Samuel Rodriguez, president of the National Hispanic Christian Leadership Conference, was quoted as observing, "The priorities of this [ethnic Pentecostal] community are issues of life, biblical marriage, education, sex trafficking, immigration reform, poverty alleviation—all under the canopy of the Great Commission."[122]

Conclusion

Two facts become clear from the study of church member giving trends.

First, there is a prolonged declining trend in the portion of income that church members in the U.S. are willing to share with their churches, while national and local church leaders have not organized financial campaigns to increase global missions at a scale commensurate with the need.

Second, there is great potential for church members to increase their giving. This confidence in the potential is based on past behavior of church members, on the current behavior of people such as the level of remittances sent by foreign-born residents to their home countries, and on the available numbers themselves that demonstrate, for example, the growth of after-tax per capita income in inflation-adjusted dollars over the past decades.

Added to that confidence about the potential is the moral imperative presented by Jesus in, among other places, Matthew 25:31-46. In these verses, seemingly not long before his crucifixion, Jesus Christ was trying to plainly communicate the priorities of His coming kingdom to those who would be disciples. His words were simple. His intention was clear.

Jesus took the disciples' attachment to himself and transferred it to the "least."

The church in the U.S. has a choice about the degree to which the least will become our increased priority. Based on what's in the Bible, this is a choice that will affect millions now, and demonstrate the heart's condition plainly, a condition that will have consequences for eternity.

John Calvin made the following observations about the king's statement in verse 41 in the Matthew 25:31-46 passage:

> 41. *Depart from me, you cursed.* He now comes to the reprobate, who are so intoxicated by their fading prosperity, that they imagine they will always be happy... For promises are necessary for us, to excite and encourage us to holiness of life, so threatenings are likewise necessary to restrain us by anxiety and fear. We are therefore taught how desirable it is to be united to the Son of God; because everlasting destruction and the torment of the flesh await all those whom he will drive from his presence at the last day. He will then order the wicked to *depart* from him, because many hypocrites are now mixed with the righteous, as if they were closely allied to Christ [emphasis in original].[123]

Or as a good and wise friend, the Rev. Dr. W. H. Donaldson, once observed, "The sheep say 'Baa' and the goats say, 'But . . .' "

There is reason to hope that denominational and congregational leaders will not refuse to mobilize church members on behalf of the least, by instead raising one "But..." after another. The potential is great. Judging from reports about the interest of younger church members, there appears to be a willingness among them to care for others through the church. This willingness could be tapped, encouraged and directed through the institutional church channels already in place. The very revitalization of the church in the U.S. might depend on embracing Jesus by embracing the least.

Until that Last Day of which Calvin speaks, the dying children, and their aggrieved parents, wait to see what the response of the church in the U.S. will be. Ephesians 3:10-11 suggests that powers in Heaven are also watching with interest what we who claim Christ's name will do: "His intent was that now, through the church, the manifold wisdom of God should be made known to the rulers and authorities in the heavenly realms, according to his eternal purpose which he accomplished in Christ Jesus our Lord" (NIV).

Bill Donaldson also related the old parable that bears retelling yet once more. When Jesus returned to Heaven, he was greeted by those in the heavenly realms with much celebration. During the festivity, one was bold enough to ask, "Jesus, if you are here, who is taking care of your interests on earth?" Jesus replied, "I have left my work in the hands of my church." A silence fell. Then another spoke up somewhat timidly, "But Jesus, what will you do if the church fails to carry out your will?" Jesus replied quietly, "I have no other plan."

Notes for Chapter 8

[1]   msnbc.com staff and news service reports; "World's Most Popular Bible to Be Revised"; msnbc.com; 9/1/2009; <http://www.msnbc.msn.com/id/32644719/ns/us_news_faith/t/worlds-most-popular-bible-be-revised/#.TILdxq79Ws0>; p. 1 of 8/22/11 5:53 PM printout.

[2]   "Preface to the New American Bible"; The Vatican; 11/11/2002 <http://www.vatican.va/archive/ENG0839/__P1.HTM>; p. 1 of 8/23/2011 10:23 AM printout.

[3]   "About the RSV" and "About the NRSV"; National Council of the Churches of Christ in the U.S.A.; n.d.; <http://www.nccusa.org/newbtu/aboutrsv.html> and <http://www.nccusa.org/newbtu/aboutnrs.html>; p. 1 of 8/23/2011 10:27 AM and 10:28 AM printouts.

[4]   John Calvin, *Commentary on a Harmony of the Evangelists, Matthew, Mark and Luke*, William Pringle, trans. (Edinburgh, Scotland: The Calvin Translation Society, 1846), p.181.

[5]   John Wesley; "Wesley's Notes on the Bible"; Christian Classics Ethereal Library; 7/13/2005; <http://www.ccel.org/ccel/Wesley/notes.i.ii.xxvii.html>; p. 3 of 8/17/2011 8:07 AM printout.

[6]   "About Us"; The World Bank; 2011; <http://web.worldbank.org/WBSITE/EXTERNAL/EX TABOUTUS/0,,contentMDK:20104132~menuPK:250991~pagePK:43912~piPK:44037~theSite PK:29708,00.html>; p. 1 of 8/18/2011 10:14 AM printout.

[7]   Howard LaFranchi; "UN Millennium Development Goals: Are They Being Reached?"; Christian Science Monitor; 9/21/2010; <http://www.csmonitor.com/layout/set/print/content/view/print/327185>; p. 2 of 9/21/2010 2:26 PM printout.

[8]   "Goal 4: Reduce Child Mortality"; United Nations; 2011; <http://www.un.org/millennium goals/childhealth.shtml>; p. 1 of 8/18/2011 10:26 AM printout.

[9]   Anthony Lake, Executive Director, "Basic Indicators," *The State of the World's Children 2011* (New York: UNICEF, 2011), 83.

    empty tomb, inc. licensed use of the photos illustrating Figure 22 from the Associated Press after seeing the two photos displayed in World magazine, August, 27, 2011, edition, p. 18.

[10]   Mo Hong'e; UN Chief Sees MDGs Achievable, Calls on World Leaders to Keep Promise"; Xianhua; 9/20/2010; <http://news.xianhuanet.com/english2010/world/2010-09/20/c_13521977.

htm>. For further discussion of the promises made by world leaders in the MDGs, see John Ronsvalle and Sylvia Ronsvalle, *The State of Church Giving through 2006:Global Triage, MDG 4, and Unreached People Groups* (Champaign, IL: empty tomb, inc., 2008), p. 113. The document is also available at <http://www. emptytomb.org/SCG06.ch8excerpt.pdf>.

[11]   Countdown to 2015 Coordinating Committee; *Countdown to 2015 Decade Report (2000-2010): Taking Stock of Maternal, Newborn and Child Survival*; World Health Organization and UNICEF; created 5/21/2010; modified 6/3/2010; <http://www.countdown2015mnch.org/documents/2010report/CountdownReportAnd Profiles.pdf>; pp. 1, 8-9 of 7/29/2010 printout: "… 'no progress' indicates that the under-five mortality rate for 2008 is 40 or more with an average annual rate of reduction of less than 1% for 1990-2008." Note: Although Swaziland is listed among the "no progress" countries in *Countdown to 2015 Decade Report (2000-2010)*, it was not listed in Table 47 because of its rate of reduction improvement since 2000.

[12]   David Barrett, ed., *World Christian Encyclopedia: A Comparative Study of Churches and Religions in the Modern World, AD 1900-2000* (New York: Oxford University Press, 1982), p. 47.

[13]   David B. Barrett, George T. Kurian, Todd M. Johnson, eds., *World Christian Encyclopedia, A Comparative Survey of Churches and Religions in the Modern World, Second Edition,* Volume 1 (New York: Oxford University Press, 2001), pp. 62, 160, 166, 179, 208, 211, 426, 675, 817, 821. The communions included in the Christian tradition column were those that had figures for "affiliated Christians" that rounded to more than 0.0% for any given country. The categories of "Independents" and/or "Marginal Christians" are not listed in the table, but are listed in the *Encyclopedia* for a given country.

[14]   Associated Press, "Fleeing Famine Making for Cruel Choices," appearing in *Champaign (Ill.) News-Gazette*, 8/12/2011, p. A-3.

[15]   Associated Press, "Kenyans United in Helping Hungry," appearing in *Champaign (Ill.) News-Gazette*, 8/8/2011, p. A-5.

[16]   The 2009 figures were obtained from "Table 1: Basic Indicators," *The State of the World's Children 2011* (New York: UNICEF, 2011), p.p. 88-90.

[17]   Rodney Stark, *The Rise of Christianity: How the Obscure, Marginal Jesus Movement Became the Dominant Religious Force in the Western World in a Few Centuries* (New York: HarperOne, HarperCollins Publishers, 1997), p. 62.

[18]   Stark, *The Rise of Christianity*, pp. 88, 89, 90-91.

[19]   Stark, *The Rise of Christianity*, pp. 84, 87.

[20]   Stark, *The Rise of Christianity*, p. 86.

[21]   Stark, *The Rise of Christianity*, p. 17.

[22]   Francis Chan, *Crazy Love* (Colorado Springs, CO: David C. Cook, 2008), p. 119.

[23]   Thomas J. Tierney and Joel L. Fleishman, Give $mart (New York: PublicAffairs™ , the Perseus Books Group, 2011), p. 77.

[24]   David Platt, *Radical Together* (Colorado Springs, CO: Multnomah Books, 2011), p. 25.

[25]   Chan, *Crazy Love*, p. 68.

[26]   G. Jeffrey MacDonald, *Thieves in the Temple* (New York: Basic Books, 2010), p. 64.

[27]   Gabe Lyons, *The Next Christians* (New York: Doubleday, 2010), p. 30-31.

[28]   Chuck Colson; "A Sign for the Times"; Christian Post; 11/19/2010; <http://www.christianpost.com/ article/20101119/a-sign-for-the-times/>; p. 1 of 11/19/2010 2:46 PM printout.

[29]   J. Gerald Harris, "Reclaiming Our First Love," *SBC Life*, August-September 2011, p. 4.

[30]   Peter Seewald, *Benedict XVI, Light of the World* (San Francisco: Ignatius Press, 2010), p. 56.

[31]   Mario Morino, *Leap of Reason: Managing to Outcomes in an Era of Scarcity* (Washington, DC: Venture Philanthropy Partners, 2011), p. 1.

[32]   Tierney and Fleishman, *Give $mart*, p. 115.

[33]   Stark, *The Rise of Christianity*, p. 165.

[34]   Chan, *Crazy Love*, p. 135.

35   The Barna Group; "Six Themes from Barna Group Research 2010"; Church Executive; n.d. <http://church executive.com/archives/six-themes-from-barna-group-research-2010>; pp. 2, 3 of 12/27/2010 8:42 AM printout.

36   MacDonald, *Thieves in the Temple*, p. 20.

37   MacDonald, *Thieves in the Temple*, p. 23.

38   Charles Ferguson, "Deleted Scenes, Eliot Spitzer #3," *Inside Job*, Sony Pictures Classics, Inc., 2010, 1:56-2:45.

39   Agence France Presse; "US Borrowing Tops 100% of GDP: Treasury"; Yahoo! News; 8/3/2011; <http://news.yahoo.com/us-aaa-rating-still-under-threat-204040123.html>; p. 1 of 8/3/2011 5:57 PM printout.

40   Polina Vlasenko, American Institute for Economic Research, "Recession's Impact Greater If Country Has a Large Debt," *Champaign (Ill.) News-Gazette*, 6/23/3011, p. A-8.

41   "Church-Backed Bonds May Be Cut by Mood's on Defaults"; The Church Report; 12/8/2010; <http://www.thechurchreport.com/index.cfm?fuseaction=siteContent.default&objectID=100719>; p. 1 of 12/10/2010 9:20 AM printout.

42   John M. Buchanan, "Wilderness of Uncertainty," *Christian Century*, April 7, 2009, p. 3.

43   Seewald, *Benedict XVI, Light of the World*, pp. 41.

44   MacDonald, *Thieves in the Temple*, p. 7-8.

45   Platt, *Radical Together*, p. 106.

46   Stark, *The Rise of Christianity*, p. 86.

47   Chan, *Crazy Love*, p. 61.

48   Seewald, *Benedict XVI, Light of the World*, pp. 49.

49   David Neff, "Signs of the End Times," *Christianity Today*, August 2011, p. 49.

50   Platt, *Radical Together*, p. 28, 29.

51   John Ronsvalle and Sylvia Ronsvalle, "The Theological Implications of Church Member Giving Patterns," *The State of Church Giving through 1995* (Champaign, Ill.: empty tomb, inc., 1997), pp. 83-96. The chapter is also available at: < http://www.emptytomb.org/implications.html>.

52   Clyde Meador; "First-Person: 'How Are They to Hear?'"; Baptist Press; 12/3/2010; <http://www.bpnews.net/printerfriendly.asp?ID-34204>; p. 1 of 12/3/2010 3:59 PM printout.

53   For a discussion of this effort, see John Ronsvalle and Sylvia Ronsvalle, *The State of Church Giving through 2008: Kudos to Wycliffe Bible Translators and World Vision for Global At-Scale Goals, But Will Denominations Resist Jesus Christ And Not spend $1 to $26 Per Member to reach The Unreached When Jesus Says, "You Feed Them"?* (Champaign, Ill.: empty tomb, inc., 2010), p. 151.

54   Erich Bridges; "Elliff Elected Unanimously to Lead International Mission Board"; Baptist Press; 3/16/2011; <http://www.bpnews.net/printerfriendly.asp?ID=34848>; p. 1 of 3/16/2011 3:37 PM printout.

55   J. Gerald Harris, "Reclaiming Our First Love," *SBC Life*, August/September 2011, p. 4.

56   Tammi Reed Ledbetter; "Editors Hear from SBC Entity Leaders"; Baptist Press; 2/21/2011; <http://www.bpnews.net/printerfriendly.asp?ID=34696>; p. 1 of 2/21/2011 5:00 PM printout.

57   Table 51: Southern Baptist Convention Lottie Moon Christmas Offerings, 1921-2009, and SBC Membership, 1921-1967.

Table 51 Year	Lottie Moon Christmas Offering $	SBC Membership	Year	Lottie Moon Christmas Offering $	SBC Membership	Year	Lottie Moon Christmas Offering $	Year	Lottie Moon Christmas Offering $
1921	28,615.78	3,220,000	1945	1,201,962.24	5,866,000	1968	15,159,206.92	1989	80,197,870.78
1922	29,583.67	3,366,000	1946	1,381,048.76	6,079,000	1969	15,297,558.63	1990	79,358,610.87
1923	42,206.37	3,494,000	1947	1,503,010.12	6,271,000	1970	16,220,104.99	1991	81,358,723.00
1924	48,677.00	3,575,000	1948	1,669,683.38	6,489,000	1971	17,833,810.22	1992	80,980,881.11
1925	306,376.21	3,649,000	1949	1,745,682.81	6,761,000	1972	19,664,972.53	1993	82,899,291.40
1926	246,152.84	3,617,000	1950	2,110,019.07	7,080,000	1973	22,232,757.09	1994	85,932,597.88
1927	172,457.36	3,674,000	1951	2,668,051.30	7,373,000	1974	23,234,093.89	1995	89,019,719.75
1928	235,274.31	3,706,000	1952	3,280,372.79	7,634,000	1975	26,169,421.12	1996	93,089,179.27
1929	190,130.81	3,771,000	1953	3,602,554.86	6,999,275	1976	28,763,809.71	1997	100,064,318.10
1930	200,799.84	3,850,000	1954	3,957,821.00	7,246,233	1977	31,938,553.04	1998	101,713,066.69
1931	170,724.87	3,945,000	1955	4,628,691.03	7,517,653	1978	35,919,605.40	1999	105,443,786.95
1932	143,331.24	4,066,000	1956	5,240,745.39	7,725,486	1979	40,597,113.02	2000	113,175,191.96
1933	172,512.86	4,174,000	1957	6,121,585.14	7,952,397	1980	44,700,339.76	2001	113,709,471.17
1934	213,925.81	4,277,000	1958	6,762,448.63	8,221,384	1981	50,784,173.38	2002	115,015,216.49
1935	240,455.12	4,389,000	1959	7,706,847.29	8,413,859	1982	54,077,464.49	2003	136,204,648.17
1936	292,401.57	4,482,000	1960	8,238,471.07	8,631,627	1983	58,025,336.79	2004	133,886,221.58
1937	290,219.74	4,596,000	1961	9,315,754.78	9,978,139	1984	64,775,763.83	2005	137,939,677.59
1938	315,000.40	4,770,000	1962	10,323,591.69	10,192,451	1985	66,862,113.65	2006	150,178,098.06
1939	330,424.70	4,949,000	1963	10,949,857.35	10,395,264	1986	69,412,195.09	2007	150,409,653.86
1940	363,746.30	5,104,000	1964	11,870,649.15	10,601,935	1987	69,912,637.50	2008	141,315,110.24
1941	449,162.48	5,238,000	1965	13,194,357.32	10,770,573	1988	78,787,726.26	2009	148,984,819.41
1942	562,609.30	5,367,000	1966	13,760,146.80	10,947,389				
1943	761,269.79	5,493,000	1967	14,664,679.30	11,140,486				
1944	949,844.17	5,668,000							

Source:
1921-2009 Lottie Moon Christmas Offering: "Lottie Moon Christmas Offering from Its Beginning in 1888"; International Mission Board, SBC; "LMCO Historical Campaign Year.XLS" attachment from David Steverson email response to author inquiry to IMB; June 9, 2010 6:54 AM; p. 1 of 6/9/2010 11:53 AM printout.
1921-1952 Southern Baptist Convention Membership: Historical Statistics of the United States: Colonial Times to 1970, Bicentennial Edition, Part 1 (Washington Bureau of the Census, 1975), Series H 805, pp. 391-92.
1953-1967 Southern Baptist Convention Membership: Yearbook of American and Canadian Churches series.
1968-2009 Southern Baptist Convention Membership: See Appendix B-1.

58   John Ronsvalle and Sylvia Ronsvalle, *The State of Church Giving through 2004: Will We Will?* (Champaign, IL: empty tomb, inc., 2006), pp. 107-110. Also available at: < http://www.emptytomb.org/SCG04.ch8excerpt.pdf>.

59   Jerry Filteau; "Getting Catholics Invested in the Mission"; National Catholic Reporter; 12/31/2009; <http://ncronline.org/news/faith-parish/getting-catholics-invested-mission>; pp. 1, 3 of 1/5/2010 7:24 AM printout.

60   Tierney and Fleishman, *Give $mart*, p. 79.

61   Chan, *Crazy Love*, p. 168.

62   Chan, *Crazy Love*.

63   David Platt, *Radical: Taking Back Your Faith from the American Dream* (Colorado Springs: Multnomah, 2010).

64   Richard Stearns, *The Hole in Our Gospel* (Nashville: Thomas Nelson, 2009).

65   Lyons, *The Next Christians*, p. 51.

66   "Pray Tell: Americans Stretching the Truth about Church Attendance"; University of Michigan News Service; 12/1/2010; < http://ns.umich.edu/htdocs/releases/story.php?id=8155>; p. 1 of 8/18/2011 4:49 PM printout.

67   Associated Press, "Super Bowl Advertisers Using New Strategies This Year," appearing in *Champaign (Ill.) News-Gazette*, 2/4/2011, p. D-2.

68   Michelle A. Vu; "Survey: 3 in 5 Unchurched Americans Are Christians"; Christian Post; 4/13/2010; <http://www.christianpost.com/article/20100413/majority-of-unchurched-are-christians-survey-finds/index.html>; p. 1 of 4/13/2010 1:37 PM printout.

69   Holly Hall, "Most Donors Intend to Give More in 2011, New Study Finds," *The Chronicle of Philanthropy*, May 5, 2011, p. 9.

70   Roger S. Oldham, "The Cooperative Program, Shared Ministry Expenses, and the Spirit of Cooperation," *SBC Life*, June/July 2011, pp. 6, 7.

71   John Ronsvalle and Sylvia Ronsvalle, *Behind the Stained Glass Windows: Money Dynamics in the Church* (Grand Rapids, MI: Baker Books, 1996), pp. 342, 335.

72   For a discussion of this issue, see John Ronsvalle and Sylvia Ronsvalle, *The State of Church Giving through 2005: Abolition of the Institutional Enslavement of Overseas Missions* (Champaign, IL: empty tomb, inc., 2007), pp. 105-131. The chapter is also available at <http://www.emptytomb.org/SCG05.ch8excerpt.pdf>.

73   Tammi Reed Ledbetter; "Elliff, in Teleconference, Answers Questions"; Baptist Press; 3/21/2011; <http://bpnews.net/printerfriendly.asp?ID=34882>; p. 3 of 3/21/2011 5:41 PM printout.

74   John Kenneth Galbraith, *The Affluent Society*, Third Edition, Revised (New York: The New American Library, Inc., 1976), pp. 1, 4.

75   Barrett, ed., *World Christian Encyclopedia*, p. 3.

76   Nathan Black; "Poll: Religion's Influence Waning in America"; Christian Post; 12/30/2010; <http://www.christianpost.com/article/20101230/poll-religions-influence-waning-in-america/>; p. 1 of 12/30/2010 1:42 PM printout.

77   Frank Newport; "This Easter, Smaller Percentage of Americans Are Christian"; Gallup Organization; 4/10/2009; <http://www.gallup.com/poll/117409/Easter-Smaller-Percentage-Americans-Christian.aspx>; p. 1 of 6/21/2011 2:05 PM printout.

78   Michelle A. Vu; "Few Millennials Interested in Religion, Study Finds"; Christian Post; 1/12/2011; <http://www.christianpost.com/article/20110112/few-millenials-interested-in-religion-study-finds/>; p. 1 of 1/13/11 8:47 AM printout.

79   Bradley N. Hill, "Missing the Signs," *Christian Century*, April 5, 2011, pp. 28, 29.

80   C. L Lopez, "A More Social Gospel," *Christianity Today*, December 2009, p. 18.

81   MacDonald, *Thieves in the Temple*, pp. 25, 26.

82   Ronsvalle, *Behind the Stained Glass Windows*, p. 79.

83   MacDonald, *Thieves in the Temple*, p. 26.

84   MacDonald, *Thieves in the Temple*, p. 191.

85   Peter L. Steinke, "Buckle Up: Congregational Change Isn't Easy," *Christian Century*, November 16, 2010, p. 34.

86   Morino, *Leap of Reason*, p. 23.

[87]   "What *Reveal* Reveals"; Christianity Today; 2/27/2008 8:09 AM; <http://www.christianitytoday.com/ct/2008/march/11.27.html>; p. 1 of 8/13/2011 4:09 PM printout.

[88]   Morino, *Leap of Reason*, p. 5.

[89]   Stark, *The Rise of Christianity*, p. 165, 169, 173.

[90]   André Nauta; "Stark, Rodney"; Hartford Seminary, *Encyclopedia of Religion and Society*, William H. Swatos, Jr., Editor; n.d.; <http://hirr.hartsem.edu/ency/StarkR.htm>; p. 1 of 8/13/2011 4:41 PM printout.

[91]   Platt, *Radical Together*, p. 15.

[92]   Stark, *The Rise of Christianity*, p. 78.

[93]   Ronsvalle, *The State of Church Giving through 2006: Global Triage, MDG 4, and Unreached People Groups*, pp. 107-148,

[94]   Ronsvalle, *The State of Church Giving through 2008*, pp. 119-166.

[95]   Patrick Worsnip and Lesley Wroughton; "U.N. Unveils Plan to Help Women, Children"; Reuters; 9/22/2010; <http://www.reuters.com/assets/print?aid=USTRE68L3UV20100922>; p. 1 of 9/22/2010 5:00 PM printout.

[96]   Lake, "Foreword," *The State of the World's Children 2011*, p. iii.

[97]   Email exchange with a representative of the World Health Organization, dated July 27, 2011 2:23 AM, regarding an update of the *Countdown to 2015* document.

[98]   The information was analyzed as follows. The annual number of under-5 child deaths for each country was entered on that country's row of a spreadsheet. The sum of the under-5 child deaths in these 68 countries totaled 8,343,000 in 2008. With a UNICEF figure of 8,772,000 under-5 deaths in 2008, it was calculated that these 68 countries accounted for 95% of the under-5 child deaths in 2005.

Next, the percent of the under-5 deaths due to each cause was entered in the spreadsheet row for each of the 68 nations.

Each country's percent of the total number of child deaths was then calculated.

Having calculated a percent of the total under-5 child deaths for each country, that individual percent was used as a multiplier for $5 billion, which served as a base cost figure for preventing the 8.772 million annual under-5 child deaths. The result was the cost-per-country dollar figure that would be needed to address causes of under-5 mortality in that country. The total calculated cost for the 68 countries was $4.76 billion, or 95% of the $5 billion total.

The cost estimate of $5 billion is the same figure used to develop a cost-per-child death figure cited in chapter 6. The Bulletin of the World Health Organization cited a figure of $52.4 billion that will be needed over the ten years, from 2006 through 2015, to "address the major causes of mortality among children aged < 5 years." [Karin Stenberg, Benjamin Johns, Robert W. Scherpbier, & Tessa Tan-Torres Edejer; "A Financial Road Map to Scaling Up Essential Child Health Interventions in 75 Countries"; Bulletin of the World Health Organization; April 2007, 85 (4); <http://www.who.int/bulletin/volumes/85/4/06-032052.pdf>; p. 1 of 8/8/2009 printout.]

The annual average for that estimate was $5.2 billion a year, thus providing support for the use of $5 billion for the present purpose.

Once a dollar figure was developed for each country, that dollar figure was multiplied by the percent of each cause of under-5 child deaths within that country. The result was a dollar-cost estimate by country per cause of death for each of the measured categories. Those categories included: Pneumonia; Diarrhea; Measles; Malaria; HIV/AIDS; Injuries; Other; and Neonatal.

Similarly, a dollar-cost estimate was calculated for each of the seven "Causes of neonatal deaths." The "Neonatal" categories included: Diarrhea; Other; Congenital; Tetanus; Asphyxia; Preterm; and Infection.

[99]   *The State of the World's Children Special Edition Statistical Tables* [2010] "Table 1. Basic Indicators"; UNICEF; 9/4/09; <http://www.unicef.org/publications/files/SOWC_Spec._Ed._CRC_Main_Report_EN_090409.pdf>; pp. 8-11 of 12/22/2009 printout.

[100] *Countdown to 2015 Decade Report (2000-2010)*, pp. 8-9, 42-177.

[101] Luisa Kroll, List Editor.; "The Forbes 400: Methodology"; Forbes.com; publication date 09.25.2010 10:40 AM ET [Forbes Magazine dated October 11, 2010]; <http://www.forbes.com/2010/1011/rich-list-10-buffett-gates-zuckerberg-oprah-methodology.html>; pp. 1 of 9/23/2010 2:02 PM printout.

[102] Tammi Reed Ledbetter; "Elliff: IMB to Be Biblical, Balanced, Bold"; Baptist Press; 3/16/2011; <http://www.bpnews.net/printerfriendly.asp?ID=34854>; pp. 1, 2 of 3/17/2011 3:17 PM printout.

[103]   Alan James; "Elliff to 'Newly Introduce' IMB to Young Pastors at SBC"; Baptist Press; 5/23/2011; <http://www.bpnews.net/printerfriendly.asp?ID=35359>; pp. 1 of 5/23/2011 5:54 PM printout.

[104]   J. Gerald Harris; "Wright Urges Adoption of 3,800 Unengaged Peoples"; Baptist Press; 6/14/2011; <http://www.bpnews.net/printerfriendly.asp?ID=35534>; p. 2 of 6/15/2011 10:12 Am printout.

[105]   Alan James; "EMBRACE: Southern Baptists Begin Engaging 3,800 People Groups"; Baptist Press; 6/29/2011; <http://www.bpnews.net/printerfriendly.asp?ID=35660>; pp. 1, 3 of 6/30/2011 4:10 PM printout.

[106]   Tammi Reed Ledbetter; "$1M to Embrace Unreached Voted by SBTC"; Baptist Press; 8/9/2011; <http://www.bpnews.net/printerfriendly.asp?ID=35908>; p. 1 of 8/9/2011 5:08 PM printout.

[107]   Imagine No Malaria; The United Methodist Church; n.d.; <http://www.imaginenomalaria.org/site/c.4dlBlLOnGalQE/b.5948247/k.EE2B/Imagine_No_Malaria__About_the_Initiative.htm>; p. 1 of 9/29/2010 11:50 AM printout.

[108]   Linda Bloom, United Methodist News Service, "Imagine No Malaria Has First Release of Funds," appearing in the Illinois Great Rivers Conference *The Current*, December 2010, p. 14.

[109]   "Simplicity for Generosity"; Lazarus at the Gate; n.d.; <http://lazarusatthegate.org/>; p. 1 of 7/11/2011 2:37 PM printout.

[110]   G. Jeffrey MacDonald, RNS, "Christians Shatter Taboos on Talking about Money," appearing in *Christian Century*, July 12, 2011, p. 17. See also <http://lazarusatthegate.org/>.

[111]   "About 58:"; 58:; n.d.; http://live58.org/about-58/>; p. 1 of 8/24/2011 6:20 PM printout.

[112]   John Nduna; "A new Alliance: John Ndunas launch speech.doc"; March 24, 2010; <http://www.actalliance.org/resources/launch/John%20Ndunas%20launch%20speech.doc/?searchterm=Nduna>; unnumbered pp. 2, 4 of 3/30/2010 printout.

[113]   "UN Troops Must Remain"; ACT Alliance; 5/11/2010; <http://www.actalliance.org/stories/act-un-troops-must-remain-in-congo>; p. 2, 3 of 8/13/2011 1:49 PM printout.

[114]   "Caritas Internationalis"; n.d.; <http://www.caritas.org/about/Caritas_Internationalis.html>; p. 1 of 1/14/2010 8:47 AM printout.

[115]   Patrick Nicholson; "Every Voice Counts to save Millennium Development Goals from Failure">; Caritas Internationalis; 8/31/2010; <http://www.caritas.org/newsroom/press_releases/PressRelease31_08_10.html>; p. 1 of 9/21/2010 9:05 AM printout.

[116]   "There Has Been Great Support: More Is Needed": Wycliffe Last Languages Campaign; n.d.; <http://www.lastlanguagescampaign.org/LLC/LLCmain/GreatSupport.aspx>; p. 1 of 11/14/2008 2:19 PM printout.

[117]   Michelle A. Vu; "Wycliffe Raises $250M for Last 2,000 Bible Translations"; Christian Post; 11/17/2010; <http://www.christianpost.com/article/20101117/wycliffe-raises-250-million-for-last-2000-bible-translations/>; pp. 1, 2 of 2/1/2011 4:59 PM printout.

[118]   "Child Health Now: Prioritising Simple, Low Cost Interventions Could Save Millions of Children's Lives Every Year, Says Aid Agency": World Vision International; Nov. 13, 2009; <http://www.childhealthnow.org/docs/pdf/Press_Release.pdf>; p. 2 of 11/25/2009 printout.

[119]   "Child Health Now: Together We Can End Preventable Deaths"; World Vision International; October 2009; <http://www.worldvision.org.uk/upload/pdf/CHN_Launch_Report.pdf>; pp. 5, 62 of April 26, 2010 printout.

[120]   Platt, *Radical Together*, p. 88-89.

[121]   Lyons, *The Next Christians*, p. 60.

[122]   Robert C. Crosby, "A New Kind of Pentecostal," *Christianity Today*, August 2011, pp. 51, 54.

[123]   John Calvin, *Commentary on a Harmony of the Evangelists, Matthew, Mark, and Luke*, p.181-82.

APPENDIXES

APPENDIX A: *List of Denominations*

Church Member Giving, 1968-2009, Composite Set

American Baptist Churches in the U.S.A.

The American Lutheran Church (through 1986)

Associate Reformed Presbyterian Church (General Synod)

Brethren in Christ Church

Christian Church (Disciples of Christ)

Church of God (Anderson, Ind.) (through 1997)

Church of God General Conference (Oregon, Ill., and Morrow, Ga.)

Church of the Brethren

Church of the Nazarene

Conservative Congregational Christian Conference

Cumberland Presbyterian Church

Evangelical Congregational Church

Evangelical Covenant Church

Evangelical Lutheran Church in America
  The American Lutheran Church (merged 1987)
  Lutheran Church in America (merged 1987)

Evangelical Lutheran Synod

Fellowship of Evangelical Bible Churches

Fellowship of Evangelical Churches (formerly Evangelical Mennonite Church)

Free Methodist Church of North America

Friends United Meeting (through 1990)

General Association of General Baptists

Lutheran Church in America (through 1986)

Lutheran Church-Missouri Synod

Mennonite Church USA (1999)
  Mennonite Church (merged 1999)
  Mennonite Church, General Conference (merged 1999)

Moravian Church in America, Northern Province

North American Baptist Conference (through 2006)

The Orthodox Presbyterian Church

Presbyterian Church (U.S.A.)

Reformed Church in America

Seventh-day Adventist Church, North American Division of

Southern Baptist Convention

United Church of Christ

Wisconsin Evangelical Lutheran Synod

Church Member Giving, 2008–2009

The Composite Set Denominations included in the 1968-2009 analysis with data available for both years, plus the following:

Allegheny Wesleyan Methodist Connection

Apostolic Faith Mission Church of God

Baptist Missionary Association of America

Bible Fellowship Church

Brethren Church (Ashland, Ohio)

Christ Comunity Church (Evangelical-Protestant)

Christian and Missionary Alliance

Church of Christ (Holiness) U.S.A.

Church of the Lutheran Brethren of America

Church of the Lutheran Confession

Churches of God General Conference

The Episcopal Church

The Missionary Church

Presbyterian Church in America

Primitive Methodist Church in the U.S.A.

The United Methodist Church

The Wesleyan Church

By Organizational Affiliation: NAE, 1968-2009

Brethren in Christ Church

Church of the Nazarene

Conservative Congregational Christian Conference

Evangelical Congregational Church

Fellowship of Evangelical Bible Churches

Fellowship of Evangelical Churches (formerly Evangelical Mennonite Church)

Free Methodist Church of North America

General Association of General Baptists

By Organizational Affiliation: NCC, 1968-2009

American Baptist Churches in the U.S.A.

Christian Church (Disciples of Christ)

Church of the Brethren

Evangelical Lutheran Church in America

Moravian Church in America, Northern Province

Presbyterian Church (U.S.A.)

Reformed Church in America

United Church of Christ

11 Denominations, 1921-2009

American Baptist (Northern)
Christian Church (Disciples of Christ)
Church of the Brethren
The Episcopal Church
Evangelical Lutheran Church in America
   The American Lutheran Church
      American Lutheran Church
      The Evangelical Lutheran Church
      United Evangelical Lutheran Church
      Lutheran Free Church
   Evangelical Lutheran Churches, Assn. of
   Lutheran Church in America
      United Lutheran Church
         General Council Evangelical Lutheran Ch.
         General Synod of Evangelical Lutheran Ch.
         United Synod Evangelical Lutheran South
      American Evangelical Lutheran Church
      Augustana Lutheran Church
      Finnish Lutheran Church (Suomi Synod)
Moravian Church in America, Northern Province
Presbyterian Church (U.S.A.)
   United Presbyterian Church in the U.S.A.
      Presbyterian Church in the U.S.A.
      United Presbyterian Church in North America
   Presbyterian Church in the U.S.
Reformed Church in America
Southern Baptist Convention
United Church of Christ
   Congregational Christian
   Congregational
   Evangelical and Reformed
      Evangelical Synod of North America/German
      Reformed Church in the U.S.
The United Methodist Church
   The Evangelical United Brethren
   The Methodist Church
      Methodist Episcopal Church
      Methodist Episcopal Church South
      Methodist Protestant Church

Trends in Membership, 11 Mainline Protestant Denominations, 1968-2009

American Baptist Churches in the U.S.A.
Christian Church (Disciples of Christ)
Church of the Brethren
The Episcopal Church
Evangelical Lutheran Church in America
Friends United Meeting

Moravian Church in America, Northern Prov.
Presbyterian Church (U.S.A.)
Reformed Church in America
United Church of Christ
The United Methodist Church

Trends in Membership, 15 Evangelical Denominations, 1968-2009

Assemblies of God
Baptist General Conference
Brethren in Christ Church
Christian and Missionary Alliance
Church of God (Cleveland, Tenn.)
Church of the Nazarene
Conservative Congregational Christian Conference
Evangelical Congregational Church
Fellowship of Evangelical Churches (formerly
   Evangelical Mennonite Church)
Fellowship of Evangelical Bible Churches
Free Methodist Church of North America
General Association of General Baptists
Lutheran Church-Missouri Synod
Salvation Army
Southern Baptist Convention

Trends in Membership, 36 Protestant Denominations and the Roman Catholic Church, 1968-2009

11 Mainline Protestant Denominations (above)
15 Evangelical Denominations (above)
The Roman Catholic Church
10 Additional Composite Denominations:
Associate Reformed Presbyterian Church (General
   Synod)
Church of God (Anderson, Ind.)
Church of God General Conference (Oregon, Ill.
   and Morrow, Ga.)
Cumberland Presbyterian Church
Evangelical Covenant Church
Evangelical Lutheran Synod
Mennonite Church USA
The Orthodox Presbyterian Church
Seventh-day Adventist Church, North American
   Division of
Wisconsin Evangelical Lutheran Synod

APPENDIX B SERIES: *Denominational Data Tables*

Introduction

The data in the following tables is from the *Yearbook of American and Canadian Churches* (*YACC*) series unless otherwise noted. Financial data is presented in current dollars.

Data in italics indicates a change from the previous edition in *The State of Church Giving* (*SCG*) series.

The Appendix B tables are described below.

Appendix B-1, Church Member Giving, 1968-2009: This table presents aggregate data for the denominations which comprise the data set analyzed for the 1968 through 2009 period.

Elements of this data are also used for the analyses in chapters two through seven.

In Appendix B-1, the data for the Presbyterian Church (U.S.A.) combined data for the United Presbyterian Church in the U.S.A. and the Presbyterian Church in the United States for the period 1968 through 1982. These two communions merged to become the Presbyterian Church (U.S.A.) in 1983, data for which is presented for 1983 through 2009.

Also in Appendix B-1, data for the Evangelical Lutheran Church in America (ELCA) appears beginning in 1987. Before that, the two major component communions that merged into the ELCA—the American Lutheran Church and the Lutheran Church in America—are listed as individual denominations from 1968 through 1986.

In the Appendix B series, the denomination listed as the Fellowship of Evangelical Bible Churches was named the Evangelical Mennonite Brethren Church prior to July 1987.

For 1999, the Mennonite Church (Elkhart, IN) provided information for the Mennonite Church USA. This communion is the result of a merger passed at a national convention in July 2001 between the Mennonite Church and the Mennonite Church, General Conference. The latter's 1968-1998 data has been added to the composite set series. The Mennonite Church USA dollar figures for 1999, and membership through 2001, combine data for the two predecessor communions.

The 1999, 2000, 2001, and 2002 data for the Southern Baptist Convention used in the 1968-2009 analysis includes data only for those State Conventions that provided a breakdown of total contributions between Congregational Finances and Benevolences for that year. For the 11 Denominations 1921-2009 analysis, 1999, 2000, 2001, and 2002, Southern Baptist Convention Total Contributions is $7,772,452,961, $8,437,177,940, $8,935,013,659, and $9,461,603,271 respectively. For the 11 Denominations 1921-2009 analysis, and the Membership Trends analysis, 1999, 2000, 2001, and 2002, Southern Baptist Convention Membership is 15,581,756, 15,960,308, 16,052,920, and 16,137,736 respectively.

Data for the American Baptist Churches in the U.S.A. has been obtained directly from the denominational office as follows. In discussions with the American Baptist Churches Office of Planning Resources, it became apparent that there had been no distinction made between the membership of congregations reporting financial data, and total membership for the denomination, when reporting data to the *YACC*. Records were obtained from the denomination for a smaller membership figure that reflected only those congregations reporting financial data. While this revised membership data provided a more useful per member giving figure for Congregational Finances, the total Benevolences figure reported to the *YACC*, while included in the present data set, does reflect contributions to some Benevolences categories from 100% of the American Baptist membership. The membership reported in Appendix B-1 for the American Baptist Churches is the membership for congregations reporting financial data, rather than the total membership figure provided in editions of the *YACC*. However, in the sections that consider membership as a percentage of population, the Total Membership figure for the American Baptist Churches is used.

Appendix B-2, Church Member Giving for 42 Denominations, 2008-2009: Appendix B-2 presents the Full or Confirmed Membership, Congregational Finances and Benevolences data for the 17 additional denominations included in the 2008-2009 comparison.

Appendix B-3, Church Member Giving for 11 Denominations, In Current Dollars, 1921-2009: This appendix presents additional data which is not included in Appendix B-1 for the 11 Denominations.

The data from 1921 through 1928 in Appendix B-3.1 is taken from summary information contained in the *YACC, 1949 Edition*, George F. Ketcham, ed. (Lebanon, PA: Sowers Printing Company, 1949, p. 162). The summary membership data provided is for Inclusive Membership. Therefore, giving as a percentage of income for the years 1921 through 1928 may have been somewhat higher had Full or Confirmed Membership been used. The list of denominations that are summarized for this period is presented in the *YACC, 1953 Edition*, Benson Y. Landis, ed. (New York: National Council of the Churches of Christ in the U.S.A., 1953, p. 274).

The data from 1929 through 1952 is taken from summary information presented in the *YACC, Edition for 1955*, Benson Y. Landis, ed. (New York: National Council of the Churches of Christ in the U.S.A., 1954, pp. 286-287). A description of the list of denominations included in the 1929 through 1952 data summary on page 275 of the *YACC Edition for 1955* indicated that the Moravian Church, Northern Province is not included in the 1929 through 1952 data.

The data in Appendix B-3.2 for 1953 through 1964 was obtained for the indicated denominations from the relevant edition of the *YACC* series. Giving as a percentage of income was derived for these years by dividing the published Total Contributions figure by the published Per Capita figure to produce a membership figure for each denomination. The Total Contributions figures for the denominations were added to produce an aggregated Total Contributions figure. The calculated membership figures were also added to produce an aggregated membership figure. The aggregated Total Contributions figure was then divided by the aggregated membership figure to yield a per member giving figure which was used in calculating giving as a percentage of income.

Data for the years 1965 through 1967 was not available in a form that could be readily analyzed for the present purposes, and therefore data for these three years was estimated by dividing the change in per capita Total Contributions from 1964 to 1968 by four, the number of years in this interval, and cumulatively adding the result to the base year of 1964 and the succeeding years of 1965 and 1966 to obtain estimates for the years 1965 through 1967.

In most cases, this procedure was also applied to individual denominations to avoid an artificially low total due to missing data. If data was not available for a specific year, the otherwise blank entry was filled in with a calculation based on surrounding years for the denomination. For example, this procedure was used for the American Baptist Churches for the years 1955 and 1996, the Christian Church (Disciples of Christ) for the years 1955 and 1959, and the Evangelical United Brethren, later to merge into The United Methodist Church, for the years 1957, 1958 and 1959. Data for the Methodist Church was changed for 1957 in a similar manner.

Available Total Contributions and Full or Confirmed Members data for The Episcopal Church and The United Methodist Church for 1968 through 2009 is presented in Appendix B-3.3. These two communions are included in the 11 Denominations. The United Methodist Church was created in 1968 when the Methodist Church and the Evangelical United Brethren Church merged. While the Methodist Church filed summary data for the year 1968, the Evangelical United Brethren Church did not. Data for these denominations was calculated as noted in the appendix. However, since the 1968 data for The Methodist Church would not have been comparable to the 1985 and 2009 data for The United Methodist Church, this communion was not included in the more focused 1969-2009 composite analysis. The United Methodist Church Connectional Clergy Support 1968-2008 data used in Chapter 5 was obtained directly from the denominational source and is also presented in this appendix.

Appendix B-4, Membership for Seven Denominations, 1968-2009: This appendix presents denominational membership data used in the membership analyses presented in chapter five that is not available in the other appendixes. Unless otherwise indicated, the data is from the *YACC* series.

Appendix B-5, Overseas Missions Income, 2003, 2004, 2005, 2006, 2007, 2008, and 2009: This appendix presents numbers provided on the four lines of the Overseas Missions Income form completed by the respective denominations. Also provided is Overseas Missions Income for two denominations which are not included in the analyses (see chapter 6, note 9).

Appendix B-6, Estimates of Giving: This appendix provides the data used in the comparison presented in chapter 7 of the Consumer Expenditure Survey, the Form 990 series, and the *Giving USA* series, for 1989-2007.

APPENDIX B-1: *Church Member Giving, 1968-2009*

Key to Denominational Abbreviations: Data Years 1968-2009

Abbreviation	Denomination
abc	American Baptist Churches in the U.S.A.
alc	The American Lutheran Church
arp	Associate Reformed Presbyterian Church (General Synod)
bcc	Brethren in Christ Church
ccd	Christian Church (Disciples of Christ)
cga	Church of God (Anderson, IN)
cgg	Church of God General Conference (Oregon, IL and Morrow, GA)
chb	Church of the Brethren
chn	Church of the Nazarene
ccc	Conservative Congregational Christian Church
cpc	Cumberland Presbyterian Church
ecc	Evangelical Congregational Church
ecv	Evangelical Covenant Church
elc	Evangelical Lutheran Church in America
els	Evangelical Lutheran Synod
emc	Evangelical Mennonite Church
feb	Fellowship of Evangelical Bible Churches
fec	Fellowship of Evangelical Churches
fmc	Free Methodist Church of North America
fum	Friends United Meeting
ggb	General Association of General Baptists
lca	Lutheran Church in America
lms	Lutheran Church-Missouri Synod
mch	Mennonite Church
mgc	Mennonite Church, General Conference
mus	Mennonite Church USA
mca	Moravian Church in America, Northern Province
nab	North American Baptist Conference
opc	The Orthodox Presbyterian Church
pch	Presbyterian Church (U.S.A.)
rca	Reformed Church in America
sda	Seventh-day Adventist, North American Division of
sbc	Southern Baptist Convention
ucc	United Church of Christ
wel	Wisconsin Evangelical Lutheran Synod

Appendix B-1: Church Member Giving, In Current Dollars, 1968-2009

	Data Year 1968			Data Year 1969			Data Year 1970		
	Full/Confirmed Members	Congregational Finances	Benevolences	Full/Confirmed Members	Congregational Finances	Benevolences	Full/Confirmed Members	Congregational Finances	Benevolences
abc	1,179,848 a	95,878,267 a	21,674,924 a	1,153,785 a	104,084,322	21,111,333	1,231,944 a	112,668,310	19,655,391
alc	1,767,618	137,260,390	32,862,410	1,771,999	143,917,440	34,394,570	1,775,573	146,268,320	30,750,030
arp	28,312 a	2,211,002 a	898,430 a	28,273	2,436,936 a	824,628 a	28,427 a	2,585,974 a	806,071 a
bcc	8,954	1,645,256	633,200 a	9,145	1,795,859	817,445	9,300 a	2,037,330 a	771,940 a
ccd	994,683	105,803,222	21,703,947	936,931	91,169,842	18,946,815	911,964	98,671,692	17,386,032
cga	146,807	23,310,682	4,168,580	147,752	24,828,448	4,531,678	150,198	26,962,037	4,886,223
cgg	6,600	805,000	103,000	6,700	805,000	104,000	6,800	810,000	107,000
chb	187,957	12,975,829	4,889,727	185,198	13,964,158	4,921,991	182,614	14,327,896	4,891,618
chn	364,789	59,943,750 a	14,163,761 a	372,943	64,487,669 a	15,220,339 a	383,284	68,877,922 a	16,221,123 a
ccc	15,127	1,867,978	753,686	16,219	1,382,195	801,534	17,328	1,736,818	779,696
cpc	87,044 a	6,247,447 a	901,974 a	86,435 a	7,724,405 a	926,317 a	86,683 a	7,735,906 a	1,011,911 a
ecc	29,582 a	3,369,308 a	627,731 a	29,652 a	3,521,074 a	646,187 a	29,437 a	3,786,288 a	692,428 a
ecv	66,021	14,374,162 a	3,072,848	67,522	14,952,302 a	3,312,306	67,441	15,874,265 a	3,578,876
elc	ALC & LCA	ALC & LCA	ALC & LCA	ALC & LCA	ALC & LCA	ALC & LCA	ALC & LCA	ALC & LCA	ALC & LCA
els	10,886 a	844,235 a	241,949 a	11,079	1,003,746	315,325	11,030	969,625	242,831 a
emc	2,870 a	447,397	232,331	NA	NA	NA	NA	NA	NA
feb	1,712 a	156,789 a	129,818 a	3,324	389,000	328,000	3,698	381,877	706,398
fec	see EMC	see EMC	see EMC	see EMC	see EMC	see EMC	see EMC	see EMC	see EMC
fmc	47,831 a	12,032,016 a	2,269,677 a	47,954 a	13,187,506 a	2,438,351 a	64,901	9,641,202	7,985,264
fum	55,469	3,564,793	1,256,192	55,257	3,509,509	1,289,026	53,970	3,973,802	1,167,183
ggb	65,000	4,303,183 a	269,921 a	NA	NA	NA	NA	NA	NA
lca	2,279,383	166,337,149	39,981,858	2,193,321	161,958,669	46,902,225	2,187,015	169,795,380	42,118,870
lms	1,877,799	178,042,762	47,415,800	1,900,708	185,827,626	49,402,590	1,922,569	193,352,322	47,810,664
mch	85,682 a	7,078,164 a	5,576,305 a	85,343	7,398,182	6,038,730	83,747 a	7,980,917 a	6,519,476 a
mgc	36,337 a	2,859,340 a	2,668,138 a	35,613	2,860,555 a	2,587,079 a	35,536	3,091,670	2,550,208
mus	MCH & MGC	MCH & MGC	MCH & MGC	MCH & MGC	MCH & MGC	MCH & MGC	MCH & MGC	MCH & MGC	MCH & MGC
mca	27,772	2,583,354	444,910	27,617	2,642,529	456,182	27,173	2,704,105	463,219
nab	42,371 a	5,176,669 a	1,383,964 a	55,100	6,681,410	2,111,588	55,080	6,586,929	2,368,288
opc	9,197	1,638,437	418,102	9,276	1,761,242	464,660	9,401 a	1,853,627 a	503,572 a
pch	4,180,093	375,248,474	102,622,450	4,118,664	388,268,169	97,897,522	4,041,813	401,785,731	93,927,852
rca	226,819 b	25,410,489 b	9,197,642 b	224,992 b	27,139,579 b	9,173,312 b	223,353 b	29,421,849 b	9,479,503 b
sda	395,159 a	36,976,280	95,178,335	407,766	40,378,426	102,730,594	420,419	45,280,059	109,569,241
sbc	11,332,229 a	666,924,020 a	128,023,731 a	11,487,708	709,246,590	133,203,885	11,628,032	753,510,973	138,480,329
ucc	2,032,648 a	152,301,536	18,869,136	1,997,898	152,791,512	27,338,543	1,960,608	155,248,767	26,934,289
wel	259,649 a	18,982,244 a	6,572,250 a	264,710 a	20,761,838 a	6,414,099 a	270,073 a	22,525,244 a	6,781,600 a
Total	27,852,248	2,126,599,624	569,206,727	27,738,884	2,200,875,738	595,650,854	27,879,411	2,310,446,837	599,147,126

a Data obtained from denominational source.

b empty tomb review of RCA directory data.

Appendix B-1: Church Member Giving, In Current Dollars, 1968-2009 (continued)

	Data Year 1971			Data Year 1972			Data Year 1973		
	Full/Confirmed Members	Congregational Finances	Benevolences	Full/Confirmed Members	Congregational Finances	Benevolences	Full/Confirmed Members	Congregational Finances	Benevolences
abc	1,223,735 [a]	114,673,805	18,878,769	1,176,092 [a]	118,446,573	18,993,440	1,190,455 [a]	139,357,611	20,537,388
alc	1,775,774	146,324,460	28,321,740	1,773,414	154,786,570	30,133,850	1,770,119	168,194,730	35,211,440
arp	28,443 [a]	2,942,577 [a]	814,703 [a]	28,711 [a]	3,329,446 [a]	847,665 [a]	28,763 [a]	3,742,773 [a]	750,387 [a]
bcc	9,550	2,357,786	851,725	9,730	2,440,400	978,957	9,877 [a]	2,894,622 [a]	1,089,879 [a]
ccd	884,929	94,091,862	17,770,799	881,467	105,763,511	18,323,685	868,895	112,526,538	19,800,843
cga	152,787	28,343,604	5,062,282	155,920	31,580,751	5,550,487	157,828	34,649,592	6,349,695
cgg	7,200	860,000	120,000	7,400	900,000	120,000	7,440	940,000	120,000
chb	181,183	14,535,274	5,184,768	179,641	14,622,319 [c]	5,337,277 [c]	179,333	16,474,758	6,868,927
chn	394,197	75,107,918 [a]	17,859,332 [a]	404,732	82,891,903 [a]	20,119,679 [a]	417,200	91,318,469 [a]	22,661,140 [a]
ccc	19,279 [a]	1,875,010 [a]	930,485 [a]	20,081 [a]	1,950,865 [a]	994,453 [a]	20,712 [a]	2,080,038 [a]	1,057,869 [a]
cpc	86,945 [a]	7,729,131 [a]	1,009,657 [a]	88,200 [a]	8,387,762 [a]	1,064,831 [a]	88,203 [a]	9,611,201 [a]	1,220,768 [a]
ecc	29,682 [a]	4,076,576 [a]	742,293 [a]	29,434 [a]	4,303,406 [a]	798,968 [a]	29,331 [a]	4,913,214 [a]	943,619 [a]
ecv	68,428	17,066,051 [a]	3,841,887	69,815	18,021,767 [a]	4,169,053	69,922	18,948,864 [a]	4,259,950
elc	ALC & LCA	ALC & LCA	ALC & LCA	ALC & LCA	ALC & LCA	ALC & LCA	ALC & LCA	ALC & LCA	ALC & LCA
els	11,426 [a]	1,067,650 [a]	314,335 [a]	11,532	1,138,953	295,941 [a]	12,525	1,296,326	330,052 [a]
emc	NA	NA	NA	NA	NA	NA	3,131	593,070	408,440
feb	NA	NA	NA	NA	NA	NA	NA	NA	NA
fec	see EMC	see EMC	see EMC	see EMC	see EMC	see EMC	see EMC	see EMC	see EMC
fmc	47,933 [a]	13,116,414 [a]	2,960,525 [a]	48,400 [a]	14,311,395 [a]	3,287,000 [a]	48,763 [a]	15,768,216 [a]	3,474,555 [a]
fum	54,522	3,888,064	1,208,062	54,927	4,515,463	1,297,088	57,690	5,037,848	1,327,439
ggb	NA	NA	NA	NA	NA	NA	NA	NA	NA
lca	2,175,378	179,570,467	43,599,913	2,165,591	188,387,949	45,587,481	2,169,341	200,278,486	34,627,978
lms	1,945,889	203,619,804	48,891,368	1,963,262	216,756,345	50,777,670	1,983,114	230,435,598	54,438,074
mch	88,522	8,171,316	7,035,750	89,505	9,913,176	7,168,664	90,967	9,072,858	6,159,740
mgc	36,314	3,368,100	2,833,491	36,129	3,378,372	3,219,439	36,483	3,635,418	3,392,844
mus	MCH & MGC	MCH & MGC	MCH & MGC	MCH & MGC	MCH & MGC	MCH & MGC	MCH & MGC	MCH & MGC	MCH & MGC
mca	26,101	2,576,172	459,447	25,500	2,909,252	465,316	25,468	3,020,667	512,424
nab	54,997	7,114,457	2,293,692	54,441	7,519,558	2,253,158	41,516	6,030,352	1,712,092
opc	9,536 [a]	2,054,448 [a]	533,324 [a]	9,741 [a]	2,248,969 [a]	602,328 [a]	9,940 [a]	2,364,079 [a]	658,534 [a]
pch	3,963,665	420,865,807	93,164,548	3,855,494	436,042,890	92,691,469	3,730,312 [d]	480,735,088 [d]	95,462,247 [d]
rca	219,915 [b]	32,217,319 [b]	9,449,655 [b]	217,583 [b]	34,569,874 [b]	9,508,818 [b]	212,906 [b]	39,524,443 [b]	10,388,619 [b]
sda	433,906	49,208,043	119,913,879	449,188	54,988,781	132,411,980	464,276	60,643,602	149,994,942
sbc	11,824,676	814,406,626	160,510,775	12,065,333	896,427,208	174,711,648	12,295,400	1,011,467,569	193,511,983
ucc	1,928,674	158,924,956	26,409,521	1,895,016	165,556,364	27,793,561	1,867,810	168,602,602	28,471,058
wel	274,635 [a]	24,315,801 [a]	7,456,829 [a]	277,628 [a]	26,585,530 [a]	8,204,262 [a]	282,355 [a]	29,377,447 [a]	8,623,460 [a]
Total	27,958,221	2,434,469,498	628,423,554	28,043,907	2,612,675,352	667,708,168	28,170,075	2,873,536,079	714,366,386

[a] Data obtained from denominational source.
[b] empty tomb review of RCA directory data.
[c] YACC Church of the Brethren figures reported for 15 months due to fiscal year change: adjusted here to 12/15ths.
[d] The Presbyterian Church (USA) data for 1973 combines United Presbyterian Church in the U.S.A. data for 1973 (see YACC 1975) and an average of Presbyterian Church in the United States data for 1972 and 1974, since 1973 data was not reported in the YACC series.

Appendix B-1: Church Member Giving, In Current Dollars, 1968-2009 (continued)

	Data Year 1974			Data Year 1975			Data Year 1976		
	Full/Confirmed Members	Congregational Finances	Benevolences	Full/Confirmed Members	Congregational Finances	Benevolences	Full/Confirmed Members	Congregational Finances	Benevolences
abc	1,176,989 a	147,022,280	21,847,285	1,180,793 a	153,697,091	23,638,372	1,142,773 a	163,134,092	25,792,357
alc	1,764,186	173,318,574	38,921,546	1,764,810	198,863,519	75,666,809	1,768,758	215,527,544	76,478,278
arp	28,570	3,935,533 a	868,284 a	28,589	4,820,846 a	929,880 a	28,581	5,034,270 a	1,018,913 a
bcc	10,255	3,002,218	1,078,576	10,784	3,495,152	955,845	11,375	4,088,492	1,038,484
ccd	854,844	119,434,435	20,818,434	859,885	126,553,931	22,126,459	845,058	135,008,269	23,812,274
cga	161,401	39,189,287	7,343,123	166,259	42,077,029	7,880,559	170,285	47,191,302	8,854,295
cgg	7,455	975,000	105,000	7,485	990,000	105,000	7,620	1,100,000	105,000
chb	179,387	18,609,614	7,281,551	179,336	20,338,351	7,842,819	178,157	22,133,858	8,032,293
chn	430,128	104,774,391	25,534,267 a	441,093	115,400,881	28,186,392 a	448,658	128,294,499	32,278,187 a
ccc	21,661 a	2,452,254 a	1,181,655 a	22,065 a	2,639,472 a	1,750,364 a	21,703 a	3,073,413 a	1,494,355 a
cpc	87,875 a	9,830,198 a	1,336,847 a	86,903 a	11,268,297 a	1,445,793 a	85,541 a	10,735,854 a	1,540,692 a
ecc	29,636 a	4,901,100 a	1,009,726 a	28,886 a	5,503,484 a	1,068,134 a	28,840 a	6,006,621 a	1,139,209 a
ecv	69,960	21,235,204 a	5,131,124	71,808	23,440,265 a	6,353,422	73,458	25,686,916 a	6,898,871
elc	ALC & LCA	ALC & LCA	ALC & LCA	ALC & LCA	ALC & LCA	ALC & LCA	ALC & LCA	ALC & LCA	ALC & LCA
els	13,097	1,519,749	411,732 a	13,489 a	1,739,255	438,875 a	14,504	2,114,998	521,018 a
emc	3,123	644,548	548,000	NA	NA	NA	3,350	800,000	628,944
feb	NA	NA	NA	NA	NA	NA	NA	NA	NA
fec	see EMC	see EMC	see EMC	see EMC	see EMC	see EMC	see EMC	see EMC	see EMC
fmc	49,314 a	17,487,246 a	3,945,535 a	50,632	19,203,781 a	4,389,757 a	51,565	21,130,066 a	4,977,546 a
fum	NA	NA	NA	56,605	6,428,458	1,551,036	51,032	6,749,045	1,691,190
ggb	NA	NA	NA	NA	NA	NA	NA	NA	NA
lca	2,166,615	228,081,405	44,531,126	2,183,131	222,637,156	55,646,303	2,187,995	243,449,466	58,761,005
lms	2,010,456	249,150,470	55,076,955	2,018,530	266,546,758	55,896,061	2,026,336	287,098,403	56,831,860
mch	92,930 a	13,792,266	9,887,051	94,209	15,332,908	11,860,385	96,092 a	17,215,234	12,259,924
mgc	35,534	4,071,002 a	4,179,003 a	35,673 a	3,715,279 a	3,391,943 a	36,397	4,980,967	4,796,037 a
mus	MCH & MGC	MCH & MGC	MCH & MGC	MCH & MGC	MCH & MGC	MCH & MGC	MCH & MGC	MCH & MGC	MCH & MGC
mca	25,583	3,304,388	513,685	25,512	3,567,406	552,512	24,938	4,088,195	573,619
nab	41,437	6,604,693	2,142,148	42,122	7,781,298	2,470,317	42,277	8,902,540	3,302,348
opc	10,186 a	2,627,818 a	703,653 a	10,129 a	2,930,128 a	768,075 a	10,372	3,288,612 a	817,589 a
pch	3,619,768	502,237,350	100,966,089	3,535,825	529,327,006	111,027,318	3,484,985	563,106,353	125,035,379
rca	210,866 b	41,053,364 b	11,470,631 b	212,349 b	44,681,053 b	11,994,379 b	211,628 b	49,083,734 b	13,163,739 b
sda	479,799	67,241,956	166,166,766	495,699	72,060,121	184,689,250	509,792	81,577,130	184,648,454
sbc	12,513,378	1,123,264,849	219,214,770	12,733,124	1,237,594,037	237,452,055	12,917,992	1,382,794,494	262,144,889
ucc	1,841,312	184,292,017	30,243,223	1,818,762	193,524,114	32,125,332	1,801,241	207,486,324	33,862,658
wel	286,083 a	32,596,319 a	9,974,758 a	292,431 a	35,807,415 a	11,173,226 a	297,037 a	39,932,827 a	11,260,203 a
Total	28,221,828	3,126,649,528	792,432,543	28,466,918	3,371,964,491	903,376,672	28,578,340	3,690,813,518	963,759,610

a Data obtained from denominational source .

b empty tomb review of RCA directory data.

178

Appendix B-1: Church Member Giving, In Current Dollars, 1968-2009 (continued)

	Data Year 1977			Data Year 1978			Data Year 1979		
	Full/Confirmed Members	Congregational Finances	Benevolences	Full/Confirmed Members	Congregational Finances	Benevolences	Full/Confirmed Members	Congregational Finances	Benevolences
abc	1,146,084[a]	172,710,063	27,765,800	1,008,495[a]	184,716,172	31,937,862	1,036,054[a]	195,986,995	34,992,300
alc	1,772,227	231,960,304	54,085,201	1,773,179	256,371,804	57,145,861	1,768,071	284,019,905	63,903,906
arp	28,371[a]	5,705,295[a]	1,061,285[a]	28,644	6,209,447[a]	1,031,469[a]	28,513	6,544,759[a]	1,125,562[a]
bcc	11,915[a]	4,633,334[a]	957,239[a]	12,430[a]	4,913,311[a]	1,089,346[a]	12,923	5,519,037	1,312,046
ccd	817,288	148,880,340	25,698,856	791,633	166,249,455	25,790,367	773,765	172,270,978	27,335,440
cga	171,947	51,969,150	10,001,062	173,753	57,630,848	11,214,530	175,113	65,974,517	12,434,621
cgg	7,595	1,130,000	110,000	7,550	1,135,000	110,000	7,620	1,170,000	105,000
chb	177,534	23,722,817	8,228,903	175,335	25,397,531	9,476,220	172,115	28,422,684	10,161,266
chn	455,100	141,807,024	34,895,751[a]	462,124	153,943,138	38,300,431[a]	473,726	170,515,940[a]	42,087,862[a]
ccc	21,897[a]	3,916,248[a]	1,554,143[a]	22,364[a]	4,271,435[a]	1,630,565[a]	23,481[a]	4,969,610[a]	1,871,754[a]
cpc	85,227[a]	11,384,825[a]	1,760,117[a]	84,956[a]	13,359,375[a]	1,995,388[a]	85,932[a]	13,928,957[a]	2,192,562[a]
ecc	28,712[a]	6,356,730[a]	1,271,310[a]	28,459[a]	6,890,381[a]	1,454,826[a]	27,995[a]	7,552,495[a]	1,547,857[a]
ecv	74,060	28,758,357[a]	7,240,548	74,678	32,606,550[a]	8,017,623	76,092	37,118,906[a]	9,400,074
elc	ALC & LCA	ALC & LCA	ALC & LCA	ALC & LCA	ALC & LCA	ALC & LCA	ALC & LCA	ALC & LCA	ALC & LCA
els	14,652	2,290,697	546,899[a]	14,833	2,629,719	833,543[a]	15,081	2,750,703	904,774[a]
emc	NA	NA	NA	3,634	1,281,761	794,896	3,704	1,380,806	828,264
feb	NA	NA	NA	3,956	970,960	745,059	NA	NA	NA
fec	see EMC	see EMC	see EMC	see EMC	see EMC	see EMC	see EMC	see EMC	see EMC
fmc	52,563	23,303,722[a]	5,505,538[a]	52,698[a]	25,505,294[a]	5,869,970[a]	52,900[a]	27,516,302[a]	6,614,732[a]
fum	52,599	6,943,990	1,895,984	53,390	8,172,337	1,968,884	51,426	6,662,787	2,131,108
ggb	72,030	9,854,533	747,842	NA	NA	NA	73,046	13,131,345	1,218,763
lca	2,191,942	251,083,883	62,076,894	2,183,666	277,186,563	72,426,148	2,177,231	301,605,382	71,325,097
lms	1,991,408	301,064,630	57,077,162	1,969,279	329,134,237	59,030,753	1,965,422	360,989,735	63,530,596
mch	96,609	18,540,237	12,980,502	97,142	22,922,417	14,124,757[a]	98,027	24,505,346	15,116,762
mgc	35,575[a]	5,051,708[a]	4,619,590[a]	36,775[a]	5,421,568[a]	5,062,489[a]	36,736[a]	6,254,850[a]	5,660,477[a]
mus	MCH & MGC	MCH & MGC	MCH & MGC	MCH & MGC	MCH & MGC	MCH & MGC	MCH & MGC	MCH & MGC	MCH & MGC
mca	25,323	4,583,616	581,200	24,854	4,441,750	625,536	24,782	4,600,331	689,070
nab	42,724	10,332,556	3,554,204	42,499	11,629,309	3,559,983	42,779	13,415,024	3,564,339
opc	10,683[a]	3,514,172	931,935	10,939	4,107,705	1,135,388	11,306[a]	4,683,302	1,147,191
pch	3,430,927	633,187,916	130,252,348	3,382,783	692,872,811	128,194,954	3,321,787	776,049,247	148,528,993
rca	210,637[b]	53,999,791[b]	14,210,966[b]	211,778[b]	60,138,720[b]	15,494,816[b]	210,700[b]	62,997,526[b]	16,750,408[b]
sda	522,317	98,468,365	216,202,975	535,705	104,044,989	226,692,736	553,089	118,711,906	255,936,372
sbc	13,078,239	1,506,877,921	289,179,711	13,191,394	1,668,120,760	316,462,385	13,372,757	1,864,213,869	355,885,769
ucc	1,785,652	219,878,772	35,522,221	1,769,104	232,593,033	37,789,958	1,745,533	249,443,032	41,100,583
wel	301,125[a]	44,378,032[a]	11,600,902[a]	303,134[a]	50,123,714[a]	12,907,953[a]	305,454[a]	54,789,339[a]	14,178,008[a]
Total	28,712,962	4,026,289,028	1,022,117,088	28,531,163	4,414,992,094	1,092,914,696	28,723,160	4,887,695,615	1,213,581,556

a Data obtained from denominational source.
b empty tomb review of RCA directory data.

179

Appendix B-1: Church Member Giving, In Current Dollars, 1968-2009 (continued)

	Data Year 1980			Data Year 1981			Data Year 1982		
	Full/Confirmed Members	Congregational Finances	Benevolences	Full/Confirmed Members	Congregational Finances	Benevolences	Full/Confirmed Members	Congregational Finances	Benevolences
abc	1,008,700 a	213,560,656	37,133,159	989,322 a	227,931,461	40,046,261	983,580 a	242,750,027	41,457,745
alc	1,763,067	312,592,610	65,235,739	1,758,452	330,155,588	96,102,638	1,758,239	359,848,865	77,010,444
arp	28,166 a	6,868,650 a	1,054,229 a	28,334 a	7,863,221 a	1,497,838 a	29,087 a	8,580,311 a	1,807,572 a
bcc	13,578 a	6,011,465 a	1,490,334 a	13,993	6,781,857	1,740,711	14,413 a	7,228,612 a	1,594,797 a
ccd	788,394	189,176,399	30,991,519	772,466	211,828,751	31,067,142	770,227	227,178,861	34,307,638
cga	176,429	67,367,485	13,414,112	178,581	78,322,907	14,907,277	184,685	84,896,806	17,171,600
cgg	NA	NA	NA	5,981	1,788,298	403,000	5,781 a	1,864,735 a	418,000 a
chb	170,839	29,813,265	11,663,976	170,267	31,641,019	12,929,076	168,844	35,064,568	12,844,415
chn	483,101	191,536,556	45,786,446 a	490,852	203,145,992	50,084,163 a	497,261	221,947,940	53,232,461 a
ccc	24,410 a	6,017,539 a	2,169,298 a	25,044 a	8,465,804	2,415,233	26,008	9,230,111	2,574,569
cpc	86,941 a	15,973,738 a	2,444,677 a	87,493 a	16,876,846 a	2,531,539 a	88,121 a	17,967,709 a	2,706,361 a
ecc	27,567 a	8,037,564 a	1,630,993 a	27,287 a	8,573,057 a	1,758,025 a	27,203 a	9,119,278 a	1,891,936 a
ecv	77,737	41,888,556 a	10,031,072	79,523	45,206,565 a	8,689,918	81,324	50,209,520 a	8,830,793
elc	ALC & LCA	ALC & LCA	ALC & LCA	ALC & LCA	ALC & LCA	ALC & LCA	ALC & LCA	ALC & LCA	ALC & LCA
els	14,968	3,154,804	876,929 a	14,904	3,461,387	716,624	15,165	3,767,977	804,822
emc	3,782	1,527,945	1,041,447	3,753	1,515,975	908,342	3,832	1,985,890	731,510
feb	4,329	1,250,466	627,536	NA	NA	NA	2,047	696,660	1,020,972
fec	see EMC	see EMC	see EMC	see EMC	see EMC	see EMC	see EMC	see EMC	see EMC
fmc	54,145 a	30,525,352 a	6,648,248 a	54,764 a	32,853,491 a	7,555,713 a	54,198	35,056,434	8,051,593
fum	51,691	9,437,724	2,328,137	51,248	9,551,765	2,449,731	50,601	10,334,180	2,597,215
ggb	74,159	14,967,312	1,547,038	75,028	15,816,060	1,473,070	NA	NA	NA
lca	2,176,991	371,981,816	87,439,137	2,173,558	404,300,509	82,862,299	2,176,265	435,564,519	83,217,264
lms	1,973,958	390,756,268	66,626,364	1,983,198	429,910,406	86,341,102	1,961,260	468,468,156	75,457,846
mch	99,511	28,846,931	16,437,738	99,651	31,304,278	17,448,024	101,501	33,583,338	17,981,274
mgc	36,644 a	6,796,330 a	5,976,652 a	36,609 a	7,857,792 a	7,203,240 a	37,007 a	8,438,680 a	7,705,419 a
mus	MCH & MGC	MCH & MGC	MCH & MGC	MCH & MGC	MCH & MGC	MCH & MGC	MCH & MGC	MCH & MGC	MCH & MGC
mca	24,863	5,178,444	860,399	24,500	5,675,495	831,177	24,669	6,049,857	812,015
nab	43,041	12,453,858	3,972,485	43,146	15,513,286	4,420,403	42,735	17,302,952	4,597,515
opc	11,553 a	5,235,294	1,235,849	11,884 a	5,939,983	1,382,451	11,956 a	6,512,125 a	1,430,061 a
pch	3,262,086	820,218,732	176,172,729	3,202,392	896,641,430	188,576,382	3,157,372	970,223,947	199,331,832
rca	210,762	70,733,297	17,313,239 b	210,312	77,044,709	18,193,793 b	211,168	82,656,050	19,418,165 b
sda	571,141	121,484,768	275,783,385	588,536	133,088,131	297,838,046	606,310	136,877,455	299,437,917
sbc	13,600,126	2,080,375,258	400,976,072	13,782,644	2,336,062,506	443,931,179	13,991,709	2,628,272,553	486,402,607
ucc	1,736,244	278,546,571	44,042,186	1,726,535	300,730,591	48,329,399	1,708,847	323,725,191	52,738,069
wel	307,810 a	60,458,213 a	15,989,577 a	310,553 a	67,830,319 a	18,198,804 a	311,364 a	71,611,865 a	18,608,914 a
Total	28,906,733	5,402,773,866	1,348,940,701	29,020,810	5,953,679,479	1,492,832,600	29,102,779	6,517,015,172	1,536,193,341

a Data obtained from denominational source.
b empty tomb review of RCA directory data.

Appendix B-1: Church Member Giving, In Current Dollars, 1968-2009 (continued)

	Data Year 1983			Data Year 1984			Data Year 1985		
	Full/Confirmed Members	Congregational Finances	Benevolences	Full/Confirmed Members	Congregational Finances	Benevolences	Full/Confirmed Members	Congregational Finances	Benevolences
abc	965,117 [a]	254,716,036	43,683,021	953,945 [a]	267,556,088	46,232,040	894,732 [a]	267,694,684	47,201,119
alc	1,756,420	375,500,188	84,633,617	1,756,558	413,876,101	86,601,067	1,751,649	428,861,660	87,152,699
arp	31,738	10,640,050 [a]	2,180,230 [a]	31,355	11,221,526 [a]	3,019,456 [a]	32,051	12,092,868 [a]	3,106,994 [a]
bcc	14,782	7,638,413	1,858,632	15,128	8,160,359	2,586,843	15,535 [a]	8,504,354 [a]	2,979,046 [a]
ccd	761,629	241,934,972	35,809,331	755,233	263,694,210	38,402,791	743,486	274,072,301	40,992,053
cga	182,190	81,309,323	13,896,753	185,404	86,611,269	14,347,570	185,593	91,078,512	15,308,954
cgg	5,759	1,981,300	412,000	4,711	2,211,800	504,200	4,575	2,428,730	582,411
chb	164,680	39,726,743	14,488,192	161,824	37,743,527	15,136,600	159,184	40,658,904	16,509,718
chn	506,439	237,220,642 [a]	57,267,073 [a]	514,937	253,566,280	60,909,810 [a]	520,741	267,134,078	65,627,515 [a]
ccc	26,691 [a]	9,189,221 [a]	2,980,636	28,383	10,018,982	3,051,425	28,624	11,729,365	3,350,021
cpc	87,186 [a]	19,252,942 [a]	3,028,953 [a]	86,995 [a]	20,998,768 [a]	3,331,065 [a]	85,346 [a]	22,361,332 [a]	3,227,932 [a]
ecc	26,769 [a]	9,505,479 [a]	2,019,373 [a]	26,375 [a]	10,302,554 [a]	2,220,852 [a]	26,016	8,134,641 [a]	1,777,172
ecv	82,943	53,279,350 [a]	10,615,909	84,185	60,295,634 [a]	11,243,908	85,150	63,590,735 [a]	13,828,030
elc	ALC & LCA	ALC & LCA	ALC & LCA	ALC & LCA	ALC & LCA	ALC & LCA	ALC & LCA	ALC & LCA	ALC & LCA
els	15,576	3,842,625	838,788	15,396	4,647,714	931,677 [a]	15,012	4,725,783	791,586
emc	3,857	1,930,689	738,194	3,908	2,017,565	862,350	3,813	2,128,019	1,058,040
feb	2,094	622,467	1,466,399	NA	NA	NA	2,107 [a]	1,069,851 [a]	402,611 [a]
fec	see EMC	see EMC	see EMC	see EMC	see EMC	see EMC	see EMC	see EMC	see EMC
fmc	56,442 [a]	36,402,355 [a]	8,334,248 [a]	56,667 [a]	39,766,087 [a]	8,788,189 [a]	56,242	42,046,626 [a]	9,461,369 [a]
fum	49,441	11,723,240	2,886,931	48,713	11,549,163	2,875,370	48,812	12,601,820	3,012,658
ggb	75,133	17,283,259	1,733,755	75,028	17,599,169	1,729,228	73,040	18,516,252	1,683,130
lca	2,176,772	457,239,780	88,909,363	2,168,594	496,228,216	99,833,067	2,161,216	539,142,069	103,534,375
lms	1,984,199	499,220,552	76,991,991 [a]	1,986,392	539,346,935	81,742,006 [a]	1,982,753	566,507,516	83,117,011 [a]
mch	103,350 [a]	34,153,628	17,581,878	90,347	37,333,306	16,944,094	91,167	34,015,200	25,593,500
mgc	36,318 [a]	8,702,849 [a]	7,661,415 [a]	35,951 [a]	9,197,458 [a]	7,795,680 [a]	35,356 [a]	9,217,964 [a]	7,070,700 [a]
mus	MCH & MGC	MCH & MGC	MCH & MGC	MCH & MGC	MCH & MGC	MCH & MGC	MCH & MGC	MCH & MGC	MCH & MGC
mca	24,913	6,618,339	911,787	24,269	7,723,611	1,183,741	24,396	8,698,949	1,170,349
nab	43,286	18,010,853	5,132,672	43,215	19,322,720	5,724,552	42,863	20,246,236	5,766,686
opc	12,045	6,874,722	1,755,169	12,278 [a]	7,555,006	2,079,924	12,593 [a]	8,291,483	2,204,998
pch	3,122,213	1,047,756,995	197,981,080	3,092,151	1,132,098,779	218,412,639	3,057,226 [a]	1,252,885,684 [a]	232,487,569 [a]
rca	211,660	92,071,986	20,632,574	209,968 [b]	100,378,778	21,794,880	209,395	103,428,950	22,233,299
sda	623,563	143,636,140	323,461,439	638,929	155,257,063	319,664,449	651,594	155,077,180	346,251,406
sbc	14,178,051	2,838,573,815	528,781,000	14,341,822	3,094,913,877	567,467,188	14,477,364	3,272,276,486	609,868,694
ucc	1,701,513	332,613,396	55,716,557	1,696,107	385,786,198	58,679,094	1,683,777	409,543,989	62,169,679 [a]
wel	312,974 [a]	75,825,104 [a]	24,037,480 [a]	314,559 [a]	82,507,020 [a]	22,845,856 [a]	315,374 [a]	86,879,662 [a]	22,275,822 [a]
Total	29,345,743	6,974,997,453	1,638,426,440	29,459,327	7,589,485,763	1,726,941,611	29,476,782	8,045,641,883	1,841,797,146

[a] Data obtained from denominational source.
[b] empty tomb review of RCA directory data.

Appendix B-1: Church Member Giving, In Current Dollars, 1968-2009 (continued)

	Data Year 1986			Data Year 1987			Data Year 1988		
	Full/Confirmed Members	Congregational Finances	Benevolences	Full/Confirmed Members	Congregational Finances	Benevolences	Full/Confirmed Members	Congregational Finances	Benevolences
abc	862,582 a	287,020,378 a	49,070,083 a	868,189 a	291,606,418 a	55,613,855	825,102 a	296,569,316 a	55,876,771
alc	1,740,439	434,641,736	96,147,129	See ELCA	See ELCA	See ELCA	See ELCA	See ELCA	See ELCA
arp	32,438 a	12,336,321 a	3,434,408 a	32,289	13,553,176 a	3,927,030 a	31,922	13,657,776 a	5,063,036 a
bcc	15,911	10,533,883	2,463,558	16,136	11,203,321	3,139,949	16,578 a	13,522,101 a	4,346,690 a
ccd	732,466	288,277,386	42,027,504	718,522	287,464,332	42,728,826	707,985	297,187,996	42,226,128
cga	188,662	91,768,855	16,136,647	198,552	124,376,413	20,261,687	198,842	132,384,232	19,781,941
cgg	NA	NA	NA	4,348	2,437,778	738,818	4,394	2,420,600 a	644,000 a
chb	155,967	43,531,293	17,859,101	154,067	45,201,732	19,342,402	151,169	48,008,657	19,701,942 a
chn	529,192	283,189,977	68,438,998 a	541,878	294,160,356	73,033,568 a	550,700	309,478,442	74,737,057 a
ccc	28,948	15,559,846 a	3,961,037	29,429	15,409,349 a	3,740,688	29,015	13,853,547	4,120,974
cpc	84,579 a	22,338,090 a	3,646,356 a	85,781	22,857,711	3,727,681	85,304	23,366,911 e	3,722,607
ecc	25,625	10,977,813 a	2,422,879 a	25,300	14,281,140 a	2,575,415 a	24,980	12,115,762	2,856,766 a
ecv	86,079	67,889,353 a	14,374,707	86,741	73,498,123 a	14,636,000	87,750	77,504,445 a	14,471,178
elc	ALC & LCA	ALC & LCA	ALC & LCA	3,952,663	1,083,293,684	169,685,942	3,931,878	1,150,483,034	169,580,472
els	15,083 a	4,996,111 a	1,050,715 a	15,892	5,298,882	1,082,198	15,518 a	5,713,773 a	1,043,612 a
emc	NA	NA	NA	3,841	2,332,216	1,326,711	3,879	2,522,533	1,438,459
feb	NA	NA	NA	NA	NA	NA	NA	NA	NA
fec	see EMC	see EMC	see EMC	see EMC	see EMC	see EMC	see EMC	see EMC	see EMC
fmc	56,243	46,150,881	9,446,120	57,262	47,743,298	9,938,096	57,432	48,788,041	9,952,103
fum	48,143	12,790,909	2,916,870	47,173	13,768,272	3,631,353	48,325	14,127,491	3,719,125
ggb	72,263	19,743,265	1,883,826	73,515	20,850,827	1,789,578	74,086	21,218,051	1,731,299
lca	2,157,701	569,250,519	111,871,174	See ELCA	See ELCA	See ELCA	See ELCA	See ELCA	See ELCA
lms	1,974,798	605,768,688	87,803,646 a	1,973,347	620,271,274	86,938,723 a	1,962,674	659,288,332	88,587,175 a
mch	91,467 a	40,097,500 a	24,404,200 a	92,673 a	43,295,100	25,033,600	92,682	47,771,200	27,043,900
mgc	35,170	10,101,306 a	7,717,998 a	34,889	11,560,998	8,478,414	34,693	11,399,995	9,638,417
mus	MCH & MGC	MCH & MGC	MCH & MGC	MCH & MGC	MCH & MGC	MCH & MGC	MCH & MGC	MCH & MGC	MCH & MGC
mca	24,260	8,133,127	1,155,350	24,440	9,590,658	1,174,593	23,526	9,221,646	1,210,476
nab	42,084	20,961,799	5,982,391	42,150 a	23,773,844 a	7,873,096 a	42,629	24,597,288	6,611,840
opc	12,919 a	9,333,328 a	2,347,928 a	13,013 a	9,884,288	2,425,480	13,108 a	10,797,786 a	2,648,375 a
pch	3,007,322	1,318,440,264	249,033,881	2,967,781	1,395,501,073	247,234,439	2,929,608	1,439,655,217	284,989,138
rca	207,993	114,231,429	22,954,596	203,581	114,652,192 b	24,043,270	200,631	127,409,263	25,496,802 b
sda	666,199	166,692,974	361,316,753	675,702	166,939,355	374,830,065	687,200	178,768,967	395,849,223
sbc	14,613,638	3,481,124,471	635,196,984	14,722,617	3,629,842,643	662,455,177	14,812,844	3,706,652,161	689,366,904
ucc	1,676,105	429,340,239	63,808,091	1,662,568	451,700,210	66,870,922	1,644,787	470,747,740	65,734,348
wel	315,510 a	92,309,279 a	22,354,781 a	316,393 a	97,179,349 a	22,112,031 a	316,098 a	101,545,536 a	22,323,451 a
Total	29,499,786	8,517,531,020	1,931,227,711	29,640,732	8,943,528,012	1,960,389,607	29,605,339	9,270,777,839	2,054,514,209

a Data obtained from denominational source.
b empty tomb review of RCA directory data.
e A YACC prepublication data table listed 23,366,911 for Congregational Finances which, added to Benevolences, equals the published Total of 27,089,518.

Appendix B-1: Church Member Giving, In Current Dollars, 1968-2009 (continued)

	Data Year 1989			Data Year 1990			Data Year 1991		
	Full/Confirmed Members	Congregational Finances	Benevolences	Full/Confirmed Members	Congregational Finances	Benevolences	Full/Confirmed Members	Congregational Finances	Benevolences
abc	789,730 a	305,212,094 a	55,951,539	764,890 a	315,777,005 a	54,740,278	773,838 a	318,150,548 a	52,330,924
alc	See ELCA	See ELCA	See ELCA	See ELCA	See ELCA	See ELCA	See ELCA	See ELCA	See ELCA
arp	32,600	16,053,762 a	4,367,314 a	32,817 a	17,313,355 a	5,031,504 a	33,494 a	17,585,273 a	5,254,738 a
bcc	16,842	12,840,038	3,370,306	17,277	13,327,414	3,336,580	17,456 a	14,491,918 a	3,294,169 a
ccd	690,115	310,043,826	42,015,246	678,750	321,569,909	42,607,007	663,336	331,629,009	43,339,307
cga	199,786	134,918,052	20,215,075	205,884	141,375,027	21,087,504	214,743 a	146,249,447 a	21,801,570 a
cgg	4,415	3,367,000	686,000	4,399	3,106,729	690,000	4,375	2,756,651	662,500
chb	149,681	51,921,820	19,737,714 a	148,253	54,832,226	18,384,483 a	147,954 a	55,035,355 a	19,694,919 a
chn	558,664	322,924,598	76,625,913 a	563,756 a	333,397,255 a	77,991,665 a	572,153	352,654,251	82,276,097 a
ccc	28,413	18,199,823	4,064,111	28,355	16,964,128	4,174,133	28,035	17,760,290	4,304,052
cpc	84,994 a	25,867,112 a	4,086,994 a	85,025 a	27,027,650 a	4,139,967 a	84,706 a	28,069,681 a	5,740,846 a
ecc	24,606	13,274,756 a	2,703,095 a	24,437	12,947,150 a	2,858,077 a	24,124 a	13,100,036 a	3,074,660 a
ecv	89,014	80,621,293 a	15,206,265	89,735	84,263,236 a	15,601,475	89,648	87,321,563 a	16,598,656
elc	3,909,302	1,239,433,257	182,386,940	3,898,478	1,318,884,279	184,174,554	3,890,947	1,375,439,787	186,016,168
els	15,740	6,186,648	1,342,321	16,181	6,527,076	1,193,789	16,004	6,657,338	1,030,445
emc	3,888	2,712,843	1,567,728	4,026	2,991,485	1,800,593	3,958	3,394,563	1,790,115
feb	NA	NA	NA	NA	NA	NA	2,008 a	1,398,968 a	500,092 a
fec	see EMC	see EMC	see EMC	see EMC	see EMC	see EMC	see EMC	see EMC	see EMC
fmc	59,418 a	50,114,090 a	10,311,535 a	58,084	55,229,181	10,118,505	57,794	57,880,464	9,876,739
fum	47,228	16,288,644	4,055,624	45,691	10,036,083	2,511,063	50,803 f	NA	NA
ggb	73,738	23,127,835	1,768,804	74,156	23,127,835	1,737,011	71,119 a	22,362,874 a	1,408,262 a
lca	See ELCA	See ELCA	See ELCA	See ELCA	See ELCA	See ELCA	See ELCA	See ELCA	See ELCA
lms	1,961,114	701,701,168 a	90,974,340 a	1,954,350	712,235,204	96,308,765 a	1,952,845	741,823,412	94,094,637 a
mch	92,517	55,353,313	27,873,241	92,448 a	65,709,827	28,397,083	93,114 a	68,926,324	28,464,199
mgc	33,982	12,096,435	9,054,682	33,535	13,669,288	8,449,395	33,937	13,556,484	8,645,993
mus	MCH & MGC	MCH & MGC	MCH & MGC	MCH & MGC	MCH & MGC	MCH & MGC	MCH & MGC	MCH & MGC	MCH & MGC
mca	23,802	10,415,640	1,284,233	23,526	10,105,037	1,337,616	22,887	10,095,337	1,205,335
nab	42,629	28,076,077	3,890,017	44,493	31,103,672	7,700,119	43,187 a	27,335,239 a	7,792,876 a
opc	12,573 a	11,062,590 a	2,789,427 a	12,177 a	10,631,166 a	2,738,295 a	12,265	11,700,000	2,700,000
pch	2,886,482	1,528,450,805	295,365,032	2,847,437	1,530,341,707	294,990,441	2,805,548	1,636,407,042	311,905,934 a
rca	198,832	136,796,188 b	29,456,132 b	197,154	144,357,953 b	27,705,029 b	193,531 b	147,532,382 b	26,821,721 b
sda	701,781	196,204,538	415,752,350	717,446	195,054,218	433,035,080	733,026	201,411,183	456,242,995
sbc	14,907,826	3,873,300,782	712,738,838	15,038,409	4,146,285,561	718,174,874	15,232,347	4,283,283,059	731,812,766
ucc	1,625,969	496,825,160	72,300,698	1,599,212	527,378,397	71,984,897	1,583,830	543,803,752	73,149,887
wel	316,163 a	110,112,151 a	22,717,491 a	315,840 a	115,806,027 a	23,983,079 a	315,853 a	121,159,792 a	24,160,350 a
Total	29,581,844	9,793,502,338	2,134,659,005	29,616,221	10,261,375,080	2,166,982,861	29,718,062	10,658,972,022	2,225,990,952

a Data obtained from denominational source.
b empty tomb review of RCA directory data.
f Inclusive membership, obtained from the denomination and used only in Chapter 5 analysis; not included in the Total sum on this page.

Appendix B-1: Church Member Giving, In Current Dollars, 1968-2009 (continued)

	Data Year 1992			Data Year 1993			Data Year 1994		
	Full/Confirmed Members	Congregational Finances	Benevolences	Full/Confirmed Members	Congregational Finances	Benevolences	Full/Confirmed Members	Congregational Finances	Benevolences
abc	730,009 a	310,307,040 a	52,764,005	764,657 a	346,658,047 a	53,562,811	697,379 a	337,185,885 a	51,553,256 a
alc	See ELCA	See ELCA	See ELCA	See ELCA	See ELCA	See ELCA	See ELCA	See ELCA	See ELCA
arp	33,550	18,175,957 a	5,684,008 a	33,662 a	20,212,390 a	5,822,845 a	33,636	22,618,802 a	6,727,857
bcc	17,646 a	15,981,118 a	3,159,717 a	17,986	13,786,394	4,515,730 a	18,152	14,844,672	5,622,005
ccd	655,652	333,629,412	46,440,333	619,028	328,219,027	44,790,415	605,996	342,352,080	43,165,285
cga	214,743	150,115,497	23,500,213	216,117	158,454,703	23,620,177	221,346 a	160,694,760 a	26,262,049 a
cgg	4,085	2,648,085	509,398	4,239	2,793,000	587,705	3,996	2,934,843	475,799
chb	147,912	57,954,895	21,748,320	146,713	56,818,998	23,278,848	144,282	57,210,682	24,155,595
chn	582,804 a	361,555,793 a	84,118,580 a	589,398	369,896,767	87,416,378 a	595,303	387,385,034	89,721,860
ccc	30,387	22,979,946 a	4,311,234	36,864	24,997,736 a	5,272,184	37,996 a	23,758,101 a	5,240,805 a
cpc	85,080 a	27,813,626 a	4,339,933 a	84,336 a	27,462,623 a	4,574,550 a	83,733 a	29,212,802 a	4,547,149 a
ecc	24,150	13,451,827 a	3,120,351 a	23,889	13,546,159 a	3,258,595 a	23,504	13,931,409	3,269,986
ecv	90,985 a	93,071,869 a	16,732,701 a	89,511	93,765,006 a	16,482,315	90,919 a	101,746,341 a	17,874,955 a
elc	3,878,055	1,399,419,800	189,605,837	3,861,418	1,452,000,815	188,393,158	3,849,692	1,502,746,601	187,145,886
els	15,929 a	6,944,522 a	1,271,058 a	15,780	6,759,222 a	1,100,660	15,960	7,288,521	1,195,698
emc	4,059	3,839,838 a	1,403,001 a	4,130 a	4,260,307 a	1,406,682 a	4,225 a	4,597,730 a	1,533,157 a
feb	1,872 a	1,343,225 a	397,553 a	1,866 a	1,294,646 a	429,023 a	1,898 a	1,537,041 a	395,719 a
fec	see EMC	see EMC	see EMC	see EMC	see EMC	see EMC	see EMC	see EMC	see EMC
fmc	58,220	60,584,079	10,591,064	59,156	62,478,294	10,513,187	59,354 a	65,359,325 a	10,708,854 a
fum	50,005 f	NA	NA	45,542 f	NA	NA	44,711 f	NA	NA
ggb	72,388 a	21,561,432 a	1,402,330 a	73,129 a	22,376,970 a	1,440,342 a	71,140 a	19,651,624 a	2,052,409 a
lca	See ELCA	See ELCA	See ELCA	See ELCA	See ELCA	See ELCA	See ELCA	See ELCA	See ELCA
lms	1,953,248	777,467,488	97,275,934 a	1,945,077	789,821,559	96,355,945 a	1,944,905	817,412,113	96,048,560 a
mch	94,222 a	68,118,222	28,835,719 a	95,634	71,385,271	27,973,380	87,911 a	64,651,639	24,830,192
mgc	34,040	14,721,813 a	8,265,700	33,629	14,412,556	7,951,676	32,782	16,093,551	8,557,126 a
mus	MCH & MGC	MCH & MGC	MCH & MGC	MCH & MGC	MCH & MGC	MCH & MGC	MCH & MGC	MCH & MGC	MCH & MGC
mca	22,533	10,150,953	1,208,372	22,223	9,675,502	1,191,131	21,448	9,753,010	1,182,778
nab	43,446	28,375,947	7,327,594	43,045	30,676,902	7,454,087	43,236	32,800,560	7,515,707
opc	12,580 a	12,466,266 a	3,025,824 a	12,924 a	13,158,089 a	3,039,676 a	13,970	14,393,880	3,120,454
pch	2,780,406	1,696,092,968	309,069,530	2,742,192	1,700,918,712	310,375,024	2,698,262	1,800,008,292	307,158,749
rca	190,322 b	147,181,320 b	28,457,900 b	188,551 b	159,715,941 b	26,009,853 b	185,242	153,107,408	27,906,830
sda	748,687	191,362,737	476,902,779	761,703	209,524,570	473,769,831	775,349	229,596,444	503,347,816
sbc	15,358,866	4,462,915,112	751,366,698	15,398,642	4,621,157,751	761,298,249	15,614,060	5,263,421,764	815,360,696
ucc	1,555,382	521,190,413	73,906,372	1,530,178	550,847,702	71,046,517	1,501,310	556,540,722	67,269,762
wel	315,062 a	127,139,400 a	26,239,464 a	314,757 a	136,405,994 a	24,403,323 a	314,141 a	142,238,820 a	23,825,002 a
Total	29,756,320	10,958,560,600	2,282,981,522	29,730,434	11,313,481,653	2,287,334,297	29,791,127	12,195,074,456	2,367,771,996

a Data obtained from denominational source.

b empty tomb review of RCA directory data.

f Inclusive membership, obtained from the denomination and used only in Chapter 5 analysis; not included in the Total sum on this page.

Appendix B-1: Church Member Giving, In Current Dollars, 1968-2009 (continued)

	Data Year 1995			Data Year 1996			Data Year 1997		
	Full/Confirmed Members	Congregational Finances	Benevolences	Full/Confirmed Members	Congregational Finances	Benevolences	Full/Confirmed Members	Congregational Finances	Benevolences
abc	726,452 a	365,873,197 a	57,052,333 a	670,363 a	351,362,401 a	55,982,392 a	658,731 a	312,860,507 a	54,236,977 a
alc	See ELCA	See ELCA	See ELCA	See ELCA	See ELCA	See ELCA	See ELCA	See ELCA	See ELCA
arp	33,513	23,399,372 a	5,711,882 a	34,117	23,419,989 a	5,571,337 a	34,344	25,241,384	6,606,829
bcc	18,529	16,032,149	5,480,828	18,424	16,892,154	4,748,871	19,016 a	17,456,379 a	5,934,414 a
ccd	601,237	357,895,652	42,887,958	586,131	370,210,746	42,877,144	568,921	381,463,761	43,009,412
cga	224,061	160,897,147	26,192,559	229,240	180,581,111	26,983,385	229,302	194,438,623	29,054,047
cgg	3,877	2,722,766	486,661	3,920	2,926,516	491,348	3,877	2,987,337	515,247
chb	143,121	60,242,418	22,599,214	141,811	60,524,557 a	19,683,035 a	141,400	60,923,817 a	19,611,047 a
chn	598,946	396,698,137	93,440,095	608,008	419,450,850	95,358,352	615,632	433,821,462	99,075,440
ccc	38,853 a	24,250,819 a	5,483,659 a	38,469 a	25,834,363 a	4,989,062 a	38,956	28,204,355	5,167,644
cpc	81,094 a	31,072,697 a	4,711,934 a	80,122 a	31,875,061 a	5,035,451 a	79,576 a	32,152,971 a	5,152,129 a
ecc	23,422	14,830,454	3,301,060	23,091	14,692,608	3,273,685	22,957	15,658,454	3,460,999
ecv	91,458	109,776,363 a	17,565,085 a	91,823 a	115,693,329 a	18,726,756 a	93,414	127,642,950	20,462,435
elc	3,845,063	1,551,842,465	188,107,066	3,838,750	1,629,909,672	191,476,141	3,844,169	1,731,806,133	201,115,441
els	16,543	7,712,358 a	1,084,136	16,511	8,136,195	1,104,996	16,444	8,937,103	1,150,419
emc	4,284 a	5,321,079 a	1,603,548 a	4,201	5,361,912 a	1,793,267 a	4,348 a	7,017,588 a	2,039,740 a
feb	1,856 a	1,412,281 a	447,544 a	1,751 a	1,198,120 a	507,656 a	1,763 a	1,120,222 a	518,777 a
fec	see EMC	see EMC	see EMC	see EMC	see EMC	see EMC	see EMC	see EMC	see EMC
fmc	59,060	67,687,955	11,114,804	59,343 a	70,262,626	11,651,462	62,191 a	78,687,325	12,261,465
fum	43,440 f	NA	NA	42,918 f	NA	NA	41,040 f	NA	NA
ggb	70,886 a	24,385,956 a	1,722,662 a	70,562 a	27,763,966 a	1,832,909 a	72,326	28,093,944	1,780,851
lca	See ELCA	See ELCA	See ELCA	See ELCA	See ELCA	See ELCA	See ELCA	See ELCA	See ELCA
lms	1,943,281	832,701,255	98,139,835 a	1,951,730	855,461,015	104,076,876 a	1,951,391	887,928,255	110,520,917
mch	90,139 a	71,641,773	26,832,240	90,959	76,669,365	27,812,549	92,161 a	76,087,609 a	25,637,872 a
mgc	35,852	15,774,961 a	7,587,049 a	35,333	18,282,833	7,969,999	34,731	14,690,904	6,514,761
mus	MCH & MGC	MCH & MGC	MCH & MGC	MCH & MGC	MCH & MGC	MCH & MGC	MCH & MGC	MCH & MGC	MCH & MGC
mca	21,409	10,996,031	1,167,513	21,140	11,798,536	1,237,349	21,108	12,555,760	1,148,478
nab	43,928	37,078,473	7,480,331	43,744 a	37,172,560 a	7,957,860 a	43,850	37,401,175	7,986,099
opc	14,355	16,017,003	3,376,691	15,072 a	17,883,915 a	3,467,207 a	15,072	20,090,259	3,967,490
pch	2,665,276	1,855,684,719	309,978,224	2,631,466	1,930,179,808	322,336,258	2,609,191	2,064,789,378	344,757,186
rca	183,255	164,250,624	29,995,068	182,342	183,975,696 a	31,271,007	180,980 a	181,977,101 a	32,130,943 a
sda	790,731	240,565,576	503,334,129	809,159	242,316,834	524,977,061	825,654	249,591,109	552,633,569
sbc	15,663,296	5,209,748,503	858,635,435	15,691,249 a	5,987,033,115	891,149,403 a	15,891,514	6,098,933,137	930,176,909
ucc	1,472,213	578,042,965	67,806,448	1,452,565	615,727,028	69,013,791	1,438,181	651,176,773	70,180,193
wel	312,898 a	150,060,963 a	33,096,069 a	313,446 a	156,363,694 a	47,334,098 a	314,038 a	163,568,990 a	52,241,401 a
Total	29,818,888	12,404,616,111	2,436,422,060	29,754,842	13,488,960,575	2,530,690,707	29,925,238	13,947,304,765	2,649,049,131

a Data obtained from denominational source.

f Inclusive membership, obtained from the denomination and used only in Chapter 5 analysis; not included in the Total sum on this page.

Appendix B-1: Church Member Giving, In Current Dollars, 1968-2009 (continued)

	Data Year 1998			Data Year 1999			Data Year 2000		
	Full/Confirmed Members	Congregational Finances	Benevolences	Full/Confirmed Members	Congregational Finances	Benevolences	Full/Confirmed Members	Congregational Finances	Benevolences
abc	621,232 a	326,046,153 a	53,866,448 a	603,014 a	331,513,521 a	58,675,160 a	593,113 a	359,484,902 a	63,042,002 a
alc	See ELCA	See ELCA	See ELCA	See ELCA	See ELCA	See ELCA	See ELCA	See ELCA	See ELCA
arp	34,642 a	28,831,982 a	7,378,121 a	35,643 a	33,862,219 a	7,973,285 a	35,022 a	33,004,995 a	8,048,586 a
bcc	19,577	24,116,889	5,274,612	20,010	22,654,566	5,913,551	20,587	25,148,637	5,703,506
ccd	547,875 a	395,699,954 a	45,576,436 a	535,893	410,583,119	47,795,574	527,363	433,965,354	48,726,390
cga	234,311 f	NA	NA	235,849 f	NA	NA	238,891 f	NA	NA
cgg	3,824	3,087,000	689,756	4,083	3,357,300	503,365	4,037	3,232,160	610,113
chb	140,011 a	57,605,960 a	22,283,498 a	138,304 a	63,774,756 a	21,852,687 a	135,978	67,285,361	25,251,272 a
chn	623,028	460,776,715	104,925,922	626,033	487,437,668 a	110,818,743 a	633,264	516,708,125	122,284,083
ccc	38,996	28,976,122	5,194,733	40,414	31,165,218	5,931,456	40,974 a	33,537,589 a	6,360,912 a
cpc	80,829 a	33,623,232 a	5,412,917 a	79,452 a	36,303,752 a	5,879,014 a	86,519	39,533,829	6,591,617
ecc	22,868	15,956,209	3,599,440	22,349	16,574,783	3,587,877	21,939	17,656,789	1,982,328
ecv	96,552	140,823,872	20,134,436	98,526 a	161,361,490 a	23,237,513 a	101,317 a	181,127,526 a	25,983,315 a
elc	3,840,136	1,822,915,831	208,853,359	3,825,228	1,972,950,623	220,647,251	3,810,785	2,067,208,285	231,219,316
els	16,897	9,363,126	1,120,386	16,734	10,062,900	1,129,969	16,569	10,910,109	949,421
emc	4,646 a	6,472,868 a	1,854,222 a	4,511 a	7,528,256 a	1,982,985 a	4,929	8,289,743 a	2,085,475 a
feb	1,828 a	1,433,305 a	502,839 a	1,936 a	1,496,949 a	534,203 a	1,764 a	1,360,133 a	373,057 a
fec	see EMC	see EMC	see EMC	see EMC	see EMC	see EMC	see EMC	see EMC	see EMC
fmc	62,176	82,254,922	12,850,607	62,368 f	86,906,899	12,646,064	62,453	98,853,770	13,430,274
fum	33,908 f	NA	NA	34,863 f	NA	NA	41,297 f	NA	NA
ggb	67,314 a	28,533,439 a	2,594,098 a	55,549 a	22,857,097 a	2,331,087 a	66,296 a	30,470,298 a	2,950,915 a
lca	See ELCA	See ELCA	See ELCA	See ELCA	See ELCA	See ELCA	See ELCA	See ELCA	See ELCA
lms	1,952,020	975,113,229	121,536,226	1,945,846	986,295,136	123,632,549	1,934,057	1,101,690,594	127,554,235
mch	92,002 a	75,796,469 a	26,452,444 a	See MUS	See MUS	See MUS	See MUS	See MUS	See MUS
mgc	36,600	14,786,936 a	5,853,292 a	See MUS	See MUS	See MUS	See MUS	See MUS	See MUS
mus	MCH & MGC	MCH & MGC	MCH & MGC	123,404 a	95,843,112 a	34,821,702 a	120,381 l	NA	NA
mca	20,764	13,082,671	1,131,742	20,400	11,527,684	849,837	20,925 a	13,224,765 a	1,014,314 a
nab	43,844 a	41,939,978 a	7,731,550 a	45,738	47,207,867	9,055,128	47,097	54,866,431	9,845,352
opc	15,936	22,362,292	4,438,333	17,279 a	24,878,935	4,920,310	17,914	28,120,325	5,978,474
pch	2,587,674	2,173,483,227	355,628,625	2,560,201	2,326,583,688	384,445,608	2,525,330	2,517,278,130	398,602,204
rca	179,085	189,390,759	33,890,048	178,260 a	216,305,458 a	36,158,625 a	177,281	226,555,821	37,221,041
sda	839,915	269,679,595	588,227,010	861,860	301,221,572	629,944,965	880,921	316,562,375	675,000,508
sbc	15,729,356	6,498,607,390	953,491,003	14,001,690 g	6,001,443,051 g	795,207,316 g	15,221,959 g	7,037,516,273 g	936,520,388 g
ucc	1,421,088	678,251,694	74,861,463	1,401,682	700,645,114	76,550,398	1,377,320	744,991,925	78,525,195
wel	314,265 a	177,633,393 a	44,584,079 a	314,217 a	181,513,283 a	49,143,360 a	314,941 a	193,625,639 a	52,918,434 a
Total	29,454,980	14,596,645,212	2,719,937,645	27,640,624	14,593,856,016	2,676,169,582	28,680,654	16,162,209,883	2,888,772,727

a Data obtained from denominational source.

f Inclusive membership, obtained from the denomination and used only in Chapter 5 analysis; not included in the Total sum on this page.

g The 1999 and 2000 data for the Southern Baptist Convention used in the 1968-2002 analysis includes data only for those State Conventions that provided a breakdown of Total Contributions between Congregational Finances and Benevolences for that year. For the Eleven Denominations 1921-2005 analysis, the 1999 and 2000 Southern Baptist Convention Total Contributions are $7,772,452,961 and $8,437,177,940, respectively. For the Eleven Denominations 1921-2005 analysis, and the Membership Trends analysis, 1999 and 2000 Southern Baptist Convention Membership is 15,851,756 and 15,960,308, respectively.

l Data obtained from denominational source and used only in Chapter 5 analysis; not included in Total sum on this page.

Appendix B-1: Church Member Giving, In Current Dollars, 1968-2009

Appendix B-1: Church Member Giving, In Current Dollars, 1968-2009 (continued)

	Data Year 2001			Data Year 2002			Data Year 2003		
	Full/Confirmed Members	Congregational Finances	Benevolences	Full/Confirmed Members	Congregational Finances	Benevolences	Full/Confirmed Members	Congregational Finances	Benevolences
abc	631,771 a	381,080,930 a	74,228,212 a	617,034 a	396,380,200 a	65,103,943 a	572,218	391,456,166 a	60,965,853 a
alc	See ELCA	See ELCA	See ELCA	See ELCA	See ELCA	See ELCA	See ELCA	See ELCA	See ELCA
arp	35,181	36,976,653	7,707,456	35,556	37,394,125	8,091,930	35,418	36,664,331	7,615,661
bcc	20,739	29,566,287	6,864,936	20,579 a	29,069,369 a	5,619,911 a	21,538 a	30,219,066 a	6,090,287 a
ccd	518,434	437,447,942	48,609,107	504,118	438,378,385	46,708,737	491,085	456,513,192 a	45,243,300 a
cga	237,222 l	NA	NA	247,007 k	NA	NA	250,052 l	NA	NA
cgg	4,155	3,436,200	477,457	3,860 k	NA	NA	3,694 a	3,786,000 a	511,394 a
chb	134,828	68,790,933	22,869,690	134,844	70,524,998	22,730,417	132,481	73,120,173	20,756,646
chn	639,296 a	557,589,101 a	121,203,179 a	639,330	587,027,991	132,183,078	616,069	595,552,079	133,379,908
ccc	40,857	34,483,917	6,754,192	40,041	36,747,983	8,190,510	42,032 a	46,340,288 a	6,232,465 a
cpc	85,427	41,216,632	6,744,757	84,417	42,570,586	6,876,097	83,742	41,950,671	7,218,214
ecc	21,463	17,932,202	2,011,619	21,208	18,195,387	2,002,028	20,743	17,648,320	1,980,327
ecv	103,549 a	198,202,551 a	25,137,813 a	105,956 a	211,733,299 a	22,644,569 a	108,594 a	222,653,578 a	24,786,692 a
elc	3,791,986 a	2,166,061,437 a	239,796,502 a	3,757,723	2,238,773,875	233,875,597	3,724,321	2,285,110,767 a	231,916,904 a
els	16,815	11,361,255	1,246,189	16,849	11,787,432	1,010,416	16,674	12,018,180	995,710
emc	5,278 a	10,563,872 a	2,335,880 a	see FEC	see FEC	see FEC	see FEC	see FEC	see FEC
feb	1,271 a	1,086,582 a	246,296 a	1,896 a	1,651,056 a	512,269 a	1,861 a	1,723,143 a	673,694 a
fec	see EMC	see EMC	see EMC	5,686 a	10,457,231 a	1,811,985 a	5,780 a	11,862,813 a	2,275,726 a
fmc	61,202 a	111,415,741	14,595,290	62,742 a	117,340,008 a	16,194,960 a	64,726 a	122,723,869	14,281,867 a
fum	40,197 f	NA	NA	38,764 f	NA	NA	37,863 f	NA	NA
ggb	66,636 a	30,152,750 a	3,091,252 a	67,231	31,000,633	2,922,004	62,377 a	32,581,954 a	2,846,173 a
lca	See ELCA	See ELCA	See ELCA	See ELCA	See ELCA	See ELCA	See ELCA	See ELCA	See ELCA
lms	1,920,949	1,092,453,907	124,703,387	1,907,923	1,086,223,370	117,110,167	1,894,822	1,131,212,373	125,169,844
mch	See MUS	See MUS	See MUS	See MUS	See MUS	See MUS	See MUS	See MUS	See MUS
mgc	See MUS	See MUS	See MUS	See MUS	See MUS	See MUS	See MUS	See MUS	See MUS
mus	113,972 l	NA	NA	112,688 k	NA	NA	111,031 l	NA	NA
mca	21,319 a	13,237,006 a	1,054,515 a	20,583 a	13,037,136 a	971,527 a	19,456	16,939,268	925,302
nab	49,017	50,871,441	9,742,646	47,692	56,813,620	8,952,067	47,812 a	55,566,213 a	9,602,812 a
opc	18,414	30,012,219	6,077,752	18,746	29,251,600	5,216,600	19,725	30,972,500	5,671,600
pch	2,493,781	2,526,681,144	409,319,291	2,451,969	2,509,677,412	392,953,913	2,405,311	2,361,944,688	381,693,067
rca	173,463	228,677,098	39,313,564	171,361	229,560,092	39,393,056	168,801	235,422,160	39,932,078
sda	900,985	329,285,946	707,593,100	918,882	346,825,034	725,180,278	935,428	348,219,525	740,463,422
sbc	15,315,526 g	7,477,479,269 g	980,224,243	15,394,653 g	7,935,692,549 g	1,028,650,682	16,205,050 a	8,546,166,798	1,102,363,842
ucc	1,359,105	772,191,485	80,464,673	1,330,985	789,083,286	78,157,356	1,296,652	802,327,537	76,647,374
wel	314,360 a	203,334,779 a	53,455,670 a	313,690 a	211,121,810 a	49,035,869 a	313,330 a	227,521,597 a	50,687,438 a
Total	28,745,807	16,861,589,279	2,995,868,668	28,691,694	17,486,318,467	3,022,099,966	29,309,740	18,138,217,249	3,100,927,600

a Data obtained from denominational source.
f Inclusive membership, obtained from the denomination and used only in Chapter 5 analysis; not included in the Total sum on this page.
g The 2001 and 2002 data for the Southern Baptist Convention used in the 1968-2002 analysis includes data only for those State Conventions that provided a breakdown of Total Contributions between Congregational Finances and Benevolences for that year. For the Eleven Denominations 1921-2004 analysis 2001 and 2002 Southern Baptist Convention Total Contributions is $8,935,013,659 and $9,461,603,271, respectively. For the Eleven Denominations 1921-2004 analysis, and the Membership Trends analysis, 2001 and 2002 Southern Baptist Convention Membership is 16,052,920 and 16,137,736, respectively.
k Data used only in Chapter 5 analysis; not included in Total sum on this page.
l Data obtained from denominational source and used only in Chapter 5 analysis; not included in Total sum on this page.

Appendix B-1: Church Member Giving, In Current Dollars, 1968-2009 (continued)

	Data Year 2004			Data Year 2005			Data Year 2006		
	Full/Confirmed Members	Congregational Finances	Benevolences	Full/Confirmed Members	Congregational Finances	Benevolences	Full/Confirmed Members	Congregational Finances	Benevolences
abc	498,407 a	372,241,219 a	60,493,722 a	375,917 a	277,122,001 a	59,772,842	343,301 a	261,159,450	51,325,563
alc	See ELCA	See ELCA	See ELCA	See ELCA	See ELCA	See ELCA	See ELCA	See ELCA	See ELCA
arp	35,640 a	43,324,132 a	5,965,950 a	35,209 a	41,256,621 a	9,664,612 a	34,939 a	40,305,680 a	8,286,494 a
bcc	22,818 a	27,218,450 a	5,016,990 a	23,498 a	34,920,636 a	4,879,420 a	22,168 a	37,146,168 a	5,211,550 a
ccd	479,075 a	447,535,858 a	45,841,497 a	431,365 a	453,623,467 a	49,421,931 a	450,057 a	489,840,866 a	49,271,591 a
cga	252,419 k	NA	NA	255,771 l	NA	NA	249,845 k	NA	NA
cgg	3,267 a	3,966,000 a	479,000 a	3,200 a	4,115,400 a	381,422 a	3,080 a	4,030,000 a	391,793 a
chb	131,201	71,402,128	19,038,122	128,820	73,982,601	23,958,373	126,994 a	72,676,903	20,157,405
chn	623,774	610,902,447	132,624,279	630,159	622,257,466	143,177,276	633,154	655,937,953	136,893,238
ccc	42,725	51,335,963	8,459,095	42,838 j	50,845,153 j	8,501,074 j	42,862 a	55,997,723 a	9,419,501 a
cpc	83,007 a	42,431,192	7,368,979	81,464 a	45,769,458 a	8,379,379 a	81,034	46,396,330	8,331,581
ecc	20,745 a	19,402,040 h	3,429,948 h	20,169 a	17,880,135 a	3,528,552 a	19,166 a	18,741,363 a	3,432,641 a
ecv	113,002 a	244,040,438 a	23,226,589	114,283 a	266,614,225 a	25,232,786 a	120,030 a	290,965,669 a	22,805,559 a
elc	3,685,987	2,329,793,744	238,220,062	3,636,948	2,348,010,569 a	256,787,436 a	3,580,402	2,413,738,345 a	250,408,865
els	16,407	11,808,028	1,118,456	15,917	12,581,651	1,250,120 a	16,319	15,105,802	1,306,478
emc	See FEC	See FEC	See FEC	See FEC	See FEC	See FEC	See FEC	See FEC	See FEC
feb	1,844 a	2,023,545 a	511,470 a	1,664 a	2,043,940 a	595,313 a	1,434 a	2,265,710 a	427,685 a
fec	6,496	13,855,056 a	2,670,733	6,694 a	15,751,410 a	2,675,422 a	6,786 a	16,301,682 a	2,729,537 a
fmc	65,272	131,576,527	15,440,418	65,816	138,619,962	15,905,067	65,802	142,861,676	15,958,866
fum	34,323 f	NA	NA	38,121 f	NA	NA	43,612 f	NA	NA
ggb	78,863 a	30,631,505 a	3,140,132 a	60,559 a	36,990,479 a	3,156,104 a	52,279 a	32,918,373 a	2,987,587 a
lca	See ELCA	See ELCA	See ELCA	See ELCA	See ELCA	See ELCA	See ELCA	See ELCA	See ELCA
lms	1,880,213	1,186,000,747	121,763,263	1,870,659	1,176,649,592	120,169,146	1,856,783	1,229,305,441	126,153,117 a
mch	See MUS	See MUS	See MUS	See MUS	See MUS	See MUS	See MUS	See MUS	See MUS
mgc	See MUS	See MUS	See MUS	See MUS	See MUS	See MUS	See MUS	See MUS	See MUS
mus	110,420 l	NA	NA	109,808 l	NA	NA	109,385 l	NA	NA
mca	19,021	17,545,228	969,697	18,529	16,738,701	1,096,554	17,955	16,729,153 a	1,051,451
nab	46,995 a	59,832,412 a	10,342,080 a	46,671 l	NA	NA	47,150	62,175,197	10,104,273
opc	19,993 a	32,760,800 a	5,899,500 a	19,965	34,520,600	6,215,800	20,850	38,642,300	7,241,000
pch	2,362,136	2,387,317,945	387,589,903	2,313,662	2,425,999,953	388,271,070	2,267,118	2,459,679,132	395,040,718
rca	166,761	256,915,687	39,941,147	164,697	267,082,267	43,827,424	163,160	286,075,445	42,718,072
sda	948,787 a	347,797,864 a	773,751,848 a	964,811	427,285,012	846,114,329	980,551	426,686,109	863,635,364
sbc	16,267,494	8,971,390,824	1,199,806,224	16,270,315	9,487,900,433	1,233,644,135	16,306,246	10,086,992,362	1,285,616,031
ucc	1,266,129 a	822,172,566 a	73,481,544 a	1,224,297	827,237,883	81,488,911	1,218,541	846,482,513 a	73,611,594 a
wel	313,088 a	245,098,070 a	51,692,943 a	311,950 a	244,718,123 a	54,606,362 a	310,338 a	250,589,183 a	63,427,503 a
Total	29,199,147	18,780,320,415	3,238,283,591	28,833,405	19,350,517,738	3,392,700,860	28,788,499	20,299,746,528	3,457,945,057

a Data obtained from denominational source.

f Inclusive membership, obtained from the denomination and used only in Chapter 5 analysis; not included in the Total sum on this page.

h Data obtained from the denomination included the following note: "2004 figures differ substantially due to change in accounting procedures."

i 2004 membership data is an average of 2003 and 2005 data obtained from the denomination; used only in Chapter 5 analysis; not included in Total sum on this page.

j The denomination stated that the data appearing in *YACC* 2007 as 2004 data was actually for 2005.

k Data used only in Chapter 5 analysis; not included in Total sum on this page.

l Data obtained from denominational source and used only in Chapter 5 analysis; not included in Total sum on this page.

Appendix B-1: Church Member Giving, In Current Dollars, 1968–2009 (continued)

	Data Year 2007			Data Year 2008			Data Year 2009		
	Full/Confirmed Members	Congregational Finances	Benevolences	Full/Confirmed Members	Congregational Finances	Benevolences	Full/Confirmed Members	Congregational Finances	Benevolences
abc	345,588 [a]	272,304,732 [a]	53,636,473	331,262 [a]	268,264,419 [a]	49,073,811	305,486 [a]	241,316,884 [a]	47,522,456
alc	See ELCA	See ELCA	See ELCA	See ELCA	See ELCA	See ELCA	See ELCA	See ELCA	See ELCA
arp	34,954 [a]	40,442,600 [a]	8,981,600 [a]	34,911	32,784,800 [a]	14,163,289 [a]	34,977 [a]	43,677,370 [a]	11,123,351 [a]
bcc	22,732 [a]	38,797,921 [a]	5,138,646 [a]	22,967 [a]	39,993,609 [a]	4,678,366 [a]	23,014 [a]	35,229,064 [a]	5,141,733 [a]
ccd	447,340	473,677,625	45,405,339	434,008	479,485,251	44,728,431	417,068	453,043,802	42,944,443
cga	252,905 [k]	NA	NA	251,429 [l]	NA	NA	250,202	NA	NA
cgg	3,039 [a]	4,066,200 [a]	312,545 [a]	3,122 [a]	3,655,813 [a]	400,946 [a]	3,010	3,568,750	445,000
chb	125,418	68,434,534	20,233,969	123,855	69,331,885	18,163,083	121,781	72,679,289	16,952,618
chn	635,526	677,586,886	140,135,344	636,923	690,867,740	138,934,121	639,182 [a]	690,753,074 [a]	133,162,454 [a]
ccc	41,772	64,471,078	9,996,077	42,149	62,792,643	9,885,002	42,296	60,595,568	9,900,687
cpc	78,451	49,306,468	8,460,302	78,074	49,052,918	8,593,296	77,811 [a]	48,174,829 [a]	8,208,372
ecc	19,339	15,731,559 [a]	1,449,196 [a]	18,710	16,658,718	2,077,928	17,834	17,551,723	2,042,520
ecv	123,150 [a]	301,961,227 [a]	21,955,749 [a]	126,351 [m]	NA	NA	129,635 [m]	NA	NA
elc	3,533,956	2,470,777,573 [a]	254,571,455 [a]	3,483,336	2,507,117,689	256,892,032	3,444,041	2,474,851,188	241,234,666
els	15,734	14,738,808	1,365,828	15,672	14,565,105	1,070,176	15,672	14,271,293	1,648,567
emc	See FEC	See FEC	See FEC	See FEC	See FEC	See FEC	See FEC	See FEC	See FEC
feb	1,248 [a]	2,261,292 [a]	400,589 [a]	1,799 [a]	3,361,033 [a]	544,127 [a]	1,721 [a]	2,794,938 [a]	653,235 [a]
fec	6,834 [a]	17,646,038 [a]	2,300,708 [a]	6,933	22,705,650	1,741,233	7,137	22,451,650	1,871,850
fmc	67,259	149,855,328	18,778,761 [a]	66,878	146,736,387	24,940,690	67,472	150,143,041	23,486,606
fum	43,647 [k]	NA	NA	35,302 [a]	NA	NA	35,302 [a]	NA	NA
ggb	46,242 [a]	27,179,045 [a]	4,206,088 [a]	45,721 [a]	29,433,584 [a]	4,087,132 [a]	54,088 [a]	34,438,595 [a]	3,822,657 [a]
lca	See ELCA	See ELCA	See ELCA	See ELCA	See ELCA	See ELCA	See ELCA	See ELCA	See ELCA
lms	1,835,064	1,278,836,855	120,937,847	1,803,900	1,223,607,882	119,478,393	1,784,139	1,234,616,467	126,921,340
mch	See MUS	See MUS	See MUS	See MUS	See MUS	See MUS	See MUS	See MUS	See MUS
mgc	See MUS	See MUS	See MUS	See MUS	See MUS	See MUS	See MUS	See MUS	See MUS
mus	108,651 [l]	NA	NA	106,617 [a]	NA	NA	105,768 [a]	NA	NA
mca	17,554	17,869,301	1,152,271	16,733	17,264,555	1,003,550	16,352	17,198,636	1,043,314
nab	NA	NA	NA	NA	NA	NA	NA	NA	NA
opc	21,031	38,486,700	7,243,700	21,243	39,118,505	6,917,483	21,608	39,785,674	6,790,182
pch	2,209,546	2,518,402,119	398,386,295	2,140,165	2,542,921,235	378,650,258	2,077,138	2,414,721,917	358,621,774
rca	162,182	294,008,651	44,438,226	157,570	283,598,231	46,305,818	154,977	258,802,017	43,036,743
sda	1,000,472	368,356,521	890,924,215	1,021,777	321,184,421	874,235,374	1,043,606	413,465,740	862,030,314
sbc	16,266,920	10,779,240,776	1,327,856,082	16,228,438	10,762,418,889	1,358,802,036	16,160,088	10,578,021,610	1,334,157,703
ucc	1,145,281	859,744,628	77,117,434	1,111,691	869,869,656	71,683,884	1,080,199	861,387,225	67,251,700
wel	309,658 [a]	255,887,929 [a]	67,194,722 [a]	307,452	251,506,951 [a]	68,481,343 [a]	306,881 [a]	255,254,310 [a]	59,728,209 [a]
Total	28,516,290	21,100,072,394	3,532,579,461	28,155,289	20,748,297,569	3,505,531,802	27,917,578	20,438,794,654	3,409,742,494

a Data obtained from or confirmed by denominational source.
k Data used only in Chapter 5 analysis; not included in Total sum on this page.
l Data obtained from denominational source and used only in Chapter 5 analysis; not included in Total sum on this page.
m 2008 membership data is calculated on the percent change from 2006 to 2007 in membership data obtained from the denomination; 2009 is calculated on the 2007 and 2008 data; used only in Chapter 5 analysis; not included in Total sum on this page.

Appendix B-2: Church Member Giving for 42 Denominations, in Current Dollars, 2008-2009

	Data Year 2008			Data Year 2009		
	Full/Confirmed Members	Congregational Finances	Benevolences	Full/Confirmed Members	Congregational Finances	Benevolences
Allegheny Wesleyan Methodist Connection (Original Allegheny Conference)	1,367	3,605,777	1,150,632	1,334	3,917,928	1,135,354
Apostolic Faith Mission Church of God	5,200	579,120	604,226	5,300	576,200	578,486
Baptist Missionary Association of America	126,056	25,615,760 [a]	23,818,065	131,117 [a]	37,643,096 [a]	11,926,068 [a]
Bible Fellowship Church	7,621	13,387,979	3,525,319	7,661	17,410,199	3,779,833
Brethren Church (Ashland, Ohio)	10,106	447,012	796,723	10,227	569,985	939,527
Christ Community Church (Evangelical-Protestant)	684 [a]	1,051,187 [a]	258,571 [a]	753 [a]	1,107,777 [a]	206,222 [a]
Christian and Missionary Alliance	194,473	398,507,989	67,880,411	197,653	394,870,984	69,823,423
Church of Christ (Holiness) U.S.A.	12,158 [a]	11,702,328 [a]	863,511 [a]	12,626 [a]	11,354,544 [a]	637,642 [a]
Church of the Lutheran Brethren of America	9,070	21,667,832	2,160,264	8,988 [a]	21,182,632 [a]	2,177,485 [a]
Church of the Lutheran Confession	6,241 [a]	5,963,501 [a]	1,110,029 [a]	6,217 [a]	5,876,870 [a]	1,097,931 [a]
Churches of God General Conference	31,315 [a]	27,123,906 [a]	6,115,919 [a]	32,691	29,663,156	5,668,387
The Episcopal Church	1,666,202	1,963,911,105	331,030,116	1,624,025	1,860,343,176	321,987,283
The Missionary Church	38,206	77,967,320	10,266,469	35,384 [a]	72,082,930 [a]	9,822,171 [a]
Presbyterian Church in America	266,988	587,328,486	127,027,647	272,323	577,511,961	119,168,926
Primitive Methodist Church in the U.S.A.	3,574	4,205,155 [a]	622,673	3,430	4,086,029	578,301
The United Methodist Church	7,819,668 [a]	5,079,086,476 [a]	1,221,635,905 [a]	7,724,821 [a]	5,020,514,489 [a]	1,197,495,141 [a]
The Wesleyan Church	117,147	291,780,474	41,987,071	122,359	281,124,382	41,937,062

[a] Data obtained from denominational source.

190

Appendix B-3.1: Church Member Giving for 11 Denominations, in Current Dollars, 1921-1952

Year	Total Contributions	Members	Per Capita Giving
1921	$281,173,263	17,459,611	$16.10
1922	345,995,802	18,257,426	18.95
1923	415,556,876	18,866,775	22.03
1924	443,187,826	19,245,220	23.03
1925	412,658,363	19,474,863	21.19
1926	368,529,223	17,054,404	21.61
1927	459,527,624	20,266,709	22.67
1928	429,947,883	20,910,584	20.56
1929	445,327,233	20,612,910	21.60
1930	419,697,819	20,796,745	20.18
1931	367,158,877	21,508,745	17.07
1932	309,409,873	21,757,411	14.22
1933	260,366,681	21,792,663	11.95
1934	260,681,472	22,105,624	11.79
1935	267,596,925	22,204,355	12.05
1936	279,835,526	21,746,023	12.87
1937	297,134,313	21,906,456	13.56
1938	307,217,666	22,330,090	13.76
1939	302,300,476	23,084,048	13.10
1940	311,362,429	23,671,660	13.15
1941	336,732,622	23,120,929	14.56
1942	358,419,893	23,556,204	15.22
1943	400,742,492	24,679,784	16.24
1944	461,500,396	25,217,319	18.30
1945	551,404,448	25,898,642	21.29
1946	608,165,179	26,158,559	23.25
1947	684,393,895	27,082,905	25.27
1948	775,360,993	27,036,992	28.68
1949	875,069,944	27,611,824	31.69
1950	934,723,015	28,176,095	33.17
1951	1,033,391,527	28,974,314	35.67
1952	1,121,802,639	29,304,909	38.28

Appendix B-3.2: Church Member Giving for 11 Denominations, in Current Dollars, 1953-1967

	Data Year 1953		Data Year 1954		Data Year 1955	
	Total Contributions	Per Capita Total Contributions	Total Contributions	Per Capita Total Contributions	Total Contributions	Per Capita Total Contributions
American Baptist (Northern)	$66,557,447 a	$44.50 b	$65,354,184	$43.17	$67,538,753 d	$44.19 d
Christian Church (Disciples of Christ)	60,065,545 c	32.50 b	65,925,164	34.77	68,611,162 d	35.96 d
Church of the Brethren	7,458,584	43.78	7,812,806	45.88	9,130,616	53.00
The Episcopal Church	84,209,027	49.02	92,079,668	51.84	97,541,567 d	50.94 b
Evangelical Lutheran Church in America						
The American Lutheran Church						
American Lutheran Church	30,881,256	55.24	34,202,987	58.83	40,411,856	67.03
The Evangelical Lutheran Church	30,313,907	48.70	33,312,926	51.64	37,070,341	55.29
United Evangelical Lutheran Ch.	1,953,163	55.85	2,268,200	50.25	2,635,469	69.84
Lutheran Free Church	Not Reported: YAC 1955, p. 264		2,101,026	44.51	2,708,747	55.76
Evan. Lutheran Churches, Assn. of	Not Reported: YAC 1955, p. 264		Not Reported: YAC 1956, p. 276		Not Reported: YAC 1957, p. 284	
Lutheran Church in America						
United Lutheran Church	67,721,548	45.68	76,304,344	50.25	83,170,787	53.46
General Council Evang. Luth. Ch.						
General Synod of Evan. Luth. Ch.						
United Syn. Evang. Luth. South						
American Evangelical Luth. Ch.	Not Reported: YAC 1955, p. 264		Not Reported: YAC 1956, p. 276		Not Reported: YAC 1957, p. 284	
Augustana Lutheran Church	18,733,019	53.98	22,203,098	62.14	22,090,350	60.12
Finnish Lutheran Ch. (Suomi Synod)	744,971	32.12	674,554	29.47	1,059,682	43.75
Moravian Church in Am. No. Prov.	1,235,534	53.26	1,461,658	59.51	1,241,008	49.15
Presbyterian Church (U.S.A.)						
United Presbyterian Ch. in U.S.A.						
Presbyterian Church in the U.S.A.	141,057,179	56.49	158,110,613	61.47	180,472,698	68.09
United Presbyterian Ch. in N.A.	13,204,897	57.73	14,797,353	62.37	16,019,616	65.39
Presbyterian Church in the U.S.	56,001,996	73.99	59,222,983	75.54	66,033,260	81.43
Reformed Church in America	13,671,897	68.57	14,740,275	71.87	17,459,572	84.05
Southern Baptist Convention	278,851,129	39.84	305,573,654	42.17	334,836,283	44.54
United Church of Christ						
Congregational Christian	64,061,866	49.91	71,786,834	54.76	80,519,810	60.00
Congregational						
Evangelical and Reformed	31,025,133	41.24	36,261,267	46.83	41,363,406	52.74
Evangelical Synod of N.A./German						
Reformed Church in the U.S.						
The United Methodist Church						
The Evangelical United Brethren	36,331,994	50.21	36,609,598	50.43	41,199,631	56.01
The Methodist Church	314,521,214	34.37	345,416,448	37.53	389,490,613	41.82
Methodist Episcopal Church						
Methodist Episcopal Church South						
Methodist Protestant Church						
Total	$1,318,601,306		$1,446,219,640		$1,600,655,226	

aIn data year 1953, $805,135 has been subtracted from the 1955 *Yearbook of American Churches* (*YAC*) (Edition for 1956) entry. See 1956 *YAC* (Edition for 1957), p. 276, n.1.

bThis Per Capita Total Contributions figure was calculated by dividing (1) revised Total Contributions as listed in this Appendix, by (2) Membership that, for purposes of this report, had been calculated by dividing the unrevised Total Contributions by the Per Capita Total Contributions figures that were published in the *YAC* series.

cIn data year 1953, $5,508,883 has been added to the 1955 *YAC* (Edition for 1956) entry. See 1956 *YAC* (Edition for 1957), p. 276, n. 4.

dTotal Contributions and Per Capita Total Contributions, respectively, prorated based on available data as follows: American Baptist Churches, 1954 and 1957 data; Christian Church (Disciples of Christ), 1954 and 1956 data; and The Episcopal Church, 1954 and 1956 data.

Appendix B-3.2: Church Member Giving for 11 Denominations, in Current Dollars, 1953-1967 (continued)

	Data Year 1956		Data Year 1957		Data Year 1958	
	Total Contributions	Per Capita Total Contributions	Total Contributions	Per Capita Total Contributions	Total Contributions	Per Capita Total Contributions
American Baptist (Northern)	$69,723,321 e	$45.21 e	$71,907,890	$46.23	$70,405,404	$45.03
Christian Church (Disciples of Christ)	71,397,159	37.14	73,737,955	37.94	79,127,458	41.17
Church of the Brethren	10,936,285	63.15	11,293,388	64.43	12,288,049	70.03
The Episcopal Church	103,003,465	52.79	111,660,728	53.48	120,687,177	58.33
Evangelical Lutheran Church in America						
The American Lutheran Church						
American Lutheran Church	45,316,809	72.35	44,518,194	68.80	47,216,896	70.89
The Evangelical Lutheran Church	39,096,038	56.47	44,212,046	61.95	45,366,512	61.74
United Evangelical Lutheran Ch.	2,843,527	73.57	2,641,201	65.46	3,256,050	77.38
Lutheran Free Church	2,652,307	53.14	3,379,882	64.70	3,519,017	66.31
Evan. Lutheran Churches, Assn. of	Not Reported: YACC 1958, p. 292		Not Reported: YACC 1959, p. 277		Not Reported: YACC 1960, p. 276	
Lutheran Church in America						
United Lutheran Church	93,321,223	58.46	100,943,860	61.89	110,179,054	66.45
General Council Evang. Luth. Ch.						
General Synod of Evan. Luth. Ch.						
United Syn. Evang. Luth. Ch. South						
American Evangelical Luth. Ch.	Not Comparable YACC 1958, p. 292		935,319	59.45	1,167,503	72.98
Augustana Lutheran Church	24,893,792	66.15	28,180,152	72.09	29,163,771	73.17
Finnish Lutheran Ch. (Suomi Synod)	1,308,026	51.56	1,524,299	58.11	1,533,058	61.94
Moravian Church in Am. No. Prov.	1,740,961	67.53	1,776,703	67.77	1,816,281	68.14
Presbyterian Church (U.S.A.)						
United Presbyterian Ch. in U.S.A.					243,000,572	78.29
Presbyterian Church in the U.S.A.	204,208,085	75.02	214,253,598	77.06		
United Presbyterian Ch. in N.A.	18,424,936	73.30	19,117,837	74.24		
Presbyterian Church in the U.S.	73,477,555	88.56	78,426,424	92.03	82,760,291	95.18
Reformed Church in America	18,718,008	88.56	19,658,604	91.10	21,550,017	98.24
Southern Baptist Convention	372,136,675	48.17	397,540,347	49.99	419,619,438	51.04
United Church of Christ						
Congregational Christian	89,914,505	65.18	90,333,453	64.87	97,480,446	69.55
Congregational						
Evangelical and Reformed	51,519,531	64.88	55,718,141	69.56	63,419,468	78.56
Evangelical Synod of N.A./German						
Reformed Church in the U.S.						
The United Methodist Church						
The Evangelical United Brethren	44,727,060	60.57	45,738,332 e	61.75 e	46,749,605 e	62.93 e
The Methodist Church	413,893,955	43.82	462,826,269 e	48.31 e	511,758,582	52.80
Methodist Episcopal Church						
Methodist Episcopal Church South						
Methodist Protestant Church						
Total	$1,753,253,223		$1,880,324,622		$2,012,064,649	

eTotal Contributions and Per Capita Total Contributions, respectively, prorated based on available data as follows: American Baptist Churches, 1954 and 1957 data; The Evangelical United Brethren, 1956 and 1960 data; and The Methodist Church, 1956 and 1958 data.

Appendix B-3.2: Church Member Giving for 11 Denominations, in Current Dollars, 1953-1967 (continued)

	Data Year 1959		Data Year 1960		Data Year 1961	
	Total Contributions	Per Capita Total Contributions	Total Contributions	Per Capita Total Contributions	Total Contributions	Per Capita Total Contributions
American Baptist (Northern)	$74,877,669	$48.52	$73,106,232	$48.06	$104,887,025	$68.96
Christian Ch (Disciples of Christ)	Not Comparable YAC 1961, p. 273		$86,834,944	$63.26	$89,730,589	$65.31
Church of the Brethren	$12,143,983	$65.27	$12,644,194	$68.33	$13,653,155	$73.33
The Episcopal Church	$130,279,752	$61.36	$140,625,284	$64.51	$154,458,809	$68.30
Evangelical Lutheran Church in Am.						
The American Lutheran Church	$50,163,078	$73.52	$51,898,875	$74.49	$113,645,260	$73.28
American Lutheran Church	$49,488,063	$65.56	$51,297,348	$66.85		
The Evangelical Lutheran Church	Not Reported: YAC 1961, p. 273		Not Reported: YAC 1963, p. 273			
United Evangelical Lutheran Ch.	$3,354,270	$61.20	$3,618,418	$63.98	$4,316,925	$73.46
Lutheran Free Church	Not Reported: YAC 1961, p. 273		Not Reported: YAC 1963, p. 273			
Evan. Lutheran Churches, Assn of						
Lutheran Church in America						
United Lutheran Church	$114,458,260	$68.29	$119,447,895	$70.86	$128,850,845	$76.18
General Council Evang Luth Ch						
General Synod of Evan Luth Ch						
United Syn Evang Luth South						
American Evangelical Luth. Ch	$1,033,907	$63.83	$1,371,600	$83.63	$1,209,752	$74.89
Augustana Lutheran Church	$31,279,335	$76.97	$33,478,865	$80.88	$37,863,105	$89.37
Finnish Luth. Ch (Suomi Synod)	$1,685,342	$68.61	$1,860,481	$76.32	$1,744,550	$70.60
Moravian Church in Am. No. Prov.	$2,398,565	$89.28	$2,252,536	$82.95	$2,489,930	$90.84
Presbyterian Church (U.S.A.)						
United Presbyterian Ch in U.S.A.	$259,679,057	$82.30	$270,233,943	$84.31	$285,380,476	$87.90
Presbyterian Ch in the U.S.A.						
United Presbyterian Ch in N.A.						
Presbyterian Church in the U.S.	$88,404,631	$99.42	$91,582,428	$101.44	$96,637,354	$105.33
Reformed Church in America	$22,970,935	$103.23	$23,615,749	$104.53	$25,045,773	$108.80
Southern Baptist Convention	$453,338,720	$53.88	$480,608,972	$55.68	$501,301,714	$50.24
United Church of Christ	$100,938,267	$71.12	$104,862,037	$73.20	$105,871,158	$73.72
Congregational Christian						
Congregational						
Evangelical and Reformed	$65,541,874	$80.92	$62,346,084	$76.58	$65,704,662	$80.33
Evangelical Synod of N.A./German						
Reformed Church in the U.S.						
The United Methodist Church						
The Evangelical United Brethren	$47,760,877 d	$64.10	$48,772,149 d	$65.28	$50,818,912 d	$68.12
The Methodist Church	$532,854,842 d	$53.97	$553,951,102 d	$55.14	$581,504,618 d	$57.27
Methodist Episcopal Church						
Methodist Episcopal Ch South						
Methodist Protestant Church						
Total	$2,042,651,427		$2,214,409,136		$2,365,114,612	

d Total Contributions averaged from available data as follows: Evangelical United Brethren, 1956 and 1960 data; The United Methodist Church, 1958 and 1960 data.

Appendix B-3.2: Church Member Giving for 11 Denominations, in Current Dollars, 1953-1967

Appendix B-3.2: Church Member Giving for 11 Denominations, in Current Dollars 1953-1967* (continued)

	Data Year 1962		Data Year 1963		Data Year 1964	
	Total Contributions	Per Capita Total Contributions	Total Contributions	Per Capita Total Contributions	Total Contributions	Per Capita Total Contributions
American Baptist (Northern)	$105,667,332	$68.42	$99,001,651	$68.34	$104,699,557	$69.99
Christian Church (Disciples of Christ)	91,889,457	67.20	96,607,038	75.81	102,102,840	86.44
Church of the Brethren	14,594,572	77.88	14,574,688	72.06	15,221,162	76.08
The Episcopal Church	155,971,264	69.80	171,125,464	76.20	175,374,777	76.66
Evangelical Lutheran Church in America						
The American Lutheran Church	114,912,112	72.47	136,202,292	81.11	143,687,165	83.83
American Lutheran Church						
The Evangelical Lutheran Church						
United Evangelical Lutheran Ch.						
Lutheran Free Church	4,765,138	78.68				
Evan. Lutheran Churches, Assn. of						
Lutheran Church in America	185,166,857	84.98	157,423,391	71.45	170,012,096	76.35
United Lutheran Church						
General Council Evang. Luth. Ch.						
General Synod of Evan. Luth. Ch.						
United Syn. Evang. Luth. South						
American Evangelical Luth. Ch.						
Augustana Lutheran Church						
Finnish Lutheran Ch. (Suomi Synod)						
Moravian Church in Am. No. Prov.	2,512,133	91.92	2,472,273	89.29	2,868,694	103.54
Presbyterian Church (U.S.A.)						
United Presbyterian Ch. in U.S.A.	288,496,652	88.08	297,582,313	90.46	304,833,435	92.29
Presbyterian Church in the U.S.A.						
United Presbyterian Ch. in N.A.						
Presbyterian Church in the U.S.	99,262,431	106.96	102,625,764	109.46	108,269,579	114.61
Reformed Church in America	25,579,443	110.16	26,918,484	117.58	29,174,103	126.44
Southern Baptist Convention	540,811,457	53.06	556,042,694	53.49	591,587,981	55.80
United Church of Christ	164,858,968	72.83	162,379,019	73.12	169,208,042	75.94
Congregational Christian						
Congregational						
Evangelical and Reformed						
Evangelical Synod of N.A./German						
Reformed Church in the U.S.						
The United Methodist Church						
The Evangelical United Brethren	54,567,962	72.91	49,921,568	67.37	56,552,783	76.34
The Methodist Church	599,081,561	58.53	613,547,721	59.60	608,841,881	59.09
Methodist Episcopal Church						
Methodist Episcopal Church South						
Methodist Protestant Church						
Total	$2,448,137,339		$2,486,424,360		$2,582,434,095	

*Note: Data for the years 1965 through 1967 was not available in a form that could be readily analyzed for the present purposes, and therefore data for 1965-1967 was estimated as described in the introductory comments to Appendix B. See Appendix B-1 for 1968-1991 data except for The Episcopal Church and The United Methodist Church, available data for which is presented in the continuation of Appendix B-3 in the table immediately following.

Appendix B-3.3: Church Member Giving for 11 Denominations, in Current Dollars, The Episcopal Church and The United Methodist Church, 1968-2009

The Episcopal Church			The United Methodist Church			
Data Year	Total Contributions	Full/Confirmed Membership	Data Year	Total Contributions	Full/Confirmed Membership	Connectional Clergy Support [c]
1968	$202,658,092 [c]	2,322,911 [c]	1968	$763,000,434 [a]	10,849,375 [b]	NA
1969	209,989,189 [c]	2,238,538	1969	800,425,000	10,671,774	44,416,000
1970	248,702,969	2,208,773	1970	819,945,000	10,509,198	48,847,000
1971	257,523,469	2,143,557	1971	843,103,000	10,334,521	52,731,000
1972	270,245,645	2,099,896	1972	885,708,000	10,192,265	56,968,000
1973	296,735,919 [c]	2,079,873 [c]	1973	935,723,000	10,063,046	62,498,997
1974	305,628,925	2,069,793	1974	1,009,760,804	9,957,710	67,344,298
1975	352,243,222	2,051,914 [c]	1975	1,081,080,372	9,861,028	75,220,496
1976	375,942,065	2,021,057	1976	1,162,828,991	9,785,534	82,681,376
1977	401,814,395	2,114,638	1977	1,264,191,548	9,731,779	94,705,448
1978	430,116,564	1,975,234	1978	1,364,460,266	9,653,711	107,508,214
1979	484,211,412	1,962,062	1979	1,483,481,986	9,584,771	116,405,701
1980	507,315,457	1,933,080 [c]	1980	1,632,204,336	9,519,407	126,442,425
1981	697,816,298	1,930,690	1981	1,794,706,741	9,457,012	136,991,942
1982	778,184,068	1,922,923 [c]	1982	1,931,796,533	9,405,164	162,884,181
1983	876,844,252	1,906,618	1983	2,049,437,917	9,291,936	172,569,488
1984	939,796,743	1,896,056	1984	2,211,306,198	9,266,853	188,372,446
1985	1,043,117,983	1,881,250	1985	2,333,928,274	9,192,172	203,047,650
1986	1,134,455,479	1,772,271 [c]	1986	2,460,079,431	9,124,575	211,121,271
1987	1,181,378,441	1,741,036	1987	2,573,748,234	9,055,145	217,708,718
1988	1,209,378,098	1,725,581	1988	2,697,918,285	8,979,139	230,013,885
1989	1,309,243,747	1,714,122	1989	2,845,998,177	8,904,824	245,281,392
1990	1,377,794,610	1,698,240	1990	2,967,535,538	8,853,455	261,434,709
1991	1,541,141,356 [c]	1,613,825 [c]	1991	3,099,522,282	8,789,101	269,248,639
1992	1,582,055,527 [c]	1,615,930 [c]	1992	3,202,700,721 [c]	8,726,951 [c]	278,990,363
1993	1,617,623,255 [c]	1,580,339 [c]	1993	3,303,255,279	8,646,595	284,654,147
1994	1,679,250,095 [c]	1,578,282 [c]	1994	3,430,351,778	8,584,125	293,637,514
1995	1,840,431,636 [c]	1,584,225 [c]	1995	3,568,359,334 [c]	8,538,808 [c]	295,102,097
1996	1,731,727,725 [c]	1,637,584 [c]	1996	3,744,692,223	8,496,047 [c]	296,944,022
1997	1,832,000,448 [c]	1,757,972 [c]	1997	3,990,329,491 [c]	8,452,042 [c]	310,347,506
1998	1,977,012,320 [c]	1,807,651 [c]	1998	4,219,596,499 [c]	8,411,503 [c]	319,721,285
1999	2,146,835,718 [c]	1,843,108 [c]	1999	4,523,284,851	8,377,662	328,089,751
2000	2,143,238,797 [c]	1,877,271 [c]	2000	4,761,148,280	8,340,954	338,798,893
2001	2,070,493,919 [c]	1,897,004 [c]	2001	5,043,693,838 [c]	8,298,460 [c]	359,734,860
2002	2,090,536,512 [c]	1,902,525 [c]	2002	5,242,691,229	8,251,042	401,465,727
2003	2,133,772,253	1,866,157	2003	5,376,057,236 [c]	8,186,274 [c]	444,210,401
2004	2,132,774,534	1,834,530	2004	5,541,540,536	8,120,186 [d]	462,206,590
2005	2,180,974,503 [c]	1,796,017 [c]	2005	5,861,722,397 [c]	8,040,577 [c]	466,588,268
2006	2,187,308,798 [c]	1,749,073 [c]	2006	6,012,378,898 [c]	7,976,985 [c]	481,453,754
2007	2,221,167,438	1,720,477	2007	6,295,942,455 [c]	7,899,147 [c]	478,982,491
2008	2,294,941,221	1,666,202	2008	6,300,722,381 [c]	7,819,668 [c]	477,863,600
2009	2,182,330,459	1,624,025	2009	6,218,009,630 [c]	7,724,821 [c]	Not Available

a The Evangelical United Brethren Data Not Reported: *YACC* 1970, p. 198-200. This figure is the sum of The Methodist Church in 1968, and the Evangelical United Brethren data for 1967.

b This membership figure is an average of the sum of 1967 membership for The Methodist Church and the Evangelical United Brethren and 1969 data for The United Methodist Church.

c Data obtained directly from denominational source.

d Data obtained from the denomination included this note: "Combines 2004 local church data with 2004 clergy data. In the past 2004 lay would be combined with 2005 clergy. We've been delayed in finalizing clergy figures for 2005... [Based on a check of] the past few years, that will mean a difference of less than 300 for the total number."

Appendix B-4: Membership for Seven Denominations, 1968-2009

Year	American Baptist Churches (Total Mem.)	Assemblies of God	Baptist General Conference	Christian and Missionary Alliance	Church of God (Cleveland, TN)	Roman Catholic Church	Salvation Army
1968	1,583,560	610,946	100,000	71,656	243,532	47,468,333	329,515
1969	1,528,019	626,660	101,226	70,573	257,995	47,872,089	331,711
1970	1,472,478	625,027	103,955	71,708	272,276	48,214,729	326,934
1971	1,562,636	645,891	108,474	73,547	287,099	48,390,990	335,684
1972	1,484,393	679,813	111,364	77,991	297,103	48,460,427	358,626
1973	1,502,759	700,071	109,033	77,606	313,332	48,465,438	361,571
1974	1,579,029	751,818	111,093	80,412	328,892	48,701,835	366,471
1975	1,603,033	785,348	115,340	83,628	343,249	48,881,872	384,817
1976	1,593,574	898,711	117,973	83,978	365,124	49,325,752	380,618
1977	1,584,517	939,312	120,222	88,763	377,765	49,836,176	396,238
1978	1,589,610	932,365	131,000	88,903	392,551	49,602,035	414,035
1979	1,600,521	958,418	126,800	96,324	441,385	49,812,178	414,659
1980	1,607,541	1,064,490	133,385	106,050	435,012	50,449,842	417,359
1981	1,621,795	1,103,134	127,662	109,558	456,797	51,207,579	414,999
1982	1,637,099	1,119,686	129,928	112,745	463,992	52,088,774 [a]	419,475
1983	1,620,153	1,153,935	131,594 [a]	117,501	493,904	52,392,934	428,046
1984	1,559,683	1,189,143	131,162 [a]	120,250	505,775	52,286,043	420,971
1985	1,576,483	1,235,403	130,193 [a]	123,602	521,061 [b]	52,654,908	427,825
1986	1,568,778 [a]	1,258,724	132,546 [a]	130,116	536,346 [b]	52,893,217	432,893
1987	1,561,656 [a]	1,275,146	136,688 [a]	131,354	551,632 [b]	53,496,862	434,002
1988	1,548,573 [a]	1,275,148	134,396 [a]	133,575	556,917 [b]	54,918,949 [a]	433,448
1989	1,535,971 [a]	1,266,982	135,125 [a]	134,336	582,203	57,019,948	445,566
1990	1,527,840 [a]	1,298,121	133,742 [a]	138,071	620,393	58,568,015	445,991
1991	1,534,078 [a]	1,324,800	134,717 [a]	141,077	646,201 [b]	58,267,424	446,403
1992	1,538,710 [a]	1,337,321	134,658 [a]	142,346	672,008	59,220,723	450,028 [a]
1993	1,516,505	1,340,400	134,814 [a]	147,367	700,517	59,858,042	450,312 [a]
1994	1,507,934 [a]	1,354,337	135,128	147,560 [a]	722,541	60,190,605	443,246
1995	1,517,400	1,377,320	135,008	147,955	753,230	60,280,454	453,150
1996	1,503,267 [a]	1,407,941	136,120	143,157	773,483 [a]	61,207,914	462,744 [a]
1997	1,478,534 [a]	1,419,717	134,795	146,153	815,042 [a]	61,563,769 [a]	468,262 [a]
1998	1,507,824 [a]	1,453,907	141,445	163,994	839,857 [a]	62,018,436	471,416
1999	1,454,388	1,492,196	142,871 [a]	164,196	870,039	62,391,484	472,871
2000	1,436,909	1,506,834	141,781 [a]	185,133	895,536	63,683,030 [a]	476,887 [a]
2001	1,442,824	1,532,876	144,365 [a]	191,318	920,664 [a]	65,270,444	454,982
2002	1,484,291	1,585,428	145,148	190,573	944,857	66,407,105	457,807 [a]
2003	1,433,075	1,584,076	145,436 [a]	194,074	961,390	67,259,768	449,634 [a]
2004	1,418,403 [a]	1,594,062	145,000 [a]	197,764	989,965	67,820,833	427,027
2005	1,396,700	1,612,336	140,494 [a]	201,009	1,013,488	69,135,254	422,543 [a]
2006	1,371,278	1,627,932	140,000 [a]	189,969	1,032,550	67,515,016	414,054 [a]
2007	1,358,351 [a]	1,641,341	147,500	195,481	1,053,642	67,117,016	413,028
2008	1,331,127	1,662,632	167,500 [a]	194,473	1,072,169	68,115,001	405,967 [a]
2009	1,310,505	1,710,560	164,500 [a]	197,653	1,076,254	68,503,456	400,055

a Data obtained from a denominational source.
b Extrapolated from *YACC* series.
Note regarding American Baptist Churches in the U.S.A. Total Membership data: Total Membership is used for the American Baptist Churches in the U.S.A. for analyses that consider membership as a percentage of U.S. population. The ABC denominational office is the source for this data in the years 1968 and 1970. The year 1978 Total Membership data figure is an adjustment of *YACC* data based on 1981 *YACC* information.

Appendix B-5.1: Overseas Missions Income, 34 Denominations, In Current Dollars, 2003 and 2004

Denomination	2003 Overseas Missions Income				2004 Overseas Missions Income			
	Line 1.	Line 2.	Line 3.	Line 4.	Line 1.	Line 2.	Line 3.	line 4.
Allegheny Wesleyan Methodist Connection	$262,260	$0	$0	$262,260	$266,299	$0	$0	$266,299
American Baptist Churches in the U.S.A.	$20,562,505	$12,048,667	$0	$8,513,838	$17,250,939	$7,759,091	$0	$9,491,848
Associate Reformed Presbyterian Church (General Synod)	$3,508,682	$0	$175,690	$3,332,992	$4,453,573	$15,183	$483,815	$3,954,575
Brethren in Christ Church	$1,651,911	$45,000	$0	$1,606,911	$1,850,963	$50,000	$0	$1,800,963
Christian Church (Disciples of Christ)	$5,960,892	$1,881,873	$0	$4,079,019	$5,347,401	$1,515,309	$0	$3,832,092
Christian and Missionary Alliance [1]	$43,160,960	$0	$0	$43,160,960	$43,534,066	$0	$0	$43,534,066
Church of the Brethren [2]	$1,767,447	$203,824	$0	$1,563,623	$1,702,267	$143,947	$0	$1,558,320
Church of God General Conf. (Oregon, Ill., and Morrow, Ga.)	$67,193	$0	$0	$67,193	$113,497	$0	$0	$113,497
Church of the Lutheran Confession	$182,156	$27,000	$0	$155,156	$246,896	$40,000	$0	$206,896
Church of the Nazarene	$46,334,499	$694,019	$0	$45,640,480	$49,715,273	$1,542,188	$0	$48,173,085
Churches of God General Conference [3]	$899,679	$0	$0	$899,679	$1,068,665	$21,517	$0	$1,047,148
Conservative Congregational Christian Conference [4]	$147,805	$0	$0	$147,805	$149,299	$0	$0	$149,299
Cumberland Presbyterian Church	$303,000	$12,236	$0	$290,764	$338,314	$14,974	$0	$323,340
The Episcopal Church [5]	$21,120,265	$3,507,225	$4,419,185	$13,193,855	$23,281,000	$3,000,000	$5,500,000	$14,781,000
Evangelical Congregational Church	$1,264,969	$219,732	$0	$1,045,237	$1,135,224	$193,815	$0	$941,409
Evangelical Covenant Church	$7,913,682	$0	$0	$7,913,682	$8,591,574	$0	$0	$8,591,574
Evangelical Lutheran Church in America [6]	$22,590,206	$2,952,825	$0	$19,637,381	$27,173,066	$3,741,985	$0	$23,431,081
Evangelical Lutheran Synod	$912,460	$665,873	$0	$246,587	$945,470	$679,229	$0	$266,241
Fellowship of Evangelical Churches	$912,689	$0	$0	$912,689	$847,526	$0	$0	$847,526
Free Methodist Church of North America	$9,848,924	$727,325	$0	$9,121,599	$10,817,138	$630,519	$0	$10,186,619
General Association of General Baptists	$1,893,585	$34,719	$0	$1,858,866	$1,817,715	$49,178	$0	$1,768,537
Lutheran Church-Missouri Synod [7]	$14,960,928	$1,881,887	$0	$13,079,041	$15,548,240	$2,370,861	$0	$13,177,379
Moravian Church in America, Northern Province [8]				$467,570				$528,733
The Orthodox Presbyterian Church [9]	$1,254,678	$40,229		$1,214,449	$1,417,758	$43,504	$0	$1,374,254
Presbyterian Church in America	$24,070,885	$0	$0	$24,070,885	$24,319,185	$0	$0	$24,319,185
Presbyterian Church (U.S.A.) [10]	$34,348,000	$11,046,000	$47,000	$23,255,000	$36,900,000	$12,190,000	$122,000	$24,588,000
Primitive Methodist Church in the U.S.A. [11]	$542,252	$5,349	$0	$536,903	$532,337	$5,697	$0	$526,640
Reformed Church in America	$8,159,552	$307,088	$0	$7,852,464	$7,610,120	$325,560	$0	$7,284,560
Seventh-day Adventist, North Am. Division [12]	$50,790,392	$2,565,158	$0	$48,225,234	$48,209,196	$1,456,611	$0	$46,752,585
Southern Baptist Convention	$239,663,000	$0	$0	$239,663,000	$242,140,000	$0	$0	$242,140,000
United Church of Christ	$12,990,011	$4,616,927	$0	$8,373,084	$12,125,594	$4,189,916	$0	$7,935,678
The United Methodist Church [13]	$124,800,000	$20,000,000	$22,800,000	$82,000,000	$138,700,000	$19,800,000	$27,700,000	$91,200,000
The Wesleyan Church	$8,507,914	$0	$0	$8,507,914	$8,881,386	$0	$0	$8,881,386
Wisconsin Evangelical Lutheran Synod	$11,534,079	$754,916	$0	$10,779,164	$10,707,496	$402,633	$0	$10,304,863

See Notes on page 202.

Appendix B-5.2: Overseas Missions Income, 34 Denominations, In Current Dollars, 2005 and 2006

Denomination	2005 Overseas Missions Income				2006 Overseas Missions Income			
	Line 1.	Line 2.	Line 3.	Line 4.	Line 1.	Line 2.	Line 3.	Line 4.
Allegheny Wesleyan Methodist Connection	$399,514	$0	$0	$399,514	$286,781	$0	$0	$286,781
American Baptist Churches in the U.S.A.	$18,837,736	$7,741,255	$0	$11,096,481	$14,701,486	$5,922,316	$0	$8,779,170
Associate Reformed Presbyterian Church (General Synod)	$4,920,208	$139,231	$264,675	$4,516,302	$4,682,925	$689,152	$172,476	$3,821,297
Brethren in Christ Church	$1,980,000	$60,000	$0	$1,920,000	$2,200,000	$82,406	$0	$2,117,594
Christian Church (Disciples of Christ)	$5,810,205	$1,587,428	$0	$4,222,777	$6,134,200	$1,712,531	$0	$4,421,669
Christian and Missionary Alliance [1]	$54,267,422	$0	$0	$54,267,422	$52,505,044	$0	$0	$52,505,044
Church of the Brethren [2]	$2,417,349	$147,215	$0	$2,270,134	$2,087,021	$199,819	$0	$1,887,202
Church of God General Conf. (Oregon, Ill. and Morrow, Ga.)	$80,000	$0	$0	$80,000	$63,355	$0	$0	$63,355
Church of the Lutheran Confession	$329,823	$20,000	$0	$309,823	$314,804	$125,987	$0	$188,817
Church of the Nazarene	$54,653,601	$1,899,919	$0	$52,753,682	$52,721,095	$1,751,130	$0	$50,969,965
Churches of God General Conference [3]	$1,146,044	$15,944	$0	$1,130,100	$1,282,333	$48,490	$0	$1,233,843
Conservative Congregational Christian Conference [4]	$166,875	$0	$0	$166,875	$123,509	$0	$0	$123,509
Cumberland Presbyterian Church	$306,428	$13,082	$0	$293,346	$306,035	$15,728	$0	$290,307
The Episcopal Church [5]	$23,871,967	$3,000,000	$5,500,000	$15,371,967	$24,334,083	$3,000,000	$6,527,290	$14,806,793
Evangelical Congregational Church	$767,359	$42,270	$0	$725,089	$1,326,393	$0	$0	$1,326,393
Evangelical Covenant Church	$9,008,719	$0	$0	$9,008,719	$8,530,245	$0	$0	$8,530,245
Evangelical Lutheran Church in America [6]	$29,109,564	$3,025,562	$0	$26,084,001	$25,484,714	$3,942,905	$0	$21,541,809
Evangelical Lutheran Synod	$1,211,101	$988,897	$0	$222,204	$1,214,815	$884,164	$0	$330,651
Fellowship of Evangelical Churches	$785,676	$0	$0	$785,676	$700,159	$0	$0	$700,159
Free Methodist Church of North America	$10,831,707	$111,467	$0	$10,720,240	$12,578,589	$699,714	$0	$11,878,875
General Association of General Baptists	$1,945,215	$20,707	$0	$1,924,508	$2,082,916	$34,346	$0	$2,048,570
Lutheran Church-Missouri Synod [7]	$18,897,894	$1,722,316	$0	$17,175,578	$16,170,108	$2,737,162	$0	$13,432,946
Moravian Church in America, Northern Province [8]	$568,497	$86,340	$0	$482,157	$561,849	$49,021	$0	$512,828
The Orthodox Presbyterian Church [9]	$2,212,525	$355,996	$0	$1,856,529	$2,064,820	$358,528	$0	$1,706,292
Presbyterian Church in America	$25,890,591	$0	$0	$25,890,591	$27,627,770	$0	$0	$27,627,770
Presbyterian Church (U.S.A.) [10]	$47,223,000	$15,540,000	$65,000	$31,618,000	$35,539,000	$14,575,000	$0	$20,964,000
Primitive Methodist Church in the U.S.A. [11]	$503,286	$5,441	$0	$497,845	$568,032	$1,916	$0	$566,116
Reformed Church in America	$10,727,347	$0	$0	$10,727,347	$7,891,745	$405,218	$0	$7,486,527
Seventh-day Adventist, North Am. Division [12]	$53,745,101	$1,614,134	$0	$52,130,967	$51,459,266	$2,553,650	$0	$48,905,616
Southern Baptist Convention	$259,394,000	$0	$0	$259,394,000	$275,747,000	$0	$0	$275,747,000
United Church of Christ	$11,299,684	$3,647,313	$0	$7,652,371	$10,834,552	$3,295,428	$0	$7,539,124
The United Methodist Church [13]	$177,000,000	$23,400,000	$26,000,000	$127,600,000	$120,400,000	$21,600,000	$15,700,000	$83,100,000
The Wesleyan Church	$9,769,938	$0	$0	$9,769,938	$13,105,882	$0	$0	$13,105,882
Wisconsin Evangelical Lutheran Synod	$8,957,945	$163,652	$0	$8,794,293	$10,886,785	$418,225	$0	$10,468,560

See Notes on page 202

Appendix B-5.3: Overseas Missions Income, In Current Dollars,
34 Denominations, 2007, and 33 Denominations, 2008

Denomination	2007 Overseas Missions Income				2008 Overseas Missions Income			
	Line 1.	Line 2.	Line 3.	Line 4.	Line 1.	Line 2.	Line 3.	Line 4.
Allegheny Wesleyan Methodist Connection	$332,511	$0	$0	$332,511	$306,946	$0	$0	$306,946
American Baptist Churches in the U.S.A.	$15,703,238	$5,837,228	$0	$9,866,010	$16,099,000	$6,253,000	$0	$9,846,000
Associate Reformed Presbyterian Church (General Synod)	$5,088,825	$254,533	$14,670	$4,819,622	$5,838,994	$0	$0	$5,838,994
Brethren in Christ Church	$2,264,672	$92,850	$0	$2,171,822	*$2,569,054*	*$116,556*	$0	*$2,452,498*
Christian Church (Disciples of Christ)	$6,645,790	$1,871,786	$0	$4,774,004	$6,436,974	$1,909,503	$0	$4,527,471
Christian and Missionary Alliance [1]	$55,964,407	$0	$0	$55,964,407	$52,012,830	$0	$0	$52,012,830
Church of the Brethren [2]	$1,943,631	$206,977	$0	$1,736,654	$1,807,162	$58,642	$0	$1,748,520
Church of God General Conf. (Oregon, Ill. and Morrow, Ga.)	$103,495	$0	$0	$103,495	$101,028	$0	$0	$101,028
Church of the Lutheran Confession	$313,700	$36,100	$0	$277,600	$361,641	$1,318	*$0*	$360,323
Church of the Nazarene	$52,195,781	$1,604,626	$0	$50,591,155	$54,573,954	$812,861	$0	$53,761,093
Churches of God General Conference [3]	$1,148,045	$29,124	$0	$1,118,921	$1,153,166	($34,087)	$0	$1,187,253
Conservative Congregational Christian Conference [4]	$169,508	$0	$0	$169,508	$84,460	$0	$0	$84,460
Cumberland Presbyterian Church	$368,334	$15,690	$0	$352,644	$322,815	$21,570	$0	$301,245
The Episcopal Church [5]	$26,940,269	$3,400,000	$8,511,710	$15,028,559	$27,589,783	$3,517,957	$9,472,472	$14,599,354
Evangelical Congregational Church	$1,464,523	$0	$0	$1,464,523	$1,583,478	$0	$0	$1,583,478
Evangelical Covenant Church	$7,954,834	$0	$0	$7,954,834	NA	NA	NA	NA
Evangelical Lutheran Church in America [6]	$26,161,433	$4,414,055	$0	$21,747,378	$27,518,419	$3,358,245	$0	$24,160,174
Evangelical Lutheran Synod	$1,389,221	$885,203	$0	$504,018	$1,070,241	$450,487	$0	$619,754
Fellowship of Evangelical Churches	$700,590	$0	$0	$700,590	$724,626	$0	$0	$724,626
Free Methodist Church of North America	$13,705,466	$1,226,998	$0	$12,478,468	$13,581,459	$336,594	$0	$13,244,864
General Association of General Baptists	$2,246,653	$67,605	$0	$2,179,048	$2,158,514	$52,673	$0	$2,105,841
Lutheran Church-Missouri Synod [7]	$16,086,361	$2,899,441	$0	$13,186,920	$17,473,964	$2,968,153	$0	$14,505,811
Moravian Church in America, Northern Province [8]	$542,968	$18,819	$0	$524,149	$504,041	$30,521	$0	$473,520
The Orthodox Presbyterian Church [9]	$1,899,674	$75,285	$0	$1,824,389	$1,820,552	$20,247	$0	$1,800,305
Presbyterian Church in America	$28,456,453	$0	$0	$28,456,453	$29,173,722	$0	$0	$29,173,722
Presbyterian Church (U.S.A.) [10]	$45,301,000	$4,935,000	$0	$40,366,000	$24,839,000	$4,920,000	$0	$19,919,000
Primitive Methodist Church in the U.S.A. [11]	$568,612	$1,802	$0	$566,810	$543,570	$1,132	$0	$542,438
Reformed Church in America	$7,931,523	$319,910	$0	$7,611,613	$8,160,053	$517,484	$0	$7,642,569
Seventh-day Adventist, North Am. Division [12]	$53,772,765	$1,734,653	$0	$52,038,112	$53,959,359	$2,457,879	$0	$51,501,480
Southern Baptist Convention	$278,313,000	$0	$0	$278,313,000	$254,860,000	$0	$0	$254,860,000
United Church of Christ	$9,800,591	$2,493,501	$0	$7,307,090	$9,943,495	$2,698,518	$0	$7,244,977
The United Methodist Church [13]	$126,600,000	$21,400,000	$25,700,000	$79,500,000	$148,300,000	$23,800,000	$10,000,000	$114,500,000
The Wesleyan Church	$13,554,996	$0	$0	$13,554,996	$13,669,461	$0	$0	$13,669,461
Wisconsin Evangelical Lutheran Synod	$11,173,147	$500,952	$0	$10,672,195	$12,107,158	$471,779	$0	$11,635,379

See Notes on page 202

Overseas Missions Income Data for Two Additional Denominations, In Current Dollars, 2003-2009

Denomination	2003 Overseas Missions Income, Line 4	2004 Overseas Missions Income, Line 4	2005 Overseas Missions Income, Line 4	2006 Overseas Missions Income, Line 4	2007 Overseas Missions Income, Line 4	2008 Overseas Missions Income, Line 4	2009 Overseas Missions Income, Line 4
Friends United Meeting	$1,314,527	$276,887 (partial year)	$863,445	$859,750	$937,142	$1,076,400	$888,142
Mennonite Church USA	$4,155,596	$3,854,139	$3,937,548	$3,876,657	$4,054,734	$4,225,771	$3,650,453

See Chapter 6, Note 9

Appendix B-5.4: Overseas Missions Income, In Current Dollars, 32 Denominations, 2009

Denomination	2009 Overseas Missions Income			
	Line 1.	Line 2.	Line 3.	Line 4.
Allegheny Wesleyan Methodist Connection	$275,139	$0	$0	$275,139
American Baptist Churches in the U.S.A.	$14,526,000	$4,941,000	$0	$9,585,000
Associate Reformed Presbyterian Church (General Synod)	$4,359,553	$124,682	$0	$4,234,871
Brethren in Christ Church	$2,612,767	$139,173	$0	$2,473,594
Christian Church (Disciples of Christ)	$5,826,676	$1,848,084	$0	$3,978,592
Christian and Missionary Alliance [1]	$52,888,984	$0	$0	$52,888,984
Church of the Brethren [2]	$2,022,629	$118,492	$0	$1,904,137
Church of God General Conf. (Oregon, Ill. and Morrow, Ga.)	$166,433	$0	$0	$166,433
Church of the Lutheran Confession	$402,162	$0	$0	$402,162
Church of the Nazarene	$45,059,581	$1,688,702	$0	$43,370,879
Churches of God General Conference [3]	$1,355,136	$19,538	$0	$1,335,598
Conservative Congregational Christian Conference [4]	$18,397	$0	$0	$18,397
Cumberland Presbyterian Church	$300,535	$23,123	$0	$277,412
The Episcopal Church [5]	$30,493,164	$4,373,291	$10,508,830	$15,611,043
Evangelical Congregational Church	$1,462,048	$0	$0	$1,462,048
Evangelical Covenant Church	NA	NA	NA	NA
Evangelical Lutheran Church in America [6]	$27,574,196	$2,908,702	$0	$24,665,494
Evangelical Lutheran Synod	$1,964,975	$820,864	$0	$1,144,111
Fellowship of Evangelical Churches	$804,057	$0	$0	$804,057
Free Methodist Church of North America	$12,032,082	$311,563	$0	$11,720,519
General Association of General Baptists	$1,978,712	$32,563	$0	$1,946,149
Lutheran Church-Missouri Synod [7]	NA	NA	NA	NA
Moravian Church in America, Northern Province [8]	$531,872	$28,055	$0	$503,817
The Orthodox Presbyterian Church [9]	$2,293,701	$314,657	$0	$1,979,044
Presbyterian Church in America	$27,219,278	$0	$0	$27,219,278
Presbyterian Church (U.S.A.) [10]	$27,182,967	$5,196,136	$0	$21,986,831
Primitive Methodist Church in the U.S.A. [11]	$430,150	$620	$0	$429,530
Reformed Church in America	$8,367,356	$179,496	$0	$8,187,860
Seventh-day Adventist, North Am. Division [12]	$52,019,434	$2,480,790	$0	$49,538,644
Southern Baptist Convention	$255,427,000	$0	$0	$255,427,000
United Church of Christ	$9,531,462	$3,317,710	$0	$6,213,752
The United Methodist Church [13]	$124,120,000	$17,800,000	$9,400,000	$96,920,000
The Wesleyan Church	$14,139,092	$0	$0	$14,139,092
Wisconsin Evangelical Lutheran Synod	$10,706,565	($324,254)	$0.00	$11,030,819

See Notes on page 202

Line Descriptions on empty tomb, inc. Overseas Missions Income Data Request Form:

Line 1.:   What was the amount of income raised in the U.S. during the calendar or fiscal year indicated for overseas ministries?

Line 2.:   How many dollars of the total amount on Line 1. came from endowment, foundation, and other investment income?

Line 3.:   Of the total amount on Line1., what is the dollar value of government grants, either in dollars or in-kind goods for distribution?

Line 4.:   Balance of overseas ministries income: Line 1. minus Lines 2. and 3.

Notes to Appendix B-5: Overseas Missions Income, 2003, 2004, 2005, 2006, 2007, 2008, and 2009

[1] Christian and Missionary Alliance: "Since both domestic and overseas works are budgeted through the same source (our 'Great Commission Fund'), the amount on lines 1 and 4 are actual amounts spent on overseas missions."

[2] Church of the Brethren: "This amount is national denominational mission and service, i.e., direct staffing and mission support, and does not include other projects funded directly by congregations or districts, or independent missionaries sponsored by congregations and individuals that would not be part of the denominational effort."

[3] Churches of God General Conference: "[Data Year] 2008 line 2 represents a net loss in investment income included in line 1. By adding this net loss amount back, line 4 represents the amount received in contributions from donors."

[4] Conservative Congregational Christian Conference: The structure of this communion limits the national office coordination of overseas ministries activity. By design, congregations are to conduct missions directly, through agencies of their choice. The national office does not survey congregations about these activities. The one common emphasis of affiliated congregations is a focus on Micronesia, represented by the reported numbers. 2009: "The amount raised is down because we didn't have any missionary that we sent overseas."

[5] The Episcopal Church: "The Episcopal Church USA Domestic and Foreign Missionary Society does not specifically raise The Episcopal Church: "The Episcopal Church USA Domestic and Foreign Missionary Society does not specifically raise money to support our non-domestic ministries. Many of the activities included in our budget are, however, involved, directly or indirectly with providing worldwide mission...Many other expenditures (e.g., for ecumenical and interfaith relations; for military chaplaincies; for management's participation in activities of the worldwide Anglican Communion) contain an overseas component; but we do not separately track or report domestic vs. overseas expenses in those categories."

[6] Evangelical Lutheran Synod: "[Data Year 2009] Line 1 includes an estate of [$]690,764 given in '09."

[7] Lutheran Church-Missouri Synod: "LCMS World Mission is the global Gospel outreach of The Lutheran Church-Missouri Synod (LCMS), a confessional Lutheran church with more than 6,000 congregations and 2.5 million members in North America. Ministry work is focused in three areas: International Mission, National Mission, and Ministry to the Armed Forces. The information provided in this report solely represents the *international component* of LCMS World Mission work. Annual budget income; above budget income; administrative incomes; and the special, multi-year, mission funding campaign, called *Fan into Flame*, income is included in the overseas income data. The majority of LCMS World Mission funding comes from direct gifts from individuals, congregations, and organizations.

"Note, information from LCMS World Relief and Human Care, another official LCMS entity involved in international and national ministry, is not included in the statistics provided here.

"In more recent years, the 35 districts of the LCMS and a number of congregations and Lutheran mission societies began sponsoring various mission fields and projects directly—with funds not flowing through the two national LCMS entities for world mission and world relief and human care. More information regarding the international work of the 35 LCMS districts can be found at <www.lcmsdistricts.org> and the 75-plus members of Association of Lutheran Mission Agencies at <www.alma-online.org>. Therefore, millions of dollars of additional support from LCMS members is raised and spent for international ministry each year. But, since these funds are not sent through the LCMS accounting department—and not required to be—the financial totals are not verifiable."

For the 2009 data: "In July of 2010 the Lutheran Church - Missouri Synod met in regular convention and adopted a new structure for the management of all programmatic activities being performed at the national and international mission level, including the creation of a new national mission board and new international mission board. A restructuring work group was formed following the convention and delivered recommendations to the President's Office in February, 2011. The final organization structure is planned to take effect in July, 2011 at which time financial reporting functions and processes will be established."

[8] Moravian Church, Northern Province: "Data provided by the Board of World Mission, an interprovincial agency of the North American Moravian Church." The Overseas Missions Income figure was estimated for the Northern Province by the Board of World Mission of the Moravian Church. The Northern Province is the only one of the three Moravian Provinces that reports Total Contributions to the *Yearbook of American and Canadian Churches* series.

[9] Orthodox Presbyterian Church: "These figures, as in past years, reflect only what was given through our denominational committee. Local churches and individuals also give directly to a variety of overseas missions causes."

[10] Presbyterian Church (U.S.A.): For Data Year 2005: "Nos. 1 & 4 Year 2005: Higher for Asian Tsunami Relief."

[11] Primitive Methodist Church in the U.S.A.: "This only includes monies passing through our Denominational Mission Board (International). Many churches send money directly to a mission field."

[12] Seventh-day Adventist, North American Division: This estimate, prepared by the General Conference Treasury Department, is for the U.S. portion of the total donated by congregations in both Canada and the U.S.

[13] The United Methodist Church: "The above represents total income received by the General Board of Global Ministries, The United Methodist Church."

Appendix B-6: Estimates of Giving

	A.	B.	C.	D.	E.	F.	G.	H.	I.	J.	K.
Year	Form 990 Direct Public Support '000s $	Form 990 Indirect Public Support '000s $	Form 990 Donor-Advised Funds '000s $	Form 990-EZ Contributions, Gifts and Grants '000s $	Giving USA Gifts to Foundations Billion $s	Giving USA Giving by Corporations Billion $s	Giving USA Giving by Foundations Billion $s	Giving USA Giving to Bequests Billion $s	Giving USA Individual Giving, Million $s	IRS Other than Cash Contributions '000s	CE Giving to "Church, Religious Organizations" '000s
1989	35,828,100	7,008,648		463,432	4.41	5.46	6.55	6.84	79,450	7,550,914	31,739,713
1990	39,395,074	8,055,551		644,613	3.83	5.46	7.23	6.79	81,040	7,494,016	30,673,887
1991	40,282,952	7,717,705		685,538	4.46	5.25	7.72	7.68	84,270	9,681,786	36,444,100
1992	43,986,785	9,110,478		813,604	5.01	5.91	8.64	9.54	87,700	9,632,779	35,159,679
1993	47,507,722	8,335,206		769,751	6.26	6.47	9.53	8.86	92,000	12,278,893	35,495,384
1994	49,238,498	8,722,141		780,896	6.33	6.98	9.66	11.13	92,520	14,739,299	37,189,109
1995	64,148,723	9,746,924		820,036	8.46	7.35	10.56	10.41	95,360	13,521,937	39,741,542
1996	69,419,764	10,230,304		988,638	12.63	7.51	12.00	12.03	107,560	21,298,819	39,053,447
1997	74,681,875	10,945,060		977,961	13.96	8.62	13.92	16.25	124,200	27,961,174	41,201,034
1998	83,359,695	12,711,938		1,053,669	19.92	8.46	17.01	12.98	138,350	29,255,985	44,831,015
1999	91,696,783	13,519,909		1,011,289	28.76	10.23	20.51	17.37	154,630	38,286,580	49,102,106
2000	103,453,445	15,176,512		1,086,099	24.71	10.74	24.58	19.88	174,510	47,256,104	48,737,216
2001	108,065,595	14,561,940		1,087,365	25.67	11.66	27.22	19.80	*173,360*	37,997,546	57,321,111
2002	102,802,550	15,223,713		1,095,317	19.16	10.79	26.98	20.90	174,440	34,293,125	62,476,667
2003	112,808,019	16,330,097		1,188,783	21.62	11.06	26.84	18.19	181,970	38,041,067	65,108,080
2004	124,575,951	16,947,398		1,397,630	20.32	11.36	28.41	18.46	202,970	43,373,209	65,712,121
2005	140,348,374	21,624,408		1,469,440	24.46	16.59	32.41	23.45	221,990	48,056,520	82,948,394
2006	150,214,837	26,049,161	10,368,453	1,551,098	27.10	14.89	34.91	21.65	224,760	52,631,443	89,469,764
2007	157,337,807	31,074,073	10,902,610	1,465,577	37.43	14.24	40.00	23.22	233,110	58,747,438	82,288,294

Source:
Columns A., B., and C.

1989	"Form 990 Returns of Nonprofit Charitable Section 501(c)(3) Organizations: Selected Income Statement and Balance Sheet Items, by Size of Total Assets, 1989"; downloaded 6/12/2007; <http://www.irs.gov/pub/irs-soi/89eo01as.xls>; p. 2 of 6/13/2007 12:26 PM printout.
1990	"Table 1.--1990, Form 990 Returns of Organizations Tax-Exempt Under Internal Revenue Code Sections 501(c)(3)-(9): Selected Income Statement and Balance Sheet Items, by Code Section"; downloaded 6/13/2007; <http://www.irs.gov/pub/irs-soi/90np01fr.xls>; p. 3 of 6/13/2007 1:48 PM printout.
1991	"Form 990 Returns of Nonprofit Charitable Internal Revenue Code Section 501(c)(3) Organizations: Selected Income Statement and Balance Sheet Items, by Asset Size, 1991"; IRS *SOI Bulletin*, Pub. 1136 (Rev. 8-96); downloaded 6/12/2007; <http://www.irs.gov/pub/irs-soi/91eo01as.xls>; p. 2 of 6/13/2007 2:48 PM printout.
1992-1999	"Table 1.--[Year], Form 990 Returns of Nonprofit Charitable Internal Revenue Code Section 501(c)(3) Organizations: Selected Income Statement and Balance Sheet Items, by Asset Size"; IRS *SOI Bulletin*, Pub. 1136; downloaded 6/12/2007;
1992	(Rev. 8-96); <http://www.irs.gov/pub/irs-soi/92eo01as.xls>; p. 2 of 6/13/2007 3:21 PM printout.
1993	(Rev. 4-97); <http://www.irs.gov/pub/irs-soi/93eo01as.xls>; p. 2 of 6/13/2007 3:39 PM printout.
1994	Spring 1998 (Rev. 5-98); <http://www.irs.gov/pub/irs-soi/94eo01as.xls>; p. 2 of 6/13/2007 4:12 PM printout.
1995	Winter 1998/1999 (Rev. 2/99); <http://www.irs.gov/pub/irs-soi/95eotab1.xls>; p. 2 of 6/14/2007 9:25 AM printout.
1996	Winter 1999/2000 (Rev. 2/00); <http://www.irs.gov/pub/irs-soi/96eo01c3.xls>; p. 1 of 6/14/2007 9:55 AM printout.
1997	Fall 2000 (Rev. 11-2000); <http://www.irs.gov/pub/irs-soi/97eotb1.xls>; p. 1 of 6/14/2007 10:09 AM printout.
1998	Fall 2001 (Rev. 11-01); <http://www.irs.gov/pub/irs-soi/98eo01as.xls>; p. 1 of 6/14/2007 10:17 AM printout.
1999	Fall 2002 (Rev. 12-02); <http://www.irs.gov/pub/irs-soi/99eo01as.xls>; p. 1 of 6/14/2007 10:29 AM printout.
2000	"Table 1.--2000, Form 990 Returns of Nonprofit Charitable Section 501(c)(3) Organizations: Selected Balance Sheet and Income Statement Items, by Size of Total Assets"; IRS *SOI Bulletin*, Fall 2003, Pub. 1136, (Rev. 12-03); downloaded 6/12/2007; <http://www.irs.gov/pub/irs-soi/00eo01ta.xls>; p. 2 of 6/14/2007 10:43 AM printout.
2001	"Form 990 Returns of Nonprofit Charitable Section 501(c)(3) Organizations: Selected Balance Sheet and Income Statement Items, by Asset Size, Tax Year 2001"; downloaded 6/12/2007; <http://www.irs.gov/pub/irs-soi/01eo01as.xls>; p. 1 of 6/14/2007 10:55 AM printout.
2002	"Table 1.--Form 990 Returns of Nonprofit Charitable Section 501(c)(3) Organizations: Selected Balance Sheet and Income Statement Items, by Asset Size, Tax Year 2002"; IRS, *SOI Bulletin*, Fall 2005, Pub. 1136, (Rev.12-05); downloaded 6/12/2007; <http://www.irs.gov/pub/irs-soi/02eo01as.xls>; p. 2 of 6/14/2007 4:31 PM printout.
2003	"Table 1: Form 990 Returns of Nonprofit Charitable Section 501 (c)(3) Organizations: Selected Balance Sheet and Income Statement Items, by Asset Size, Tax Year 2003"; IRS SOI Division, August 2006; downloaded 6/12/2007; <http://www.irs.gov/pub/irs-soi/03eo01as.xls>; p. 1 of 6/14/2007 4:42 PM printout.
2004-2005	Table 1: Form 990 Returns of 501(c)(3) Organizations: Balance Sheet and Income Statement Items, By Asset Size, Tax Year [Year]; IRS, SOI Division,
2004	August 2007; downloaded 3/15/2008; <http://www.irs.gov/pub/irs-soi/04eo01as.xls>; p. 1 of 3/15/2008 9:59 AM printout.
2005	August 2008; downloaded 3/5/2009; <http://www.irs.gov/pub/irs-soi/05eo01as.xls>; p. 1 of 3/5/2009 3:59 PM printout.
2006-2007	"Table 1. Form 990 Returns of 501(c)(3) Organizations: Balance Sheet and Income Statement Items, by Asset Size, Tax Year [Year]"; IRS, SOI Division,
2006	August 2009; downloaded 4/29/2010; <http://www.irs.gov/pub/irs-soi/06eo01as.xls>; p. 1 of 4/29/2010 3:27 PM printout.
2007	July 2010; downloaded 4/28/2011; <http://www.irs.gov/pub/irs-soi/07eo01.xls>; p. 1 of 4/29/2011 9:10 AM printout.

Col. D.

1989	"Form 990EZ Returns of Organizations Tax-Exempt Under Internal Revenue Code Sections 501(c)(3)-(9): Selected Income Statement and Balance Sheet Items, by Code Section, 1989"; IRS, SOI Tax Stats; downloaded 6/15/2007; <http://www.irs.gov/pub/irs-soi/89eo04cs.xls>; p. 1 of 6/16/2007 8:56 AM printout.
1990	"Table 2.--1990, Form 990EZ Returns of Organizations Tax-Exempt Under Internal Revenue Code Sections 501(c)(3)-(9): Selected Income Statement and Balance Sheet Items, by Code Section"; IRS, SOI Tax Stats; downloaded 6/15/2007; <http://www.irs.gov/pub/irs-soi/90np02ro.xls>; p.1 of 6/16/2007 9:11 AM printout.
1991	"Form 990EZ Returns of Organizations Tax-Exempt Under Internal Revenue Code Sections 501(c)(3)-(9): Selected Income Statement and Balance Sheet Items, by Code Section, 1991"; IRS, *SOI Bulletin*, Pub. 1136 (Rev. 8-96); downloaded 6/15/2007; <http://www.irs.gov/pub/irs-soi/91eo04cs.xls>; p.1 of 6/16/2007 9:22 AM printout.
1992-1993	"Table 4.--[Year], Form 990EZ Returns of Organizations Tax-Exempt Under Internal Revenue Code Sections 501(c)(3)-(9): Selected Income Statement and Balance Sheet Items, by Code Section"; IRS, *SOI Bulletin*, Pub.1136; downloaded 6/15/2007;
1992	(Rev. 8-96); <http://www.irs.gov/pub/irs-soi/92eo04cs.xls>; p.1 of 6/16/2007 9:39 AM printout.
1993	(Rev. 4-97); <http://www.irs.gov/pub/irs-soi/93eo04cs.xls>; p.1 of 6/16/2007 9:48 AM printout.
1994-1995	"Table 4.--[Year], Form 990-EZ Returns of Organizations Tax-Exempt Under Internal Revenue Code Sections 501 (c)(3)-(9): Selected Balance Sheet and Income Statement Items, by Code Section"; IRS, *SOI Bulletin,* Pub. 1136; downloaded 6/15/2007;
1994	Spring 1998, (Rev. 5-98); <http://www.irs.gov/pub/irs-soi/94eo04cs.xls>; p. 1 of 6/16/2007 9:58 AM printout.
1995	Winter 1998/99, (Rev. 2/99); <http://www.irs.gov/pub/irs-soi/95eotab4.xls>; p. 1 of 6/16/2007 10:09 AM printout.
1996	"Table 3.--1996, Form 990-EZ Returns of Nonprofit Charitable Section 501(c)(3) Organizations: Selected Balance Sheet and Income Statement Items, by Asset Size"; IRS, *SOI Bllletin,* Winter 1999/2000; Pub. 1136, (Rev. 2/00); downloaded 6/15/2007; <http://www.irs.gov/pub/irs-soi/96eo03c3.xls>; p. 1 of 6/16/2007 10:28 AM printout.
1997-2000	"Table 4.--[Year], Form 990-EZ Returns of Organizations Tax-Exempt Under Internal Revenue Code Sections 501(c)(3)-(9): Selected Balance Sheet and Income Statement Items, by Code Section"; IRS, *SOI Bulletin*, Pub. 1136; downloaded 6/15/2007;
1997	Fall 2000, (Rev. 11-2000); <http://www.irs.gov/pub/irs-soi/97eotb4.xls>; p. 1 of 6/16/2007 10:36 AM printout.
1998	Fall 2001, (Rev. 11-2001); <http://www.irs.gov/pub/irs-soi/98eo04cs.xls>; p. 1 of 6/16/2007 10:43 AM printout.
1999	Fall 2002, (Rev. 12-02); <http://www.irs.gov/pub/irs-soi/99eo04cs.xls>; p. 1 of 6/16/2007 11:22 AM printout.
2000	Fall 2003, (Rev. 12-03); <http://www.irs.gov/pub/irs-soi/00eo04cs.xls>; p. 1 of 6/16/2007 11:29 AM printout.
2001	"Form 990-EZ Returns of Organizations Tax-Exempt Under Internal Revenue Code Sections 501(c)(3)-(9): Selected Balance Sheet and Income Statement Items, by Code Section, Tax Year 2001"; IRS, SOI Tax Stats, downloaded 6/15/2007; <http://www.irs.gov/pub/irs-soi/01eo04cs.xls>; p. 1 of 6/16/2007 11:34 AM printout.
2002	"Table 4.--Form 990-EZ Returns of Organizations Tax-Exempt Under Internal Revenue Code Sections 501(c)(3)-(9): Selected Balance Sheet and Income Statement Items, by Code Section, Tax Year 2002"; IRS, *SOI Bulletin,* Fall 2005, Pub. 1136 (Rev. 12-05); downloaded 6/15/2007; < http://www.irs.gov/pub/irs-soi/02eo04ty.xls>; p. 1 of 6/17/2007 7:50 AM printout.
2003	"Table 4: Form 990-EZ Returns of Organizations Tax-Exempt Under Internal Revenue Code Sections 501(c)(3)-(9): Selected Balance Sheet and Income Statement Items, by Code Section, Tax Year 2003"; IRS, SOI Division, August 2006; downloaded 6/15/2007; <http://www.irs.gov/pub/irs-soi/03eo04ty.xls>; p. 1 of 6/17/2007 8:07 AM printout.
2004	"Table 4: Form 990-EZ Returns of 501(c)(3)-(9) Organizations: Balance Sheet and Income Statement Items, by Code Section, Tax Year 2004"; IRS, SOI Divison, August 2007; downloaded 3/14/2008; <http://www.irs.gov/pub/irs-soi/04eo04ty.xls>; p. 1 of 3/14/2008 3:50 PM printout.
2005	"Table 4: Form 990-EZ Returns of 501(c)(3)-(9) Organizations: Selected [I]tems, by Code Sectrion, Tax Year 2005"; IRS, SOI Division, August 2008; downloaded 3/5/2009; <http://www.irs.gov/pub/irs-soi/05eo04ty.xls>; p. 1 of 3/5/2009 4:11 PM printout.
2006-2007	"Table 4: Form 990-EZ Returns of 501(c)(3)-(9) Organizations: Selected Items, by Code Section, Tax Year [Year]"; IRS, SOI Division; downloaded 4/29/2010;
2006	August 2009; <http://www.irs.gov/pub/irs-soi/06eo04ty.xls>; p. 1 of 4/29/2010 5:34 PM printout.
2007	July 2010; <http://www.irs.gov/pub/irs-soi/07eo04.xls>; p. 1 of 4/29/2011 3:41 PM printout.

Col. E.

1989-2007	*Giving USA 2011;* Created: 6/20/2011; published by Giving USA Foundation, Chicago, Ill. ;<www.givingusareports.org/dowonloads.php>; p. 56 of 6/20/2011 printout.

Columns F., G., H., and I.

1989-2007	*Giving USA 2011*, p. 53.

Col. J.

1989	Internal Revenue Service, Statistics of Income—1989, Individual Income Tax Returns, "Table 2.1—Returns with Itemized Deductions: Sources of Income, Adjustments, Itemized Deductions by Type, Exemptions, and Tax Items by Size of Adjusted Gross Income" (Internal Revenue Service: Washington, DC, 1992), p. 41.
1990-2001	"Table 1.--Individual Income Tax Returns, Selected Deductions, 1990-2001"; IRS *Statistics of Income* Winter 2003-2004 Bulletin, Pub 1136; <http://www.irs.gov/pub/irs-soi/01in01sd.xls>; pp. 1-2 of 9/6/2005 8:59 AM printout.
2002	"Table 3.--2002, Individual Income Tax Returns with Itemized Deductions, by Size of Adjusted Gross Income"; IRS, *Stastics of Income Bulletin,* Fall 2004, Pub. 1136, (Rev. 12-04); <http://www.irs.gov/pub/irs-soi/02in03ga.xls>; p. 5 of 9/6/2005 10:58 AM printout.
2003	"Table 3.---2003, Individual Income Tax Returns with Itemized Deductions, by Size of Adjusted Gross Income"; IRS, Statistics of Income Bulletin, Fall 2005, Pub. 1136, (Rev. 12-05); <http://www.irs.gov/pub/irs-soi/03in03ag.xls>; p. 5 of 6/6/2006 3:38 PM printout.
2004	"Table 3--Returns with Itemized Deductions: Sources of Income, Adjustments, Itemized Deductions by Type, Exemptions, and Tax Items, by Size of Adjusted Gross Income, Tax year 2004"; IRS, Statistics of Income Division, July 2006; <http://www.irs.gov/pub/irs-soi/04in03id.xls>; p. 3 of 8/12/2007 1:33 PM printout.
2005	"Table 3--Returns with Itemized Deductions: Itemized Deductions by Type and by Size of Adjusted Gross Income, Tax Year 2005"; IRS; <http://www.irs.gov/pub/irs-soi/05in03id.xls>; p. 3 of 4/10/2008 7:07 PM printout.
2006	"Table 3--Returns with Itemized Deductions: Itemized Deductions by Type and by Size of Adjusted Gross Income, Tax Year 2006"; IRS; <http://www.irs.gov/pub/irs-soi/06in03id.xls>; p. 3 of 3/10/2009 11:34AM printout.
2007	"Table 3. Returns with Itemized Deductions: Itemized Deductions by Type and by Size of Adjusted Gross Income, Tax Year 2007";IRS; <http://www.irs.gov/pub/irs-soi/07in03id.xls>; p. 3 of 4/28/2010 4:48 PM printout.

Col. K.

1989-2007	U.S. Department of Labor, Bureau of Labor Statistics, "Table 1800.Region of residence: Average annual expenditures and characteristics, Consumer Expenditure Survey, [Year]"

APPENDIX C: *Income, Deflators, and U.S. Population*

Appendix C.1 presents U.S. Per Capita Disposable Personal Income for 1921 through 2010.

The Implicit Price Index for Gross National Product is provided for 1921 through 2010. The deflator series keyed to 2005 dollars provided deflators from 1929, only, through 2010. Therefore, the 1921 through 1928 data was converted to inflation-adjusted 1958 dollars using the series keyed to 1958=100, and the inflation-adjusted 1958 dollar values were then converted to inflation-adjusted 2005 dollars using the series keyed to 2005 dollars.

Appendix C.2 presents U.S. Population for 1921 through 2010.

SOURCES

Income, 1921-1928, Deflator 1921-1928, and U.S. Population, 1921-1928

Historical Statistics of the United States: Colonial Times to 1970, Bicentennial Edition, Part 1 (Washington, DC: Bureau of the Census, 1975):

 1921-28 Disposable Personal Income: Series F 9, p. 224 (F 6-9).

 1921-28 Implicit Price Index GNP (1958=100): Series F 5, p. 224 (F 1-5).

 1921-28 U.S. Population: Series A-7, p. 8 (A 6-8).

Income, 1929-2010

Per Capita Disposable Personal Income in Current Dollars: U.S. Department of Commerce, Bureau of Economic Analysis; "Table 7.1. Selected Per Capita Product and Income Series in Current and Chained Dollars"; Line 4: "Disposable personal income"; National Income and Product Accounts Tables; 1969-2010: <http://www.bea.gov/national/nipaweb/SS_Data/Section7All_xls.xls>; 1929-1968: <http://www.bea.gov/national/nipaweb/SS_Data/Section7All_Hist.xls>; Data Published on March 25, 2011.

Deflator, 2005 Dollars, 1929-2010

Gross National Product: Implicit Price Deflators for Gross National Product [2005=100]: U.S. Bureau of Economic Analysis; "Table 1.1.9. Implicit Price Deflators for Gross Domestic Product"; Line 26: "Gross national product"; National Income and Product Accounts Tables; 1969-2010: <http://www.bea.gov/national/nipaweb/SS_Data/Section1All_xls.xls>; 1929-1968: <http://www.bea.gov/national/nipaweb/SS_Data/Section1All_Hist.xls>; Data Published on March 25, 2011.

Population, 1929-2010

U.S. Bureau of Economic Analysis; "Table 7.1. Selected Per Capita Product and Income Series in Current and Chained Dollars"; Line 18: "Population (midperiod, thousands)"; National Income and Product Accounts Tables; 1969-2010: <http://www.bea.gov/national/nipaweb/SS_Data/Section7All_xls.xls>; 1929-1968: <http://www.bea.gov/national/nipaweb/SS_Data/Section7All_Hist.xls>; Data Published on March 25, 2011.

Appendix C-1: Per Capita Disposable Personal Income and Deflators, 1921-2010

Year	Current $ Per Capita Disposable Personal Income	Implicit Price De-flator GNP [1958=100]	Implicit Price De-flator GNP [2005=100]		Year	Current $ Per Capita Disposable Personal Income	Implicit Price De-flator GNP [2000=100]
1921	$555	54.5	18.103		1966	$2,733	20.469
1922	$548	50.1	18.103		1967	$2,894	21.098
1923	$623	51.3	18.103		1968	$3,112	21.996
1924	$626	51.2	18.103		1969	$3,324	23.081
1925	$630	51.9	18.103		1970	$3,586	24.299
1926	$659	51.1	18.103		1971	$3,859	25.515
1927	$650	50.0	18.103		1972	$4,140	26.617
1928	$643	50.8	18.103		1973	$4,615	28.097
1929	$683		10.592		1974	$5,010	30.643
1930	$605		10.205		1975	$5,497	33.541
1931	$517		9.151		1976	$5,972	35.472
1932	$393		8.081		1977	$6,514	37.735
1933	$366		7.865		1978	$7,220	40.385
1934	$417		8.299		1979	$7,956	43.745
1935	$465		8.468		1980	$8,794	47.728
1936	$525		8.558		1981	$9,726	52.206
1937	$559		8.926		1982	$10,390	55.391
1938	$512		8.666		1983	$11,095	57.586
1939	$545		8.579		1984	$12,232	59.749
1940	$581		8.680		1985	$12,911	61.562
1941	$703		9.263		1986	$13,540	62.920
1942	$879		9.990		1987	$14,146	64.749
1943	$990		10.529		1988	$15,206	66.974
1944	$1,072		10.778		1989	$16,134	69.511
1945	$1,088		11.065		1990	$17,004	72.199
1946	$1,142		12.384		1991	$17,532	74.755
1947	$1,187		13.727		1992	$18,436	76.521
1948	$1,299		14.497		1993	$18,909	78.224
1949	$1,275		14.469		1994	$19,678	79.874
1950	$1,384		14.626		1995	$20,470	81.542
1951	$1,496		15.677		1996	$21,355	83.096
1952	$1,550		15.946		1997	$22,255	84.558
1953	$1,620		16.139		1998	$23,534	85.509
1954	$1,627		16.287		1999	$24,356	86.766
1955	$1,713		16.568		2000	$25,944	88.645
1956	$1,800		17.136		2001	$26,805	90.648
1957	$1,866		17.705		2002	$27,799	92.113
1958	$1,897		18.103		2003	$28,805	94.096
1959	$1,976		18.320		2004	$30,287	96.767
1960	$2,020		18.577		2005	$31,318	100.000
1961	$2,077		18.786		2006	$33,157	103.260
1962	$2,170		19.044		2007	$34,512	106.300
1963	$2,245		19.248		2008	$35,931	108.626
1964	$2,408		19.546		2009	$35,888	109.609
1965	$2,562		19.903		2010	$36,697	110.654

Appendix C-2: U.S. Population, 1921-2010

Year	U.S. Population	Year	U.S. Population	Year	U.S. Population
1921	108,538,000	1951	154,287,000	1981	230,008,000
1922	110,049,000	1952	156,954,000	1982	232,218,000
1923	111,947,000	1953	159,565,000	1983	234,333,000
1924	114,109,000	1954	162,391,000	1984	236,394,000
1925	115,829,000	1955	165,275,000	1985	238,506,000
1926	117,397,000	1956	168,221,000	1986	240,683,000
1927	119,035,000	1957	171,274,000	1987	242,843,000
1928	120,509,000	1958	174,141,000	1988	245,061,000
1929	121,878,000	1959	177,130,000	1989	247,387,000
1930	123,188,000	1960	180,760,000	1990	250,181,000
1931	124,149,000	1961	183,742,000	1991	253,530,000
1932	124,949,000	1962	186,590,000	1992	256,922,000
1933	125,690,000	1963	189,300,000	1993	260,282,000
1934	126,485,000	1964	191,927,000	1994	263,455,000
1935	127,362,000	1965	194,347,000	1995	266,588,000
1936	128,181,000	1966	196,599,000	1996	269,714,000
1937	128,961,000	1967	198,752,000	1997	272,958,000
1938	129,969,000	1968	200,745,000	1998	276,154,000
1939	131,028,000	1969	202,736,000	1999	279,328,000
1940	132,122,000	1970	205,089,000	2000	282,418,000
1941	133,402,000	1971	207,692,000	2001	285,335,000
1942	134,860,000	1972	209,924,000	2002	288,133,000
1943	136,739,000	1973	211,939,000	2003	290,845,000
1944	138,397,000	1974	213,898,000	2004	293,502,000
1945	139,928,000	1975	215,981,000	2005	296,229,000
1946	141,389,000	1976	218,086,000	2006	299,052,000
1947	144,126,000	1977	220,289,000	2007	302,025,000
1948	146,631,000	1978	222,629,000	2008	304,831,000
1949	149,188,000	1979	225,106,000	2009	307,483,000
1950	151,684,000	1980	227,726,000	2010	310,106,000

LINCOLN CHRISTIAN UNIVERSITY

LINCOLN CHRISTIAN UNIVERSITY